D0100304

PRODUCING GREAT SOUND for DIGITAL VIDEO

Jay Rose

Digital Video

DV

EXPERT SERIES

CMP**Books**

San Francisco, CA • New York, NY • Lawrence, KS

Published by CMP Books
an imprint of CMP Media LLC
Main office: 600 Harrison Street, San Francisco, CA 94107 USA
Tel: 415-947-6615; fax: 415-947-6015
Editorial office: 4601 West 6th Street, Suite B, Lawrence, KS 66049 USA
www.cmpbooks.com
email: books@cmp.com

Designations used by companies to distinguish their products are often claimed as trademarks. In all instances where CMP is aware of a trademark claim, the product name appears in initial capital letters, in all capital letters, or in accordance with the vendor's capitalization preference. Readers should contact the appropriate companies for more complete information on trademarks and trademark registrations. All trademarks and registered trademarks in this book are the property of their respective holders.

The publisher does not offer any warranties and does not guarantee the accuracy, adequacy, or completeness of any information herein and is not responsible for any errors or omissions. The publisher assumes no liability for damages resulting from the use of the information in this book or for any infringement of the intellectual property rights of third parties that would result from the use of this information.

Acquisitions editor: Dorothy Cox
Managing editor: Michelle O'Neal
Layout design: Justin Fulmer
Cover layout design: Damien Castaneda

Distributed to the book trade in the U.S. by: Distributed in Canada by:
Publishers Group West   Jaguar Book Group
1700 Fourth Street   100 Armstrong Avenue
Berkeley, CA 94710   Georgetown, Ontario M6K 3E7 Canada
1-800-788-3123   905-877-4483

For individual orders and for information on special discounts for quantity orders, please contact:
CMP Books Distribution Center, 6600 Silacci Way, Gilroy, CA 95020
Tel: 1-800-500-6875 or 408-848-3854; fax: 408-848-5784
email: cmp@rushorder.com; Web: www.cmpbooks.com

Printed in the United States of America

04 05 06 07   5 4 3 2

ISBN: 1-57820-208-6

Table of Contents

Dedication

Still to my cat

Acknowledgments

A lot of people helped with this book and its first edition. Matt Kelsey and Dorothy Cox of CMP Books, and Jim Feeley of *DV* magazine, helped me bridge the tremendous gap between thinking about a book and actually publishing the first edition; Dorothy and CMP Books' Michelle O'Neal provided tremendous support for this second edition. Jim also took the time to read through various versions of the original manuscript and to offer useful suggestions on content and style. I'm grateful for the working professionals who let me pick their brains about the techniques they use. First among them would be Boston-based location sound expert, fellow DV author, and Cinema Audio Society member G. John Garrett (among other things, he co-wrote some of the material about wireless mics). But I also got help from *Videography* magazine's Bob Turner, veteran boom operator Chris O'Donnell (who posed for some photos in Chapter 8), and PBS narrators Wendie Sakakeeny and Don Wescott. Don and Omnimusic president Doug Wood also contributed audio examples for the book's CD.

Special thanks to Richard Pierce, noted audio design consultant, author, and reviewer for the Audio Engineering Society, for the countless times he answered my phone calls about the finer points of acoustics and digital audio. And thanks to Dave Moulton, Grammy-nominated engineer, nationally-respected audio educator and researcher, and author of *Total Recording*, for reviewing the first edition's manuscript and offering suggestions. Of course, anything I misinterpreted from either of these gentlemen is my own fault.

Thanks also to readers of my column at *DV* magazine, members to the online *Audio Solutions* forum at DV.com, e-mail correspondents, and readers who have posted critical comments of the first edition at Amazon.com. Your suggestions (and brickbats) helped shape the changes in this second edition.

It's customary for authors to thank their families, but mine went far beyond the norm. My son Dan is Assistant Chief Engineer at NPR powerhouse WBUR, and has a deeper math background than mine. He spotted and cleaned up some ambiguities in the early chapters, did a lot of the research in the section on camera audio, and is always available to talk technical with me. And my wife, Carla, did much more than provide the usual spousal patience and support: As author of more than 30 successful books on computers and digital graphics, she was able to teach me the practical realities of getting a manuscript out the door . . . while also running a studio.

Introduction

There's a good chance you picked up this book because you're working on a project and having trouble with one aspect of its sound. So the first thing we've included is a list of Frequently Asked Questions: a bunch of common audio problems, and either how to fix them or—if the fix is complicated—where in this book you'll find a complete solution.

Consult Chapter 1's FAQ if you have to put out fires in a hurry.

Read the rest of this book if you want tracks that are truly hot.

I'm going to try to guess some things about you. You may have taken a few film or video courses, but most of your production knowledge is self-taught. You improve your skills by watching the videos you've produced, seeing what you don't like, and changing it the next time. You look at still frames to analyze your lighting or composition, or compare your editing techniques with what's on television and the movies you rent. Because you're primarily an artist, your eyes are your guide. You can see what you've done wrong.

One other guess: you've discovered it's almost impossible to learn how to create a good soundtrack that way. There are too many variables. If the finished mix has dialog that's hard to understand, there's no intuitive way to guess whether it was because the boom was placed badly . . . or levels weren't set properly during digitization . . . or if it was mixed on the wrong kind of speakers. Often, trying to fix one sound problem makes other aspects of the track worse.

Even if you also play a musical instrument, your sense of aesthetics doesn't bail you out when the track isn't working. There's a reason for this:

Good soundtracks aren't just a question of art. You also have to understand the science.

In this book, we cover both.

It's Not Rocket Science

Don't be scared about the science part. The math is mainly stuff you learned in elementary school, and the physics is common sense.

Don't be scared of the art, either. This is not a book on the aesthetics of sound (there *are* books like that, filled with critical essays about classic film directors, and they're completely irrelevant to what we're trying to do here). I'm not going to try to change what you think is good.

And don't be scared of me. The "art" of this book is the tricks, shortcuts, and industry practices that have been developed over 75 years of talking pictures, and that I've been working with since the late 1960s. There's a lot to be shared after years of creating tracks for everything from corporate videos to national spots, working in every kind of facility from local stations to large post houses, contributing to the design of some of the industry's standard pieces of digital audio equipment, and seeing projects I've worked on win Clios, an Emmy, and hundreds of other awards.

How This Book is Organized

The first section of this book, after the FAQ, is an explanation of how sound works. It covers the physics of sound in space and the technology of digital recording. I've put this material in front because it's important. I've also put it in plain English, without jargon or complicated formulas, and with plenty of drawings and examples. It shouldn't take more than a couple of evenings to read.

Then we get to step-by-step advice—the bulk of these pages. First, pre-production: how to plan the track, figure the budget, and pick the location. Second, acquisition: how microphones work and are affected by practical acoustics, how to use them on location and in the studio, how to get the best audio results from cameras and recorders, and how to work with the people and things that make sound. Finally, postproduction: editing voices, adding and editing music and effects, processing for the best possible sound, and mixing for various viewing situations.

There's also an accompanying CD with examples and tutorials. I made it an audio CD, playable on any standard stereo, rather than a CD-ROM because I wanted you to be able to hear it on the best speakers you own. There should be no problem importing the tutorials into your editing system.

About This Book and *Audio Postproduction for Digital Video*

The first edition of *Producing Great Sound* sold well enough that CMP Books had me write a companion piece in 2002, with much more detail about the postproduction process. That book, *Audio Postproduction for Digital Video,* includes almost 150 pages just about processing: tutorials, explanations, examples, practical tips, and specific recipes for equalization, compression, and the other processes necessary to build a good mix, including a chapter on removing noise from bad recordings. It also has long sections about editing, postproduction sound and music sources, debugging sync and NLE problems, and soundproofing and wiring an audio post setup. It comes with a one-hour audio CD of new diagnostics, examples, and tutorials aimed at postproduction. But it doesn't cover any aspect of location sound at all.

With *Audio Postproduction* on the shelf, I felt free to expand the *production* section of this book. There are new and expanded sections on choosing microphones, boom and lav technique, and wireless mics. There's also a completely new chapter on getting the best results with in-camera sound and separate audio recorders, including specific measurements and tips for some popular camera models. I've kept the chapters about audio postproduction that were in the first edition (with some minor updates), so *Producing Great Sound* can still serve as a guide to the entire production process.

Some parts of the two books necessarily overlap. The basics of sound, digital recording, accurate monitoring, and editing belong in both books. But I've written about them differently in each, to give you a better chance of understanding these important concepts.

In other words, it's entirely reasonable to own both *Audio Postproduction* and this edition of *Producing Great Sound*. But if you can get only one, choose this book for an overview of the entire audio process with a strong emphasis on sound at the shoot; choose *Audio Postproduction* for a complete discussion of turning that sound into a polished, finished soundtrack.

Staying Up-to-date

While styles change, the techniques behind good audio remain constant. The physics of sound isn't going to change without a major overhaul of the universe. You should be able to hang onto this book for a while.

While there are recommendations for using some popular DV cameras and suggestions about some high-end mics and other field equipment, I also explain the principles involved so you can apply the information to other models. This kind of hardware stays on the market for years, and lasts a long time. However, I've stayed away from step-by-step software instructions based on a particular program or platform, because these things change faster. The tutorials are appropriate for any decent program, Windows or Mac, and just about any collection of software or hardware processors. You can use this book with tools you have now, and keep using it when you upgrade.

For the most current information, check *DV* magazine and their Web site DV.com. They've got up-to-date product reviews, recommendations, and how-to features. There's a good chance I'll still be writing a monthly audio tutorial column (I've been in almost every issue since late 1995). Check the DV.com Community section as well: it's an on-line forum of professionals and amateurs sharing techniques and solving problems. I moderate the Audio section.

Or ask a friendly professional: we're not at all territorial, and are usually willing to share ideas and information. You can reach me through my studio's Web site: www.dplay.com.

How to Create a Great Soundtrack (in a quarter page)

Here are the rules:

- Know what you're doing before you start.
- Plan the audio as carefully as you plan the video.
- Get good elements.
- Treat them with respect.
- Do as little processing as possible until the mix.
- Listen very carefully while you mix.
- Follow the tips in this book.

The rest is just details.

Chapter 1

"Help! It Doesn't Sound Right!"

If you're hearing a specific problem in your project and need to find out how to fix it in a hurry, this section of Frequently Asked Questions is for you.

As an engineer, I'd prefer you read the whole book. That way you'll learn how sound really works and be able to make choices that get you the best possible track with the least amount of effort. But as a pragmatist—and someone who's lived with years of project deadlines—I understand this may not be possible right now.

So flip through this section until you find the problem that's bothering you. If it can be repaired easily, you'll find the instructions right here. If the fix is slightly more complicated, I'll point you to which chapter in this book has the answers. One or the other will probably be enough to get you back on track.

Then, when you have time, read the rest of the book. It'll save you from this kind of panic on your next job.

Problems with On-camera Dialog

Don't feel bad; this happens all the time in Hollywood. Unfortunately, often the only way to fix a bad dialog track is to re-record in the actors in sync with their pictures. This is standard practice in feature films and TV movies. It's also time-consuming, annoys the actors, introduces problems of its own, and can cost a bundle. And it's also not usable in documentaries and other talking-head productions.

You can avoid the need to replace dialog by listening carefully during the shoot, either on a good speaker in a separate control room or with high-quality headphones. Play back the first and last take as well, so you can catch equipment or tape troubles. Then follow the steps below to fix any problems you hear.

It's not easy to remember during the heat of production, but "wasting" five minutes on the set to move a microphone or hang a sound blanket over a window can save you hours in postproduction—and possibly keep a day's shooting from ending up in the scrap heap.

If you've already got bad tracks and reshooting isn't an option, you may have to live with the problems. I'll give you what advice I can to clean them up, but don't expect miracles. The section on dialog replacement in sync with picture is in Chapter 10.

1. "It's hard to understand the words!"

If the actors are mumbling, send them to acting school. If you can hear them clearly on the set but have to strain to hear them on the tape, here are some likely causes:

Too much room echo around their voices

This is the most common problem with dialog tracks. You need to either treat the room with *lots* of sound-absorbing material (Chapter 7) or get the mic closer to their mouths (Chapter 8). Moving the mic is probably more practical.

A camera-mounted shotgun mic will almost always be too far away for effective dialog recording indoors. (It may be usable outdoors, but only if the camera is close to the subject and there isn't too much background noise.) If you can place a shotgun on a boom, in front of and no more than a foot or so above the talent's head, you'll get the most realistic dialog. Where you put the mic and how you aim it is critical: it has to be close to the actors' mouths and pointed towards them, without getting close to or pointing towards reflective surfaces.

If you don't have the time or resources to use a boom mic effectively, a lavaliere or tie tack will do a better job. Get the mic as close as possible to the talent's mouth, hiding it in their clothing or hair if necessary. Remember: you can make a close mic sound distant by adding reverberation in postproduction. But the only way to make a distant mic sound close-up is to move it at the shoot.

There is a lot of information about using boom mics and lavalieres in Chapter 8.

Too much echo and more random room noises than seem appropriate, but voices seem okay

Your camera's automatic volume control is lowering the recording volume while the actors talk, and raising it whenever they pause. Turn it off.

If you can't defeat the automatic control, try lowering the microphone signal level with a simple attenuator or mixer. You may have to experiment to find a level that doesn't make the automatic control work so hard, but still avoids electronic noise. Don't attempt to defeat the automatic volume control by moving the mic farther from the talent. That just increases room echo. There's more on this in Chapter 9.

More echo on one actor than on another

If you're using a single mic, make sure it's aimed properly. If it's on a boom, someone has to pan it between the actors. If that doesn't help, try adding some strategically placed absorption (Chapter 7).

If you're using multiple body mics, there's a good chance Sue's microphone is picking up George's voice and vice versa. If this is the situation, you'll hear echoes when they're across the room from each other and a hollowness when they come close together. Set up a mixer and assign someone to turn each actor's mic down whenever they don't have a line. Or assign each mic to a separate track in your recorder, and sort them out in postproduction.

2. Too Many Background Noises

Too much machinery noise, traffic, footsteps . . .

Acoustic noise problems are similar to echo ones and almost always improved by moving the mic closer.

The most common acoustic noises in business videos are air conditioners and computer fans. If you can't turn a building air conditioner off, try removing its grill. The only cure for computer fans is isolation: move the tower, or throw a sound-absorbing blanket over it. (If you do that, watch out for heat build-up under the blanket. Take the blanket off whenever you're not shooting.)

If actors' footsteps are a problem, throw a blanket down for them to walk on when their feet aren't in camera range, put foam pads (available from film sound suppliers) under their shoes, or let them work in socks. If prop-handling noises are a problem, block the scene so the noises occur during pauses in dialog; then you'll be able to reduce them in postproduction. Put a piece of foam-core board or a foam placemat on a table to dampen the sound when a prop is put on it.

If traffic noises are a problem in an interior, make sure all the windows are closed tightly. Then hang sound blankets over the windows. Low-frequency traffic rumbles can be controlled by a mic's low-end rolloff switch, and further filtered in post.

Noise in a wireless mic

These things can be unpredictable, so always bring a wired alternative.

Before you give up on a radio mic, make sure you're using fresh batteries: it's not unusual to have to replace the batteries two or even three times during a long shoot day. Get the receiving antenna as close to the mic as possible while maintaining line-of-sight (large metal objects can disrupt the signal), and orient it in the same direction as the transmitter's antenna.

If the signal fades or distorts as talent walks around, it's probably bouncing unpredictably between metal elements in the building: get a diversity receiver. There's a lot more about getting good results from wireless in Chapter 8.

Electronic hum during the recording

Hum can be introduced by the mic cable, particularly when you're using small digital cameras with mini-jack mic inputs. Get an XLR balancing adapter (Chapter 9): the improvement, with a good mic, will amaze you.

Even with a balancing transformer, a microphone's tiny signal is easily polluted by electronic noise. Keep all mic cables away from AC power or video lines. If the cable must cross one of these noisy wires, do it at a right angle to minimize the area where pickup can occur. Star-Quad, an inexpensive upgrade to standard XLR mic cables, can reduce noise pickup.

If you're borrowing signals from a computer, PA system, or playback device and things start to hum, you may have a voltage mismatch—these things should never be plugged into a mic input—but a ground loop is more likely. The best solution is an isolation transformer in the audio line. If one isn't available, you might be able to get a clean signal by running the camera on a battery instead of AC supply. Disconnect the camera from monitors or anything else plugged into an AC outlet. Try to arrange things so that the only item plugged into the wall is the house sound system.

We often refer to ground loop noise as "60-cycle hum," but its effects extend throughout the audio band and are almost impossible to eliminate with standard filters.

3. Dialog Problems Introduced by the Recorder

Playback doesn't sound like the recording

Make sure the camera or recorder is properly adjusted. If you're using an analog recorder, the heads must be clean or you'll hear a muffled sound. If you're using a digital recorder, set it for the highest possible quality (16 bits rather than 12).

Set the recording volume very carefully (Chapter 9). MiniDV cameras have a limited range between noise and distortion.

Use good isolating earphones at the shoot, ones that surround the ear and block outside sounds. A lot of "playback" problems turn out to be operator error in the original recording.

Dialog seems uneven from shot to shot during editing

If you're using a lavaliere, this probably won't happen unless your actors are changing their projection on different shots. If you're using a boom that had to be pulled too far away for the long shot, try using audio from a close-up take . . . or at least do an L-cut (audio and video cut on different frames) to disguise the changes.

You may need to equalize or process the dialog track to smooth out these variations. Resist the temptation to do this during the editing process: it'll save time and be more effective to tweak the sound at the mix, where you'll have better monitors and be able to concentrate more on the track. Keep the mismatched camera angles' dialog on different audio tracks while editing, so you can apply global corrections during the mix instead of changing things clip by clip.

Background noises seem uneven from shot to shot during editing

If the noise level on the set changed during the shoot, fade in some background tone from the noisiest shots over the quieter ones. If noise levels stayed relatively constant during the shoot but are jumping around in the edited track, either the camera's automatic level control or some production assistant's fingers were too active. L-cuts and a little extra ambiance—either from the shoot or a library—will help you smooth over the changes.

Audio is too quiet in the editor. When I boost it, I hear hiss and buzzing.

If you've transferred from the camera using FireWire, this was most likely a problem in the original footage. MiniDV cameras have to be set very carefully to make sure they're not generating noise. See Chapter 9.

If you've transferred via an analog connection, check the original tape. It may have been recorded properly but the settings were wrong when you transferred it to the computer. See Chapter 12.

No matter which kind of transfer you did, check the computer's system-level input volume controls. They can override the settings in your NLE software.

Postproduction Audio Issues

If your system uses an analog audio connection into the editor, it's essential that you set digitizing levels properly. Don't trust an on-screen meter. Instead, calibrate your system using the tips in Chapter 12.

4. Lipsync Problems

If the track is largely in sync but you see errors on specific edits, it's probably an operator error. Some desktop systems are notoriously unintuitive for anything other than straight cuts. If this happens only once or twice in a project, it'll be faster to manually nudge the track rather than take an advanced software course.

Sync drift

If it's impossible to get stable sync—if you can get the first line to look right, but other lines in the scene vary from being early to being late—it's probably a software problem. If the track stays in sync for the first five minutes or so, but then jumps wildly out and never comes back, you've most likely got hardware issues. Either way, contact the editing system manufacturer. There may be an update or workaround. You may have to reconfigure your computer, and restart. It's also possible you're using audio and video boards the manufacturer didn't qualify to work together.

If a track starts out in sync but seems to jump earlier from time to time, suspect dropped video frames. Check the settings, defragment the hard drive, quit any other programs, and turn off all network services.

If a track drifts out of sync at a constant rate, getting worse over time but never making any obvious jumps, you've probably got incompatible references. Is video sync or blackburst being distributed everywhere it's supposed to go? Do timecode or frame rate settings agree throughout your system? Manually sync the front and back of the video and measure how much it's drifted over time: this can help you or the manufacturer diagnose the problem (for example, an error of just under two frames per minute is almost always related to differences between 30 fps audio and 29.97 fps NTSC video). If nothing else, figuring the error as a percentage will let you apply a speed correction to the track and finish the job that way.

Some prosumer cameras are built with their audio sample rate a tiny bit off-speed to take advantage of cheaper components. This can cause sync errors when the material is transferred via FireWire to a properly designed NLE. Redigitizing through an analog connection solves this problem, though it may lower the quality.

Many of these errors are cumulative and don't show up until the middle of a film. If so, try breaking the project into shorter pieces. Export each as a QuickTime or AVI. Then string those finished and properly synchronized pieces together in the editor.

Separate audio and video recorders

If you recorded double-system—using separate digital audio and video recorders—you may have to go back to original footage and use the slate to resync.

If you recorded without a slate, or used a totally nonsync medium like analog audio cassettes or DC-motorized film cameras, you're in for a nightmare of manual resyncing and trimming. A sound engineer with lipsync experience and a good audio-for-video workstation may be able to save you time and money.

5. Hum and Noise

If a track gets noisy but the original footage is clean, it's best to redigitize. But first, check the connections between recorder and computer (Chapter 11). Make sure the computer is set for 16-bit or higher resolution. Even if your final goal is a low-resolution medium like the Internet, always record at the highest possible bit setting.

Background noises that couldn't be eliminated at the shoot

If you're willing to sacrifice realism for intelligibility, get a good filter and start with settings like this:

- Sharp rolloff (at least 12 dB/octave) below 200 Hz and above 8 kHz
- Consonant peak, 6 dB around one octave wide, at 1.75 kHz
- Optional warmth boost around 2 dB at 250 Hz

Fine-tune the settings with a good audio monitor, always listening for distortion. If you're not sure what things like dB and Hz are, check Chapter 2. If you're not sure how to use a filter, check Chapter 16. If you don't have good monitor speakers, don't do anything. You'll have to go to a sound studio for the final mix—it's impossible to do a good mix without accurate speakers—and you can put off the corrections until then.

Power-line hum is seldom just at power-line frequencies and can't be fixed with a standard filter. A comb filter, with mathematically related notches like the teeth of a comb, can help a lot (see Chapter 16).

Hum and hiss that don't obscure the dialog, but are annoying during pauses, can be eliminated with sliding filters and multi-band noise gates. That's in Chapter 16 also.

There's a separate chapter devoted to Noise Reduction, additional pages on using equalizers and expanders for noise control, and cookbook examples with CD samples of various kinds of noise, in my *Audio Postproduction for Digital Video* (CMP Books, 2002). It was too much material to include in this book.

6. Narration Problems

Radio and TV have conditioned us to expect voice-overs to be cleanly recorded, disembodied voices speaking directly to us from limbo (hey, I don't make the rules). You can't record them in the kind of real-world reverberant spaces that are appropriate for dramatic dialog. Read Chapter 10 for some tips on recording them properly.

Voice-over recording lacks clarity

If an analog tape recorded in a professional studio sounds dull or muffled, suspect your playback deck's heads. Sometimes all that's needed is a good cleaning with a cotton swab and alcohol. Make sure the alcohol is wiped off with a clean swab before rethreading the tape. If that doesn't help, suspect head alignment: a tiny screw near the playback head can be adjusted to tilt the head for maximum high-frequency transfer. But if you're not familiar with the procedure and it's not covered in the recorder's manual, it's best to call a technician.

If an analog tape sounds very weak and muffled, check to make sure it hasn't been inadvertently flipped and you're trying to play through the back of the tape (I've seen this happen in major radio stations). The recording is on the smooth side with the eggshell semigloss surface. Depending on the tape, the back is either very glossy or very dull: this side should face away from the heads.

If an analog tape sounds squeezed, with breaths and mouth noises unnaturally emphasized or high frequencies that are very spitty, it may have been recorded with analog noise reduction encoding. Contact the studio for advice; they may be able to lend you a decoder or supply an unencoded version. On the other hand, it may have been recorded through inappropriate processing: this was a bad decision by the announcer, director, or recording engineer and can't be undone.

If you've recorded narration by pointing a camera mic directly at the speaker's mouth, try using just one channel of the stereo pair. Use the Take Right or Take Left command in your NLE's audio clip options.

Voice-over sounds fine by itself but is weaker than other elements

A little processing is a good thing. See Chapter 16 for advice on using equalization and compression to make a voice punchier.

7. Computer Doesn't Play Audio Well

If you hear skipping, pops, or brief silences when you play from hard disk but not from the original track, suspect data-flow problems. Don't assume that because you see relatively good video, the drive or CPU is capable of handling audio. The eye can forgive momentary lapses or uneven motion a lot more easily than the ear can.

Either the hard disk isn't accessing audio quickly enough, or the CPU is trying to do too many other things at the same time. Try defragmenting the hard disk or copying the audio file to a faster drive. Contact the editing system manufacturer: you may need to change your computer's startup configuration and reboot. As a last resort, lower the sample rate or use mono instead of stereo.

If individual clips sound fine but playback stutters or distorts when you try to play from the timeline, there's a sample rate issue. Check clip info to make sure every clip is at the same rate as the overall project. If not, export those clips to an audio program and convert their sample rate.

Periodic clicking in a file

This is almost always the result of digital audio being out of sync with itself. Check that your sound card and software settings match. If you copied the audio digitally from a DAT, standalone CD player, or DV recorder, make sure the sound card and the source shared the same sync reference: either both should be locked to a blackburst generator, or the card must be set to use its own input as the reference.

Random squeaks, whistles, or edginess mixed with the high-pitched sounds

This is aliasing distortion. The file was recorded at a sample rate that the sound card doesn't properly support (no matter what the manufacturer printed on its box). See Chapter 3.

Maybe you're lucky and the problem is in the card's playback filters. Try playing the file on a different computer. If it sounds okay, get a different brand of sound card.

But it's more likely the problem was created during the original recording, and the file can't be repaired. Try rerecording at the highest sample rate your software will support. If that results in a cleaner file, you may then convert to a lower rate in software and avoid this problem. The best solution is to get a card that was properly designed in the first place. Don't just let price be your guide: a thousand-dollar unit from a leading manufacturer of editing systems had this problem. (And this was their flagship Macintosh card well into the mid-1990s; fortunately, they've since corrected the problem.)

Aliasing can also occur when very bright sounds are recorded in a MiniDV camera or pocket MiniDisc recorder. The only solution is to use a separate DAT or CD recorder at the shoot.

8. Editing Problems

Sound effects or dialog edits seem fine in previews, but are out of sync in the final movie

You can't edit sound at anything less than the full frame rate. A 15 fps preview or timeline set to larger than one-frame resolution will hide a lot of problems. Kick your software up a notch and try re-editing.

Some problems may be hardware or software related; see the discussion of lipsync at the start of this section.

Music edits don't sound smooth

While there's an art to music editing (one you can learn easily; see Chapter 14), the problem may be mechanical. Single-frame resolution may be fine for sound effects and most dialog, but a thirtieth of a second can be an eternity in music. Export the music to an audio program to cut its length. Most will display picture while you're cutting.

Mix Problems

If you don't have good monitor speakers in a well-designed environment, the ability to process sounds in real time, and a system that will let you independently adjust the level of many tracks at the same time, it might be worthwhile to hire a studio to mix critical projects. An experienced engineer with the right equipment can save you time, assure a polished overall sound, and fix audio problems that aren't repairable in a desktop video-editing system. Mixing on the wrong equipment, or trying to do a complex mix with a mouse and "rubber band" volume lines is not worth the effort.

Besides, it's how I make my living.

The mix sounded great on the desktop or mixing studio, but bad on the air or in the conference room

If the music disappears but dialog sounds okay, chances are you're using home hi-fi speakers optimized for pop music, or small multimedia speakers supplemented by subwoofers. The speakers emphasized the extreme highs and lows, so you turned down the music track to compensate. This problem can also result from too reverberant a mixing room: since reverb is more obvious on voice than on music, you may have turned down the music so it wouldn't interfere.

If the dialog disappears and the music sounds too loud, your speakers emphasized the midrange. This is common with midsized multimedia speakers and the cube speakers often placed on top of mixing consoles.

The solution for both problems is to remix using good speakers in a proper environment, but tweaking an equalizer during playback can provide a temporary fix. It can also generate distortion that fights intelligibility, so making an equalized dub of a bad mix isn't a good option.

The mix proportions were right, but it was too soft/loud/distorted on the air or when professionally duplicated

Make sure the line-up tone at the head of your tape is accurate. Not only should it match the standard zero setting on your recorder, it also has to match the "average loud" level of your program. Most broadcasters and dub houses rely on the tone exclusively when setting levels, and don't try to compensate if program audio doesn't match.

Broadcast audio on digital videotape is standardized with tone and average program level at –20 dBFS, and no peaks higher than –10 dBFS. MiniDV cameras and some NLEs use a –12 dBFS average standard, which can cause distortion if the broadcaster or dub house isn't used to it. "dBFS" (decibels related to full scale) is defined in Chapter 3.

Broadcast audio on analog videotape is usually standardized with tone and average level at the magnetic level represented by 0 VU on the recorder's meter, with peaks no higher than +6 VU. The average-to-peak difference appears smaller on analog meters than digital ones because analog meters can't respond to fast peaks as well.

If you're having trouble keeping the average level in the right place while peaks stay below the maximum, try moderate compression on individual elements in your track as well as peak limiting on the overall mix. Tips for using these processors appear in Chapter 16.

Some elements sound fine in stereo, but completely disappear when the tape is broadcast in mono

Something is out of phase. The signal on the left channel is pushing while the one on the right is pulling by exactly the same amount. (If that doesn't make sense to you, you'll either have to trust me or read Chapter 2.) When the two channels for that element are combined, they cancel each other out.

This most often happens because of a cable problem, where two wires in a balanced cable are reversed. It doesn't cause a problem when the cable is being used by itself for a mono signal, but shows up when stereo channels are combined. Some low-cost synthesizers and effects processors reverse the phase of one channel intentionally, to hype the "stereoness" of their output.

This can also happen when the monaural balanced output of a mixer appears on phone jacks, and a stereo-to-mono phone plug adapter is used to split its signal to two channels.

You need to go back to the original tracks and check individual stereo pairs by combining them to mono. When you hear the pair that disappears in mono, use the phase-invert function of your mixing console or software to invert just one channel. If you don't have that ability, redub the original source through a correctly wired cable. Then remix.

In a pinch, you can play the project in mono by using just one channel of your original stereo mix.

The entire mix sounds very wide in stereo, but disappears in mono

This is a variation of the above problem, but much easier to fix. It probably occurred when you dubbed the output of your editing system to a final videotape master because one of the two balanced cables was miswired. Redub, using two correctly wired cables. Or if you can tolerate the generation loss, make a submaster by copying the stereo tracks from the original master with one correctly wired cable and the miswired one. This will flip things back the way they should be. It doesn't matter which channel you reverse when making the submaster.

If the miswired cable was also feeding your monitor speakers during the mix, the result could have suppressed mono elements somewhat when the two speakers combined in the room. This could fool you into making the dialog and narration too loud, or—because the effect is more pronounced at low frequencies—equalize those tracks badly. Remix.

Other Common Questions

Where can I find cheap talent/music/sound effects?

Voice-over casting advice is in Chapter 10. Music scoring is Chapter 14. You usually get what you pay for, but there are some strategies for stretching the budget.

Sound effects are free if you record them yourself or create them on a synthesizer. But even professionally recorded, fully licensed ones are cheap—often only a few dollars per minute—if you buy them individually over the Internet. Check http://www.sound-ideas.com and http://www.sounddogs.com.

Is it a copyright violation to use pop music recordings in an educational or nonprofit video? How about classical music?

Yes. It doesn't matter how noble the intended use is. And while most classical compositions are no longer protected by copyright, the recorded performances probably are.

Only an attorney can give legal advice, but as a general rule "fair use" applies only to private viewing at home or brief excerpts in a critical review of the music itself. This does not include the use of pop music in a professionally-produced wedding video, even if the clients already owned the CD. I've heard of video companies being shut down because of the high legal fees a copyright defense can involve.

What software should I use? What brand of sound card? Mac or PC?

The science of sound and the technique of the sound track—what this book is really about—have taken most of a century to develop and are well understood. Digital recording hasn't been around as long, but radical developments in the technology take many years to make it from lab to common practice. So it's my expectation that you'll be able to use this book for a while.

On the other hand, new computer and digital video products are introduced every month. Rather than risk misleading you with outdated information, I've avoided specific brand and model recommendations in this book. If you want to keep up, read *DV* magazine: it's remarkably free from hype and rehashed press releases. Besides, I'm a contributing editor. (*DV* magazine is available at most large newsstands and computer stores, and back issues are posted at www.dv.com.)

For what it's worth, you can reach me (or check a frequently updated list of the gear I use) at my studio's Web site: www.dplay.com.

Section I

Audio Basics

This is the technical stuff: How sound exists and is perceived by the brain, how it can be turned into computer data, and how it gets conducted over wires in a studio. This is the foundation everything else in this book is built on.

I've avoided formulas. You should be able to understand these concepts using no more than grade-school science and math, and your own common-sense understanding of how things work. A lot of it is based on visual analogies, on the assumption that videographers are pretty good at looking at the world.

But it *is* technical, and I don't want to trigger any deep-seated phobia. You can skip this material—if you must—and go directly to the practical tips and techniques that comprise this book's other chapters. But I promise that if you *do* read it, the rest of the book will make a lot more sense. In fact, since you'll know how sound actually works, you'll find yourself getting better tracks without having to memorize a bunch of rules.

And that will make it easier to concentrate on the fun stuff.

Chapter 2

How Sound Works

A brief note . . . This is the most technical chapter of the book. However, I've avoided complex formulas and theorems—the only math and science you'll need is the kind you learned in grade school. Instead, you'll use your visual imagination and common-sense knowledge of how the world works.

Skip this chapter, if you must. But if you read through it, you'll understand what sound really is, how it moves around a shooting stage or editing room, and how the words that describe it relate to reality. And once you have that knowledge, the rest of this book—the practical tips for making sound do what you want in a production—will be a piece of cake.

Rose's Rules:
- ✔ Sound is messy stuff. It spreads out, bends around corners, and bounces off objects. The way it bounces can hurt your track.
- ✔ As sound spreads out, it gets drastically weaker. If you know how this happens, you'll find it easier to control the bouncing.

Music-sicle?

"Architecture is frozen music." When Friedrich von Schelling wrote that, he was being poetic. The scientific truth is if there were such a thing as frozen music, or any kind of sound, it would be *pressure*. This is usually air pressure, but it can also be pressure in water, wood, or anything else that conducts sound. It's not precisely the kind of pressure you feel when deadlines approach, but the pressure that compresses molecules together. Sound travels through the medium of molecules bumping into each other. They can be air molecules, iron molecules, helium molecules, or just about any other substance.

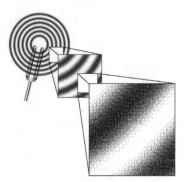

2.1 If we could see sound, it would look like this. Air molecules are squeezed together and pulled apart by the vibrations of the tuning fork.

If the pressure keeps changing repeatedly within certain speed ranges, you've got sound. Something—a drum skin, human vocal cords, the cone of a loudspeaker, or anything else that makes noise—starts vibrating back and forth. As its surface moves towards us, it squeezes air molecules together. As it moves away from us, it creates a very slight vacuum that pulls the molecules apart.

If we *could* freeze sound and see the individual molecules, they'd look like Figure 2.1.

Think of Figure 2.1 as a snapshot of a single moment in the life of a sound. Air molecules are represented as tiny black dots, and as we enlarge sections of the picture, we can see individual ones.

The Life of a Sound

The tuning fork vibrates back and forth. When its surface moves towards the air molecules next to it, it squeezes them together. Those compressed molecules push against the ones a little farther from the tuning fork, and that squeezes the farther molecules together. The farther molecules now push against ones even farther, and so on: as the squeezing spreads out to successive layers of molecules, the pressure spreads out.

Air molecules, like everything else in the physical universe, take time to move from one place to another. So even while the pressure is spreading outward, the tuning fork—which is vibrating back and forth—may start moving back in the other direction. The air molecules next to the fork rush back in to fill the space where it was, pulling them a little further apart than normal. This very slight vacuum—engineers call it *rarefaction*—pulls on the next layer of molecules a little farther from the tuning fork, spacing them apart. And the process repeats to successive layers.

Everybody Feels the Pressure

As you can imagine, pent-up molecules try to push away from what's squeezing them together. They don't necessarily push in a straight line from the sound source, so the sound spreads in all directions. Because of this basic principle:

- You can point a light, but you can't point a sound.
- You can aim a lens to avoid something out-of-frame, but you can't effectively aim a microphone to "miss" a distracting sound.

Eventually the waves of pressure and rarefaction reach our ears. The eardrum vibrates in response, and the vibration is carried across tiny bones to a canal filled with nerves. Different nerves are sensitive to vibrations at different speeds, so they tell the brain how fast the vibrations are occurring. Those nerve messages about the speed of the vibrations, how strong the vibrations are, and how their strength changes over time, are what we hear as sound.

It Matters How Frequently You Do It

Since sound is changes of pressure, its only characteristics can be how much pressure exists at any moment, and how often the pressure changes. Let's deal with the "how often" part first.

Think back to the imaginary world of Figure 2.1, where we could see individual molecules. If we stand in one place, we would see waves of pressure and rarefaction go past us. With an imaginary stopwatch, we could measure the time from the most intense pressure of one wave to the most intense pressure of the next. This timing reflects how quickly the tuning fork is vibrating, changing from pushing molecules in one direction to pulling them back in the other.

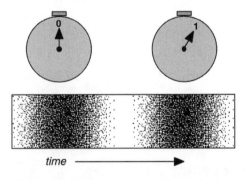

2.2 Timing from one pressure peak to the next.

Figure 2.2 shows two peaks that are one second apart. If the vibration continues at this rate, we could say it's vibrating with a frequency of one cycle per second. That's a mouthful, so we use the term Hertz—named after a 19th-century German physicist—or its abbreviation Hz instead.

A Hertz is one complete cycle per second. That's too slow for us to hear as a sound. Another measurement—kiloHertz, or kHz—represents 1,000 cycles per second.

Fast Pressure Changes are Heard as Sounds

It's generally accepted that humans can hear sounds in a range between 20 Hz and 20 kHz. This is a little like saying, "Humans can run a mile in four minutes." A few exceptional humans can hear this range, and even the best hearing deteriorates as you get older. Fortunately, very few useful sounds extend to these limits. If all you consider are basic vibrations:

- The highest note of a violin is about 3.5 kHz.

- The highest note on an oboe is around 1.8 kHz.

- In fact, of all the instruments in the orchestra, only the pipe organ can vibrate faster than 5 kHz.

Figure 2.3 shows the basic vibration of various instruments.

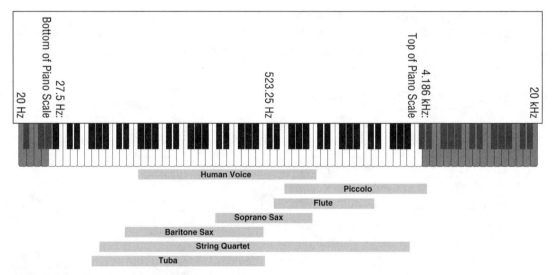

2.3 Basic vibrations of common instruments.

Harmonics

The fastest that a violin string or oboe reed can vibrate is considerably less than 5 kHz. But frequencies higher than that are still important. To see how, we need to refine how we look at the pressure waves.

A microphone converts sound pressure into electrical voltage. If we connect the microphone to an oscilloscope—a device that displays a graph of voltage changes over time (a video waveform monitor is one form of oscilloscope)—we can see the wave with considerable detail. Figure 2.4 shows how an ideal wave looks.

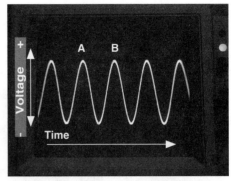

2.4 A pure wave on an oscilloscope.

Positive pressure generates a positive voltage, forming the peaks. Negative pressure generates negative voltage, forming the valleys. The two voltage peaks A and B represent the two pressure peaks in Figure 2.2.

But this is a pure wave, also known as a sine wave from its mathematical function (this may be the only time you'll see "mathematical function" in this book). I generated it electronically because pure sine waves almost never occur in nature. In the real world, most things that vibrate don't have this perfect, symmetrical back-and-forth movement.

The basic back-and-forth movement is called the *fundamental*. It carries most of the energy and is what we hear as the pitch of a sound.

But there also are imperfections in the movement, caused by how the mechanism vibrates. The imperfections take the form of softer higher-frequency waves, called *harmonics*, superimposed on the fundamental. The shape of the instrument and what it's made of determine how much of the harmonics we hear.

- These higher harmonics make the difference between an oboe and a violin when they're playing the same note. (You can even see the difference, in Figures 2.5 and 2.6.)

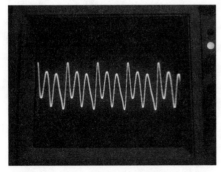

2.5 An oboe playing concert A . . .

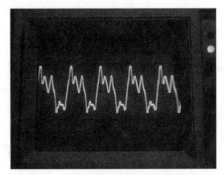

2.6 . . . and a violin playing the same note.

Notice how every third wave of the oboe is stronger than the others. This is the basic or fundamental vibrating frequency of its reed. The smaller peaks are a harmonic, three times as fast. The violin's strongest waves are exactly as far apart as the oboe's because they're both playing the same note. But it has a more complicated mixture of harmonics, ranging from two to eight times the fundamental. They combine to produce the complex pattern of the violin's wave, which is why you can tell an oboe from a fiddle when they're playing the same note.

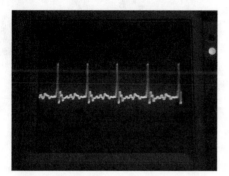

2.7 A trumpet's A shows a very different pattern.

Just for fun, here's the same note on a trumpet: the fundamental is much stronger than its very complex harmonic pattern (Figure 2.7).

You can hear harmonics at work. Track 1 of the CD that came with this book has the four waves you've just seen, played first at full fidelity, and then through a sharp filter that eliminates frequencies above the fundamental. Listen to it on a good hi-fi system: you'll find it's easy to tell the instruments apart when you can hear the harmonics, but very difficult when you can't hear them. Then if you can, play the same track through a low-quality speaker—perhaps the one built into your computer's tower—and you'll find it's a lot harder to tell the difference between violin and oboe, even when the filter is turned off!

Unpitched Sounds

Many sounds don't have regularly repeating waves at all. You can't pick a note for the sounds of an explosion or rustling leaves because they're caused by random movements. Instead of any particular pitch, each wave is a different length. The lengths can fall within certain limits: when we talk about a high-pitched noise (such as a hissing air) or a low-pitched one (like thunder), we're really describing its frequency limits.

(?) Say What?

Human speech has highly complex harmonic patterns. We control them by changing the shape of the mouth. Try singing "eee," "ooo," and "aah" on the same note. The fundamental pitch stays the same for each, but the harmonics change as you move your tongue back and forth.

Human speech is a combination of pitches with harmonics (the vowels), unpitched noises (about half of the consonants), and noises at the same time as pitches (the other consonants).

The Myths of Frequency Response

One of the ways to rate the quality of a sound system is to measure the highest frequency it can carry. For a system to be considered "high fidelity," we usually expect it to be able to handle harmonics up to 20 kHz. But in a lot of cases, this much range isn't necessary.

- Until digital TV becomes a strong force in the marketplace, the upper limit for television and FM radio broadcasting in the United States is 15 kHz. Frequencies higher than that cause problems with the transmission system.

- Most Hollywood films made before the 1970s—including all the great musicals—carried harmonics only up to about 12.5 kHz, and most theater sound systems weren't designed to handle much more than that.

- We don't need high frequencies to recognize people's voices or understand speech. Telephones don't carry anything above 3.5 kHz . . . but most people would describe a telephone as lacking bass notes, not high ones. Syndicated radio talk shows, even on FM stations, are often limited to 7.5 kHz to save transmission costs.

- Even most high-fidelity systems aren't hi-fi. While it's easy to build an amplifier with 20 kHz response, very few speakers can handle those high-frequency sounds accurately. Manufacturers regularly manipulate ratings, or use deliberately imprecise measurements, when describing their speakers.

Track 2 of this book's CD can help you tell how well your own systems handle high frequencies. It consists of musical selections that alternate between being played at full fidelity and through different filters that eliminate various high frequencies. If your speakers (and ears) are capable of handling the highest tones, you'll notice a distinct difference when the filters are switched on and off. But if those frequencies aren't making it through your system anyway, the filters won't have any effect.

Most people won't hear any difference between the unfiltered version and the version with an 18 kHz cutoff. Depending on their age, many won't even hear a significant loss with a 15 kHz cutoff.

Try playing this part of the CD at your editing station as well. You might be amazed how much you're missing through typical multimedia or personal monitoring speakers.

Somewhat Slower Pressure Changes are Heard as Envelopes

We know that fast pressure changes—above 1/20th of a second or so—are heard as sounds. But if we compare the peak pressure from one wave to the next, we'll also see slower changes over time. This is the sound's *envelope*, how it varies between loud and soft over a period as short as a fraction of a second. Figure 2.8 shows the envelope of about a second and a half of dialog. This is too long a period to display on an oscilloscope, so I'm using a screen shot from an audio-editing program instead. But the display is exactly the same: the vertical axis is sound pressure translated into voltage, and the horizontal axis is time.

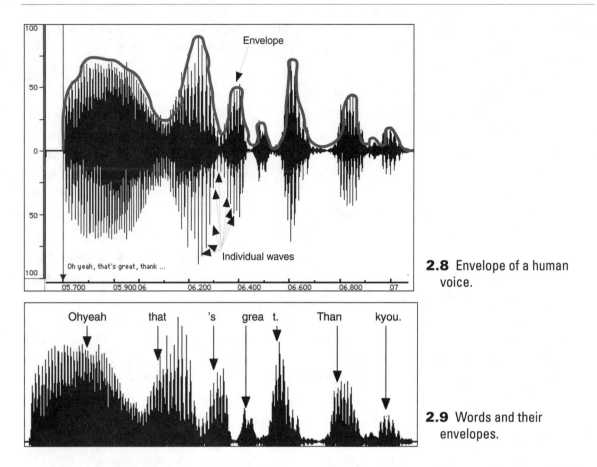

2.8 Envelope of a human voice.

2.9 Words and their envelopes.

If you look closely you can see individual waves. But if you look at the larger picture—which I've traced with a heavy gray line—you can see the slower changes of volume that make up the envelope.

Speech envelopes are very seldom related to individual words because people tend to elide words together: We. Don't. Talk. Like. This. The voice in Figure 2.8 is saying "Oh yeah, that's great . . . thank you," but it's difficult to correlate those sounds with the peaks of the envelope unless you've had a lot of editing experience. I've done it for you in Figure 2.9: note how some peaks are shared by more than one word, while some words have more than one peak.

This suggests two rules:

- You don't edit words in a soundtrack. You edit envelopes.
- Unless you're doing the most rudimentary cutting—moving whole paragraphs that have big pauses between them—it's impossible to mark edits just by examining an envelope. You have to listen.

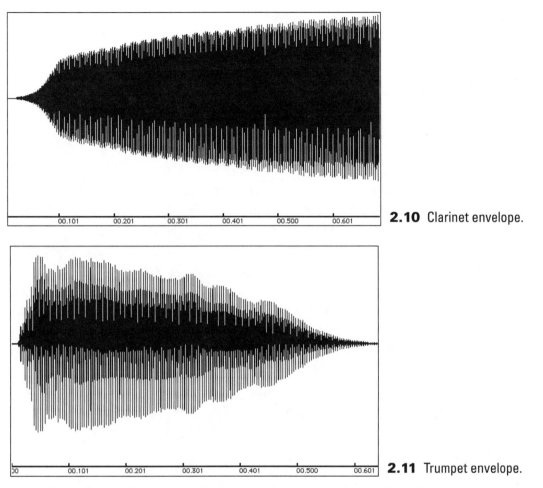

2.10 Clarinet envelope.

2.11 Trumpet envelope.

Obviously, envelope plays a large part in how we understand speech. But it's also important in how we differentiate musical instruments. Compare the clarinet in Figure 2.10 with the trumpet in Figure 2.11: The clarinet starts its sound slowly, as the reed's vibrations get reinforced by the resonance of the tube. The trumpet starts with a burst that's characteristic of all brass instruments, as the musician's lips start vibrating from built-up air pressure (it's often called a *brass blip* by people who work with synthesizers).

In Chapter 16, you'll see how devices like a compressor can manipulate the envelope to make a sound stronger—or to completely change its character.

When Envelopes and Frequencies Overlap

The time scale in the previous screenshots is calibrated in seconds. If you look closely at Figure 2.11, you can see that the "blip" takes about .03 second. But we've already learned that frequencies higher than 20 Hz—or 0.05 second per wave—are audible. So is the blip part of the envelope or a sound by itself?

In this case, it's part of the envelope because the repeating wave is a lot faster: 0.0038 second (261 Hz), corresponding to C4 on the piano. But the issue becomes important when you're dealing with predominantly low-frequency sounds, including many male voices, because the equipment can't differentiate between envelopes and waves unless you adjust it carefully.

Slow Changes of Pressure are Loudness

You can play that trumpet note through a pocket radio at its lowest volume, or blast it out of a giant stadium sound system, and still hear it as a trumpet. The range of overall sound levels we can hear is amazing. A jet plane landing is about ten trillion times more powerful than the quietest sound audiologists use to test your ears.

Our brains can handle such a wide range of pressure because they deal with volume changes as ratios rather than absolute amounts. A sound that would be absolutely jarring in a quiet setting is practically ignored in a noisy one. (A crying baby is a major distraction in a public library—but put that baby in a noisy factory, and you can't hear it at all.) The standard way to think about loudness ratios is to use decibels. Here's how they work.

> ⚠ **Warning**
> The following dozen paragraphs contain some math. It's simple math, but it's numbers nonetheless. If this scares you, just skip down to the box labeled "Bottom Line."

The Need for a Reference

Since our brains hear loudness as ratios, we can't describe how loud a sound is unless we relate it to some other sound. Scientists have agreed on a standardized "other" sound, nominally the softest thing an average healthy person can hear. It's often called the *threshold of hearing*. A quiet living room may have a sound-pressure level about a thousand times the standard. The level at a busy city street is about five million times the standard.

Adjusting a sound's volume means multiplying its positive and negative pressure by a specific ratio. But its original volume was measured as a ratio to the threshold of hearing, so the new volume is the product of both ratios combined. You start with the ratio between the original sound and the standard, and then multiply it by another ratio that represents the volume change. These ratios are usually fairly complex (rather than something easy, like the ratio of 3:1) so the math can get messy. We use a shortcut—logarithms—to make life easier.

The Logarithm

"Help! I don't know a thing about logarithms!"

Just remember two rules:

- Any logarithm is a ratio expressed as a single number. The ratio "three to one" is the log "0.477". (Nobody remembers all the logarithms; you look them up in tables or use a calculator or spreadsheet.)

- If you have to multiply two ratios, you can just add their logs instead. If you have to divide two ratios, just subtract their logs. Complex problems involving multiple ratios become simple matters of addition or subtraction.

Here's an example of how logarithms save you time: A reasonable pressure level for an announcer's voice, standing one foot away, is 349,485 times the threshold of hearing, or a ratio expressed as log 5.8. Suppose we have to make that voice twice as loud. Loudness is influenced by a lot of subjective factors, but if we're considering just sound pressure, we'd want to multiply it by two. The ratio 2:1 is the logarithm 0.3010299957 (close enough to 0.3 for any practical purpose).

Sound pressure is the product of two factors: power and the area it occupies. To give something twice as much pressure, we either have to double both factors, or double just the power *twice*.

So we have to multiply the ratio of the announcer's voice to the threshold of hearing, times two, times two. On a piece of paper it would look like

```
ratio of one to    349,485
                 x       2
                 x       2
                 ----------
ratio of one to  1,397,940
```

Logs make the job a lot easier:

```
   5.8
+   .3
+   .3
  ----
   6.4
```

So if we turn up an amplifier so the voice is mathematically twice as loud as it was before, the result is log 6.4 times as loud as the threshold of hearing.

The Decibel

The engineering term for the logarithm of any two acoustic or electric power levels is the *Bel*, named for the fellow who invented telephones. A decibel is actually 1/10th of a Bel, which is why it's abbreviated dB. We use a tenth of a Bel because it multiplies the log by 10, making it easier to think about (trust me, that's how logs work). So the announcer's voice at one foot had a sound-pressure level with a ratio of 58 dB to the standard reference, commonly written as 58 dB SPL *(Sound Pressure Level)*.

Bottom line: The software and equipment you use to manipulate sounds work in terms of voltage, representing pressure. So to double an electrical volume, we turn its knob up 6 dB.

The Speed of Sound Matters to a Videographer

Sound pressure travels through the air, as one molecule bumps the one next to it. This takes time: roughly a thousandth of a second to go one foot. (In nonrough numbers, 1,087 feet/second at 32° Fahrenheit, speeding up as things get warmer.)

A thousandth of a second doesn't seem like much when you're producing a video. But it adds up: when an object is 30 feet away, its sound takes about a frame to reach us. This can be critical if you're shooting distant events with a long lens and a camera-mounted mic because the visual distance to the image won't match the timing to its sound. This is made worse by the conventions of the small screen: we expect to hear an effect exactly in sync with the picture, no matter how far away they're supposed to be. An explosion a hundred feet away, placed realistically, will strike most viewers as being three frames late. Science-fiction adventure films carry this to extremes: you can blow up a planet thousands of miles away and hear it explode instantly . . . through the vacuum of space.

Sync errors because of distance also affect how we hear sound in a large theater. An effect that's perfectly in sync for the front row can appear two or three frames late in the back of the hall. There's nothing film producers can do about this.

Echoes and Colorations

The speed of sound also determines how we (or our microphones) hear sounds in enclosed spaces. Sound bounces off hard surfaces—air molecules can't relieve their pressure by moving the wall or ceiling, so they spring back in the opposite direction—and the reflected waves mix with the original ones.

If we hear the reflection later than about a tenth of a second after the original sound, it's perceived as an echo. In some cases, the sound keeps bouncing between surfaces in the room: many echoes, randomly spaced, are heard as reverberation. If the sound can travel a distance between bounces, and the space has lots of different surfaces to bounce off, the reverb sounds richer. But almost any enclosed shooting space—not just cathedrals and courtrooms—will have some form of echoes. You might not hear them as reverberation, but they can add realism to a scene. They can also interfere with intelligibility and are one of the main causes of amateur-sounding tracks. We'll devote a lot of pages to them in later chapters.

Echoes in small rooms

We're usually not aware of how sound bounces in small spaces like offices or editing rooms because the reflections arrive very quickly. But they can cause major problems if you want to record or critically listen in the room, because of how they combine with the original sound.

Think of the compression-rarefaction cycle of a sound wave like the phases of the moon. A moon goes through continuous cycles from dark to bright and back, just as a sound wave cycles between pressure and partial vacuum. In fact, the word *phase* refers to the timing of any repeating phenomenon: the moon, sound waves, or even rotating engine parts.

Now, if we had two moons in our sky and each was in its full phase at the same time, we'd have a very bright night. But if one moon was new while the other was full—if the phases didn't match—it wouldn't be as bright.

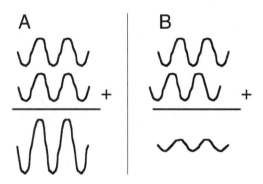

When two sound waves are in the same phase, they add together the same way. Figure 2.12A shows how this works with our familiar pressure-over-time graph. Where both waves are providing positive pressure, we have twice as much pressure; where both are in their vacuum phase, we have twice as much vacuum.

2.12 Sounds add differently depending on their phase

But Figure 2.12B shows what happens if one of the sounds is later in its cycle. Where the top sound has pressure, the bottom one is almost at its strongest vacuum and absorbs the pressure. Where the bottom one is pushing, the top one is pulling. The two forces cancel each other, leaving very little sound. Since both sounds are at the same frequency, this cancellation continues for each wave.

This is more than just an academic exercise. These cancellations happen all the time in the real world. In Figure 2.13, our listener hears both a direct sound from the tuning fork and a reflected one from a nearby wall. Unfortunately, since the reflected path is a different length than the direct one, the reflection takes longer to arrive and is at a different phase when it gets to the listener. The reflected sound is compressing while the direct sound is in rarefaction. The two paths cancel each other's sound.

If you moved the listener's head in the drawing, the relationship between direct and reflected sound would be different. At some positions the waves reinforce; at others, they'll cancel.

If you want to actually hear this happening, grab a hard-surfaced object like a clipboard or a notebook. Then play Track 3 of the CD: a steady high-frequency tone (7.5 kHz) recorded on one channel only. Set it so the sound comes out of one speaker at a moderately low volume, and get three or four feet away from the speaker. Move your head a foot or so in either direction, and you'll hear the sound get louder and softer. Hold your head steady with the hard-surfaced object parallel to your ear and about a foot away, and then move it farther and closer. You'll hear the sound change volume as you do.

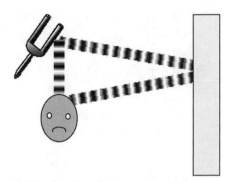

2.13 A reflection can arrive at a different phase from the original sound.

The situation gets worse when you start dealing with complex sounds. Different frequencies will be at different phases, depending on how far they've traveled. So when the direct path's sound mixes with its reflection, some frequencies will cancel, but others will reinforce. In Figure 2.14, a loudspeaker generating two tones replaces the tuning fork.

Over the direct path, the high frequency (closely spaced waves) and the low frequency (waves are farther apart) both happen to be compressing when they reach the lis-

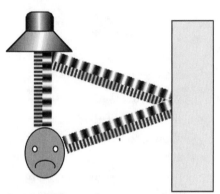

2.14 Different frequency sounds get canceled differently by their echoes.

tener. When the reflected low frequency reaches the listener, it also happens to be compressing: the two paths reinforce each other. But when the reflected high frequency reaches the listener, it's in rarefaction. It cancels the direct path. As far as Figure 2.14's listener is concerned, the sound has a lot less treble.

Track 4 of the CD demonstrates this, with a 400 Hz low frequency added to the 7.5 kHz high one. Play it like you did Track 3, get at least four feet from the speaker, and start moving your head around. Unless you're in a room with very few reflections, at some positions you'll hear the high frequency predominate. At others, the lower frequency will seem louder.

Real-world sounds have a lot more frequencies, and real rooms have lots of reflecting paths. Full and partial cancellations occur at random places throughout the spectrum. So what you hear at any given point in the room depends a lot on the size and shape of the room. (Ever notice how the inside of a phone booth sounds "boxy"? That's why.)

We get used to rooms very quickly (as soon as you're into the conversation, you forget how boxy the phone booth sounds). That's because we can use our eyes and ears together to correlate the sound of a room with its shape.

But if we put a microphone in one room, and then listen to the playback somewhere else, the cancellations become more obvious. And if the characters are moving around as they talk, the cancellations are constantly changing—just as they did when you moved around the room while listening to Track 4. The result is a distracting hollowness or boxiness. That's why a lot of soundtracks sound less than professional.

The Inverse Square Law

Fortunately, physics is on our side. As sound spreads out from a source, the pressure waves have to cover a larger area. But the total amount of power doesn't change, so the pressure at any one point is less. Light works the same way: as you get farther from a spotlight, the size of the beam increases but its brightness diminishes.

2.15 As you get farther away, the pressure gets less intense.

In fact, under ideal conditions (a nondirectional sound source and an echo-free listening environment), the intensity of a sound diminishes with the square of the distance. This is called the inverse square law. Figure 2.15 puts it in graphic terms.

Since decibels compare the loudness of two sounds, and they use logarithms to make things like squares easier to compute, the inverse square law can be very simply stated:

Each time you double the distance from a sound source, its sound pressure becomes 6 dB less.

If a microphone hears an instrument as 58 dB SPL at one foot, it'll hear it as 52 dB SPL at two feet, or 46 dB SPL at four feet.

The inverse square law applies to ideal conditions, with a nondirectional sound source and no hard surfaces to stop sound from spreading. Most sources are directional at some frequencies, and anywhere you shoot is going to have hard surfaces. But the law still holds up fairly well in the real world:

> If you can get closer to a sound source—and farther from interfering sounds or reflective surfaces—you'll record it better.

If we take our bad-sounding setup in Figure 2.14, but increase the distance to the wall, the inverse square law reduces the amount of cancellation. Figure 2.16 shows how this works.

The first rule explains why camera-mounted microphones rarely do a good job of rejecting interference or echoes. The camera is usually too far away from the sound source.

The second rule is the principle behind the "nearfield" speakers that sit on the console of just about every recording studio in the world.

2.16 When we get farther from a reflecting surface, there's much less cancellation.

Make the inverse square law your friend:

- Try to place a microphone at least three times closer to the sound source than it is to any source of interference.

- If you want to listen to a playback in a less-than-perfect editing room, try to be at least three times closer to the speakers than to any reflecting walls.

"Soundproofing"

The wedge-shaped foam panels, special tiles, or tuned cavities you see in recording studios aren't there to stop sound from entering or leaving the room. It's to reduce reflections by absorbing sound energy and turning it into mechanical motion. Sound studios also frequently have rigid curved or sculpted panels along one wall, to diffuse the reflections so cancellations don't build up at a particular frequency.

Later in this book, we'll discuss specific ways to use absorption and diffusion for better sound when you're shooting, recording voice-overs, and mixing.

We'll also discuss the use (and limitations) of portable sound barriers and how to take advantage of existing building features to block sound. But true soundproofing—stopping outside noises from getting into a room, or keeping a loud mixing session from disturbing the neighbors—requires special construction techniques and belongs in a different book. You'll find some explanations in my book *Audio Postproduction for Digital Video*, in a section about building a new audio or editing room.

- For the practical video producer, the best soundproofing is understanding:

- Know how to avoid situations where reflected or incidental sounds will interfere with what you're trying to do.

Very Slow Changes of Pressure are Weather

Barometric pressure—the stuff reported in the evening weather forecast—is exactly the same kind of molecular pressure as sound, changing over hours and days instead of seconds and milliseconds. I include it here for the sake of completeness, to suggest there's a cosmic continuum that links all things, and because, after this chapter, you could use some comic relief.

Chapter 3

How Digital Audio Works

Why Digital?

Audio, when it's vibrating through the air, is definitely not digital. Pressure varies smoothly between compression and rarefaction, rather than in steps that can be related to specific numbers. Or to put it another way, the tines of a tuning fork don't click back and forth like the one on the left of Figure 3.1; they vibrate continuously like the one on the right.

A microphone turns this changing sound pressure into continuously changing voltage. If we want, we can store these voltage changes for later playback:

- We can use them to wiggle a needle and cut grooves in a moving phono disk.

- We can use them to wiggle a shutter and cast shadows on a moving film track.

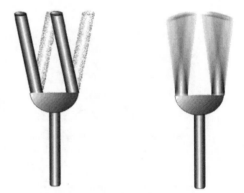

3.1 A digital tuning fork—if there were such a thing—could instantly click between two positions *(left)*. But real ones *(right)* move smoothly between the extremes.

- We can send them through a coil and make patterns of varying magnetism on a moving tape that's been covered with iron particles.

Then we can reverse the process, create a varying voltage from what we've stored, and send it to a speaker diaphragm that pushes or pulls the air, recreating a sound. What we've really stored is a mechanical, optical, or magnetic analogy of the sound. Analog recording is a century old, well refined, and works pretty well.

So why complicate matters by turning the sound into computer data?

We Don't Use Digital Audio Because it's Nonlinear; We Use it Because it's Robust

The nonlinear revolution primarily affected video production. Film and audio tape have always been nonlinear: you could open any scene or sequence, any time, and trim or add new material. Computerized sound editing may be faster or less messy than splicing tape (in some cases, it's slower), but that's not why the industry adopted digital sound.

Historically, media production is the process of copying images or sound from one place onto another. Pieces of movie film are copied onto others for special effects, composite masters, and release prints. Videotape can't be spliced, so it's edited by copying from one deck to another. Music originates on multi-track recorders, is copied to a master tape, and then dubbed again before being turned into a cassette or CD. A movie soundtrack may go through six or more copies between the shooting stage and the theater.

Step 1: Original   Step 2: Copy of Step 1   Step 3: Copy of Step 2   Step 4: Copy of Step 3

3.2 A multigenerational cat, analog and digital.

But analog doesn't copy well. When analog images are copied, grain builds up and subtle shadings are lost. A similar thing happens when you copy analog audio: noise builds up and high frequencies are lost. Each time you play an analog tape, it wears out a little and sounds a tiny bit worse.

Digital data doesn't slowly deteriorate. When you copy a number, you get exactly that number—never a little more or less. You can store digital data, play it countless times, manipulate various aspects of it, transmit it across great distances, and it'll always be the numbers you expect. Digits are ideal for the "copy-after-copy" style of media production.

Figure 3.2 shows a simple visual analogy. If we photocopy the cat, and then copy the copy, we start to lose details. After a few generations, we have nothing left but a blob with whiskers. But if we invent a digital code that spells the word CAT, we can make as many successive copies as we want. Those three letters aren't enough information to identify Mr. Whiskers, there, as well as the photos do. But if we can tolerate longer codes, we can spell out every one of his feline details.

Digital Audio Hides its Mistakes

If one of the analog pictures got scratched before its copy was made, we'd be stuck with the scratch forever . . . but we'd still recognize the cat. If that copy got scratched, *its* copy would be even worse.

Digital audio handles data loss differently:

- Small data errors are reconstructed perfectly. The system uses checking digits to find out what the missing data should have been, and recreates it.

- Medium data errors are hidden. The checking digits let the system know that *something* is missing, but it doesn't have enough data to make a perfect reproduction. Instead, the system guesses the missing data by interpolating from the numbers it knows are good. In almost every case, the repair is transparent.

- Large data errors are also detected because of the checking digits. But since there isn't enough known-good data, the whole signal deteriorates into noise or is turned off.

In an analog system, even slight problems cause noise or distortion. But large problems may still leave recognizable—if not attractive—signals. In digital you can't

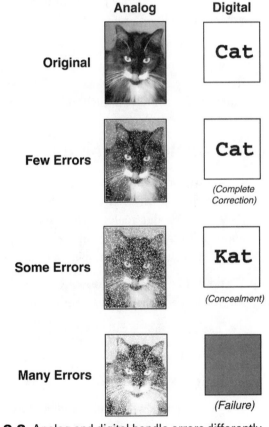

3.3 Analog and digital handle errors differently.

hear the small problems at all, and the big ones are catastrophic. Figure 3.3 charts this difference.

As with any other data, it's just common sense to back up anything you may ever want to keep:

- Make copies of all masters. If a digital audio tape gets damaged, it may not be recoverable.

- After a few years, it may be a good idea to make copies of the *copies* on truly important projects.

The idea behind making periodic copies of important backups is to catch errors before they become too large to accurately correct. If a tape or CD-ROM has deteriorated so much that error concealment is taking place, you might not hear there's a problem . . . but subsequent generations can make it a lot worse.

The jury's still out on the useful life of various media. I have DAT tapes from 1988 that are still playable, but colleagues at that time were seeing tapes die after three or four years. When recordable CDs came out in the mid-90s, there were reports of media deteriorating very quickly (but my archives from that era are fine). Now, CD-R manufacturers claim lives of 25–75 years. The accelerated life tests rely primarily on heat cycling; the discs haven't been around long enough for anybody to tell for sure.

It appears as though early adopters suffer the most in this regard. As media manufacturers gain experience, they can turn out more reliable products. But any medium is subject to failure—analog tapes recorded in the early 1980s were literally falling apart by the mid-90s, because of "improved" formulas in their manufacture.

Turning Analog to Digital

Digital circuits are immune to gradual noise because they ignore ambiguity. A bit of information is either zero or one. If a signal falls between those two values, the circuit picks one and ignores the difference. But analog signals are always changing. They seldom are precisely one value or another. To take advantage of the digital process, we have to change a smoothly varying, often fractional voltage into unambiguous numbers.

We do this by taking a snapshot of the voltage at a particular moment, measuring and reporting the voltage, and then taking another snapshot.

- Each snapshot is called a *sample*.

- How often we take these snapshots is the *sample frequency*.

- How precisely we measure the voltage is the *sample depth*.

Those two qualities—sample depth and frequency—determine the limits of how accurately a digital stream can represent a sound.

Sample Depth

We used an oscilloscope in Chapter 1 to show sound waves. This analog gadget displays varying voltage along the vertical and ongoing time along the horizontal. Aside from being a vital piece of test equipment, it's handy for visualizing audio processes.

In Figure 3.4, I've drawn horizontal lines across the oscilloscope to represent voltage levels. (These lines are actually printed on the faces of most scopes, but don't show up well in the photo.) The numerical units I've assigned to them are completely arbitrary, but, for the sake of simplicity, we'll call them volts. The signal is an oboe, amplified so it's approximately +10 volts where the microphone picked up its highest compression and –10 volts where it picked up its deepest rarefaction.

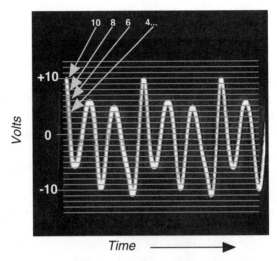

3.4 An oscilloscope displays voltage over time.

The arrows in the upper left show how the waveform reaches different voltages at different times.

It's very easy to build an electrical comparator: a circuit that turns on when an input reaches a particular level, and off when the input falls below the level. If we had a bunch of comparators, each one set to turn on at a different voltage, we could change the analog signal into a digital one. The highest-voltage comparator that's turned on is the unambiguous digital value.

But if we zoom in on the waveform, we can see there might be problems.

Figure 3.5 shows the same waveform, redrawn twice as large. The value at time A is six volts. But what about time B? Five and a half volts is an illegal value in a system that requires whole numbers. The comparators would say it's five volts, but they'd be wrong.

The solution is to use a *lot* of comparators, spaced very closely together. Computer designers combine bits together to represent high numbers, and each time they add another bit, they double the number of possibilities.

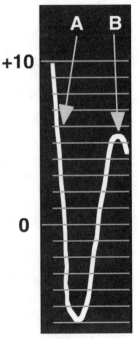

3.5 An ambiguous voltage at B

Adding bits can make a big difference. Figure 3.6 shows our cat in both two- and three-bit versions. With two bits, there are four possible values: black, white, and two grays. But a three-bit photo has eight possible values: black, white, and *six* different grays. It makes a big difference to kitty.

Bits don't have intrinsic value

It's wrong to think of a bit as representing a specific voltage or sound-pressure level. Digital systems don't care what you assign to a single bit. In a vending machine, it might be a nickel. In a cash register, it might be a penny. In a traffic control system, it could be a car. The very first video games assigned each bit the presence of light on a pixel: 1 for on, 0 for off. Today's games assign that smallest bit a value of 1/65,536th the maximum brightness on a pixel. Go ahead—open the color picker in a modern graphics program, and you'll see that big a range for each primary.

3.6 2-bit cat *(upper left)* has only black, white, and two grays. 3-bit cat *(lower right)* has four more grays, for more detail.

The difference between those ancient video games and a modern color computer is the number of bits that are strung together in one word, to express a single number. Teletypes used 6 bits for 64 different characters. Early communication protocols used 7 bits to represent 128 possible ASCII characters, and saved the eighth bit of that byte for other purposes. Today's word processors devote 8 bits for each letter, with 256 possible values, enough to cover most typographic symbols.

The 16-bit solution

The minimum standard for professional digital audio is to use 16 bits, representing 65,536 possible different values for each sample. In terms of sound, that's a pressure change of about 0.00013 dB. Real audio circuits round up as well as down, so the worst error will occur when an analog signal falls precisely between two of those tiny slices: the digital value will be wrong by exactly half a slice, or less than 0.00007 dB.

Note

Radio and TV news used to be transmitted from press associations via teletype. The limited number of characters ruled out lower-case, so news scripts were formatted all-capitals.

That's why scripts were typed upper-case. Not to make them more readable—countless studies have determined they're actually *less* readable than proper upper- and lower-case.

Trust me: an error that tiny doesn't matter in media production.

The error can get worse, however. Once you've digitized that signal, you'll probably want to do things to it: change the level, or equalize it, or do other mathematical processing. Each time you do, there's another chance for the result to fall between two sample levels. The errors that can result sound like random noise. Professionals avoid noise by doing their processing at 24 bits or higher, for a possible error of roughly 0.00000026 dB. (As far as I'm concerned, an error of a quarter-millionth of a dB is pretty accurate. But my digital audio workstation uses 32-bit precision for mixing—I can't print that in precise decibels, because my calculator doesn't handle logarithms that small.)

Bits as dynamic range

You can also look at bit depth another way. Each bit doubles the possible values for a sample. We know from the previous chapter that doubling a voltage means increasing it just about 6 dB. So each bit represents a 6 dB range between the lowest and highest level the system can handle. An 8-bit signal (common in early computers, and still used on the Internet) has a 48 dB range between its loudest sound and where the signal gets buried by ambiguous noise. This is similar to the range for AM radio or 16mm film.

A 16-bit signal has twice the range, or 96 dB (16 × 6 = 96). This is considerably better than FM radio, and close to the limits of human hearing. A 24-bit signal has 144 dB dynamic range, well beyond the limits of even the most golden-eared listener. Those extra bits provide a margin for calculation errors.

Prosumer cameras often have a 12-bit mode as well. It's noisier (12 × 6 = 72 dB), and, considering that most of them recommend setting aside 12 dB for sudden loud sounds, doesn't leave much margin for error. This mode should be avoided.

Most software converts 12-bit signals to 16 bits when you transfer them digitally. This doesn't make existing noise any quieter, but does reduce rounding errors in subsequent processing.

An Analog Myth: "Analog audio is better than digital because digital is 'steppy': some voltages will fall between steps and get lost."

The logic of that statement on the left is correct, but the conclusion is wrong. While a 24-bit system has nearly 17 million possible voltage levels, the sound wave itself can have an infinite number of values. So, yes, some subtle variations will fall between possible digital levels and get lost: this is called a *quantizing error*. It doesn't happen in an analog system.

But analog systems have a random background noise that doesn't exist in digital. You can see, with an oscilloscope, how this noise can have the same effect as quantizing errors. Compare the smooth wave in Figure 3.7 with the quantized one in Figure 3.8.

I used a 7-bit digital signal, with 128 possible levels, to make the quantization error more obvious. Obviously, some detail is getting lost among the stair steps of the digital version. We know the original waveform falls *somewhere* between those steps, but for any given step we can't know whether the original was at the top, the bottom, or anywhere in between. (By the way, the steps are perfectly flat in the digital domain. Some of them look slanted in the figure because I photographed an analog oscilloscope.)

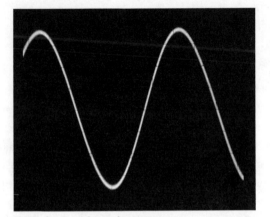

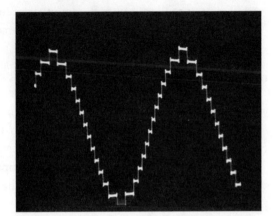

3.7 A smooth analog wave . . .   **3.8** . . . and its 7-bit quantized version.

But remember, this particular digital signal is a pretty awful one: at 6 dB per bit, a 7-bit signal has only a 42 dB range between the loudest and the softest sound possible—less than an AM radio broadcast. It's unfair to compare this low-quality digital signal with what you could achieve with the finest analog system, so let's level the playing field.

An analog system's dynamic range is the difference between the loudest signal it can handle and the noise made by the system itself. If we raise the analog noise to −42 dB below the maximum we can see on the scope—matching the range of our 7-bit digital signal—it looks like Figure 3.9.

In analog systems, the noise mixes with the signal and appears to "ride on top of it," as in Figure 3.10.

This is a much broader scope trace than what we saw in Figure 3.7. It's ambiguous, because the analog noise obscures some of the wave's details. We know the original wave falls *somewhere* in that broad trace; but, at any given moment, we can't tell whether the original was at the top, the bottom, or anywhere in between.

Sound familiar? That's exactly the problem we had with the digital stair steps in Figure 3.8. Once you level the playing field—once you compare audio systems of identical quality—quantization errors aren't any more or less of a problem than analog noise.

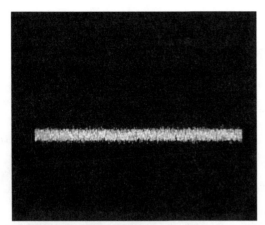

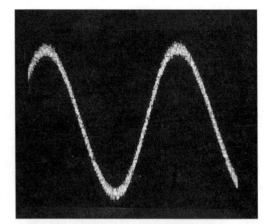

3.9 Analog noise at -42 dB, a quality equivalent to 7-bit digital audio.

3.10 Analog signal with –42 dB noise

By the way, the audio output of a complete digital circuit will never have the kind of steps as in our scope photo. A filter in the circuit smoothes the signal from the midpoint of one step to the midpoint of the next.

Dither: making the most of those bits

The analog myth-mongers are right about one thing: Even with the best digital systems, you'll eventually encounter signal details at the tiny level represented by only one bit. The quantization error is small—it takes trained ears and excellent monitors to hear it in a 16-bit system—but it can be ugly. That's because it creates a distortion that follows the signal but isn't harmonically related.

The solution is to add the same stuff that causes so much trouble in analog circuits: noise. Digital designers add a tiny amount of analog noise, at a level about one-third what a single bit represents. When this random noise has a positive voltage, it pushes the signal details to where the comparator sees it as a 1. When it's negative, it pulls the details down to 0. Because this happens totally randomly, it adds distortion across the entire band . . . not following the desired signal.

This process—called *dithering*—not only reduces distortion at low levels, it even makes it possible to hear some details that are smaller than the lowest possible value! The ear is good at picking up specific sounds even when they're obscured by random noise, something you've probably noticed if you've ever tried to follow a conversation at a noisy cocktail party.

It's easy to understand dither with a visual analogy. Hold your hand in front of this page (as in Figure 3.11), and some of the words are obscured . . . just as if they'd fallen below the lowest level of a digital signal and were zeroed out.

Now start waving your fingers rapidly side-to-side (Figure 3.12). The fingers don't go away—they still cover as much of the page at any one time—but your mind can pick the meaningful words out from the randomly obscuring fingers.

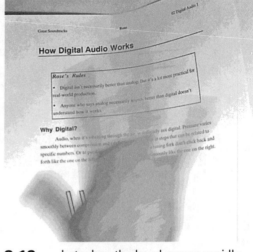

3.11 A steady hand obscures some of the page . . .

3.12 . . . but when the hand moves rapidly, you can "see behind it."

Dither is best used when going from a high-resolution medium to a lower one. Well-designed professional systems apply it during the initial quantization, and on the output of high-bitrate processes. Most desktop video editors never reach this kind of precision, and dither isn't available. Either way, you usually don't have to make decisions about its use.

But if a program gives you the option of dither when converting 16-bit files to 8 bits for older multimedia systems, turn it on. As 20- and 24-bit digital audio equipment becomes more common in the video studio, you'll want to use dithering every time you move to a lower bit depth.

- Avoid low bit depths. The 12-bit recording supported by some digital video equipment *will* be noisy.

- You can't improve a low-bit signal by converting it to a higher depth, because the damage is already done. But changing to a higher bit depth will keep it from getting worse in subsequent processing.

Track 5 of this book's CD lets you hear the effect of different bit depths. The same recording was truncated to 7 bits, 8 bits, and 12 bits. It was then re-encoded at 16 bits so it could be included on a standard CD, but this process doesn't affect the damage done by the lower bit depths.

Sample Rate

Bit rate is only half the equation for digital audio. Because audio only exists as changes of pressure or voltage *over time*, you have to measure it repeatedly if you want to recreate the sound. The more often you measure, the more accurately you'll be able to reproduce the sound.

We'll start with another scope photo. In Figure 3.13, I've added eight vertical lines spaced evenly apart. The scope's electron beam sweeps horizontally across its face at a controlled speed, so each vertical line marks a different time in its sweep. For simplicity, we'll say the vertical lines are one millisecond apart.

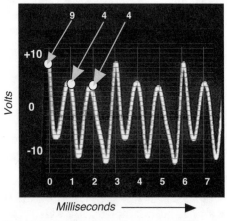

3.13 Sampling over time, at a low sample rate.

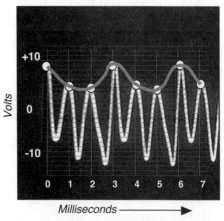

3.14 Badly recreated signal from a very low sample rate.

At the start of this section of sound, the signal is 9 volts. A millisecond later, it's 4 volts. And a millisecond after that, it's 4 volts again. These are the first three samples, and what a digital system would store at this sample rate. Since the samples are one millisecond apart, this system has a sample rate of a thousand times per second (usually written as 1 kHz s/r).

On playback, the system averages these values to produce an output like the gray line in Figure 3.14. This output doesn't look very much like the input, and it wouldn't sound like it either. Obviously this is a bad recording (1 kHz s/r is a ridiculously low rate for digital audio).

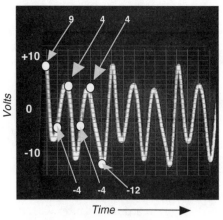

3.15 Doubling the sample rate gives us more data.

But suppose we check the voltage *twice* each millisecond. This raises the sample rate to 2 kHz, doubling the amount of data generated (Figure 3.15).

When we average these samples, we get a somewhat more accurate result (Figure 3.16). Still not perfect, but better.

As you add more samples, you get a better representation of the sound. An older multimedia computer system may check slightly more than 22 samples each millisecond, or a sample rate of 22.050 kHz. Compact discs double that, for a sample rate of 44.1 kHz. Professional digital broadcast formats operate at 48 kHz s/r, and DVD doubles that to 96 kHz. Many sound engineers doubt that a 96 kHz sample rate is necessary (except as marketing hype), but there's a definite relationship between sample rate and sound quality.

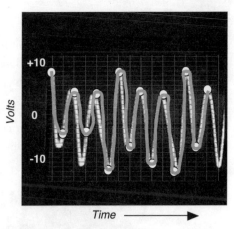

3.16 More samples give us a more faithful picture.

The Nyquist limit and aliasing

In the 1920s Harry Nyquist, an engineer at Bell Labs, proved mathematically that the highest frequency you can faithfully reproduce has to be less than one-half the sample rate. Since U.S. analog FM and TV don't carry audio higher than 15 kHz (to protect other parts of the broadcast signal), the Nyquist theorem suggests a broadcaster doesn't need a sample rate of more than 30 kHz. In fact, a lot of what you hear on the air has been sampled at 32 kHz.

Unfortunately, all Nyquist guarantees is that sounds *below* this limit will be reproduced accurately. A broadcaster's microphone could easily pick up a sound at 17 kHz. Above the Nyquist limit, digital recording does very strange things: it combines the signal with the sample frequency, implying additional signals that are totally unrelated to any harmonics. A simple sine wave will have two additional *aliases*—other waves that could fit the same data. A complex musical signal, with lots of harmonics, may have thousands of aliases. The playback system turns them all back into analog audio, creating a combination of squeaks and whistles accompanying the high frequencies. It isn't pretty, as you can hear from the example on Track 6 of this book's CD.

The only solution is to use an *aliasing filter*: an equalizer that absolutely blocks any frequency higher than half the sample rate and doesn't affect any frequency below it. With no frequencies above the Nyquist limit, there can't be any aliases. The only problem is that a perfect filter like this can't exist.

You can't design a filter with infinite cutoff at one frequency and absolutely no effect on frequencies below it. Any real-world hi-cut filter will have two characteristics:

- A slope between what passes through and what's blocked. As the frequency rises, the volume is slowly turned down—not instantly turned off.

- Some degradation to signals below but close to the cutoff frequency. Even though those lower-frequency signals are passed, they get distorted.

Early digital devices were designed with a safety margin—usually around 10% of the sample rate—to allow for that first characteristic. The first compact disc recorders started their filters sloping slightly below 20 kHz, so they could achieve a good cutoff by they time they reached half the 44.1 kHz sample rate. Many computer sound cards are still designed the same way.

But there's no way to compensate for the second characteristic. The sharper a filter gets, the more it affects sounds below its nominal cutoff frequency. You can put multiple filters in series, or use other techniques to sharpen their rejection, but this inevitably adds distortion as sounds approach the limit. And affordable analog filter components lose their calibration as they get older, further compounding the problem. Depending on what compromises the designer made, early digital devices suffered from high-frequency distortion, aliasing, or both. They earned a reputation for having less-than-ideal sound, the source of many of the "analog is better" myths.

Oversampling

Modern professional equipment solves this problem by using an initial sampling frequency many times higher than the nominal sample rate, as much as two million samples a second or more. This raises the Nyquist limit so that very gentle superhigh frequency filters can be used, which have no effect on the desired audio. The high sample rate signal is then filtered using digital techniques, which are more accurate than analog ones, and down-converted to the desired rate. A similar scheme is used on the output.

Oversampling presents other advantages as well, in that digital artifacts can be spread across a much wider band and not affect the audio signal as much. But it's also more expensive to design and build circuits that use it, because the high data rates require very precise timing. So multimedia equipment seldom takes advantage of the technique. As of this writing, no prosumer camera does, either. If a piece of gear brags about that feature, use it.

The lack of oversampling in cameras isn't generally a problem, because the cameras operate at 48 kHz s/r (in their best mode), and dialog frequencies seldom go above 15 kHz. But if you need absolute best quality for music recording in the field, go *double system* and record audio on a separate device (Chapter 9).

If you're concerned with getting the best quality audio from analog sources in a desktop video-editing system, avoid the built-in inputs. Instead, use a professional external analog-to-digital converter with oversampling. Or have a good sound studio do the conversions and provide you with data on CD-ROM or removable hard drive.

Working with sample rates

Broadcast digital videotape uses a sample rate of 48 kHz, so if you're going to be broadcasting your project digitally, it may make sense to keep your equipment at that setting. But a lot of projects are intended for analog videotape, CD-ROM, or Internet delivery—or will be broadcast in analog format from a digital tape. If that's the case, you should weigh the costs of a high sample rate against its advantages.

- Samples have to be processed. A high sample rate means the CPU will take longer to do data-intensive tasks such as non-real-time effects. Since many systems give priority to audio processing (jumpy sound is a lot more distressing than an occasional skipped video frame), it diverts resources that could be used to improve the video.

- Samples have to be stored. 48 kHz, 16-bit stereo eats more than 11 megabytes of storage space per minute. While hard drive space isn't very expensive, CD-ROM real estate can be.

- Samples have to be transmitted. Data bandwidth is a precious commodity, particularly on the Internet. While MPEG compression techniques (discussed below) can help, they don't work as well on signals with very high bitrates.

The best way to choose a sample rate is to consider the final audience. You've probably already used this book's CD and some of the tests in Chapter 2 to discover that your monitoring system isn't really as wide-range as the manufacturer may have claimed. (If you're over 30, you probably discovered that your ears aren't very wide-range either.) Unless you're sure of a high-quality listening environment, it's unlikely that your audience will ever be in the presence of anything above 17 kHz.

In the U.S. and other NTSC countries, analog broadcast television cuts off at 15 kHz: this is part of the transmission standard, to leave a slice of the band for stereo and second audio channel information. Even the best home-theater systems can't get around it. Most multimedia and kiosk systems aren't very accurate above 12 kHz, and presentations that are mostly spoken word don't have much going on above 10 kHz.

Once you've decided on the highest frequency your project will need to support, double it (to allow for the Nyquist limit), add a safety margin, and choose the closest sample rate. For analog broadcast, that's 32 kHz s/r. For multimedia, it can be as low as 22 kHz.

Most modern audio software does a good job of sample rate conversion. Even if your final output has to be at 48 kHz s/r for digital video, if all of your sound sources are at 44.1 kHz (CDs, DATs, and MiniDiscs), it makes the most sense to keep your NLE at that rate as well. Assemble and mix the show, then convert its track in an audio program. But do a test first, if sync is critical—some software changes the timing slightly when converting sample rates.

- The high-frequency loss of a lower sample rate is not cumulative. Things don't get worse when you digitally dub or mix the track. This is contrary to the way analog recording works.

- Once a sound has been sampled at one rate, there's almost never any benefit to converting it to a higher rate except compatibility.

There is one exception to that second rule. *Harmonic enhancers* are processors that change the timbre of a sound, brightening it by creating artificial harmonics at frequencies an octave higher than the original recording. A very low sample rate recording can often be subjectively improved by converting it to a higher rate and then using an enhancer. But bear in mind that the equalizers provided with audio- and video-editing software are not enhancers, and won't improve low-rate recordings.

Audio Data Reduction

If the goal is simply to reduce storage space or Internet bandwidth, there are better strategies than lowering the sample rate or bit depth. Audio data reduction or compression relies on statistical and psychoacoustic principles to squeeze a lot of sound into the smallest number of bits. While they do compromise the sound quality—and are often referred to as *lossy compression* by audio engineers—they don't damage it anywhere near as much as an equivalent reduction in raw data. In fact, these techniques are considered so benign that they're part of the specification for digital television, multi-track digital film sound, and DVD.

As good as data-reduction techniques get, they're not perfect. And subsequent mixing, editing, and re-reduction make the sound a lot worse. So if you're using them, be sure to keep an uncompressed version on a backup tape or disk.

Standard redundancy-compression methods like PKZIP and Stuffit aren't much good for audio. They rely on finding repeating patterns in the data, and normal audio is just too random—in a numeric sense—to have these patterns. The best they can do with a typical track is only a few percent reduction.

Delta Encoding

Fortunately, most sounds do have one predictable element: from one sample to the next, the incremental change isn't very great. Figure 3.17 shows how this works, using a 16-bit recording of a piano.

From one extreme of this wave to the other, there's a difference of about 47,500 digital values. It would take a full 16-bit word to represent it accurately. But from one sample to the next, the biggest difference is never more than about 5,000 digital values. We need only 13 bits to record the jump from a single sample to the one after it.

This *delta encoding* is the basis of QuickTime IMA, one of the first popular multimedia compression methods and still found on many editing systems. It can cut files down to a quarter of their original size without seriously affecting the audio quality.

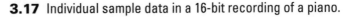

3.17 Individual sample data in a 16-bit recording of a piano.

Delta coding has the advantage of easy math, can be played back on virtually any CPU, and doesn't add much distortion to most well-recorded speech or music. But it can't cope with very sudden changes: beeps, clicks, and sharp sound effects can be surrounded by noise. Track 7 of this book's CD shows examples of IMA encoded signals.

Perceptual Encoding and Masking

Psychoacoustic researchers have known for most of the past century that our ears aren't very good at the extremes of the audio band. We evolved with our most sensitive hearing in the midrange, probably because that's where we can best hear predators or the warnings of fellow tribe members. Figure 3.18 shows a typical threshold of hearing curve. Sounds that are louder than the curve at a particular frequency will be heard; those softer than the curve at their frequency—or within the gray area—disappear for most listeners.

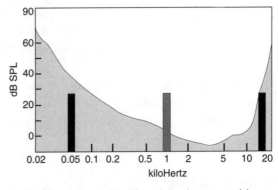

3.18 The threshold of hearing changes with frequency.

There are actually many threshold of hearing curves because the relative sensitivity to different frequencies will change based on how loud a sound is. But in almost every case, your ears will be the most sensitive within the speech range of around 350–3,500 Hz. Most people can hear more than 16 bits' worth of detail at the top of that range.

A relatively soft sound at 1 kHz (the gray bar) is perfectly audible because it falls above the curve. But at other frequencies, the threshold rises, and equally soft sounds at 500 Hz and 15 kHz (the black bars) won't be heard by most listeners. At 50 Hz, many people hear only about 6 bits' worth of detail. At 18 kHz, 2 bits may be sufficient.

But Figure 3.18 shows a static threshold with sounds superimposed on it. Researchers have discovered that real-world thresholds are constantly shifting, based on what you're listening to at the time. A loud sound raises the threshold around it, as shown in Figure 3.19. The signal at 1 kHz (gray bar) stops you from hearing the slightly softer signals at 700 Hz and 1.5 kHz (black bars). The figure is slightly exaggerated to highlight the effect, but some degree of frequency masking exists in every listener depending on their individual hearing and

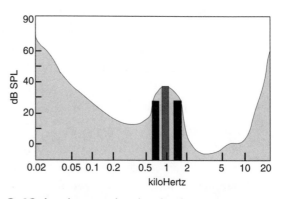

3.19 Louder sounds raise the threshold around them.

how carefully they've trained their ears. As a practical example, consider the case of an orchestra playing a full chord: one instrument may be slightly out of tune, but it's unlikely than anyone other than the conductor (and a few music critics) will notice.

Layer 3 / MP3

It takes sophisticated processing to predict how various threshold shifts will mask specific sounds. But once that's done, there's no reason you can't remove the sounds that are being hidden. One of the most popular algorithms was established by the International Standards Organization's Moving Pictures Expert Group in 1992. Its most complex implementation, ISO/MPEG Layer 3, uses 576 separate frequency bands to analyze the sound. Stereo tracks are further processed to find the details that are identical on both channels and encode them only once. The resulting sound stream not only uses fewer bits because masked or redundant sounds are eliminated, it's also more predictable, and redundancy coding can be used on it.

Layer 3 is scalable depending on how much detail you're willing to sacrifice. It's used in broadcasting and postproduction to carry high-quality audio in real time over ISDN, with data that's about 12% of its original size. But it's found the biggest application on the Internet, where it is known as the MP3 format, which became popular in the late 1990s. Well-encoded MP3 files can keep most musical values at 4% of their original size; voice tracks remain intelligible when as small as 0.5% of the original. Track 8 of this book's CD demonstrates different degrees of MP3 encoding, translated back to 16-bit noncompressed so you can play it on a standard system.

A less complex cousin, Layer 2, uses fewer bands and masks fewer details. It became popular because it could be implemented on simpler processors, and it is still preferred for high-bandwidth applications like satellites and hard-disk audio storage systems.

It takes the ear a few milliseconds to recover from loud sounds, so threshold shifts continue even after the masking sound has ended. Layer 3 takes some advantage of this as a side effect of its very sharp filters. The Advanced Audio Coding (AAC) algorithm, used in MPEG4, exploits this further and even eliminates sounds that occur slightly *before* the masking signal. AAC streams can be some 30% smaller than Layer 3.

Other encoding standards

MPEG and AAC are open standards, supported by many manufacturers. Macromedia Shockwave and Microsoft ASF also use the MPEG Layer 3 algorithm, with some additional nonaudio data functions. You may also encounter older open standards such as mu-law encoding (the Internet .au format), developed for telephone calls. And there are proprietary schemes promoted by companies including Dolby and APT, which may find their way into broadcast, DVD, theatrical, and Internet standards.

Perceptual encoding is probably the most volatile field in all of professional audio. The demands of quality, data bandwidth, and copyright protection are spurring institutional and private developers to try new schemes all the time. As a practical matter:

- Don't just assume that the encoding you use will be compatible with your viewers or clients. If you're not sure, do a test or revert to the most basic standards.

- If you want the smallest files or the fastest data transfers with the least effect on audio quality, check the Web. A new standard may have evolved while you were reading these pages.

- Always keep an unencoded version at the original sample rate and bit depth. When a new, more efficient standard is developed, you'll be able to reissue your material to match. Expanding an audio file that's been encoded, and re-encoding in the new standard, won't sound as good.

Chapter 4

Audio on a Wire

Rose's Rules:

✔ Analog audio wiring will pick up noise, unless you pay attention to some simple voltage and grounding principles.

✔ Digital audio wiring is generally free from noise issues, but its very high frequencies mean you have to treat it like video: always use impedance-matched cables and terminations.

In many professional facilities, high-resolution audio exists primarily as high-speed data: dialog that was recorded directly to hard disk or DVD on the set is opened as files in the editor, with no transfer time; audio and video workstations pass content back and forth over Ethernet; clients get their copies via internet. It's the wave of the future.

But that doesn't make real-time audio on cables obsolete. At the shoot, we have to get a microphone signal to a camera or recorder, headphones, and possibly a mixer. In even the simplest editing suite, audio has to go from NLE to monitor speakers; more complex ones have mixers, hardware-based processors, patch bays, and multiple tape decks. Until the world is completely fiber-optics based, there will be reasons to carry analog voltages and digital serial data streams on a copper wire. The trick is to do this without losing any signal quality.

Analog Wiring

When the phone company made up the rules for audio wiring, about a century ago, most devices' inputs were powered by the audio signal itself. Audio levels were measured in terms of their power, as decibels related to a standard wattage. Transferring this power efficiently meant you had to pay attention to both voltage and *impedance*, a measure of how a device draws current. This practice lasted through most of the century: Until the mid-1970s, TV stations and

53

large recording studios were wired using methods developed in the days of hand-cranked phones.

Modern analog audio equipment doesn't care very much about power transfer. Circuits use just a tiny amount of current from the input signal, and react to its voltage instead. This simplifies things a lot and lets you do things like splitting a signal to two or more different devices easily. If you pay attention to the basic voltage range, connecting things is about as complicated as hooking up Christmas tree lights.

However, current and impedance still matter for equipment that's powered by the audio signal itself. Speakers and headphones should be somewhat matched to the amplifier output. You can often connect two speakers to a single amplifier, but if you try to use more than two, you run the risk of distorting the sound (and even damaging the amp).

Microphones are a special case. Most mics used in film or video production have internal power supplies and work as voltage-based devices, but the currents are so small that major impedance mismatches can cause problems. But other mics, some of which are used in video, turn audio power directly into electricity. For them, impedance matching is critical.

Digital connections also require matched impedance. That's due to the high frequencies involved, not because of power issues.

Ohm's Law

I was an electronics geek in high school. Plaid flannel shirt, slide rule at my belt (calculators didn't exist), heavy-framed glasses, the works. Often, I used that slide rule to solve problems in Ohm's Law and its derivations, an essential set of formulas that predict how electrons will move from one place to another. Given any two electrical characteristics such as voltage or resistance, these equations let you determine things like wattage and amperage using simple math.

While The Law has many permutations, they're easy to remember if you think of the triangles in Figure 4.1. The letters stand for Volts, Amps, Ohms (Ω), and Watts. To find the value for one point on a triangle, check the locations of the other two. If they're both on

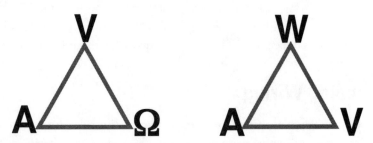

4.1 The easy way to remember Ohm's Law. Engineers use different letters, but the meaning is the same.

the bottom, multiply them. If one's on top, divide. So volts = amps x ohms, and amps = watts / volts. (Engineers prefer to write E for voltage and I for amperage, but this civilian version works just as well.)

It gets practical very quickly. If you need to know the minimum circuit-breaker amps a powerful lamp requires, divide its watts by its volts. To find how many volts will get lost in a long extension cable to that lamp, multiply its amps by the resistance of the wire (which you can find at Web sites like www.bnoack.com). If you want to calculate watts from amps and ohms, solve for volts using the first triangle and then plug the answer into the second.

Watts, of course, are the measure of electrical power—the stuff that gets things done. This is as true in audio as in lighting. When I was in high school, almost all recording used dynamic or ribbon mics, which convert the movement of air molecules directly into electricity. The resulting tiny signal was only a few dozen millionths of a watt. Even the mixers and preamps that boosted their signal operated at only around a thousandth of a watt. To use these tiny signals efficiently, you had to connect them to an input with the right number of ohms. Fortunately, that's mostly ancient history now. With most modern equipment, the source and input impedances just have to be in the same range. But a different aspect of the signal, its *voltage*, still has to match . . . and history has a lot to do with what voltages we use.

Setting the Standard

In 1940, the phone company and radio networks agreed on standard levels for long-distance broadcast and telephone lines: zero decibels would match 1/1000 watt (one milliwatt); any audio power from the tiniest microphone signal to the biggest amplifier output could be described as a ratio in dBm (decibels referred to that milliwatt). Wattage is a function of voltage and impedance, but telephone lines always had 600 ohms impedance; at that impedance, 0 dBm—or exactly one milliwatt—equals 0.775 volts. If you're not sure why something with a zero has any voltage at all, go back and read about decibels in Chapter 2.

The phone company developed meters calibrated to read zero at 0.775 volts, and added specific timing characteristics to make them respond the way we hear. They called them Volume Unit, or VU, meters. Broadcasters used them to measure program loudness and verify they were sending the phone company the right level. But they quickly discovered that the meters' internal rectifiers distorted the sound, something that didn't matter with phone calls. They reduced the distortion by isolating the meter with a resistor. But the resistor also reduced the voltage by 4 dB. Rather than design completely new VU meters, broadcasters decided that in *their* world, the standard line level would be +4 dBm, or 1.228 volts across 600 ohms. When a VU meter reads zero, that's the voltage it's seeing.

Professional sound equipment is often rated "+4 dBm line level" and operates at a nominal signal level of approximately 1.25 volts.

Of course, Ohm's Law insists that +4 dBm—a level in milli*watts*—can equal a precise voltage only at one impedance. So two other standards evolved. In the United States, the National Association of Broadcasters took just the voltage part of the phone company standard and called it 0 dBu—the "u" stands for *unterminated*: an open circuit with no impedance.

Modern pro gear may be specified as "+4 dBu" instead of "+4 dBm." This also is a nominal level of about 1.25 volts.

Note _____

Unless you're dealing with transformers or very long transmission lines—both of which seldom appear in a modern video studio—dBm and dBu are equivalent.

In Europe, the IEC said exactly 1 volt would be a more rational reference: they called it 0 dBV. It turned out that tubed hi-fi equipment worked best with an input voltage around 10 dB below this reference, about a third of a volt. This is also sometimes called the IHF standard because it was subsequently adopted by the Institute of High Fidelity in the United States.

Hi-fi, prosumer, and computer multimedia equipment is often rated "–10 dBV line level" and operates at a nominal signal level of roughly 0.3 volts.

So we have two different standards—three if your equipment is sensitive to impedance—to describe the nominal input voltage of a circuit. Because they're all based on the same rules of physics and math, they're easily related (Table 4.1).

Nominal levels

Line levels are equivalent to "zero level," where the equipment's volume unit (VU) meter (Figure 4.2) reads zero near the top of its scale. In a broadcast station or magnetic recorder, zero level relates to a precise amount of transmitter modulation or magnetism on the tape. In other equipment, it's the operating voltage that results in the best compromise between noise and distortion.

Of course analog audio is a constantly changing voltage, not a constant tone at a particular level. The dynamic range of any piece of equipment may extend from as much as 12 dB above the nominal zero to

4.2 A typical VU meter showing zero level.

between 60 dB and 80 dB below it, depending on quality. Calling something "+4 dBu" or

Table 4.1 Voltage compared to dBV and dBu

	Level in dBV	Voltage	Level in dBu (or dBm across 600 ohms)	
	+6	2.0	+8.2	
	+4	1.6	+6.2	
	+1.78	1.228	+4	(Pro standard)
	+0	1	+2.2	
	-2.2	0.775	0	
	–6	0.5	–3.8	
	–8.2	0.388	–6	
(Consumer standard)	–10	0.316	–7.8	
	–20	0.1	–17.8	

"–10 dBV" is just a convenient way to describe the normal operating voltage, so you can connect devices together with some hope of good sound.

Level and dynamic range

Figure 4.2 might look like the meter has been set precisely to a standard, but inside any piece of gear, this level is completely arbitrary.

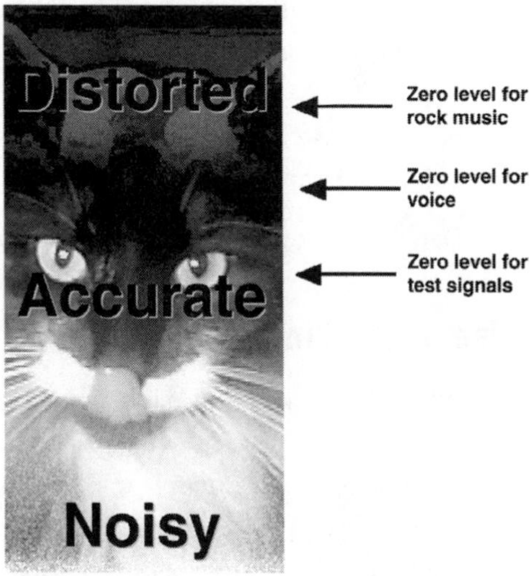

4.3 Zero can be an arbitrary level.

Analog equipment has a continuum between the lowest levels, where signals have too much noise, to the highest levels, where there's too much distortion. Since "too much" is a completely subjective term, and there's no reason you can't record an analog signal louder than zero, you can redefine the standard level depending on how much noise or distortion you want to tolerate. Figure 4.3 shows how this could work: A rock music studio might record at a higher level, moving the signal farther away from the noise floor, because distortion is already part of the sound of many rock instruments. On the other hand, a broadcast studio may be more sensitive to distortion, and it may set its nominal level slightly lower. These decisions have to do with how a signal is handled internally, not how it connects to the outside world.

Analog equipment manufacturers often make similar choices, specifying a higher level if they want to brag about low noise, or a lower one so they can brag about low distortion.

- +4 dBu and –10 dBV are just voltages. There's no physical reason why one should sound any better than the other.

- However, higher-quality equipment is usually designed for the higher voltage standard. That's a marketing decision, not physics.

Cross-connecting –10 dBV and +4 dBu equipment

If you plug the output of a consumer-level mixer into a professional recorder, such as a tape deck or camera, you may get a usable signal. As Table 4.1 indicates, the mixer's idea of zero is only about 12 dB lower than the recorder's. But since the signal will be that much closer to the recorder's noise floor, the tape will be about 12 dB (or four times) noisier. The best solution is to put a small amplifier in between the units, converting the mixer's –10 dBV output to +4 dBu.

If you plug the output of a professional-level mixer into a consumer recorder, you'll probably hear very bad distortion. Since this distortion occurs in the input stages of the recorder, lowering its volume control won't help. You need a network of resistors between the two units to lower the voltage.

Equipment with transformers in their output often need impedance matching. Connecting older equipment—or newer devices with vacuum tubes and transformers—to modern studio gear may require a 680 ohm resistor across the output to prevent hiss problems. This isn't to improve power transfer, but because a transformer output can have excessive high frequencies when it doesn't see the right impedance.

Details about these connections appear in Chapters 9 and 11.

Noise on the Line

While the idea of impedance matching has mostly been abandoned, another telephone-company idea is still very much with us. Phone calls have to travel over hundreds or thousands of miles of low-quality wire, often near power lines and other interference sources, without picking up too much noise. The technique phone companies developed to cope with this, *balanced wiring*, is used today by professional broadcast and sound studios for the same reason.

If your editing setup is plagued by noise and low-frequency hum, chances are you don't have balanced wiring. Here's what's really happening inside your equipment:

People sometimes hum when there's an awkward silence in a conversation. Circuits hum when they're not sure what silence sounds like. The sensitive circuits in audio amplifiers and processors need a reference they can be sure is zero volts. They compare the input signal to this reference, amplify and process as necessary, and generate an output signal that's also compared to the reference. Designers designate one point within a piece of equipment, usually connected to an external ground screw or the grounding pin of the power plug, and call it "ground:" all voltages within the equipment are referenced to it.

That's fine for a single piece of equipment, but problems arise when you try to connect equipment together. Both pieces have to agree on a reference zero, but if you use a wire to connect one reference point to the other, it can act as an antenna, picking up stray electric fields being radiated by all the other wires in the vicinity. Since most of the wiring in a building is carrying high-current AC to wall outlets and lights, these fields tend to be at the power-line frequency of 50 Hz or 60 Hz. This interference mixes with the reference and is amplified along with the signal.

Also, the signal wire itself acts as an antenna to pick up interference. You can eliminate some of this by wrapping a shield around the signal wire, and audio cables almost always include a copper braid or metal foil for this purpose. The shield is connected to ground and shorts out the interference before it can reach the signal wire. But now there are two

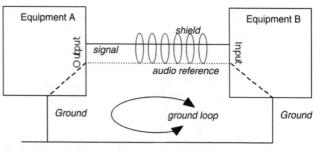

4.4 A ground loop.

ground paths—one through the shield, and one through the external ground connections or power plugs—forming an even more efficient loop antenna for the power-line interference. Figure 4.4 shows how this can happen. These ground "loops" are difficult to predict, since you don't know the internal details of all your equipment, and can appear even in very simple installations. In a practical video studio, the situation is apt to be far worse: between the ground connections of audio and video wiring, shielded FireWire or USB, RS-232 and RS-422 control, MIDI, and even cable television, there can be many ground loops.

Balanced wiring

Professional equipment solves this problem by using two closely spaced conductors twisted together. The audio is balanced equally between these wires, flowing in a positive direction on one wire while in a negative direction on the other. Equipment looks at the voltage difference between them and never references ground at all. There might still be an antenna created between the cable's shield and ground, but since it isn't part of the audio path, nobody cares. Figure 4.5 shows the basic setup.

The two conductors in a balanced wiring scheme are often labeled + and – for convenience, but they're not strictly positive and negative. Analog audio is an alternating current, with electrons flowing back and forth depending on whether the original soundwave was in compression or rarefaction

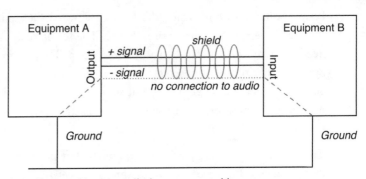

4.5 Balanced wiring eliminates ground loops.

(Chapter 2). Sometimes the current flow is positive on one wire; sometimes it's negative. Depending on the circuit design, audio current may also flow to ground . . . but this ground connection is ignored by the next device's input.

Balanced wires have another advantage that lets them reject much more than ground-loop noise. The two wires are twisted closely together in a single cable, so any interference radiated into the cable will be picked up equally by both wires. Since subsequent circuits look for voltage differences between the wires, the noise is ignored.

Figure 4.6 shows this happening in a balanced circuit. In Figure 4.6A, the top wire carries 1 volt positive while the bottom one carries 1 volt negative. The difference between them is the audio signal of 2 volts. But in Figure 4.6B, 1 volt of noise is picked up by the cable. The top wire gets an additional volt and now carries 2 volts positive. The bottom wire also gets an additional volt, which adds to its negative signal for a total of 0 volts. The difference between the wires is still exactly 2 volts.

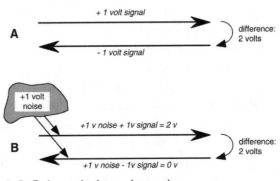

4.6 Balanced wires reject noise.

Of course both the signal and the noise are constantly switching polarity depending on the original sound wave, but the effect remains the same: since noise is added equally to both legs of a balanced circuit, it cancels itself out.

There are many different ways to build a balanced input or output circuit, and some are more successful than others at rejecting noise. But balancing will always add to cost and complexity, so it's often omitted in prosumer or music-industry audio equipment. This equipment is called *unbalanced*, or occasionally *single-ended*.

- In a simple studio setup, with only a few pieces of equipment and short cable lengths, noise pickup may be so low that balanced wiring isn't necessary for line-level signals.

- If you do hear ground loops in a simple unbalanced setup, the easiest cure might be to break the loop. See Chapter 11.

- Microphone signals are much weaker than line level, and more prone to interference. Balanced wiring is almost always necessary for microphones. The only common exception is the very short cable from a camera-mounted mic or XLR adapter.

You can't tell a wire by its connector

Balanced wiring is sometimes mistakenly called "XLR wiring" because it often uses three-pin connectors matching the Cannon XLR standard (Figure 4.7). It's dangerous to assume that an XLR plug or jack is balanced. While most manufacturers reserve these connectors for balanced circuits, there are some exceptions. Check the spec sheet to be sure.

4.7 XLR-style male connector.

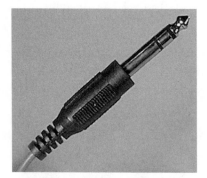

4.8 Three-conductor phone plug, sometimes used for balanced signals.

You can also get into trouble assuming that other kinds of connectors *aren't* balanced. Some manufacturers save money and space by putting balanced signals on three-conductor phone jacks. From the front panel, these jacks look identical to unbalanced two-conductor ones. But if you connect a three-conductor phone plug—known as "tip-ring-sleeve" (TRS), and also used for stereo headphones (Figure 4.8)—you can access the balanced circuit. Again, check the specs; some equipment uses TRS jacks as a way to connect unbalanced external processors.

The worst thing you can do is split a single balanced phone-jack output by using a stereo Y cable and send it to a stereo device. You'll hear a signal on each end of the Y, but the two signals will be of opposite polarity. If they're then combined for broadcast, VHS, or web use, they'll cancel each other and the audio will disappear!

Cross-connecting balanced and unbalanced wiring

You can plug a balanced output into an unbalanced input or output without damaging the signal, but this unbalances the entire connection. The connecting cable loses its noise immunity. (If the wires are short or in a benign environment, this may be perfectly acceptable.)

To make this cross-connection work, you have to make sure that both devices see the signal path they've been designed for. The best way to do this depends on how the balanced circuit was designed. Tables 4.2 and 4.3 are intended just as a starting point for systems using modern video equipment and might not always yield the best noise performance. There are tips for debugging these connections in Chapter 11.

Table 4.2   Directly connecting unbalanced sources to balanced inputs

Unbalanced Output	Balanced Input		
	Conductor	XLR	Phone
Signal	+	Pin 2	Tip
Ground	–	Pin 3	Ring
(no connection)*	Shield	Pin 1	Sleeve**

*   If you hear excessive hum, try connecting the unbalanced ground to these points as well.

**   Some balanced phone-plug inputs are designed so that you can plug an unbalanced two-conductor plug directly into them.

Table 4.3   Directly connecting balanced sources to unbalanced inputs

Balanced Output			Unbalanced Input
XLR	Phone	Conductor	
Pin 2	Tip	+	Signal
Pin 3	Ring	–	(no connection)*
Pin 1	Sleeve	Shield	Shield

*   Some transformer-balanced outputs won't work unless you connect pin 3 to the shield.

The best way to hook balanced and unbalanced equipment together is not to attempt a direct connection, but to use a separate balancing transformer or electronic interface at the unbalanced end. This lets you use balanced wiring, with its inherent noise immunity. It can also provide a necessary voltage conversion as well, since unbalanced devices are usually designed for –10 dBV and balanced ones are usually +4 dBu.

Prosumer digital cameras often have unbalanced microphone inputs. While unbalanced mic cables can be used for one or two feet, realistic distances between subject and camera are too long for this kind of wiring. A transformer or electronic adapter, or most mixers and preamps, will let you use balanced connections. Mic to camera hookups are described in Chapter 9.

Fancy Wiring?

A lot has been written in audiophile magazines about the need for special oxygen-free cables, sometimes with patented braided construction or solid-gold connectors. These allegedly add a unique audio transparency that golden-eared types can appreciate. They certainly add a unique price tag to the installation.

As of this writing, nobody has been able to show me evidence that these cables make any measurable difference to the sound, compared to more reasonably priced wire with similar electrical specifications. There isn't even a body of studies suggesting differences that can't be measured but are repeatable among trained listeners.

In my opinion, the makers of these cables should be put in special oxygen-free listening rooms, but you're welcome to spend money on the things. However, two other cable developments are worth considering with balanced wiring: *Star-Quad* and Category-5 Ethernet cable.

Star-Quad

Balanced cable typically has two conductors loosely twisted within a shield. If noise attacks it from a direction where both conductors receive it at the same level and in the same phase (Figure 4.9A), the balanced input will be able to reject the noise completely. But if noise attacks from the side (Figure 4.9B), the different distance to each conductor means each might receive a slightly different version of the noise. When this happens, the balanced input circuit can't reject it as well.

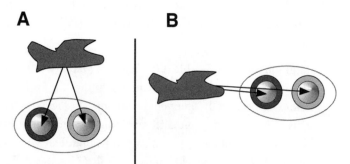

A   **B**

4.9 The effectiveness of balanced wiring depends on what direction the noise is coming from.

Star-Quad bundles four conductors inside the shield, *two* for each leg of the circuit; they're normally carried by one conductor each. This creates a round cross-section, making it much more likely that the combined conductors for each leg will pick up exactly the same noise (Figure 4.10).

Star-Quad was introduced by wire maker Canare, but they didn't trademark the name, and it's now generic and available from a number of companies, both as bulk wire and as pre-assembled XLR cables. It's also known as *double-balanced* wiring. It adds about $10 to the cost of a 50 foot cable, and is worth the price for low-voltage microphone connections. Line-level signals are strong enough that the extra noise-rejection generally isn't needed, and ordinary balanced wiring is fine for them.

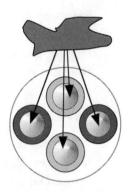

- If you're soldering your own Star-Quad cables, you'll notice that the wire has two pairs of conductors of the same color—usually one pair blue, and one white. You must connect same-colored wires together at the XLR connector. Standard practice is to connect both white wires to pin 2, both blue wires to pin 3, and shield to pin 1.

- If you don't do this, the cable loses its noise-rejection benefit.

4.10 Star-Quad has four conductors, two for each leg of the circuit. When combined, they pick up noise more evenly for better rejection.

Category 5 for audio

Balanced wiring achieves most of its noise rejection through its dual conductors, rather than its shield. So does a lot of computer wiring, which might not be shielded at all. Standard Category-5 cable (also known as UTP, and used for 100Base-T Ethernet) has four pairs of balanced twisted wires.

High-quality Cat-5 cable (like Belden's *Mediatwist*) is built to very rigorous balancing standards, usually much higher than ordinary audio cable. It can be perfectly appropriate for line-level audio in electrically quiet environments. In fact, the balancing can be so good that different signals can be carried on different pairs in the same cable, without significant crosstalk. Since there's no shielding, you don't want to bundle it with sources of high-frequency noise (like video or timecode). Mic-level signals are a little bit too delicate for unshielded wire. But +4 dBu line-level signals from tape decks, mixers, and effects can be carried perfectly. Even though data cables are built to higher specs than most audio ones, economies of scale often make them cheaper.

Category-5 can introduce losses, compared to a more standard wire. You want a cable with low capacity between conductors, so high frequencies aren't lost. This is a matter of design and what the insulation is made from. There can also be a tiny voltage loss, since the conductors are slightly thinner than most audio cables—but it's negligible because there's so little current flowing. You should also pay attention to mechanical issues: audio cables with stranded conductors and thicker insulation can take stress better than thin solid data cable. Cat-5 is designed to be crimped into RJ-45 Ethernet connectors, not stripped and soldered to an XLR, and won't stand up to repeated bending.

As you can guess, Cat-5 won't give you any noise protection on unbalanced signals. It may not even be appropriate for low-cost balanced gear that might not have good common-mode rejection. Furthermore, classic transformer-coupled balanced equipment might not like its 110-ohm characteristic—though that shouldn't be significant for short runs.

Digital Wiring

Because digital audio cables carry only ones and zeros, they're unlikely to be affected by noise and ground loops. However, digital audio uses very fast signals. Because individual bits are sent serially in bi-phase format, the frequency of a 48 kHz s/r signal can be above 6 *mega*Hertz!

At these speeds, the wire itself, and the impedances of connected devices, become significant:

- Always use a cable matched to the impedance of the digital audio signal.
- Make sure cables are properly terminated.

Impedance matching is simply a matter of using cables rated for the particular kind of digital signal, rather than just grabbing something with the right connectors. Termination occurs automatically in digital equipment, but can be ruined if you try to route a digital signal using analog wiring techniques. Ordinary patchbays, switchers, and splitters can cause drop-outs.

Digital Audio Wiring Standards

Digital audio wiring almost always follows one of two electrical standards. There are also two data formats, professional and consumer. But the data formats are virtually identical, with minor changes in such things as pre-emphasis (now obsolete), copy protection, or extra digital audio bits. Most professional equipment can read consumer-format audio without any trouble. There are absolutely no audio-quality differences among the electrical or data standards.

Both channels of a stereo pair are carried as a single, interleaved data stream. Signals travel from output to input, just as they do with analog wiring. There is none of the handshaking or data exchange used in bi-directional computer connections.

Audio levels are implicit—signals are referenced to zero decibels full-scale (dBFS), where every bit is turned on—rather than depending on particular voltages.

AES/EBU

This standard was set by the international Audio Engineering Society and the European Broadcast Union, and is found on virtually all professional digital audio equipment. It uses 5-volt balanced signals with 110-ohm impedance, almost always terminating in XLR connectors. While its cables often look like standard microphone extensions, they don't work the same way. Running AES/EBU audio over an analog cable can result in problems. However, good Category 5 cable (see previous section) can be used in most environments.

AES/EBU is electrically similar to RS-422 computer data, and to TTL logic levels.

s/pdif

This standard was invented by consumer audio manufacturers (Sony/Philips Digital Interface Format) and adopted by electronic manufacturers' associations in Europe and Japan. It's also known as *coaxial* digital, and occasionally as IEC-958. It puts a half-volt signal on 75-ohm coaxial cable, terminating in either phono or BNC video connectors. Standard RG-59 analog video cables, available from electronic chain stores, are perfectly acceptable for s/pdif.

s/pdif is electrically similar to video signals.

You may come across equipment that uses professional-format data on 75-ohm jacks, though you probably won't notice: in most applications and equipment, the two bit streams are interchangeable. A few professional CD players, CD-ROM drives, and consumer sound cards output consumer-format digital audio at AES/EBU levels. Converting them to s/pdif inputs requires a simple circuit described in the next section.

Toslink

This optical standard, named for the company that first made the transmitter and receiver, is often found on consumer equipment. It puts s/pdif data on a 1 mm plastic fiber, as red light from an LED. Because of light loss, fibers must be much shorter than AES/EBU or s/pdif cables; the maximum length with some equipment is 10 feet.

Toslink uses special optical connectors to assure good light transfer. A few MiniDisc recorders have optical inputs that are part of analog line inputs on mini-jacks; adapter cables are available.

FireWire

This electrical standard, also known as IEEE Standard 1394 and i.Link, was designed to let computers transfer large amounts of data quickly. It was adopted by digital video camera manufacturers to send audio and video simultaneously to an editing system, but can also be used for AES/EBU-format audio transfers.

However, FireWire is much more complicated and expensive than is needed for simple 2-channel audio interconnections. Rack-mounted FireWire audio adapters are often used in music production to get multi-track signals in and out of a computer in a single pass.

USB

This computer connection standard is used by a lot of high-quality stereo audio input/output devices, and can be the best way to connect audio devices to your computer. USB audio boxes are available with balanced mic- and line-level connections and with Toslink or s/pdif digital audio. Some also include mixer or jog-wheel remote controls that can be recognized by audio software.

Multi-track formats

Small multi-track digital recorders often use proprietary data formats. Since two of these recorders have become de facto standards—the Alesis ADAT in music studios, and the Tascam DA-88 in film and video—you may have to deal with their connections. The safest thing to do is buy jumper cables from the equipment manufacturers themselves, or adapters to convert their signals to standard AES/EBU or s/pdif.

Cross-connecting Digital Formats

The most common cross-connection is between s/pdif and AES/EBU. Because the impedances, balancing, and voltages are different, you can't plug one into another with a standard audio adapter. Transformers and electronic adapters designed for this purpose are available from pro audio and video dealers. Most equipment is tolerant of the tiny data differences between professional and consumer digital audio streams. However, some gear is picky. An adapter that works well in one situation might not work in another.

You can plug an AES/EBU output into a s/pdif input by building an adapter that matches their level and impedance.   Figure 4.11 shows the circuit. The resistors are 1/4- or 1/8-watt, metal film or carbon, 1% or 5% tolerance. They should cost less than 25¢ each. The values in the figure will give

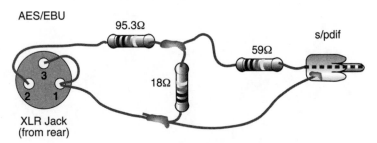

4.11 This circuit will convert an AES/EBU output to an s/pdif input. Read the text for important assembly instructions.

you the closest match, and should be available in 1/8-watt, 1% metal film at large electronics dealers. But the circuit isn't critical: you can use Radio Shack 100 Ω, 15 Ω, and 56 Ω ones instead.

Put insulating sleeves or shrink-tubing over all the resistor leads, except where they connect. This is particularly important at the XLR jack and inside the phono plug.

This circuit works with AES/EBU sources and s/pdif inputs only. It won't boost an s/pdif output to match an AES/EBU input. It's also not balanced, so the two devices should be as close together as possible.

Other signal formats always require powered adapters to sort and condition the data so it can be cross-connected.

Digital Audio Errors

If you don't treat digital audio properly, it may jump up and bite you. Some of the ways include:

- Data errors, resulting in dropouts or loud, sporadic popping. Check the cables. Chances are an AES/EBU signal is running through a microphone cord, or an s/pdif signal through an analog phono cable.

- Timing errors, heard as periodic clicking in the sound or sometimes no sound at all. This can happen when a digital input isn't in sync with a device's internal clock, and usually can be fixed by changing the equipment's settings. Sound studios often distribute a separate digital audio sync signal, called word clock, to all their equipment. Every audio signal is then aligned to this clock.

- Many digital video recorders require that digital audio timing is related to the video frame rate. In most cases this means your key audio components will also have to accept black-burst, and you'll have to give them the same signal that locks your video equipment.

A third kind of digital audio error, jitter, has gotten a reputation for causing subtle problems with stereo imaging and compatibility. But almost all modern equipment re-clocks the incoming signal to eliminate this problem.

Section II

Planning and Pre-production

When I was a kid, some friends and I decided to build a playhouse in one of our backyards. Since my father was an accomplished carpenter and had a successful business building new homes, I figured we'd have an easy time obtaining the necessary materials.

Dad asked what we'd need.

"Well, a couple of pieces of plywood and some two-by-fours, and maybe some shingles for the roof. Oh, and red paint. What do you think, Dad?"

"I think you forgot the paper and tape."

I wasn't figuring on any fancy flooring that would require rosin paper, fiber house-wrap hadn't been invented, and I *knew* nails were more appropriate than duct tape for holding buildings together. Then he handed me a tape measure and some graph paper.

"Plan first. Measure the area, and make scale drawings. Do up a bill of materials. Until you know what you're trying to accomplish, the details are just guesswork."

This from a guy who could stroll into a lumber yard, point at materials seemingly at random, and then throw together a complex bookcase or cabinet from a sketch on the back of a napkin.

• • •

Years later, I realized that Dad really did work from elaborate plans, but that they were in his head. All the napkin sketch provided was a reminder.

After a while, you'll be able to produce video tracks the same way. Until then, rely on the next two chapters. Chapter 5 describes the various elements that can be used to make an effective soundtrack, and why they're appropriate—there are probably some options you haven't thought of. Chapter 6 tells you how much it'll cost in time and cash, and what to look for when scouting locations.

Planning for Sound

Rose's Rules:

✔ The goal of a video is usually either to communicate a concept or to change someone's behavior. Sound may be the most important part of that process.

✔ If you plan ahead, it won't cost very much to have a soundtrack that adds professionalism and polish to your production. The converse—that an unplanned track will either cost extra or hurt the production—is also true.

The Need for Sound

Many videographers approach their projects as a chance to shoot interesting pictures and string them together in an effective way. Sound is secondary: after all, you weren't hired to create an *audio* cassette.

But communication isn't necessarily a visual phenomenon. Psychologists estimate that more than two-thirds of everything a person knows was experienced through their ears. The other four senses contribute less than 30%. Except for a few rare cases like some technical animations, no video can be effective unless picture and track work together. Neither is secondary.

This hasn't always been true for our medium. Obviously, early motion pictures had no sound. Producers were quick to realize the benefit of adding music, often sending suggested scores—with sound effects—to be played on piano or organ while the film was projected. It wasn't a soundtrack, but a live performance. Even some 30 years after sound films became popular, Warner Brothers still tested cartoons by showing them silently to preview audiences. If Bugs and Daffy got a laugh as mimes, Warner knew they had a hit. The genius-level contributions of voice actor Mel Blanc and composer Carl Stalling only added to the hilarity.

That was then. Today, network television is almost entirely driven by dialog. Try to imagine any popular program without sound. The most immediate and compelling use of pictures, breaking news events, is accompanied by voice-over and surrounded by talking heads. There's even less visualization in sitcoms, game shows, soaps, and, of course, late-night talk shows; most would be equally effective on radio. Even visually-rich documentaries primarily use pictures illustrating a soundtrack. The only exceptions seem to be action/adventure shows . . . and most of their screen time is filled with dialog rather than explosions or car chases.

That's what people are watching, folks. And if sound is that important to the big-time media, it deserves some careful planning in smaller projects.

The metaphors we choose tell us a lot. Ask your clients which they'd prefer: "A lot of *flash*?" Or, "More *bang* for the buck?"

People are Conditioned to Expect Good Sound

Maybe you think it's a corporate documentary or cable-access essay, but your audience knows they're watching TV. They don't have your commitment to the message, and they haven't sat through the lengthy development and production. The only yardstick they have for your project is what they saw on the tube last night.

Even if all they saw was an infomercial, it used good production techniques. The set was lit properly, shots were in focus, the editing made sense, and the sound was clean and easy to understand. The people who make a living doing this work (myself included) know their crafts, and the production process is well-defined. You need a TV show or a movie? I can call a bunch of my colleagues in other disciplines and we'll put together a darned good one. Of course, you'll have to pay us.

That may not be an option with desktop or low-budget production. There just aren't the resources to hire specialists for every job. A producer often has to write the script, simultaneously direct and shoot, and serve as both editor and mixer. This high distraction level means that sound is often neglected: video is more demanding—and more fun for producers with film or graphics training.

Wisely Invested Time Can Save a Lot of Money

Even if you don't have deep pockets, you can still have a good track. But you'll have to face the fact that you probably won't be paying proper attention to sound during the shoot, and plan accordingly. Don't expect sound to magically "happen," unless you've hired an expert sound person with experience in film or video, and even then, you should contact them for pre-production advice.

- Start prepping the track while you're still developing the script and budget. Know what it'll sound like, how you'll get the necessary elements, and what resources you won't be able to live without.

- Verify that the location and equipment will support the track you want.

- Make sure you have the skills you'll need. Know which buttons to push before you start production. Know which other buttons to push when things go wrong.

- Don't expect to point a microphone and get lucky, and don't expect that whatever you record will be fixable in post. The former never happens, and the latter can be expensive... if it's possible at all.

If you can hire someone to concentrate on audio during the shoot—even someone who isn't necessarily trained in that field—you've got a better chance of getting a good track. But you have to give them the opportunity to learn what they'll need; otherwise, they'll turn your location days into expensive learning experiences. Even a music studio or radio broadcasting background doesn't guarantee that someone will have the right skills.

This isn't rocket science. If someone has average intelligence and a cooperative attitude, they can learn how to gather good sound. But you'll have to lend them a copy of this book or some other training resource, and make sure they have adequate time to practice with the equipment they'll be using.

Take your pick:

- You can plan properly and train the people you work with.

- You can hire professionals to worry about sound for you.

- Or you can have an echoey, muffled track that says, "This video isn't as important as the average infomercial."

How a Good Soundtrack Can Help

Good sound adds believability

We spend our lives hearing the sounds around us. We've learned what voices sound like in a conversation, how environments can affect the sound of a voice, and what kind of noises everyday objects make. But a microphone doesn't hear the world the same way, and careless sound is a constant, subtle reminder that what's on the screen isn't real. It makes it harder for a viewer to identify with the character or the message.

Sound often has to be more realistic than picture. Nobody looks at a TV and assumes they're seeing a window into another world. We're constantly aware of camera movement and editing, reminding us that a director has defined reality for us. It's what dramatists call the willing suspension of disbelief. But in a properly created soundtrack, the only unbelievable element is music.

Or look at it another way. You can build a small bedroom set in a corner of a giant studio and shoot an intimate and romantic scene there. Even though we're intellectually aware there has to have been camera, lights, and a lot of people around, we accept the actors' version of things and let ourselves get wrapped up in their story. However, if one of them murmurs, "I love you," and it sounds like they're in a gymnasium, the illusion is shattered.

I've seen videos like that. If you haven't, turn on your local cable access channel.

As technology gets better, maintaining the illusion becomes harder.

- When TV was black and white, and the sound came out of a tinny speaker, it was easy to accept technical limitations. We knew that Lucy's hair and Ricky's skin weren't really gray, but we didn't care. Or we filled in the red and tan ourselves.

- Color television made it harder to suspend our disbelief. While gray hair was acceptable for Lucy, orange wasn't. Lighting and makeup became much more important

- The same thing has happened to sound. The increased audio clarity of digital tape, better speakers and amplifiers in TV sets, and the prevalence of stereo conspire to let us hear more of the track. Since it's no longer obviously canned, it has to be right.

As budgets go down, spend proportionally more on sound

If you plan audio properly, it's much more cost-effective than video. You don't need sets or locations, the equipment costs less, and it takes less time to put it together. Good sound can add the professionalism you might not be able to afford with pictures.

- Voice-overs are cheaper to record than on-camera spokespersons are to shoot. The money saved here can buy you a more experienced (and convincing) actor.

- A small buyout score will cost as little as $10 or 15 a minute. Even a full symphonic score, played by a world-class orchestra, can cost less than $50 a minute from a needle-drop library. It's the cheapest special effect you can buy.

- Sound effects cost virtually nothing and can add realism to most video scenes. A few well-placed actors backed up by a crowd recording costs a lot less than shooting a room full of extras. The noise of an explosion, a flashing light, and a horrified on-camera reaction has *got* to be cheaper than blowing up a car.

Think about the Overall Track

A track is more than the sum of its sounds. If this idea appears strange to you, you're not alone. Too many Hollywood features are nothing but continuous noise. The current idea of Sound Design is to create a track with nonstop gunshots, car crashes, explosions, and alien growls—it isn't interesting; it's just loud. After the initial adrenaline reaction to sound pressure wears off, it isn't even exciting.

A lot of sound effects isn't necessarily a lot of effective sound. On the other hand, well-chosen sounds—including pauses and quiet ambiences as well as hard effects—can almost become another character: the track builds a world around your actors and helps the viewer believe the message.

Start with the Script

Many producers believe that sound happens in postproduction. *Good* sound begins when you first start writing the script. This doesn't mean you need to work in a lot of car crashes and laser zaps—most scripts have no place for them—but you need to think about the overall sound of the video while you're writing. A couple of techniques can help.

Listen to the words in your mind

Hear the script in your head while you're writing it. Don't just type

```
Sfx:      phone rings
Sue:      Hello? George! I've been waiting to hear from you...
```

and leave it at that. That's not what's going to happen on the screen.

Instead, *hear* the sequence. You'll realize that what actually happens is

```
Sfx:      phone starts to ring
Sue looks at phone, reaches toward it, picks it up
Sfx:      ring is interrupted
handset pick-up sound
Sue holds handset, talks into it
Sue:      Hello?
Sue pauses, then reacts to voice
Sue:      George! I've been waiting to hear from you...
```

You don't have to type all that on the script, of course. But hearing it in your head makes you realize how much this simple action affects the pacing. The scene plays slower than you might have originally thought. (If you're writing a commercial, this can be critical.)

Working this way also lets you explore other sound options. Is there music under previous dialog or as a transition into the scene? Ending the music on the first ring will have a very different effect than waiting until Sue recognizes George's voice. What about her timing? Does she pick up on the first ring, because she's really eager, or wait while she finishes some quick task?

Are there background sounds? If Sue is watching TV when the phone rings, what happens to its speaker? Perhaps she was in her office. Just by maintaining the ambience and conversations, you can tell us Sue's busy life wasn't on hold. She wasn't *really* waiting to hear from George.

What about her emphasis? Was Sue '*waiting* to hear from you,' because she's eager to talk to George? Was she 'waiting to hear from *you,*' because the other members of her workgroup have already chimed in? Don't leave decisions like this, which affect meaning, entirely up to your actors.

This is real Sound Design. At first, it'll take a little longer to write scripts this way. But you'll get used to the technique quickly, write more realistic dialog, and eventually find yourself writing better scripts—with fewer time-consuming revisions.

Be aware that sounds may need a reference

Often, sounds that make sense in the script become "widowed" in the track because they're hard for the viewer to identify. Many sounds aren't obvious unless there's a visual or verbal reference to them.

Imagine a film noir sequence in a cheap hotel room on a rainy night, with the sound of a neon sign flashing. A realistic recording of rain through a tightly closed window could easily be mistaken for static. The rhythmic bzzap of a neon sign only adds to that confusion. You can solve this sound problem with an establishing shot, perhaps a point of view looking out through the window to see rain splashing on the glass and part of the sign. If that's too expensive, you could have a character comment on the weather while rhythmically flashing a red light onto the set. Either way, the sound is established. After that, you're free to block the rest of the scene any way you want; viewers will remember that the noises mean rain and neon.

It takes a special kind of mind to imagine a score in your head while also thinking dialog and effects, but now's the time to think about how music will work. Don't just write "music fades up" on the script; specify what the music is trying to convey. If it's there to build an emotion, describe the emotion. If it's a bridge, describe it in terms of the attitude and style of the scene that's coming. Including details about music in the script can help you pace the actors when you're directing. It'll also guide the composer in postproduction, or—if you're using library music—help you find appropriate pieces faster.

Make Room for Sound

Real people stop talking every now and then, and when they do, we hear the world around them. Try to avoid writing dialog over noisy actions (Sue shouldn't be talking to another character while she hangs up the phone); this complicates mic placement and makes a good mix more difficult.

Even if a sound effect will be added in post, leave room for it in the dialog. Characters shouldn't start screaming at the same moment there's supposed to be a car crash or explosion—that just detracts from both sounds. Let them scream in anticipation as the car careens towards the wall, or react after the explosion settles.

Since different sounds have different frequency ranges, consider how their brightness or deepness might conflict. The metallic crunch of car against wall has a similar timbre to an adult male shouting, so you won't hear both if they're happening at the same time. But substitute either breaking glass or a female scream and they'll coexist together.

This also affects how you specify the music. Good scoring composers are very aware of how instrumental timbres fit in the overall track. When John Williams orchestrated the rolling rock in *Raiders of the Lost Ark*, he relied almost exclusively on high, staccato strings. That way the rumbles of the rock itself could show through. The low notes of his theme for *Jaws* aren't just ominous; they also leave room for the ocean and seagull effects. Even if your budget is limited to library cuts, you can use the same kind of thinking. Solo brass and winds occupy the same range as the human voice, so avoid that lonely sax player in the window if there's simultaneous dialog.

Sound and picture also have to make room for each other. If you want viewers to follow complex visuals, lighten up on the track. Consider the classic recapitulation at the end of many mysteries: as the detective finally describes what really happened, we see a montage of flashbacks showing the murder . . . but the sound effects in that montage are almost always underplayed. We may hear a gunshot and body fall, but that's about it.

Provide Texture Changes

When people know what to expect, they stop paying attention. This even happens at the subtle level of room reverberation and background sounds.

Long dialog sequences with static actors get very boring acoustically, even if the words themselves are interesting. Let the characters move around the room, so we can hear differences as their voices bounce off different surfaces. Move some of the dialog into a hallway or another room with different acoustics. Or let them continue some of the conversation outdoors or in their car. If your budget is limited to a single setup, at least give the characters a chance to stop talking and react to an off-camera sound. Instead of just walking a new actor into the scene, let everyone else silently react as we hear the off-camera sounds of a car stopping, a door slam, and footsteps.

Music helps break up boring sequences, but may become a cliché. A stab after a dramatic line can give a soap-opera feel to a scene . . . but it might be just what's needed to let us think about a dramatic point. If a sequence is light on dialog, try specifying an underscore instead of matched sound effects to fill the pauses. If your video has a lot of music, leave some scenes unscored to make them stand out.

Remember the Medium

Even if you've got the money to spend, a business video's track has to be more limited than a theatrical film's. That's because film-sound designers have surround sound and much wider frequency and dynamic ranges to play with. Business videos have to play on a conference room TV. If you're relying on the slam-bang effects you saw in the latest adventure thriller, you'll be disappointed at the result.

Sound can be most ambitious in videos that will be shown only under controlled circumstances. If you know you'll be using high-quality digital or Betacam SP playback, in an auditorium with a good stereo system, you can rely on stereo and differences of loudness and texture to help carry your message. It's reasonable to think in terms of five or more sound layers: dialog, up-front effects, effects that aren't sharply on-camera, ambiences, and music. The stereo field and high playback quality help the viewer sort things out.

Broadcast sound is a lot less flexible. Even though most stations transmit in stereo, many cable networks are squashed to mono by the local cable system, to save money. And even if a viewer has a stereo set, it's likely to be off to one side of the room. In most stereo sets, the speakers are too close together to project a realistic stereo field; most of the smaller sets from chain retailers don't have stereo circuits, even if you can see two speaker grills on the front. Cheap VHS decks usually are stereo—but only when hooked up through their RCA connections to a stereo amplifier. The antenna output, which is how most viewers connect a VCR to their TV, is almost always mono. The truth is, *most stereo TV broadcasting isn't,* and it shouldn't be. Listen carefully to those high-priced network dramas: you'll find that most dialog is dead-center—even as the characters are moving around the room—and only music and effects are stereo.

Broadcasters also deliberately limit their dynamic range, so viewers can hear normal dialog without having to constantly compensate for screaming commercials. Don't count on more than three layers in a broadcast track, and pay careful attention to prevent dialog and foreground effects from conflicting.

The most limiting medium is Internet or CD-ROM audio. Expect many viewers' playback to be on tiny speakers, in noisy rooms. Internet compression techniques further muddy the sound. And don't try anything at all ambitious if the track may be played on a laptop: even voice and music will fight each other.

It's Not Just the Writer's Responsibility

If you're creating the script, you've got a great opportunity to write for sound. But if you're shooting someone else's script, you must still go through the process of hearing it in your head, marking sound cues, and possibly breaking things up to make room for audio. It's the best way to assure that the track will go together smoothly and predictably.

Planning and the Bottom Line

Planning a track long before production will save money you can spend elsewhere in the video.

- If you know what sounds you'll need, you can get them at the shoot. It's a lot cheaper to grab an off-camera line, crowd walla, or a specific prop noise when you've got the actors, extras, and props already there.

- If you know what you won't need, you don't have to waste time recording it.

- If you think about the final track while you're shooting, editing will be smoother because you won't be trying to fudge existing footage to make room for audio.

Elements of the Soundtrack

There are a lot of different flavors that can go into your soundtrack. Mix 'em up! Too much of anything can be boring.

It's standard practice, after mixing a TV show, to give the producer a tape with separate tracks or *stems* for voice, music, and effects. This simplifies the process of creating foreign-language versions and allows additional freedom when cutting promos or lifts.

But don't let that three-track tape fool you into thinking there are only three kinds of sound. Within the broad areas of voice, music, and effect are enough subcategories to satisfy the most ambitious sound designer. If you train yourself to think in terms of these subcategories, rather than just "we'll use a voice," you can create more interesting tracks and do a better job of engaging the viewer.

Spoken Words

Video is driven by the spoken word. It affects the visual editing rhythm and style as well as the choice of shots. But you've got a lot of freedom where those words will come from and how you'll control them.

On-camera Dialog

This is the primary way to get words across in dramatic videos, many corporate pieces, and some commercials. Obviously, on-camera voices are recorded while you're shooting picture; in digital video production, they're almost always recorded on the same tape. But that doesn't mean they have to stay together forever.

You can often improve a track by breaking the link between on-camera faces and the voices that were recorded at the same time. It's common practice in Hollywood to use voices from a close-up against pictures from a long shot, or even to re-record dialog after the shoot.

Modern audio workstations let you take the process even further: I'll frequently use words from a discarded take to fix sound problems in the take that was actually used, even if the shot is fairly tight on the actor's face. I'll also take individual syllables to fix a word that might have been mispronounced or clipped by the video editor. It's more important that the dialog be understandable than that every frame be in perfect lipsync. It takes a few seconds before sync problems become obvious, so you can have one or two words that are slightly out in an otherwise synchronized take and nobody will be the wiser.

Editing tip: The easiest way to mess with words during a cutaway without risking sync errors during on-camera segments is to split the voice onto two separate tracks in your editor. Keep on-camera segments on a track that's linked to picture, and use a temporary work track for the highly edited stuff. After you're sure it all works together, move the edited version back to the main track and discard the temporary one.

If your editing skills aren't up to replacing individual words against picture (you'll get plenty of practice in Chapter 13), there's still lots of freedom to edit the on-camera voice during cutaways. Any time we're not seeing the characters' lips, you can make their voices do anything you want. Feel free to grab a better reading from an alternate take, or to edit out long breaths. Use time compression to pick up the pace slightly so there's room to hear other sounds. Or use time expansion to stretch individual words for emphasis. The only limit is that you be back in sync within a few frames of cutting back to the actor's face.

On-camera dialog and on-camera narration have different sounds

We usually think in terms of characters talking to each other on screen because that's what we see most often in movies and episodic TV. But in corporate and commercial projects, the actor frequently talks directly to camera. This affects the texture of the sound as well as the writing and performance.

Dialog in a dramatic scene requires a sound that matches the environment where we see the actors. If they're in a normal room, they'll usually be boomed from slightly above their heads, so the mic also picks up some room reverb. If it's a long shot in a very big room where booming is impossible, they're probably wearing radio mics only a few inches from their mouths. Very little of the room is picked up when the mic is this close, so artificial reverb is added to match the shot. The idea in both cases is that we're eavesdropping on the conversation these people are having, so the room they're in is a natural part of the sound.

But if a spokesperson is in a normal room and talking directly to camera, we—the viewers—are a presumed part of the conversation. The real room where we're sitting is as much a part of that conversation's environment as the shooting stage. In that case, it's appropriate to eliminate artificial reverb, or move the boom much closer to the actor, so the set's acoustics don't completely overpower the viewing room's.

If a spokesperson is in front of a drape or in limbo, there isn't any "room" at all. Any reverb would sound unnatural. This also applies to highly staged settings that aren't trying to be real-world rooms, such as a typical news set with desk, station logo, and monitor wall or chroma key. We're perfectly comfortable with the close lavaliere sound of the evening newscast because the anchors are talking directly to us.

Vérité audio

Documentaries and some commercials often depend on ad-lib comments, directed to an interviewer who's very close to the camera lens. The texture of these voices can be very different from a trained actor or spokesperson, lending additional interest to the track. Because these people aren't polished performers, their voices are often weaker and need to be miked with a very close boom or a lavaliere that rejects most of the room sound. This is entirely appropriate, since the presumption is they're talking to camera and to us: the environment works like it would for a spokesperson.

By the way, it's almost always a mistake to ask a vérité subject to deliver a spokesperson's scripted selling line. Nothing destroys a commercial faster than having an allegedly real customer shout into the camera, "I love the variety and selection!". That's not how humans talk.

Remember the room

Staying aware of the presumed acoustic environment of on-camera dialog can help you avoid conflicts where sounds don't match their apparent location, or where insert shots don't match the master.

In his seminal book on sound design, *The Responsive Chord*, Tony Schwartz pointed out how early versions of Johnny Carson's *Tonight Show* used a close desk mic for Johnny. An overhead boom picked up the guests, plus quite a bit of the studio's natural reverb. For this reason, the host always sounded more intimate and closer to the viewer. Later incarnations of the show kept the desk mic as a nonworking prop, but put lavalieres on everybody.

But even modern, technically sophisticated shows can have similar problems. Just a month before writing this, I encountered one while mixing network promos for *Sesame Street*. One of the Muppet characters had to interact with a child. The puppeteer stood beneath a counter where the child was seated, holding his hands overhead to work the puppet. A head-mounted mic picked up his voice from an inch away. But the child was picked up by an overhead boom, at least a foot above his head. The obvious difference in room sounds hurt the fact that Muppet and child were sharing a moment. I had to split out the Muppet's voice to another track and add artificial reverb to put them in the same room again.

Historic audio

Documentary producers can take advantage of almost a century of historic audio available from archives, stock footage sources, and the Library of Congress. Some of it has accompanying video or film. If you're planning to use historic sound with sync pictures, plan for a few still photos of crowd reactions as cutaways. This kind of sound almost always needs a lot of editing, both to correct technical problems and to pick its pace up to modern expectations.

Crowd Voices

If dialog takes place in a setting where there's a crowd, it's almost universal practice for the extras playing the crowd to mime their conversations, moving their lips but not making any noise. This is the only way to get a clean, editable recording of the principal dialog.

Appropriate crowd sounds or *walla* is then added in postproduction. Walla can be recorded at the shoot, after the scene is shot but before the extras go home, but this is seldom necessary or economical. Sound effects libraries have multiple discs of crowd backgrounds and reactions in every possible setting; if you don't have such a library, you can sneak an audio recorder into a crowded restaurant or building lobby and grab what you need. If the crowd has to have unique reactions or say particular key phrases, you can simulate a large crowd with four or five people ad-libbing conversations in different voices. Record this small group in a quiet studio, so you can run two or three separate ad-lib takes simultaneously without noise buildup. Then mix the result with prerecorded walla from a library.

Voice-over Narration

In most commercials, corporate and educational videos, and documentaries, we never see who's doing most of the talking. A voice-over, by definition, exists in limbo; there shouldn't be any background ambience or room reverb around it. With nothing to suggest any distance between us and the narrator, it can become the most intimate part of the track and interpret the rest of the video for us.

Narrations should almost always be recorded in a sound studio designed for voices, or in an isolated space with plenty of absorption (see Chapters 7 and 10).

- There's a temptation, if you know a scene will be accompanied by narration, to shoot it without sound. This would be a mistake. Even if there's no dialog, point a mic at the scene. It doesn't cost any extra to record sound in a video camera, and the ambience and action noises you pick up can add another texture to the mix—or at least provide a guide track if you later want to add cleanly recorded effects.

- This is one of the few times when a camera-mounted mic can be useful in dramatic production.

The idea of an intimate announcer is a relatively modern concept, which seems to have grown out of the one-on-one style of pioneer television talk hosts like Jack Paar and Arthur Godfrey. Voice-over announcers in films prior to the mid-1950s usually had formal "speaking to the masses" deliveries and were often mixed with reverb. You may want to experiment with this style of narration as yet another texture, one that evokes a nostalgic or historic feel.

Music

It may seem obvious, after watching the latest Hollywood blockbuster with a wall-to-wall orchestral score, that music can play an important part in a production. But many video producers don't do anything with music until the end of the editing process, and then simply add an opening and closing theme.

Music can be an important element throughout a production. Aside from the obvious title and end credit themes, it can be used to explain settings, tie scenes together, emphasize emotions, call attention to important plot or visual elements, or even be an additional character with an attitude of its own. In a video, music can be everywhere.

Source Music

The most obvious place to consider music is when it's a sound effect—something we can see happening on the screen. If the characters are at a parade, we must hear a marching band. If we see someone put a CD into a player, we should hear music come out of the speakers.

Other kinds of scenes imply music even though we can't see the source. A school dance should have rock and roll, sounding either live or canned depending on the school's budget. But don't forget all the other places where canned music will make a scene more realistic: a restaurant scene can use pop, ethnic, or classical selections to establish its atmosphere quickly. And there probably isn't a shopping mall in the United States that doesn't have some kind of instrumental background at all times.

Source music—sometimes called *diegetic music* by film theorists—is an excellent way to build another layer into your soundtrack, since it occupies a place between the up-front dialog and any background scoring. The trick is that it has to sound like it's really there. You can't shoot the scene with the music playing because that would make voice pickup difficult and editing impossible. So a separate music track has to be heavily processed with echoes and equalization to put it in the same environment as the dialog. If the characters are hearing the music from a loudspeaker, remember that the viewer is hearing the *entire scene* from a loudspeaker: the music has to be extra processed, so it sounds even more canned than the dialog.

Source music also has to be chosen for musical and production values that match the scene. Background music in a supermarket has to be appropriately insipid. If the characters are listening to a pop radio station or jukebox, the music should be an authentic pop style and probably a vocal. This becomes most critical in cases like the school dance with a live band: a five-piece garage group will have a thinner sound and more inept playing than anything you're likely to find in a studio recording. Chapter 14 has some tips for getting source music.

Scoring

The kind of continuous underscoring found in theatrical films is too expensive for most video projects, but it still helps to think about music the way they do in Hollywood. Once you know exactly what the music is trying to accomplish, it's easier to find what you want in a library or hire a composer to create a few short affordable cues.

Aside from the title and end credit sequences, there are three major ways scoring can be used in your project.

Music as an emotional statement

There's no question that sad, anxious, or romantic music riding under the dialog affects how we perceive a dramatic scene. But music can convey emotions even when there is no dialog. The pounding score under a car chase or fight scene, and the whimsical ditty under a comic montage, are both filling the same purpose: to help shape the viewer's reaction to what's on the screen. By extension, a montage of widget manufacture in a corporate video can use music the same way. Rather than settle for a background track, think about what the scene is supposed to convey: Is Widgetronics including this sequence to show off their precision, or their efficiency, or their power, or the human way they care about every widget that comes off the line?

The classic film scores of the past were composed in the European tradition of *program music*, where events in a story were linked to parts of the composition. They developed along musical lines, while still being timed to important emotional moments in the scene. These days, it's more common to match every action to an appropriate chord or shimmer and then fill in the notes between (musical development may be an afterthought, if the composer even has time to deal with it), or to use a piece of music that wasn't necessarily written for the scene and add occasional punctuations in sync with the picture. While these two conventions may represent a decline in the art of Hollywood scoring, they're a blessing for video producers: the matched-chord-and-shimmer approach can be executed economically on electronic keyboards, and even if you can't afford any original music, library cuts can be edited seamlessly to fit this occasional-punctuation style (learn how in Chapter 14).

In its sparsest incarnation, this kind of scoring can punctuate dialog with just a few notes. A quick broken piano chord might be all you need to highlight a conflict; a string stab can call our attention to a dramatic foreshadowing. Even a few whimsical notes under some vaguely humorous action can help add texture to an otherwise static scene. The important thing when using music this way is to plan for it, leaving appropriate pauses during the shoot or creating them in the edit.

Music to identify a character or plot development

John Williams used motifs in the score for *Star Wars*: every major character had a unique theme, and these themes would interact and develop as the characters played out the plot. But he also used motifs in the score for *Superman*, linked to plot developments instead of characters. Whenever Superman went to fight villains, the score was based on the march music from the main title. But when he and Lois had a romantic moment, we'd hear a snippet of their love song (based, in part, on Richard Strauss' 1898 orchestral suite *A Hero's Life*).

You can do the same sort of thing when scoring a video. Recurring themes—even ones chosen from a library—can be used whenever a particular kind of plot development takes place. Using music this way isn't limited to dramatic videos: for a History Channel documentary about a city-wide construction project, I used timpani-heavy variations of an orchestral theme under the heavy-equipment sequences, an electronic piece reminiscent of the theme when we were seeing the high-tech control rooms, and classical instrumentations of the main theme during history and archeology scenes. And it all came from library cuts.

Music to set a scene

There is no faster way to establish an ethnic or nostalgic setting than to use appropriate music. Any good music library will have plenty of cuts designed for this purpose, and most composers welcome the challenge of working their music into a different style.

But scene-setting music doesn't have to be a caricature. You can use more mainstream styles to mark the passage of time, or a jump from one locale to another. You can also join two pieces of music that are related in key and texture, but different in tempo or dynamic, and use this new cue to show an abrupt change in mood.

The Pitfalls of Popular Music

It's common practice in mainstream films to include a number of pop songs either as source music or underscoring montages. These songs might be newly created for the film, be classic recordings, or be new covers of pop standards; no matter where they came from, they're sure to receive lots of radio airplay and be highlighted in the film's promotion.

It's possible there's a tiny bit of artistic justification for using these songs. But the incentive is more likely a financial one: a best-selling "soundtrack" album can contribute to the producers' and musicians' income stream. (I put "soundtrack" in quotes because these albums seldom have much to do with the film's track: they often include songs heard only peripherally in the film, and covers by big-name artists that weren't part of the track at all. It's a certainty that very little of the actual underscore will be included.)

This Hollywood practice may tempt you to use popular songs in your video the same way. If so, remember two things:

- Unless you have permission from both the copyright owner and the performer, you're running the risk of major lawsuits. The fact that a video may be nonprofit, educational, or nobly intended is not a defense. Unless you're willing to risk your production business or personal savings, talk to a lawyer before you consider breaking this rule. I've heard of record companies putting wedding videographers out of business, because of an unlicensed pop song in some couple's precious memories.

- Even if you have permission to use an existing song, your viewers have already linked it to events and feelings that have nothing to do with your video. Once you start playing *their* music, you don't control the experience any more. While there may be emotional justification for hearing "Lady in Red" when George first discovers how he feels about Sue at the company party, do you really want to remind a viewer about her own breakup with an ex-boyfriend who liked that song?

Pop music soundalikes are available from bigger music libraries, can be fully licensed to avoid lawsuits, and carry less emotional baggage.

Sound Effects

There's a rule in Hollywood: if you see it, you should probably hear it. While it's true anything that moves air molecules quickly enough will make a noise, features and episodic television have taken this to extremes. I'm sorry, folks: no matter how good the action hero is at karate, his hands don't go "woosh" when they fly through the air. And the *Enterprise* doesn't even have air molecules to move as it swoops past us in the vacuum of space.

Video producers often err in the other direction. Both documentary and dramatic videos can suffer from a silence that never occurs in the real world. (Take a listen while you're reading this . . . there's probably a symphony of muted traffic noises, distant conversation, and small machines like clocks or computer fans. Even in the quietest library reading room, you'll hear footsteps and pages turning.)

Use sound effects to add richness and believability to your track.

Sound Effects Categories

As you're thinking about sounds in your video, you can break them into three categories.

Hard effects

The most common film definition of a hard effect is any noise that's linked to an on-screen action and must stay in sync with it. This includes the tiniest footsteps as well as gunshots and car crashes. In video production, many of the smaller sounds don't need to be in perfect synchronization. The smaller screen forgives some lack of precision, and budget realities force us to paint with a broader brush. So I prefer to use "hard effects" to refer to sync effects that are big, obvious, and usually help the plot; of course, this includes the car crashes and gunshots, but also Sue's telephone or the crunch of a briefcase hitting the desk.

Natural sounds

This is a subcategory of what a Hollywood sound editor would consider hard effects. Feature films usually add them in foley sessions where specialists walk, move props around, and fake fist fights to mimic the on-screen actions.

In video production, I prefer to use this term to denote the smaller sounds that add realism to the scene. They may be foleys, but they're more likely to be lifted from the production tracks or edited in from an effects library. Many times they're created by making small edits in an existing background or ambience track so that loud sounds happen around the same time as on-screen actions. These natural sounds might be in sync, but—as in the case of most clothing rustles, footsteps, or automobile passbys—they only have to *appear* to be in sync.

By the way, TV editors often refer to any incidental noises that were recorded with the video as "Nat Sound." Their Nat Sound tracks can be an excellent source for natural sound in a scene.

Backgrounds and ambiences

Traffic, crowds, or random interior and exterior noises may be recorded at the shoot, but are more often lifted from a sound effects library or specially recorded by the sound editor.

Backgrounds usually aren't added until just before the mix because one of the purposes of these tracks is to smooth over dialog edits with continuous sound. Fading in the background a few frames earlier than a scene starts, and holding it a few frames after the scene's end, can also help smooth over visual transitions.

Special Effects and Processing

Don't forget that creative editing and technical manipulations can create additional types of elements for your soundtrack. Ideas like these might be too avant-garde for a corporate video, but certainly are appropriate in an art piece:

- Repetitive sound effects can be slowed down to a small fraction of their original speed and serve as the bass line of a piece of music.

- Musical elements can be used as sound effects. Try placing a cymbal crash or drum hit on the same frame as a hard effect, to thicken the sound. If the score uses similar cymbals or drums, it'll tie the music and action together—even if the action is nowhere near a musical beat.

- Tightly edited off-camera voices can serve as a rhythmic element that complements or replaces music. Tony Schwartz's track for the Academy Award–winning animated short *Frank Film* used a montage of individual words in the animator's voice to provide a driving rhythm under the animator's own voice-over.

- Processed off-camera voices can serve as an additional layer in the track. Ken Nordine pioneered the idea of running his own voice through a telephone filter, and mixing in the result as parenthetical comments in commercials he created; this is now common practice in radio station promos. I haven't heard or used the technique in a video project, so you might be breaking new ground.

The Layers of a Track

There's a definite order of importance of the various elements in a video track. Understanding this can help you plan the track better; assembling the track in this order can be the most efficient way to work.

- Dialog and narration come first. They have to be edited smoothly and stay in the foreground of the mix.

- Hard effects, if any, come second. They advance the plot and lend realism.

- Music comes third! This is contrary to the way feature films are often built, but in the world of video production, resources are often more limited. A well-chosen and edited piece of music can eliminate the need for backgrounds and natural sounds.

- Backgrounds should be chosen and placed before worrying too much about natural sounds. Often, random noises in a prerecorded background will appear to be in sync and can serve the same purpose.

- Natural sounds should be finally added to scenes that don't have music or much of a background, or where an action definitely appears to be missing audio.

Chapter 6

Budgeting, Scheduling, and Pre-production

Digital camcorders and desktop video systems have become enormously capable, but they're not magic. If you want good pictures, you have do more than simply point the camera and hope for the best. If you want a good track, you have to do more than simply point the camera-mounted microphone. (In fact, the camera mic is usually the *worst* way to record a track. Chapters 7 and 8 tell why, and show you the right way.)

A proper soundtrack requires a commitment of time and money—nowhere near as much as for good visuals, but a commitment nonetheless. In many cases, you can trade these resources and spend a few dollars more for the sake of convenience, or work a little harder to save money.

There are only a few basic tools you'll need to do sound properly, and they're available for rent or purchase in production cities around the world. The more important decisions are whether you want to work with the sound yourself—meaning you have to learn how to do it right—or hire professionals who already know how to do the job. These decisions can be made on a task-by-task basis: it might make sense to get a professional sound operator for the shoot, but plan to edit the music track yourself.

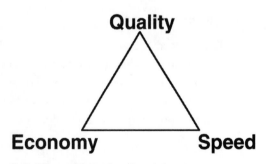

6.1 The golden triangle: pick any two.

To make these decisions efficiently, you have to know how much time or money each aspect of the track will cost. Remember: the golden triangle of production (Figure 6.1) applies to sound, just as it does to every other aspect of our business. You can have it fast, cheap, or good: choose any two. You can't have all three.

Budgeting for Sound

I'm assuming that, as a digital video producer, you already have a video-editing system and know how to work it. So we won't include any costs for basic sound editing. Using the techniques explained in this book, you should be able to do it yourself on equipment you already have.

But unless you've got a fully equipped crew at your disposal, expect to spend a few dollars on audio at the shoot. Depending on your voice-over needs, you might also have to spend money for a recording studio. Many producers rely on outside scoring, sweetening, and mixing services because desktop video-editing systems simply aren't designed to be efficient at these tasks.

Here are some of the personnel and equipment costs you can expect. They were accurate when I wrote this (late 2002) and had been stable for years. Barring major technology or economic changes, they should be accurate for a long time to come—or if we have rampant inflation, you'll at least be able to use them as a guideline.

The prices are based on nonunion corporate, feature, or documentary videos in major production centers. Smaller towns are apt to have personnel with less experience or who split their time between audio and other gigs; they usually charge less. Union rates are similar but based on a fixed-length day, so overtime can get expensive. Commercial shoots are often more demanding, and personnel expect to be paid more for them.

Production Costs

Audio mixer/recordist

Experienced operators who bring their own equipment for miking or recording the shoot may be the best investment you can make. (They're called *mixers* in professional production, for historic reasons, even if they're holding a boom instead of mixing.) They'll let you concentrate on getting good pictures and performances, and guard against the acoustic problems that plague so many amateur productions and absolutely can't be fixed in post.

Plan on a pre-production meeting where you can fully describe the project and the location. For many video productions, there's no need to have the sound recordist actually make a sound recording on separate equipment; it's more likely they'll provide you with a clean audio feed to record in your own camera. (This may not be true for feature-style productions using prosumer cameras; see Chapter 9.) But they bring something more important than equipment: you can rely on their skills to take care of mic placement, acoustic concerns, boom and level control, and the setup of electronics and wireless mics. During the prepro, make sure they're familiar with the camera or recorder you'll be using and its audio specifications; if they're not, plan for some compatibility tests before the shoot. Even the pros can get blindsided by some of the compromises in prosumer equipment.

Experienced mixers are often the most technically trained people on a set, even in Hollywood, and may be able to help you diagnose non-audio problems as well. But their experience has to be in film or video sound; live sound and music recording use totally different techniques that don't apply to making a movie.

Depending on the experience and equipment they bring, figure $250–450/day.

Boom operator

If only one mic boom is needed and it won't be actively mixed with radio or other mics, the mixer will usually handle it. But if the recordist has to be constantly balancing multiple mics, or you need more than one boom, get an additional experienced operator. Figure $150–300/day.

- Don't assume that a boom operator is merely someone tall enough to hold a pole with a mic at the end. Aside from the physical endurance required, there's a lot of skill involved in pointing a mic accurately and quickly enough to cover back-and-forth dialog, while aiming the mic to avoid noise sources and changing its distance to compensate for the actors' delivery.

- If you have to use an inexperienced boom operator, make sure they read Chapter 8 and have a chance to practice with the equipment before the shoot.

Equipment packages

The mixer may supply an equipment package as part of their basic fee or charge a nominal amount for its use. But if you're not hiring one, you'll probably need to rent equipment. Professional gear is rented on a daily basis; many rental companies price their weekly rentals at three or four times the daily rate, and allow extra time for shipping to out-of-town customers.

All of this equipment is described in the next three chapters, along with directions on how to use it.

- Lavaliere mics (nonwireless): $10–15/day

- Lavaliere mic systems (wireless analog): $45–80/day

- Lavaliere mic systems (wireless digital): $75–150/day

- Shotgun mics: $25–50/day

- Microphone booms: $10–15/day

- Microphone mixers: $25–$50/day

- XLR transformer adapters for DV cameras: $5–10/day

- Professional portable DAT recorders (non-timecode): $70–100/day.

- Professional portable DAT and hard disk recorders (timecode): $100–150/day.

- High-quality headphones: $5–10/day

Of that list, the last item is the most important. You can't count on good sound unless you're absolutely sure of what you're recording. Walkman-style phones aren't appropriate: you need a set that will isolate you from the outside world, so you can hear how room acoustics are being recorded and if there's any noise on the track. If you're using a boom mic, the boom operator should also have a set of headphones and—depending on your camera setup—may also need a separate headphone amplifier ($10–15/day).

Rental equipment usually comes with adequate cables for basic hookups; additional cables are available at trivial cost. While I've included DAT recorders on this list, they may not be necessary: choosing the right audio setting and adjusting things carefully can give you adequate sound, with most cameras, for most purposes. Decent quality MiniDisc recorders can also be an alternative. Specific information about this is in Chapter 9, but in many cases how you use the microphone—not what you record it into—has the most effect on a track's quality.

If you're doing a multi-camera shoot that relies on timecode and double-system sound, or plan to use multi-track tape to catch ad-libs on multiple wireless mics, hire a pro who can also specify the equipment. There are too many ways an inexperienced operator can ruin this kind of shoot.

Film sound rental houses usually charge less than companies specializing in video gear, because they understand how good audio equipment, when treated properly, will be serviceable for a long time. Video rental companies expect all equipment to become obsolete as quickly as digital cameras do.

Expendables

Most wireless mics use a standard 9-volt alkaline battery, but burn through them quickly: to be safe, allow three battery changes per mic per day. Wireless receivers use one to three batteries each; change them once a day. While 9-volt batteries are available almost everywhere, it's important to use fresh ones. Batteries from an electronics store are usually better because they haven't sat on the shelf as long as those from a supermarket or drug store.

Most of the wired mics used in video production also require power, but don't consume it very quickly: one battery every day or two should be sufficient. It may be possible to skip the batteries and power wired mics from the mixer. Ask the rental house about "phantom powering;" this system sends power from a properly-equipped camera or mixer to the microphone.

Other things a sound operator should have handy are non-allergenic paper surgical tape (for mics and wires that have to be hidden on an actor's body), safety pins and gaffer tape (for the ones that are hidden within clothing), alcohol prep pads (for cleaning skin before and after mounting mics), rubber bands of various sizes (strain relief for wireless mic antennas and XLR assemblies), cheesecloth (emergency wind screens), pony-tail holders (the ball-and-elastic type are great for keeping coiled cables neat, and attaching a mic wire to a boom), and anti-static spray (for carpets and clothing). You may also want a couple of condoms: while they muffle the sound slighty, they're ideal protection for mics that'll be rained on or otherwise getting wet.

If you're recording audio directly to videotape, separate audio stock isn't an issue. Otherwise, you'll need DAT tape or MiniDiscs. You'll probably also want plenty of paper for keeping track of which audio take belongs to which video one; most rental houses can sell you pads of low-cost *sound logs* that are designed for this purpose and track other vital information as well.

Voice-over Recording

The acoustics of the room become very important when recording narration, so unless you have a space specifically built for this purpose, it's best to hire a studio. Look for a studio that does a lot of spoken word; the acoustics and techniques used for music recording are different. If a studio is completely out of your budget, plan to spend a few dollars on the sound-control techniques in Chapter 10.

In large cities, a good studio with an experienced engineer will cost between $150–250/hour, plus stock. The amount of time a session takes depends on the talent's experience, how much jargon is in the script, and your own directing style. If you're efficient, you should be able to record 20 minutes' worth of material in an hour.

Most studios will normally record to DAT or directly into a computer. Make sure they'll be able to deliver a format you can use. AIFF or WAV files on CD-ROM, at the same sample rate as your production, are the most universal. DATs may be slightly cheaper because the studio doesn't have to take extra time to burn a CD. However, if your DAT player isn't connected digitally to your NLE, this introduces a needless analog conversion and another place to get the levels wrong or introduce noise. Many studios can record audio CDs in real-time and hand you a disc a minute or two after the announcer is finished.

Check the studio's policy on stock. It's standard industry practice for them to mark up all blank media: a DAT tape that costs $6 from an electronics supplier may appear on the invoice for as much as $25. Blank CDs cost less than 50¢ in quantity, and the cheap ones from warehouse clubs are perfectly good for recording audio. Some enlightened studios don't charge for CD media at all; others ask $15 per disc. Ask if you can bring your own stock (some facilities don't allow it).

media at all; others ask $15 per disc. Ask if you can bring your own stock (some facilities don't allow it).

Dial-up ISDN lets you walk into a local studio and record an announcer from a distant city, hearing them with perfect fidelity and even playing voice or music reference cues to them. The sound is carried real-time in compressed format (see Chapter 3) and recorded locally. Aside from a slight delay introduced by the encoding system, it's exactly as if they were in the next room.

Depending on the compression system used and the studio's policies, this service will add between $75–300/hour to the local studio's charge. Internationally standardized MPEG Layer 2 or Layer 3 connections are on the lower end of the price scale; proprietary connections don't offer any significant advantage for voice recording but are more expensive. The distant studio will, of course, add their own charges. They may also ask if you want them to record a backup tape, but this is seldom necessary (if there's a problem in the ISDN connection, you'll hear it immediately and can re-record).

You may be able to get the studio for free. Many professional narrators now have their own studios with good acoustics, professional equipment matched to their voices, and ISDN terminals, CD recorders, or fast internet connections. Most of them will throw in the studio services as part of their talent fee. If you're not using ISDN to a local studio, you can direct them via telephone from your desk, and have them courier or e-mail the finished tracks to you. High bitrate MP3 (over 192 kbps) is fine for voice, if the encoding is done properly.

Voice-over talent costs are described in Chapter 10, along with how to pay voices without getting into trouble with the talent unions.

Postproduction Costs

Digitizing help

If you've got a lot of nonsync elements such as narration and music, there might be both a cost and quality advantage to having a local studio convert the tapes and CDs into files your editing system can read directly. This means you don't have to tie up your editing station for digitizing, don't have to rent a DAT player, and won't worry about proper digitizing levels and analog connections. Figure $65–125/hour, plus media costs.

Music

Now we get to some real variability. Here are some guidelines for a corporate video shown to an internal audience. Music for commercials, broadcast programs, and videos for sale or public exhibition are more expensive: see Chapter 12 for a full breakdown.

Original music will cost between $200–$1,000 per screen minute, depending on how good the composer is and how quickly you want it. At the higher end, it usually includes a mix of live instruments and high-quality samplers and can sound excellent.

While music prices have remained stable over the years, technical advances in the music industry keep raising the quality standards for both library and custom music. Shop around: you may find some incredible music for the money.

Sound effects

If you gather them yourself, or use some of the tricks in this book, sound effects are free. You can also download high-quality ones from the Internet, for license fees of a few dollars per minute. Most audio post facilities have immense stock sound libraries with computerized catalogs; depending on studio policy, the cost may range from nothing (if you're mixing there) to $15 per effect. Or you can buy libraries of professionally recorded effects with license to use them in all your productions for $50–75 per CD.

All of this is covered in Chapter 15.

Postproduction audio studio

A good studio that specializes in corporate or broadcast video sound, fully equipped and with a large stock library, will cost between $150–300 per hour in major production centers. One that concentrates on feature-film sound will be a little more expensive. Studios that specialize in advertising sound are also more expensive, because of the more intense client services and glitziness expected.

Depending on your project's complexity, they should be able to do multiple dialog fixes, add all the necessary sound effects and music, process tracks to improve their cleanliness and punchiness, and completely mix a 20-minute video in about a day. The time varies, depending on what shape your tracks are in when you show up at the studio; see Chapter 17 for some tips. Any professional studio won't charge to walk through your project with you, estimate exactly what will be required, and show you ways to save money on transfers and file interchanges.

Allow Time for Sound

Again, I'm assuming you're already familiar with your editing equipment. Otherwise, all bets are off: you can waste hours rendering or processing sequences only to discover that the sound is damaged or out of sync because of a simple mis-set switch or a system conflict. Problems that are specific to particular brands or versions of editing systems are beyond the scope of this book, but there's some general trouble-shooting information in Chapter 1.

Pre-production Time

It won't take more than an hour to go through all the planning and location audio considerations in this chapter. Now is also the time to line up a location sound crew if needed, and also start thinking about postproduction audio resources: sources for music, voice-over studios, and—if you're going to use one—a mixing facility.

If you're using an experienced sound operator at the shoot, spend at least a quarter hour on the phone with them describing the location and setup. If it's a complex production, it's a good idea to schedule a full prepro meeting with the videographer or director of photography, set designer, sound mixer, wardrobe supervisor, and any other craftsperson who will have a major role at the shoot. The best pre-production meetings also include postproduction specialists, who can suggest things to do at the shoot that'll save time or money later on.

Have your meetings with the people who will actually be providing technical services, not just an agent or booking manager. The former are involved in day-to-day problem solving; the latter just want to book as many days as possible.

Training time is an important resource

If you're running sound yourself, or assigning the job to a production assistant, allow enough time to get used to the equipment. I'd suggest a quarter to half a day, doing actual recordings in similar circumstances. You may need to enlist a colleague to serve as temporary talent during practice sessions with a mic boom. Read Chapters 7 through 9 to learn what you'll have to do.

A half day practicing with a boom mic or mixer? Yes. Production sound is critical to the success of any dialog-driven project. The person responsible for sound has to know how to record a voice cleanly while compensating for room acoustics. This book explains the procedures, but hands-on—and ears-on—experience is essential.

If you can't afford the time to learn how to do this correctly, hire a professional. While almost any other kind of audio problem can be repaired (or resurrected) in postproduction, bad production sound will haunt your video forever.

Time Requirements at the Shoot

If you've hired an experienced mixer, sound shouldn't take up much extra time during the shoot; most of the setup will take place while other people are worrying about sets, lights, and camera. Concealing a wireless mic on the talent can take a few minutes and should be coordinated with wardrobe and makeup. Make sure you have enough time to check bought takes to verify that both audio and video were running properly.

Concealing a wireless mic on the talent can take a few minutes and should be coordinated with wardrobe and makeup. Make sure you have enough time to check bought takes to verify that both audio and video were running properly.

If you're using a boom mic with an inexperienced operator, allow for extra takes because the microphone or its shadow has gotten into the scene.

If you don't have a separate audio operator and are using a simple setup with one or two wired lavaliere mics, allow an extra quarter hour to get things right. If you're using wireless mics in a steel-framed building or a location you haven't tested, make it at least a half an hour. Count on a few extra takes when you notice, on playback, that a wireless battery was running down.

If you're renting sound equipment, allow enough time to test it thoroughly. Allow even more time, before and at the shoot, if you're unfamiliar with that particular model.

Postproduction Time

Capture

If you recorded audio on the videotape and are transferring digitally, sync sound won't take any extra time at all. If you're transferring sync dialog as analog audio, allow 15 or 20 minutes to calibrate your system using the steps in Chapter 12. If you've never tried sync sound with your specific editing system, allow enough time to capture a few scenes, edit them, and render them as a moderately long sync test before attempting the entire project. There are some black holes of sync incompatibility that can take days to diagnose.

Capturing audio from DAT or MiniDisc takes place in real time, plus a little extra for file management. If you're using an audio CD recorder or laptop computer to gather sound, file transfers can be dozens of times faster than real time.

Editorial

Basic layout and trimming of scenes affect audio and video simultaneously, and the additional time to render or preview unfiltered audio is insignificant compared to video.

If dialog needs to be repaired (changing words or joining takes in the middle of a sentence, as opposed to trying to clean up bad recordings), the time required depends a lot on the skill of the editor and how flexible the editing system is. Replacing a single word of on-camera dialog may take a video editor 5 or 10 minutes, in a frame-based desktop system. The same edit could take less than 30 seconds for an experienced sound editor using a high-end audio workstation. The tips in Chapter 13 will show you how to edit voices efficiently, but if you've got a lot of dialog to repair, you might want to export it to a more flexible audio program . . . or farm the whole job out to a specialist.

Sound-effects placement is easier to predict. Adding one or two hard effects and a couple of backgrounds to a 5-minute video sequence shouldn't require more than 15 minutes of editing, assuming you already have a source for the effects. Finding the effects will take only a couple of minutes in a well-indexed library or commercial on-line source. But don't expect to achieve the deeply layered richness of a feature film in that amount of time: Hollywood sound cutters allow a week per 10-minute reel of sfx.

Finding stock music is a major variable. If you have only a few CDs to look through, the job will go quickly but you're not likely to be thrilled with the choice. If you have a large library available, and use the tips in Chapter 14, plan on spending 5 or 10 minutes per cue; main title or theme music may take longer. Picking music for a one-hour, densely-scored project should take about a third of a day.

Using the music also takes time. Figure 3 to 4 times the running length of the music to capture a cut, place it against picture, and check the result. Fine-tuning stock music to match the length of a sequence depends on your skill as an editor (also in Chapter 14) but shouldn't take more than 10 or 15 minutes per scene. If you find it taking longer, try the alternatives recommended for dialog editing: export the music to an audio-only program that isn't restricted to frame boundaries or let a music editor handle the job. At least one program will edit music to a precise length in a matter of seconds; Chapter 14 explains its limitations.

Audio mixing

The time this takes depends both on your expectations and your level of equipment. If you're mixing within a basic desktop video-editing setup, you'll probably be using "rubber band" lines to indicate audio fades. Drawing and previewing them for a 5-minute video won't take more than a few minutes.

If you want to add basic compression or equalization using plug-ins, expect a minute or so to fine-tune each separate process. Chapter 16 will give you some starting points. Adding a lot of effects on multiple tracks can slow down audio rendering time by many hundred percent, but whether you'll notice this at all depends on how many video effects you're using—they take longer.

On the other hand, if you're mixing on hardware or a dedicated audio workstation with hands-on controls, effects shouldn't take any rendering at all. Simple mixes can be as fast as real time. But chances are you'll be more sensitive to the way level changes and effects interact when you can hear them in context, so you'll spend longer polishing them and get a better mix than you would with rubber bands. Mixing a 20-minute piece may take an hour before it sounds perfect. I've had some highly dramatic 20-minute pieces take three hours . . . but boy, they were good.

Transferring individual tracks from a desktop editor to a dedicated audio workstation can be instantaneous, or take up to twice real time, depending on the file systems involved.

Checking Locations

If you're producing an action film for theatrical release, you can choose locations based on how they look. If they're also good for sound, that's great; if not, you'll replace the dialog later. (And if replacing the dialog means a more stilted performance, who cares? It's an action film.)

But if you're producing on videotape instead of film, you're probably paying tighter attention to budgets. Dialog replacement is usually too expensive an option. The location has to sound as good as it looks . . . which means you have to scout with your ears as well as your eyes.

Knowing in advance how a location will affect sound means you can prepare efficiently for the shoot and be ready to fix problems as they occur. If a location is just too beautiful to pass up but has insurmountable sound problems, try rewriting the script to eliminate or reduce dialog there.

Potential Problems

I live in New England, where Autumns are particularly spectacular. You can point a camera almost anywhere and get a wonderful shot . . . unless you're shooting dialog. Even the prettiest location can have audio problems: if you don't know what to check for, that beautiful shot can cost you a lot of time and money in sound fixes.

The laws of acoustics are in full force every day of the year, indoors and out. There are only three things you have to ask about a location to determine if it's sound-worthy:

- Is it quiet enough for dialog?
- Does it have the right acoustic properties?
- Will you be able to use equipment without interference?

Other location issues—access, electrical power, legal clearance, and the like—are common to both audio and video, so you'll probably be checking them anyway.

Noise in exteriors

The microphone is a lot less selective than the lens. A city park may look as bucolic as a medieval pasture, if you avoid shooting past the trees and into the tall buildings. But you can't avoid the sounds of traffic and crowds; once they're on your track, you can't get rid of them without starting from scratch.

But while nobody would try to shoot *Robin Hood* in Central Park, other conflicts aren't as obvious. You have to visit the location, stand where the talent will, and listen. Whatever you hear will be part of your track. Here are some ways to avoid unpleasant surprises with exteriors:

- Scout at the same time of day you're planning to shoot. A suburban park that's quiet at four o'clock may be very noisy when school's in session. Traffic and crowd patterns change depending on the time of day, and major streets have been known to attract radio station helicopters during rush hour.

- Try moving 10 or 15 feet in various directions while listening to the background noise. One side of an open field might be a lot noisier than another, without any visually obvious reason. On the other hand, low-frequency sounds generally aren't directional: if there are a lot of trucks on a nearby highway, their sound will infect the whole location.

- Watch out for very large buildings in the middle distance, like the apartment house peeking over the trees in Figure 6.2. Those buildings don't make noise themselves, but mid- and high-pitched noise from nearby traffic or factories can bounce off them and into your shot. This is worst when a building's surface is mostly glass and it has two wings at an angle: they act as a corner reflector, focusing the sound right at you.

6.2 That shack in the woods would make a great rural setting—but the apartment house behind it *(inset)* can reflect traffic noises all over the "farm."

- Be aware of airline flight patterns. Some times of day have more flights than others, and runways change from one day to the next. Ask neighbors what their experience has been.

- If you're using generators, make sure they can be positioned far enough away to be quiet; ideally behind some solid structure to block the sound. And bring enough high-current extension cable.

Noise in interiors

Interior locations have fewer variables, but you still have to go to them and listen at the same time of day you'll be shooting. While scouting interiors, pay careful attention to windows: do they overlook a potential noise source, such as a loading dock or trash compactor? Can you get these operations shut down while you're shooting?

If a window lets a small amount of traffic noise through even when it's tightly shut, you can often control the sound by hanging sound-dampening blankets over it. If the window is part of the shot and can't be covered, you can cut down its transmission by sealing a piece of thick Lexan or Plexiglass to the frame. If all else fails, plan a point-of-view shot through the window showing traffic on the other side. Include it early in the edited sequence so the viewer at least has a reference for the sound.

Check every opening into the room. Unless a door is specially constructed, it won't stop most sound. If there's a potentially noisy work area or hallway on the other side of the door, make arrangements to keep it quiet while you're actually shooting. Pay attention to media walls and built-in cabinets as well: these often are openings to another potentially noisy room.

A common practice in office buildings is to build partial walls which stop at the suspended ceiling. The area above the ceiling is an open plenum—sometimes extending completely across the building—where ducts and cables can be run. It's also an open path for sounds to pass from one room to another. To check if this is the situation at a proposed location, pop a tile near a suspect wall and take a look. But you can often tell just by following the ceiling grid as it approaches a wall. On a proper wall, the grid terminates at an angle bracket (Figure 6.3A). But if the wall stops partway up, the grid will disappear above it (6.3B).

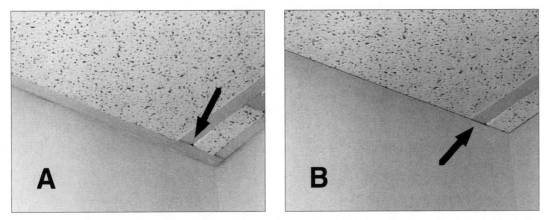

6.3 Be a ceiling detective. If the grid disappears (arrow on right), it's only part of a wall and won't stop sound.

Special fiberglass ceiling blankets can absorb some noises, but installation is difficult, and they're not totally effective. If you absolutely must shoot in a space with partial walls, you may have to shut down nearby areas or wait until after the building closes.

Air-conditioning systems can be particularly troublesome at interior locations. Listen carefully for any sounds they make; the microphone will hear them a lot louder than you do. Try removing the ventilation grill from an air duct: turbulence over the vanes that direct air around the room are a major source of noise, and air in the duct itself may be relatively quiet. The high-frequency hiss from air ducts is particularly localized, and you may find that the other side of the room is quiet enough to shoot.

The best solution is to have control over the system, and turn it off while you're rolling sound. The worst situation is a system that turns on and off automatically and can't be manually controlled: if some shots have air noise and others don't, it will be distracting when you cut between them. Plan to record some additional room tone with air conditioner running, and cut it under the quieter shots.

Air-conditioning ducts are also sound paths to other parts of the building. You might not notice it when the air is on and blowing past the grill, but once things are quieter, conversations and footsteps will be able to waft through the ductwork.

Refrigerators, water coolers, and fish tanks also have motors that make noise. The best solution is to turn them off while you're rolling. Watch out for units that turn on and off automatically: if some shots have noise and others don't, the difference will be distracting. As a last resort, record additional room tone with the motor running, and mix it under the quieter shots.

👉 *Note*

If you're turning off a refrigerator, put your car keys in it first. This guarantees you won't go home without remembering to turn it back on.

Acoustic problems

Even if you've found an incredibly quiet interior location, you still have to deal with room acoustics. Microphones pick up more reverberation than you notice when you're in the room and having a conversation. Once recorded, it can't be removed from the track.

The solution is usually a combination of added absorption, often provided by sound blankets and wrapped fiberglass panels, and close miking. Counterintuitively, larger spaces can be less of an echo problem because you can place the action in the middle of the room, where the reflecting walls are much farther from the microphone than the actors are. Specific tips for working with reverberant rooms are in the next chapter.

Reverberation is seldom a problem in exterior shooting, unless there's a large building nearby to reflect sound. If there is, it'll probably be in the shot, and viewers will expect to hear some slap from it.

Electronic interference

Wireless mics are subject to interference from television stations, police radios, video monitors, neon lights, bug zappers, and virtually anything else that relies on sparks or electronic circuits. It's not that the technology is particularly fragile; the problem is that a transmitter tiny enough to hide in somebody's sock or the small of their back isn't going to be very powerful. Their signals will also be reflected by a building's steel framework, nearby cars, or even large lights, causing the same kind of cancellations that affect sound in hard-walled rooms. Check Chapter 8 for tips on getting the best results from a wireless rig. And bring a wired backup, or adapters to use the wireless mic's pickup element with ordinary cables.

Wireless can also be affected by those rectangular cellphone antennas planted all over the place (Figure 6.4). While the phones themselves work on different frequencies than a wireless mic, the signals from the relay station can mix together in low-cost receivers to create unpredictable interference.

6.4 Those ubiquitous cellphone antennas can radiate combinations of signals that interfere with wireless mics

Some locations will even cause problems for wired mics. High-voltage transmission lines, power distribution transformers, medical equipment, and even lamp dimmers can radiate interference that's distributed by the building wiring and picked up by the mic. If you're at a location where this may be a problem, try a test first. Balanced wiring with Star-Quad (Chapter 4) and a transformer adapter at the camera (Chapter 9) can help a lot.

Location Considerations for Special Situations

Voice-overs

If a character or spokesperson is seen on camera and then intercut as a voice-over, the reverberation should match, or the edit will be distracting. The location also has to be quieter for voice-over than for on-camera dialog, since noises that might be excusable when we can see the source—such as nearby traffic at an exterior—are more objectionable when they're not identified. For compatibility, plan to record these voice-overs using the same microphone as the character's on-camera dialog.

If there's a lot of material to record this way and it can't be scheduled during down-time at the location, you may want to postpone the recording so you won't have an expensive crew standing idle. Returning to the original location (at the same time of day) will help the sounds match; but if that's impossible and you need to record in a studio, choose one with excellent acoustics and no natural reverb of its own. Then use an artifical reverb, when you mix, to match the location's sound. A studio is essential for this kind of matching: every location has its own unique sound, and trying to match a real-world shoot with a randomly chosen room near your office—even if it's roughly the same dimensions—is seldom successful.

The studio engineer will need to know how the microphone was set up at the location and should have a sample location track as a guide for processing. Hearing a location track will also help the talent match the original speaking style.

The reverse can also sometimes happen: you need just a couple of lines recorded without any room reverb, possibly for special effects or to narrate a promo that'll accompany the video. This is ideally done in a studio, but with only a few lines, it might not be worth the time or expense to go to one. Folding portable sound booths, consisting of padded rigid panels that snap into a frame, are available as an on-location substitute. They don't provide any isolation—the area will have to be kept quiet—but they do control reverberation the same way as a good voice studio. In a pinch, you can build this kind of booth by creating a frame with light stands and hanging sound blankets around its perimeter and across the top.

Industrial locations and other noisy places

If you have to interview the manager at a construction site or inside a busy office, intelligibility is more important than looks. Get the mic as close as possible—even if it's in the shot—and hope for the best. If you have to shoot dramatic dialog at the same site, a miniature lav as close to the mouth as possible—taped to the glasses or peeking out from a shirt collar—may be adequate if the talent is speaking loudly. But it's better to shut down most of the operations while shooting. A dialog replacement session (Chapter 10) may be the only cure.

Very long shots

Since there's no place to put a boom, you have to use lavalieres. Wireless mics work best when they're close to the receiver, so a long shot may present its own problems. If possible, run mic cables down the characters' pants legs. If those would show, try hiding the wireless receiver behind some object in the shot close to the actor, and run a cable to the camera. If that's not possible, you may want to try concealing a MiniDisc recorder in the character's costume.

Fortunately, when the shot is that long, you probably won't see the character's mouth distinctly. Lip sync becomes less of an issue.

On-set playback

Some sequences, particularly musical ones, require that talent work with a previously recorded track. If you don't intend to record dialog or effects during these sequences, the audio setup is simple: all you need is a stable playback medium such as DAT, portable CD, or MiniDisc (the speed of analog audio cassettes drifts too much to be useful for playback); speakers close enough so that talent isn't confused by room echoes; and a feed from the playback device to your recorder for sync reference.

But these sequences can be more effective if you're also recording natural sounds, dialog, or the characters singing along with the playback. This kind of shot requires pre-production planning, because you don't want the playback to be picked up on the characters' microphones. Room acoustics will make that pickup sound worse than a direct feed, and you'll have no control over the voice/music ratio in the mix. To get the best isolation, have an experienced production sound recordist help you sort out the options:

- Foldback. This is the simplest kind of playback. Small speakers are used with just enough volume for the talent to hear the cues. Mic placement is critical to minimize pickup from these speakers, or else there'll be problems when the mic is mixed with the original recording.

- IFB. Small radio receivers, with tiny earpieces, are hidden on the talent. The cueing signal is transmitted to them. Mic placement is less critical, but the individual receivers can get expensive if you have to equip a large cast, the earpiece may show in very tight shots, and active movement—such as dancing—can shake the whole thing loose. An alternative scheme picks up audio frequencies from a large loop of wire running around the shooting area; while cheaper, the advantages and disadvantages are pretty much the same as using radio.

- Thumper. The lowest rhythmic notes of a piece of music are played on special speakers and conducted through the floor. Dancers literally "feel the beat." Miking is very flexible; any thumps that make it to the soundtrack can be filtered in postproduction.

Shoot Now, Record Later

Some locations have too many problems to allow successful dialog recording, and a dialog replacement session may be the only way to get an acceptable soundtrack. ADR (automatic dialog replacement, but it isn't really automatic at all), also known as looping, is an accepted part of Hollywood filmmaking. So are budgets that reach a hundred million dollars.

ADR is expensive, exacting, annoys the actors, and seldom gives you a wonderful soundtrack. It's frowned upon by the feature-film sound community. When a Director of Photography says, "You can fix the sound later," mixer Randy Thom often replies, "That's not fixing it; it's replacing it." In a production sound newsgroup, mixer Jon Trebilcock adds: "If you bring your Mercedes for a repair, and the next day they give you the keys to a Ford, would you say you got your car fixed? No, you had it *replaced* with something inferior. It runs, and will get you from point A to point B, but it's not what you originally bought. That's why the *R* in *ADR* stands for 'replacement', not 'repair'."

ADR should only be considered as a last resort in video production; often, compromising slightly on the choice of location will yield a better overall project. If you must use it, *plan ahead*:

- Long shots are easier to loop than close-ups, because lipsync errors aren't as obvious.

- Quick cuts with lots of cutaways are easier than longer takes, for the same reason.

- Short phrases are easier to loop than long speeches.

- Every word counts. The less dialog in a scene, the faster you'll be able to fix it.

The decision to use ADR doesn't absolve you of the responsibility to record sound in the field. Your actors will need a guide track to work efficiently, and some of the original dialog or effects may be salvageable.

The actual techniques for ADR are discussed in Chapter 10.

Section III

Production Sound

Enough theory and planning. Here's where we get down to practical realities.

This section is about production:

- Chapter 7 discusses how to choose the right kind of microphone and deal with location acoustics. It's slightly technical, but it's not at all theoretical: the things in this chapter are as real as pointing a light or focusing a lens.

- Chapter 8 teaches the techniques of production sound. There are long sections on holding and manipulating a boom mic, where and how to hide a lavaliere or tie-tack mic, and how to get the best results from a wireless rig. It won't turn you into a professional sound recordist overnight, but it does cover all of the basics so you can record professional-quality dialog.

- Chapter 9 covers the actual field recording process: getting the signal from the mic onto tape with a minimum of noise and other problems. It includes advice for specific cameras and shooting situations, things you won't find in manufacturer's manuals. It also includes when and how you should record in something other than a camera.

Those three chapters are some of the longest in the book, because getting good sound at the shoot is critical, and there are a lot of things to consider.

- Chapter 10 explains how to record additional voices and effects after the shoot is over—the techniques are totally different from those in Chapter 8. I've also included sections on how to record sync dialog to existing picture and proven successful ways to direct a voice-over performer.

Let's make a movie.

Chapter 7

Microphones and Room Acoustics

We listen to the world through rose-colored ears. Within a few minutes of entering a room, most people learn to ignore its acoustics. The hum of machinery and computer fans that normally surrounds us seems to disappear as soon as we start paying attention to something else. It's no problem to pick out your child's voice in a crowded schoolyard or your friend's conversation at a noisy cocktail party.

The real world doesn't sound like our perception of it. That's why, if you record a scene and then play it back without the spatial and visual cues that help focus our ears, all the noise and reverb come crashing back. The only way to avoid it is to take special care in how you set up the room and the mic.

About Microphones

A camera's lens defines a precise rectangle. Point it in the right direction, and you can frame a shot that includes only what you want the viewer to see. Everything else is out of camera range.

With a lens, we could take a basic two-shot (Figure 7.1) and zoom in on just the horn-playing trickster. His bear friend would be completely gone (Figure 7.2).

But a mic doesn't work that way. When we talk about a mic's pickup pattern, we're merely indicating in which direction the mic is slightly more sensitive. It actually continues to hear things from all around the room, and there is no such thing as "just out of microphone range."

7.1 A basic 2-shot.

7.2 A longer lens lets us focus on just one character.

Figure 7.3 is a visual analogy of what a good shotgun mic would hear, focused on just one subject.

Three visual aspects of Figure 7.3 translate to what you'll hear with real-world directional microphones:

- A directional mic will make sounds coming from the front seem slightly closer. That's why our horn player is slightly larger, compared to the bear, in Figure 7.3.

- It does this by lowering the volume of sounds from other directions. That's why the rest of the scene is darker.

7.3 Unfortunately, the mic isn't as discriminating. Even the most directional shotgun won't exclude the bear.

7.4 Real-world mics continue to pick up, far beyond what we think they're pointing at.

- A directional mic will change the timbre of sound coming from other directions, adding a coloration that emphasizes some frequencies and lowers others. Note how the bear's colors are subtly changed.

The more directional a mic is, the more you hear these effects. However, better-quality mics will have less of the off-axis coloration.

Actually, Figure 7.3 is a simplification. What that directional mic *really* hears is more like Figure 7.4 . . . except it would continue beyond the photo, picking up me, my camera, and things behind me.

Try this

- Take your best directional microphone, camera, and good headphones. Turn on a radio, at conversational volume, in an average room of your house or office. Stand about three feet away from the radio, and listen to it through the mic.

- Now turn the mic 180°, so its back is pointing to the radio. Listen again . . . and you'll still hear the radio. It'll just be a little bit softer and not sound as good.

- Try the same thing at 6 feet, and the difference will be even less.

Types of Microphones

A microphone is just a pickup element to convert sound pressure into electrical voltages, mounted in a box. The construction of the pickup element determines how it translates pressure into electricity, but only a couple of methods—dynamic and condenser—are appropriate for video production. We'll cover those in a few pages.

What's much more important is how the microphone picks up pressure from different directions. This is determined by the shape of the box, its vent holes, and internal baffles. But it's also influenced by frequency: sounds of different frequencies will work their way through those holes and baffles differently.

Microphone Directionality

Polar patterns It's fairly easy for mic manufacturers to measure this phenomenon. They put the mic in a room without echoes, walk around it with a tone generator, and read the mic's output at different frequencies and directions. They plot this on a circular graph, as in Figure 7.5. Directly in front of the mic is considered 0°, at the bottom of the figure. The voltage for a sound coming from directly in front is considered 0 dB. As the voltage drops for sounds from different directions, it's plotted on the inner circles. Multiple plots are used to show how the mic reacts to different frequencies. The graph is split in half because mics are symmetrical: assume there's a matching half circle, facing in the other direction, for each side.

All of the polar patterns in this section are based on actual measurements of some highly-regarded, expensive European mics. Figure 7.5 shows the polar pattern of an *omnidirectional* mic. On the left side, you can see that the mic is equally sensitive from any direction, for any frequency between 125 Hz and 1 kHz. On the right, it's also equally sensitive from any direction between 2 kHz and 8 kHz. But the gray line on the right shows how this mic becomes slightly directional at 16 kHz: sounds at that frequency, coming from the rear, will be –5 dB softer than those from the front. This is insignificant for most purposes. It's caused by the mic's body casting an acoustic shadow. (Much thinner mics are used for lab measurements, so there's less of a shadow.)

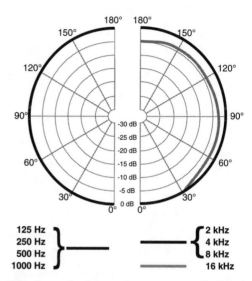

7.5 A graph of the polar response of a good omnidirectional mic.

Omnidirectional Omnidirectional mics (or *omnis*) like the one measured in Figure 7.5 have a solid box around the element's side and back. There's only a tiny hole in the back, to equalize barometric pressure (Figure 7.6). Air-pressure waves strike the front of the element and generate a signal. The air inside the box acts as a resilient spring to push the diaphragm out when the sound wave is in rarefaction. Any sound waves coming from the back refract around the mic and hit the element. Omnis are sometimes called *non-directional* for this reason.

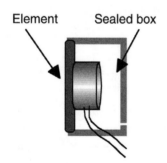

7.6 Omnidirectional mic.

Since an omnidirectional mic is mostly a sealed box, it's less sensitive to wind noise than other designs. This kind of mic is also sometimes called a *pressure mic* because it reacts to any changes in sound pressure, anywhere around it. Lavaliere microphones are often omnis because this design can be made very small. They're close to the actor's mouth, so lavs can rely on the inverse square law to pick up lots of voice with very little reverb or noise.

Full-size omnis are often used in studio recording and as handheld vocal-performance mics, but their major use in video is as handheld-close-up interview mics in very windy exteriors. They can also be used for recording background ambiences, when you want to pick up a diffuse impression of everything going on in a space.

For visual reference, an omni's pickup pattern looks like Figure 7.7. The mic is the black circle in the middle. I've emphasized the shape of the pickup in all of these drawings to make them more understandable. In reality, there's a smooth and gradual falloff of sensitivity around the shape, more like Figure 7.4. In other words, all four of the dark gray crew members around the bottom of the picture will be recorded at about the same sensitivity as the two actors at the top. It doesn't make any difference whether they're precisely inside or outside the white circle.

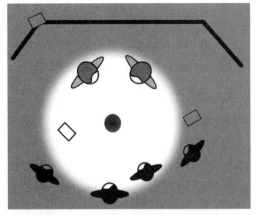

7.7 Omnis pick up everything around them. But read the text—the pattern isn't exactly like this.

Boundary mic   The boundary mic is a variation on omnidirectional mic design, which can be very useful in video production. It was originally developed by Crown International as the Pressure-Zone Microphone, and boundary mics are still referred to as *PZMs*. A very small omni element is mounted a fraction of an inch above a large rigid plate (Figure 7.8), which is then taped to a wall or other flat surface. Sound waves can reach it from only one direction, so there's less of

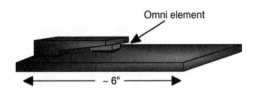

7.8 A boundary or PZM mic.

the interference caused by reflections coming from multiple paths. Because of their low profile, boundary mics can be concealed on the walls or floor of a set (placing a mousepad between the mic's plate and the floor will help isolate it from footsteps). They're also useful when you have to record in a reverberant space and can't get close enough to the source. The reverb is still there, but it doesn't color the sound as much. Some lavalieres come with mounting adapters to use them as boundary mics.

Cardioid

Cardioid mics are named for a theoretical heart-shaped pickup pattern, which rejects sounds from the rear and accepts them from the front and sides. You can see in Figure 7.9 how the pattern really works. It's reasonably heart-shaped between 250 Hz and 4 kHz, though rear rejection in the mid-band is only about –15 dB. But low frequencies (gray line on the left) are only reduced –7 dB from the rear. And high frequencies (gray lines on right) are hardly down –5 dB. Sounds coming from the rear are somewhat tubbier than those from the front.

This kind of microphone, also known as a *unidirectional*, often looks like an elongated omni with a few large holes in the sides of the box (Figure 7.10).

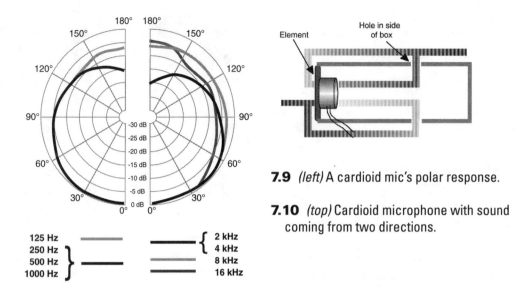

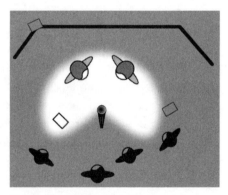

7.9 *(left)* A cardioid mic's polar response.

7.10 *(top)* Cardioid microphone with sound coming from two directions.

When a sound comes from the rear (shown as the top path in the drawing), it enters the hole and strikes the back of the element. It can also refract around the mic and strike the front of the element. Since these paths are about the same length, the front and back versions are the same volume and cancel each other out.

A sound coming from in front of the mic (bottom path) can also reach the back of the element. But in order to do so, it has to travel the length of mic to the hole, and then back again to the element. By that time, it's considerably weaker than it is at the front of the mic and doesn't cancel itself.

Figure 7.11 is a visual reference of how a cardioid mic performs. It's the black cone in the middle, parallel to the floor and pointing to the actors. The actual pickup pattern is mostly circular for three-quarters of the way around the mic and tucks in at the back. Viewed from above, it's sort of heart-shape . . . hence the name. Of

7.11 Cardioid pickup pattern.

course, the warning about Figure 7.7 also applies here: all mic patterns are much more gradual than the drawing.

This directionality makes cardioids more useful on the video set. They can be aimed so their front is pointing to the actor, while the rear is pointing to a noise source or reverberating surface. The difference between front and back sensitivity decreases as the frequency goes down, and, at very low frequencies, the design is almost omnidirectional.

The holes in the sides of a directional mic are a critical part of its design. If you block them by grabbing the mic around its middle or gaffer-taping it to a support, you can seriously hurt the sound. It's counterintuitive, but cupping your hands around the end of most microphones—the way you'd cup them around your ear to concentrate on a sound—makes them *less* directional.

Hypercardioid

A *hypercardioid* is a variation on the cardioid design, about the same size but with multiple holes in the side of the box, tuned for different frequencies. This makes it slightly more directional, and a good hypercardioid will have very little side or rear coloration except at the highest frequencies.

Figure 7.12 shows the polar pattern of a top-quality hyper (Schoeps MK41, a favorite Hollywood boom mic, about $1,000 with its powering module). The heart is tucked in, under 4 kHz, with side rejection –15 dB and down to –25 dB at 120°. There's a rear lobe, typical of very directional mics, of only –10 dB. At higher frequencies, the mic gets more directional, with about –5 dB more rejection for each octave up. Sounds from the sides will be just a bit duller than those from the front, but this effect doesn't really kick in at dialog frequencies. Lesser hypers, such as the AKG C1000 (about $250), exhibit the same tucked-in pattern but with about twice as much coloration from the sides and rear above 4 kHz and below 250 Hz. There are other differences between those two mics as well; many Hollywood mixers would say the AKG isn't worth a quarter of the Schoeps.

Figure 7.13 shows a visual reference. The hypercardioid is the short cylinder in the middle. Hypercardioids' reasonable directionality without too much coloration at dialog frequencies make them ideal for interior booming, where the mic will be close to the talent, but reflective ceilings or walls might also be close to the mic. Echoes from the actors' voices won't have their timbre changed, the way a mic with more side coloration might.

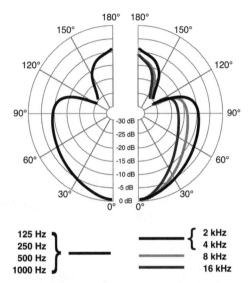

125 Hz		2 kHz
250 Hz		4 kHz
500 Hz		8 kHz
1000 Hz		16 kHz

7.12 Hypercardioid polar response.

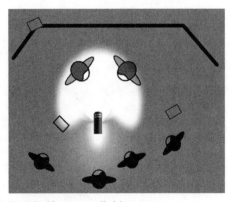

7.13 Hypercardioid pattern.

Shotgun

If you make the mic longer and add more holes of carefully calibrated dimensions, and possibly mount some tubes inside so that sounds coming in certain holes have to travel an even longer distance, you can make a mic that's more directional across more frequencies (Figure 7.14).

Short Shotgun mics are used frequently on DV shoots. Figure 7.15 shows why their results might not be what a videographer expects. The mics are reasonably directional across the band, with 15 dB or better rejection from the sides. But side rejection varies greatly with frequency: it's almost 30 dB at 125 Hz, around the vowels of most male voices. It's just 15 dB at 2 kHz, at the consonants. That's why voices or echoes hitting the side of a short shotgun can sound strange.

Oddly enough, rear rejection for the short shot is only about –5 dB at low frequencies and –10 dB at the mid-band—much less than from the sides. If the mic is on a camera while you're interviewing a subject 4' away, your voice will be considerably louder than theirs—and a little tubby sounding. This graph is from a well-respected, high-priced short shotgun; cheaper ones will be even more irregular at different frequencies. But all shotguns, long or short, have less rejection from the rear than from the sides. Figure 7.16 shows their pickup pattern.

Shotguns come in varying lengths, with longer ones having narrower pickup angles. Short shots are useful on booms in rooms without much echo, or outdoors. They can also be handheld for

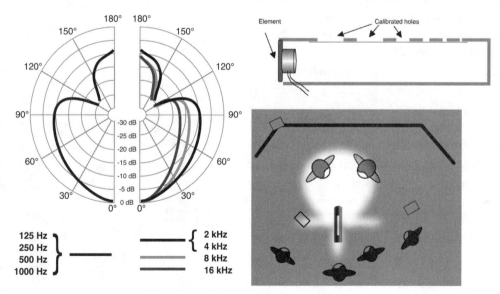

7.14 *(top right)* A shotgun mic.

7.15 *(left)* Short shotgun polar response.

7.16 *(bottom right)* Short shotgun pickup. The narrow, sensitive areas to the side and rear will vary with different mics, but some side and rear pickup will always exist.

interviews, or used for close-miking announcers or sound effects in rooms with less-than-perfect acoustics. While these rooms will have reverb, inverse square law dictates that the echoes won't be loud enough for the mics' side and rear coloration to matter. Long shotguns have even more coloration, and their use is generally reserved for exteriors, where there is no reverb.

Zoom mic

This is a marketing term, pure and simple. It's possible to make a variably directional mic, by using multiple elements back-to-back, or with an m/s configuration (discussed in a few pages). But no mic zooms like a lens does, and the term misleads a lot of beginning videographers. Furthermore, zoom mics are typically low-end consumer devices—they're certainly not purchased by professionals—and the dual elements contribute additional noise.

Hey . . . this isn't engineering class

- Why take the time to explain polar graphs in a book for video producers? Two reasons. First, I wanted to make sure you absolutely understood how a mic's response from different directions can color the sound.

- But second, you now know to look for a polar graph when buying a mic. It should be in the product literature or the manufacturer's Web site. All good mics come with this kind of information. If you can't find it, suspect that the manufacturer either doesn't understand the technology or was ashamed of the results.

- Mics also should come with frequency-response graphs, which show relative sensitivity across the band for sounds coming from the front. Without these two graphs, there's no way to tell how good a mic is. Claims like "acceptance angle 70°" or "frequency range 80 Hz–18 kHz" might sound technical, but they're meaningless.

Real-world Patterns

If you study the pattern drawings, you'll notice that the directional mics don't hear any farther into the set than the omni does. The difference is in how they reduce pickup from the sides or back. Because this tends to lower noise and reverb, we can choose to amplify the directional mic's signal more. But the extra "reach" is provided by the amplifier, not by the mic. When film sound mixers talk about the reach of a shotgun mic, they're really referring to how sensitive it is in various directions and how little electronic noise it contributes.

The best directional mics reject off-axis sounds by about 30 dB at mid and high frequencies. This is a significant amount, but certainly nothing like total rejection.

By this point, I hope you've gotten the message:

- There is no such thing as a telephoto mic.

- All microphones are wide angle and have to be brought close to the subject.

- Some mics have wider angles than others.

There are only two exceptions that I know of. Some mics are coupled with a parabolic reflector, which gathers sound pressure from a large area and focuses it in towards a small mic. Parabolics sacrifice frequency range for sensitivity, so they don't sound good for dialog recording. However, they're sometimes used in nature recording and surveillance.

One manufacturer, Audio-Technica, makes an array mic (about $2,500). Inside the body is one of their conventional short shotguns, with four additional omnis spaced around it. A separate logic box interprets the relative signal from the shotgun and omni, and applies electronic cancellation of signals that appear on both. The array mic has excellent rejection from the rear and sides, with reasonably-full frequency response. However, the multiple elements generate significant hiss, and the logic gets confused by any interior echoes. This mic's primary use is gathering sounds from the sidelines during outdoor sporting events, where the crowd noise buries the hiss.

Problems with directional mics

With nothing but patterns of holes and hollow tubes to work with, it's amazing that microphone designers can make their products as good as they are. But even the best of them are subject to physical limitations:

1. Off-axis response   The holes and tubes cause cancellations and reinforcements depending on frequency. Sounds from the rear and side will have their timbre affected. The more directional a mic is, the more pronounced this effect. Track 9 of this book's CD lets you hear on- and off-axis response for different kinds of mics.

This means shotguns have to be pointed precisely. There are some tips for learning this skill in the next chapter.

2. Proximity effect   Directional mics emphasize bass notes as you get closer to them. Radio announcers frequently take advantage of this, working close to the mic to make their voices appear deeper. This also means that directional mics are more sensitive to "popped Ps": an overload caused by the sudden blast of air from a plosive vowel spoken too closely to the mic. At normal operating distances, the proximity effect shouldn't be a problem.

3. Wind pickup   Directional mics are more sensitive to wind, because they have so many openings along their sides. Any air movement will be heard. You almost always need to use a windscreen with them, except if the mic is perfectly still and indoors. The foam windscreen supplied with many short shotguns doesn't provide enough protection for exteriors or fast-moving booms; a zeppelin-style hard windscreen, often with a furry cloth cover, is usually used instead.

4. Lack of low frequencies   It's difficult to make a very directional mic directional for bass notes, so manufacturers often limit a shotgun mic's low-frequency response. The frequencies involved are too low to be of much concern for dialog, but you should be aware of this if using a shotgun for music or deep sound effects.

Stereo mics

A few manufacturers make dual mics in a single housing, designed to pick up stereo. Stereo mics can be useful for backgrounds, large sound effects, and music recording. They're seldom used for dialog, however. Even large-screen features record the actors in mono. No matter where the actors are on the screen, their voice usually comes out of a center speaker. If some sense of direction is needed for a special effect or a distant character, the mono recording will be placed in a specific position at the mix.

Stereo mics usually come in two configurations: X/Y and M/S. In an X/Y mic, two separate cardioid elements are positioned with their fronts very close together and at a 90° angle. Their outputs are fed down a common multi-conductor cable and terminate in either a stereo mini-plug or dual balanced XLRs.

A minor problem with X/Y miking is that it's not truly mono compatible. Sounds coming from the side may add strangely when the channels are mixed together, causing colorations similar to the multiple acoustic paths discussed in Chapter 2. Mono compatibility is important for broadcast, Internet, and CD-ROM productions.

An alternative scheme, M/S (for mid/side) miking, uses a cardioid mic pointing forward, with a *bi-directional* mic close to it and pointing to the sides. Bi-directionals work like dual hypercardioids, back-to-back, but have a single element. Because of this, pressure coming from one side of the element will create a positive voltage, and pressure from the other side will create a negative voltage. In effect, the mic works equally well for both sides, but one side has its polarity reversed. The two mic signals are routed down a common multi-conductor cable, but the cardioid output is considered *middle* and the bi-directional is *side*.

A circuit then adds the two outputs, as shown in Figure 7.17, to create left and right outputs. Since the cardioid (light gray in the drawing) is facing the performers, it picks up the right and left side of the stage equally. The bi-directional (dark gray) is facing the left, so sounds from the left side of the stage reach the front of its element, with positive pressures producing a positive voltage. Sounds from the right side of the stage reach the back of its element, so positive pressures from that side produce a negative voltage. Its signal consists of +Left combined with −Right, or Left−Right.

If the two mic signals are mixed normally, the positive and negative rights cancel out, and you get the left side of the stage only. But if the bi-directional's signal is inverted before they're mixed, it consists of –Left and +Right. Mixing the two mics together now means the positive and negative lefts will cancel, and you get the right side of the stage only.

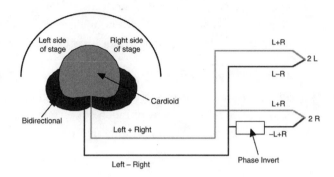

This may seem like a lot of work—it's really not—but it pays off

7.17 Mid-side miking to preserve mono compatibility.

when somebody listens in mono: when you combine the derived left and right outputs, the bi-directional mic completely cancels itself out! You're left with nothing but the cardioid's signal, and absolutely no coloration caused by time delay.

As a matter of fact, this same scheme is at the heart of analog stereo FM and TV. Using electronic inversions rather than a bi-directional mic, the left and right channels are combined into a main mono signal. This is what's broadcast in the usual band, and mono listeners hear it with no trouble. The "side" signal is broadcast in a slightly higher band that stereo receivers can get. The receiver then performs a similar translation, recreating left and right.

You can create your own M/S rig with two microphones, closely matched for sound quality. One should be an omni or cardioid for the middle, the other a bi-directional. Bi-directional (also called *figure-8*) mics are so rare in video production that most catalogs don't list them. You'll have to get them from a music studio supplier. Many multi-pattern mics (also not used in video) have a bi-directional setting.

Place the microphones as close together as possible, with the omni or cardioid facing the performers. The bi-directional mic should be aligned sideways, so that its front is facing the left side and its back is facing the right. Since the mics are close together, the time delay between them is very slight.

Stereo on a boom   An alternative, sometimes used in documentary production (favored by the BBC, but rarely heard in the U.S.), substitutes a short shotgun or hypercardioid for the cardioid. The two mics are wired as in Figure 7.17.

This configuration is useful if the subject is in an interesting-sounding place, and isn't moving. Its advantage is that, for mono listeners, most of the room disappears. Instead of an echoey sound with background noise, they hear the tight sound of a normal boom mic. Stereo listeners hear the subject centered but with a good sense of the room background and reverb coming from the sides.

Audio-Technica makes short and long shotguns with this configuration, available from broadcast dealers. Ambient (www.ambient.de) makes an *Emesser* miniature bi-directional mic, designed to fit on the shockmount of a conventional hyper or shotgun, so you can create your own. It's available from film sound specialty shops.

Stereo booming usually isn't appropriate for dramatic shoots or any situation where the boom isn't in a fixed location, because the stereo image swings around unrealistically as the mic moves.

Mid-side tricks   Mid-side techniques can be used to create a variable-width mic for some recordings. Set it up as in the figure, with a cardioid or more directional mic in the middle. But add a volume control to the output of the bi-directional mic. When that mic is turned up, the stereo effect will be wide. As its level is reduced, the recording gets narrower and narrower. When it's all the way off, the recording is mono. You can use this trick in postproduction to match the perceived width of a sound to its image, without sacrificing mono compatibility.

A variation of the technique doesn't require a bi-directional mic and doesn't create true stereo, but it can provide a spaciousness to scenes for stereo viewers. It's particularly helpful in areas where a good stereo recording would be hard to set up, such as a factory interior. Put a lavaliere on the actor or point a hyper at the dialog, and call that the Mid channel. Then put an omni somewhere else—a boundary mic on the floor, in front of the action, works well for this. Call this the Side channel, and mix them as if it were MS. It won't be true stereo, but it'll give you a lot of control during the final mix without any of the hollowness of trying to mix a typically spaced stereo pair. Check the results in mono, to make sure you haven't accidentally reversed the channels.

Camera mics

The mics built into most MiniDV cameras are awful. They're included because nobody (other than a pro) would buy a camera without one. Unless you're shooting from a foot away, they just won't do a good job on dialog. Save them for birthday parties where you don't care about sound.

Even placing a high-quality mic on the camera isn't a very good solution. Four inches from the lens is a terrible place to put a mic,

In the first edition of *Producing Great Sound*, I wrote the following:

"Are you using the camera's built-in mic? If so, you haven't been paying attention to what I've written. Here's a better use for this book: take it in one hand and whack the mic off your camera."

The drugs have kicked in, and I'm mellower now. But the principle stands.

too far from dialog and too close to camera (and videographer) noises. Save this configuration for breaking events, where it's impossible to get a mic closer, or for the kind of close-camera shouted interviews sometimes done at wedding receptions. And for best results, use a mount that lifts the mic as far above the camera as possible. Inverse square law will reduce camera noise while not lowering the dialog level.

Types of Pickup

So far, we've spoken about a microphone's pickup element but haven't explained how they work. Here's how a mic converts varying air pressure to a changing voltage.

Dynamic mics

The simplest pickup element has a coil of wire attached to a plastic or foil diaphragm, suspended in a strong magnetic field. Air pressure waves make the diaphragm vibrate, and, as the coil vibrates along with it, the magnetism creates an electric current (Figure 7.18). This is the same principle as an electric generator, except the ones in a power plant use turbines to continually rotate the coil instead of letting it just vibrate. In both cases, they turn physical movement into electricity.

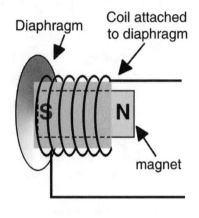

Since a dynamic mic's voltage is directly generated by sound pressure, it takes a relatively large amount of pressure to get a usable output. An internal transformer is almost always used to raise the output voltage enough so

7.18 Dynamic microphone

that it can be carried on a cable without too much noise pickup. Dynamic mics are not as sensitive as condenser mics, particularly at high frequencies. On the other hand, the simplicity of design makes them very rugged, and the lack of electronics in the mic itself means it can handle louder sounds than a condenser. The magnet in these mics can be fairly strong, so be careful with them around floppy disks.

On the other hand, since dynamics convert sound directly into electricity, they can have very low distortion and don't contribute any electronic noise. Many announcers prefer their sound, and full-sized dynamics like the Electro-Voice RE-27 and Shure SM-7 have been staples in the pro studio for years.

Performance mics, such as the classic Shure SM-57 and SM-58, have low-sensitivity dynamic elements designed to work best when they're very close to an instrument or vocalist's mouth. They are not suitable for video production, unless they're being used as a visible musician's or stand-up comic's mic.

A dynamic mic's construction is very similar to a headphone. Just as electric generators can also be used as motors, dynamic mics can be used as tiny speakers. Back when I was a radio station engineer, I'd occasionally fuddle announcers by connecting their mic to an intercom output. As they were about to read the news, I'd whisper into the 'com. Their mic—now working as a headphone—would say "Eww. You had garlic for lunch!"

Don't try this stunt unless you thoroughly understand the engineering risks involved—and the possibility of physical ones, if the announcer doesn't have a sense of humor.

Condenser mics

A condenser mic doesn't turn sound directly into output volts. A metalized plastic diaphragm is mounted close to a rigid plate, and an electric charge is applied to it. As sound pressure waves move the diaphragm closer or farther from the plate, a tiny but varying stream of electrons can jump across. This stream has a high impedance and low voltage, so it's too weak to send to a recorder—even a few feet of extra cable can damage the signal. Instead, a preamplifier is built inside the mic body (Figure 7.19). The preamp uses an exter-

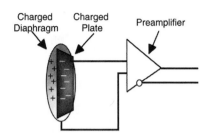

7.19 Condenser microphone

nal voltage to boost the signal to usable levels. The voltage can come from an internal battery, or be supplied by the mixer or recorder.

Most of the mics on a film or video set are condensers. Since they don't use a magnet, they can be smaller and lighter—an advantage for both booms and lavalieres. High-quality condensers can be more sensitive to subtle sounds than dynamics. Much cheaper condensers still sound better and are smaller than similarly priced dynamics.

Traditional condenser mics are *externally polarized*. The diaphragm is charged up to a couple of hundred volts, stepped up from the preamp's power supply. This means they can be highly sensitive (or create very little electrical noise of their own, which amounts to the same thing), so this design is preferred for high-quality studio mics.

You can also charge small plastic diaphragms chemically instead of electrically, with a process similar to the one used for making static-charged dust mops. The result is the ubiquitous *electret* condenser, found everywhere from cell phones to lavs. This is the technology used in most sub-$500 studio mics. While the best of them are almost as good as externally-polarized mics, they can't be as sensitive, so their internal amplifiers generate comparatively more noise. However, the lack of a high-voltage supply means they can be smaller and less expensive.

Electret condensers are virtually the only type of pickup used in video production. The ones costing between fifty and a few hundred dollars, depending on their construction and pickup patterns, are more than adequate for this kind of work. Their size means that electrets are always preferred for lavalieres—even those used in major features.

Condenser mics also lend themselves to modular construction. The pickup element and whatever arrangement of ports and tubes that give it directionality can be one module. The preamp can be another. They connect with screw threads or a bayonet arrangement. With a system like this, a videographer can carry multiple heads for different miking situations, while having to pay for only a single preamp. It's a little like a photographer carrying multiple lenses with a single camera body. This system is used in the Sennheiser K6 series, popular in video production, and the Schoeps MK41 used on most features.

Very cheap electrets—costing less than a dollar each—are found in toys, telephones, and multimedia computers. Don't expect the mic that came with your computer or sound card to be any more than a toy.

All condenser mics require some form of power supply:

- Very cheap electrets are usually powered directly from the circuits they're built into.

- Electrets designed for mounting on prosumer cameras use *plugin-power*, a low voltage applied to the mic jack.

- Full-sized electrets with XLR connectors are powered either by a small battery in their bodies or via phantom powering (See "Phantom power" on page 127.). Externally-polarized condenser mics require phantom power. Some classic used ones might be wired for T-power, which isn't directly compatible.

> **Dynamic or condenser?** Choose a condenser mic when you can for video work: the extra sensitivity translates into a better-sounding track. Use an externally polarized mic for tracks that are being recorded on a separate DAT and intended for theatrical playback. The reduced noise is worth the extra expense.
>
> If the mic is going to be subject to humidity or physical abuse, or if you're planning to record very loud sounds, choose a dynamic mic.

- High-quality music studio mics that use vacuum tubes often require dedicated power supplies, and multi-conductor cables.

- The tiny electrets used as lavalieres are powered by batteries in their plugs or phantom powering. If they're part of a wireless mic system, they'll get power from the transmitter's battery.

When power is first applied to a traditional condenser microphone, it may produce a loud "thunk" as the plate charges. Electrets may make clicking or popping noises when they're powered. As a general rule, leave a condenser mic's volume turned down when you change the battery or plug it into a phantom supply.

Other microphone types

Ribbon   Ever notice the large jellybean-shaped mic on David Letterman's desk? It's a classic RCA 77DX, one of the all-time greats for making a voice-over sound both warm and natural. It's a shame that Letterman's is only a prop—his voice is really picked up by a wireless electret lav, visible on-camera.

The 77DX and other *ribbon* mics use the same basic principle as dynamics, but without a diaphragm. Instead, a delicate foil strip is vibrated by the sound waves, while suspended in a very strong magnetic field. This produces a tiny electric current. Because the foil has so little mass, a ribbon can be extremely accurate—particularly on relatively loud sounds that lack extreme highs, like the human voice—and is often preferred by announcers.

The low output of a traditional ribbon mic requires an internal transformer and a low-noise, impedance-controlled preamplifier. Prosumer mixers usually aren't good enough; if you've got one of these classic mics, treat it to a good preamp. A few contemporary versions of the mic include an internal preamplifier; their output is similar to that of a condenser mic and will work with any mixer. They also require phantom power for the preamp. But make sure of a ribbon mic's requirements before applying power: some of the older ones may be wired in a way that phantom power could harm the ribbon.

Those tiny ribbons are also physically fragile. A strong wind or other shock can knock it out of position, requiring an expensive repair. Add the weight of the large magnet required, and it's understandable why these mics aren't used outside sound studios. There's also an economic consideration: while RCA ribbons haven't been made for years, good used ones can fetch as much as $2,000. Contemporary ribbons from Beyerdynamic, Fostex, and Royer cost between $750–2,500.

Ceramic and crystal   These used to be the cheapest mics available for home recording and two-way radio. Their quality was never very good, and they were easily damaged. Unless you want a deliberately bad sound (which is easier accomplished with processors), there's no reason to use one of these for a voice-over. In fact, they're not even used for two-way radios any more; electret condensers are cheaper and better.

Phantom power   Balanced wiring, discussed in Chapter 4, uses a positive audio signal on one wire of a two-conductor cable while there's a negative signal on the other. This way, it can reject noises that are picked up equally on both wires. A metallic shield is usually provided for additional noise protection. This scheme is used by all professional microphones that have to drive long cables.

When transistorized condenser microphones became popular for production, engineers realized the balanced microphone cables could also carry power for the diaphragm and preamplifier, without worrying about it contaminating the audio signal. A positive current (usually at 48 volts, but many mics will work at much lower voltages) is applied to *both* wires of a balanced cable, with the current's negative side returning through the cable shield. Since this causes no voltage difference between the two signal wires, the audio circuitry totally ignores it.

In most equipment, phantom power is applied with a pair of precision resistors so the voltage is equal on both wires. A pair of capacitors keep the voltage from affecting the audio circuits, since capacitors block DC voltages (Figure 7.20). This is the most common arrangement for professional cameras with XLR inputs, and small mixers. Some equipment uses a transformer to apply the voltage, in a circuit that's almost identical to the microphone's (Figure 7.21). This has the advantage of slightly better noise immunity.

At the microphone end, a center-tapped transformer winding gathers DC voltage from both wires. DC

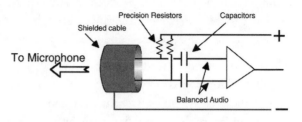

7.20 Phantom power in an input circuit.

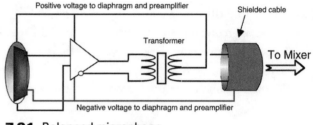

7.21 Balanced microphone

can't jump from one winding of a transformer to the other, so it doesn't affect the mic's audio circuit. Transformers can be sensitive to AC hum in the vicinity, and good-sounding ones are expensive, so some microphones use capacitors instead to sort out the phantom power.

The voltage is called "phantom" because if a mic doesn't look for it, it disappears. The output transformer of a dynamic mic (Figure 7.18) is never connected to the cable shield. If a phantom voltage is fed equally to both of that mic's signal wires, it won't create any current flow through the microphone itself. As far as the mic is concerned, there never was any powering voltage coming from the mixer.

T or Simplex Powering

Before phantom power became a standard, some condenser microphones used on film shoots were powered with a positive voltage on one wire and a negative voltage on the other. This is now obsolete, but some classic high-quality boom mics in rental inventories or on eBay may be wired this way. It's not directly compatible with any video production equipment, but adapters are available.

Beware the Phantom!

Phantom power works well in most professional applications. However, using it improperly can damage the microphone or mixer:

- If an unbalanced microphone is connected to a phantom supply, voltage will be applied across its element.

- If a cable or connector is damaged so either conductor touches the shield, the phantom supply will be shorted out. Most plug-in XLR-to-phone-plug adapters will short out a phantom voltage this way.

- If a balanced line-level signal is applied to a microphone input that has phantom power, the voltage can cause distortion and possibly damage the source's circuits.

On the other hand, phantom power lets you run wired condenser mics all day without worrying about changing batteries. If your microphones and cables are in good shape and need the voltage, leave it on. Otherwise, turn phantom power off.

Rooms and Recording

I have an actress friend who used to dub the, uh, dialog during the heavier scenes of Swedish sex films. But when she told me about it, I topped her: I've done *my* job under blankets in a hotel room, in the back of a limousine, and with a professor inside a world map. The search for good acoustics on a location can make you do strange things, but the right technique makes a big difference in your finished track.

That's also the reason for foam tiles on a sound studio's walls. They're not part of the soundproofing—foam doesn't have much mass, and it has too many holes to stop airborne noise. Their purpose is to absorb reflections, since sound bouncing around a room can make a voice sound tubby or hollow (see Chapter 2).

Testing the Space

It's not practical to put up foam tiles when you're shooting in a conference room or factory floor, but you can still use a piece of foam to find out if there are going to be echoes. Before you decide where the camera will be, stand at the talent's position. Hold a square of foam—or a folded towel, couch cushion, or anything else absorbent—about two feet in front of your face and sing "ahh" at a fairly loud volume. Then take the absorber away and keep singing. If you hear any difference in the sound of your own voice, it's caused by reflections that can interfere with the sound.

Studios often have nonparallel walls to control reflections, so that sounds don't keep echoing between them to cause hollowness by reinforcing individual frequencies. If the sound can bounce at an angle, the reflections follow different paths each time, and the hollowness gets smoothed out. You can't push the walls away where you're shooting, but you can do the next best thing by keeping the talent at an angle to any reflective surfaces.

Both the distance and the angle between talent and wall are important. Walk around the room while you're doing the sing-into-the-foam test. If light or props mean that you have to place the talent in a less-than-ideal position, try rotating the setup a few degrees so the voice strikes reflective surfaces at an angle. Figure 7.22 shows how changing the talent's position can make a big difference in a finished track.

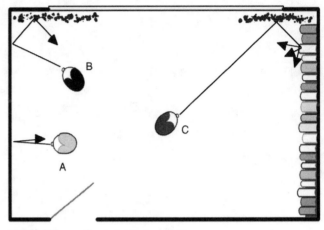

7.22 Where the talent stands in a room can make a difference.

The drawing shows a typical conference room with drapes and a bookshelf. Actor A is in the worst position, facing a wall (and close to any noise from the hallway). Actor B is better because the angle gives echoes a longer path and the drape absorbs some of the sound. Actor C is in the best position, taking advantage of distance, absorption, angles, and the way an uneven surface like a bookshelf breaks up the reflections.

Cutting Down Reflections

The reflections that really matter are the ones the talent is facing into—usually from the wall behind the camera. That location means you've got more options for lowering reflections, without worrying about how they'll look. The most common solution is *sound blankets*—heavy, padded cloths about six feet square, available from film and video supply houses. Furniture-moving pads are a close equivalent, though with a little less absorption. Hang them from the offending wall, at about the same height as the talent's mouth. Hanging a few on the sides of the room can also cut down the parallel-wall problem. You can boost their echo-cutting ability by hanging them from a light stand and boom instead of directly on the wall. A couple of inches between wall and blanket lets it trap more sound.

Sound blankets can be folded up and stored when they're not in use. A less-flexible alternative (literally) but with better absorption is Owens-Corning type 703 fiberglass. This is a specially compressed version of the fibers used for house insulation, designed specifically for acoustics. It comes in lightweight 2×4-foor panels, an inch or two thick, and can be found at acoustical-ceiling supply companies and bigger home-improvement centers. It costs about 60¢ per square foot for the 2 inch version. Wrap the panels in an old bedsheet or something similar to keep the fibers from irritating your skin. The panels are rigid enough to be leaned against a wall, and light enough that they can be hung from standard picture hooks.

You can soften a reflective surface by closing drapes, moving a sofa, or even lining up a row of heavily dressed production assistants against it. But there's another technique—diffusion—that can also conquer some of the offending echoes. That's because the biggest problem with a hard wall is that it reflects all the sound back in the same direction. If you can break up the surface so some of the reflections go elsewhere, there'll be less noticeable echo. If you don't have a book-shelf handy, try stacking up some road cases and equipment boxes at random angles. The round tubes used to ship tripods or light stands—or any large rounded objects—are particularly helpful since they diffuse sound in all directions.

If a room has a high reflective ceiling, you can provide some absorption and diffusion by filling the ceiling with helium-filled balloons. This may be the only way to get usable dialog in rooms with a domed ceiling that focuses echoes back at the actors.

Be Flexible

Keep trying different placements and angles within a room—and other recording spaces—until you get a sense of how walls affect sound. That's why some zero-budget filmmakers record voice-overs in a closet stuffed with winter coats (the coats absorb sound, and they mic very closely). It's also how I got into some of the weird places referred to at the start of this section. The blankets in the hotel room were, of course, sound blankets. The limo was parked in a dealer's show-room—but the room itself had gigantic glass windows and an opening to their machine shop, so we moved an interview into the car to gain isolation and absorption. The map was the kind with large sheets of heavy paper hanging from an easel; we were recording voice-over inserts in an echoey classroom, so we held some of the pages out to improvise a tent, and I put the professor inside of it.

Chapter 8

Production Mic Technique

Rose's Rules:

✔ You can fake almost any other aspect of the track, and undo or change it if you're not happy with the result. But bad dialog recordings are forever.

✔ You can write, direct, shoot, edit, create graphics, and mix the whole project all by yourself, all in your own sweet time, and create a solo tour-de-force. But unless you're in a position to pay full attention to sound *at the shoot*, you'll need someone else to help you.

No part of production seems more misunderstood by videographers than gathering dialog while they're shooting. This is a shame, considering the process has been refined over three-quarters of a century in Hollywood. We know how to do it right, and the information is freely available. It's not rocket science. In fact, once you understand some basics about handling a boom, rigging a lavaliere, or using a wireless rig, the rest is just common sense.

This chapter will tell you how to do those things.

A few definitions, first. In this book, *dialog* means any speech: scripted acting, spontaneous interviews, people talking at an event, or voice-over. This chapter covers dialog shot with the picture; chapter 10 is about voice-overs and other studio recordings. *Boom* is the pole that holds a mic over the actors' heads. But the term also refers to the mic itself, the technique of using one, and (in postproduction) the track that results.

Lav or *lavaliere* is a tiny mic that can be mounted near a subject's mouth, or the track that results. Most people think of lav and *wireless* as being equivalent. But they don't necessarily go together, and I cover them separately in this chapter. A good wired lav will sound better than almost any wireless one, because the radio link hurts the quality (unless you're using one of the new $3,500 digital ones). Lavs should always be wired unless the cable will be seen or seriously limit the performer's movement. On the other hand, there can be good reasons for using a wireless transmitter with a boom or hand-held mic, particularly in spontaneous documentary situations.

What Kind of Mic to Use?

Hollywood is a boom town. In dramatized feature films, there's a definite hierarchy to miking methods. In order of preference:

1. Use a hypercardioid or shotgun on a boom, over the actor's head and just out of camera range. If that's not possible . . .

2. Use those mics on a boom, but from underneath and pointing up to the actor. If you can't boom . . .

3. Plant a cardioid, hypercardioid, PZM, or shotgun on the set, where it'll cover dialog. If there's nowhere to hide a full-size mic . . .

4. Plant a lavaliere on the set. They're small and easily hidden. If you absolutely can't plant a mic . . .

5. Put a lav on the actor, and run the cable out the back of a jacket or down a pants leg. If that puts the cable in the shot . . .

6. Use a wireless lav, and hope that radio problems don't ruin the take.

In feature films, boom mics are preferred because they sound better. Since they're bigger than lavs, they can have better low-frequency and noise performance. They're also free from clothing rustles and wireless interference. But Hollywood's choice of boom mics is also artistic: because of where they're placed, overhead mics pick up more of the natural ambience and perspective of a scene than body mics can. These subtleties help create the illusion that we're overhearing real life and not just a performance.

Non-dramatic films have other priorities. Because of their closeness to the mouth, lavs concentrate on the performer's voice and help create the illusion that the person is talking directly to us. They're the best choice for a spokesperson, demonstrator, or interview subject, because their sound matches the visual perspective of a person talking to camera. They're also more convenient for productions that don't have a designated boom operator. Furthermore, the low-frequency and noise differences between a good lav (~$350) and the similarly-priced hypercardioids or short shotguns used in most DV production are minimal. Hollywood's preference for booms includes the use of much higher-quality mics.

You can also use traditional handheld or stand-mounted mics if you don't mind them being in the shot. This is common in news reporting, and the technique is simply to get the mic as close to the subject as possible. But I've never seen it done in non-news situations, except for tapes of club singers or standup comics.

The best way to get dialog from a single performer is to use both boom and lav, plugged into separate tracks in the camera or recorder. *Don't mix them.* When you edit, keep both of them in sync. Then, when you mix, choose the one that sounds most appropriate for the shot. If that's the boom track, you can use the lav as an alternative when talent turns off-mic or prop movements

There's another factor in the *boom vs. lav* decision, if you're producing for broadcast commercials. TV is a very processed medium, using lots of the equalization and compression discussed in Chapter 16.

My typical mixes don't sound squashed or distorted, and they aren't fatiguing to the listener, but they're sure up-front. Spots I do jump right out of a station break, often sounding louder—and clearer—than anything else in the cluster. That's what my clients want for TV, even though I'd never mix a theatrical film that way. (Theatrical trailers often use the same technique. That's why they're so darned loud.)

All of that processing tends to emphasize the acoustics of the room. What was a reasonable, clean boom track in the mixer's headphones becomes an airplane hanger in my studio's monitors. I'd rather start with production tracks that have very little reverb, do the processing that producers demand, and then add high-quality artificial reverb to the processed product.

are too loud. If you choose the lav track as the primary source, cut over to the boom when there's clothing noise. Since you'll be using the alternate tracks for only a syllable or two, a little equalization (plus some reverb, when lav is replacing boom) is usually all that's needed to make the sound quality match.

Videographers should note that "use the built-in camera mic" doesn't appear anywhere in this section. The mics supplied with most cameras are pretty poor. You can replace them with better ones mounted on the camera, but unless you're shooting very close (2 feet from the subject; slightly farther outdoors) they'll pick up too much noise and room reverb. Professionals use camera-mounted mics only for breaking events, when there is no time to rig something better, or for in-your-face interviews where both camera and mic are close to the subject.

These are the technical and practical realities. Your own artistic sensibilities and shooting situations may outweigh any hard-and-fast rules, but a cry of "I'm out there solo, and don't have time to rig a lav" will *not* make a camera mic sound any better.

Using Boom Mics

The downside of boom mics is that they require an operator. If you're already hiring a sound mixer who's not too busy worrying about multiple mics, he or she may be able to double on boom. Otherwise, you need a separate boom op, and good ones cost a few hundred dollars a day. It's a worthwhile investment if you want high-quality sound, but may not be practical for independent budgets. If you can afford only one professional, hire a mixer instead of a boom op. Mixers have more experience in the entire pickup-to-camera process, and can bring extra equipment.

If you can't afford trained personnel at all, you'll have to designate a production assistant or someone else on the crew, or find an intern or film student. But this only works if you give them enough support to do the job right. That costs money, too, but far less than an experienced oper-ator. It also requires a time investment from both of you.

Or you can skip the support, point to someone at random, hand them a boom, and tell them to deal with it between changing lights and getting coffee. You'll save a lot of money, and the only cost will be an echoey, uneven track that's difficult to edit and mix. And, of course, your whole film will seem amateur.

Choose Boomer and Boom

Let's assume you've picked the middle ground, and want to use inexperienced personnel but still get the best sound possible. You'll have to find the *right* inexperienced person:

- Someone with the physical strength and endurance to hold a long, unbalanced pole over their heads during a long shoot day . . . but also with the agility to make tiny movements and keep themselves in an awkward position for the length of a take.

- Someone who can hear subtle differences in sound through their headphones.

- Someone with an alert attitude. They have to pay attention during the rehearsal and the take. They have to learn how the actors will exchange lines, and good boom operators usu-ally memorize cues from the dialog. They should also pay attention to the actors' body lan-guage, to anticipate their movements. The point is having the mic in position *before* the actor begins a line. Starting a line off-mic, and then moving in during dialog, sounds awful.

- Someone who doesn't have anything else important to do at the shoot. Even though ward-robe or makeup personnel are theoretically free to hold a mic during takes, their distrac-tion levels will be too high. If they start worrying about mic placement, they won't be doing their own jobs well.

- Someone who has at least half a day to practice with boom and mic, the day before the shoot. You may need to pay for their time, and you'll definitely need the full sound package for this session, as well as somebody else to play "actor". But this is an absolutely neces-sary expense. Booming is a physical skill. You can't learn it just by reading a book. If you don't provide this practice session, be prepared to throw away most of the first day's shoot-ing. That's where the practicing will take place.

You're also going to need some equipment.

Gear for Booming

Microphone

The most critical part of a boom rig isn't the boom; it's the mic. Professionals describe boom mics in terms of "reach"—a combination of how much noise the mic itself generates, and its directional characteristics. Low self-noise is essential so the signal can be amplified without losing any subtleties. For film and HDTV, or videos using separate recorders and destined for theatrical projection, you'll want a true externally-polarized condenser element (see Chapter 7). Electret condenser mics are quiet enough for broadcast, VHS, or CD-ROM.

Too much directionality may be as bad as too little. As discussed in the last chapter, very directional shotguns suffer from uneven response along the back and sides. If a mic is close to the ceiling, reflections from that surface will color the sound. Externally-polarized condensers are almost always better than electrets in this regard as well, because they're designed and built to higher standards. Professionals working on location usually choose a relatively small hypercardioid or top-quality short shotgun of this type. It may be worth renting one for an important shoot.

If you're aiming at broadcast or lower-quality media, you can use the fairly good electret short shotguns from Audio-Technica, Beyerdynamic, Sennheiser, and Sony selling in the $350–550 range. Aside from the difference in noise level—which translates to how close they have to be to a performer—these mics are more sensitive to reflections and noisy crew members then their higher-priced cousins. But if you use them carefully, you can get a decent track. No matter what quality of mic you choose, the techniques for using it will be the same.

While you're picking a mic, get an appropriately-sized wind screen. You'll need a hard mesh windscreen, with a porous cloth cover if it'll be outdoors. A set costs about $350, but they're very cheap to rent (and occasionally thrown in as a boom/mic/windscreen kit). The foam windscreen that came with the mic is useful only indoors, in situations where the boom won't be moving through the air much.

Pole and shockmount

Of course, you'll also need a boom pole. You really will: a lightweight paint-roller extension or plastic broom handle just won't do the job.

- Professional boom poles are incredibly rigid for their weight. They won't droop because of a microphone on their end, and your operator won't droop from holding up a heavy handle. A nine-foot Gitzo metal boom weighs less than two pounds. A nine-foot Van den Bergh carbon fiber boom weighs 13 oz!

- The clutches on a professional boom lock securely when the boom is extended. This is important. Nobody cares if a paint roller or broom creaks when you move it, but the slightest squeak or rattle in a mic boom will be recorded with the dialog.

- Booms are usually matte black. Lighting a set is hard enough, without a shiny piece of metal or plastic over the actor's head.

- The shockmount is important if you're going to be moving the boom. Otherwise, even the movement of a rigid boom can turn into rumbles on the track.

Good boom poles aren't expensive. The Gitzo mentioned sells for about $225, and the Van den Bergh for about $400; shockmounts are around $175. But because these tools last so long, rentals are a bargain: boom, shockmount, and cable go for as little as $10–15 per day.

Necessary accessories

The other items you'll need might not be obvious:

1. Monitoring. Even experienced boom operators don't rely on their eyes to tell when the mic is perfectly positioned; and headphones are essential for the amateur. You'll also need some way to power them: a separate cable from the mixer or recorder, or an inline headphone amp like the Shure FP-12 (rentable for under $10).

European boom operators sometimes pride themselves on their ability to get by without headphones. In the U.S., that's considered too risky; professionals always use phones. Amateurs need them even more, since they have no experience correlating mic position and sound. Don't depend on Walkman-style ones or earbuds. You'll need a reliable isolating phone, designed for voices, like the Sony MDR-7506 (about $90, rentable for under $10 per day).

A few boom operators like a video monitor as well, and may even wear LCD screens on their chest. This helps them see if the mic gets in the shot—something even an experienced operator will occasionally do. They'll still have to glance at the actors to check body language, outside of frame, that cues them to what's coming next.

2. Some way to get the mic's signal into your recorder. See Chapter 9 for details about adapters, mixers, preamps, and other accessories.

3. Cotton gardening gloves. Clip the fingertips off, so you can manipulate clutches and other small items quickly. The cotton palms will pad your hands, so you can slide the pole without making noise.

4. Pony-tail holders, about $2 per dozen in drugstores. I'm not kidding. The plastic balls with elastic between them (Figure 8.1) can be opened or closed with one hand, and are ideal for holding hanks of cable or keeping mic wires from rattling when you move the boom. Goody Products' Ponytailers are so useful that many operators affectionately call them

8.1 Hairballs! Also known as Goody Ponytailers: you won't find anything better for keeping wires clipped to a boom.

8.2 A caribiner clip, available from theatrical rigging and rock-climbing suppliers

"hairballs," and keep some on hand at all times.

5. A rigger's caribiner clip (Figure 8.2) or Velcro strap with clip (visible in Figure 8.7), about $10. Attach it to your belt to keep a loop of excess cable handy without letting it fall noisily to the floor.

6. A small, directional flashlight. This is not just so you can see in shadows on the set. You can attach it to the boom, in place of the mic, for practice sessions in darkened rooms. Enlist a friend to be the "actor," and try to keep the light focused on their mouths while they move around. Once you get the hang of that, graduate to mic and headphone.

The Art of Going Boom

The basic concept is simple. Hold the mic above the actor, slightly in front of and pointed towards the mouth. Make it as close as physically possible without being in the frame. Unless you're in a well-designed studio or quiet outdoor setting, two feet from the actor is probably too far away. Even a difference of a couple of inches can have a major effect on the sound. Use your earphones as well as your eyes for this placement: since you're most likely coming at the actor from a sharp angle, you won't be able to see when the tip of the mic is pointing off to one side instead of directly in front.

Closer is better. Too close is impossible. On some sets, a difference of a couple of inches can turn usable dialog into something that has to be replaced in post. Some Hollywood mixers feel their boom operators aren't doing their jobs unless the mic dipped into the frame on at least a couple of takes.

Keep the mic pointed at the mouth at all times. You should be able to draw an imaginary straight line, through the center of the mic and right to the talent's lips. Otherwise, as the actor drifts into areas of the pickup pattern that aren't perfect, the quality of their voice will change. This may require adjusting the angle of the shock mount, so the mic stays in the right direction for the way you're holding the pole.

Boom mic locations

Overhead booming provides the most natural sound for dramatic dialog. Since the mouth is closest to the mic, voices are emphasized—a good thing—while the downward angle picks up prop noises and footsteps to a lesser extent. But remember that highly directional mics change the timbre of sounds coming from the back and sides. If the ceiling is too close to the mic, echoes from it may color the dialog.

If the ceiling is too short or the shot requires a lot of headroom, booming from below is often an alternative. But it requires more cooperation on the set. Prop noises and footsteps will be louder, so lines have to be delivered without too much movement. If you can, stage the shot with characters sitting down: their mouths will be closer to the mic. There's a tendency to tilt the camera down as a shot gets wider, so the videographer will have to warn the boom op before zooming out.

If two characters are close together, you can often position the mic between them—either above or below—and just rotate it slightly as they exchange lines.

Booming from directly in front, with microphone parallel to the floor, is seldom a good idea. Echoes and noises from behind the actor will be picked up almost as loudly as the voice. Mouth noises and sibilance are generally projected forward, so a close frontal mic will pick up more of them.

Two-shots

If there'll be more than one actor in the scene, things get complicated. You have to move between them in the pauses between lines, to be approximately the same distance from each, and end up in the same place each time. For occasional step-ons, when you can't swing around in time, it might sound better to stay with the first speaker rather than move during the second one's line; depending on the mic, moving during the line can be very distracting. If there are a lot of step-ons, have a production conference: something—the quality of the track, the director's vision, or the ability to use a boom at all—is going to have to be compromised. Robert Altman's incredible

How to stay out of the shot

- The boom operator wants the mic as close as possible. The videographer wants total freedom composing the shot. A reality check is always necessary, and—unless you have a video monitor available—you'll have to count on the camera operator to tell you during setup how close you can get.

- You could start with the mic high and gradually lower it until someone says "any lower and you'll be in the shot." But that almost always results in too much safety margin, and more mic distance than is necessary. A foot of extra distance to "protect the frame" doesn't look any different than an inch or two, but sounds a lot worse.

It's better to start with the mic *in* the shot and gradually raise it until it can't be seen any more.

- Some boom operators put a piece of white camera tape on the end of their windscreen, so it'll be immediately obvious in the viewfinder if the mic dips too low during a take. Others feel this compromises the sound.

simultaneous-speech scenes use lavs on individual tracks, because he knows the boom will have problems.

Stretching the distance

The reason you need to be close is to get as much of the actor's voice as possible. Competing noises are all around the shooting set, even if you're not aware of them during the take. The mic also hears prop noises and footsteps, background traffic rumbles, and reflections of the dialog off nearby surfaces (because of the delay, these reflections muddy up the voices instead of reinforcing them). Sounds fall off rapidly with distance, so by getting closer to the actor you'll hear proportionately less of the junk.

A few tricks will let you get farther away without hurting the sound:

- Soften the set. Reflections are the biggest problem, particularly when you leave the well-designed spaces of a studio and move to real-world locations. There are tips for cutting reflections at the end of Chapter 7.

- Keep things quiet. Get rid of as many environmental noises as possible. This may mean turning off HVAC or computer systems during the take, or moving generators to another location. It also means cutting down on prop noises and footsteps. Throw a sound blanket on the floor, or moleskins on the soles of actors' shoes, if they have to walk around (particularly important when booming from below). Put a piece of foam-core on the desk if the actor's going to be putting something down.

- Get a better mic. All mics generate some internal noise, and electrets are noisier than externally-powered condensers. But cheap electrets are invariably noisier than good ones. Often, the amount of noise is almost directly proportional to how much you thought you saved when you bought the mic. This noise, and additional electronic noise when low-output mics are plugged into most camcorders (Chapter 9), means you have to get the mic closer so tiny details of dialog don't get lost.

Controlling perspective

As a shot gets wider, you'll have to move the boom out so it won't be seen. This changes the ratio of direct to reflected sound, so the mic will pick up relatively more room reverberation. A small amount of this is not only acceptable, but appropriate: wide shots make the actor appear farther from us, and in real life we expect to hear more echo from a distant voice than a close one (even across a small room). The converse is also true: as the shot closes in, you have to move the mic in to pick up less echo.

If a shot is framed very wide but without much headroom, you might want to deliberately pick up more echo. Raise the mic slightly higher than usual, or point it more toward the floor.

Three tricks will help you keep mic perspective in, uh, perspective:

- The effect must be subtle. Once we're aware of changes in reverb, they become distracting. Early talking pictures changed the mic perspective with each edit: the effect was horrible, and sound operators quickly learned to leave their mics relatively stable.

- Each character's volume should stay constant during a scene. Since moving a mic farther away means less of the voice is picked up, you have to compensate by raising the recording level.

- Leave difficult decisions for postproduction. If you're not sure, stay close. It's easy to add artificial reverb in the mix, but impossible to take natural room echoes away.

Operating the Boom

It's no problem to work a mic boom (assuming you have enough stamina to hold your arms over your head for long periods of time), but it's not necessarily intuitive.

Extension

After you extend each boom section as far as it'll go, collapse the joint slightly so the pieces overlap a couple of inches. This will make it sturdier and less likely to creak at the joints. Figure 8.3 shows the wrong (top) and right (bottom) way to extend. It's better to extend three sections partway than two sections all the way.

The clutch that locks the sections of a boom when they're extended can wear out and become difficult to use. A layer of plumber's Teflon tape around the threads usually fixes things. Sometimes sections of a collapsed fiber boom can get stuck together, particularly if it was moist when stored. Gentle heating can usually get things moving again.

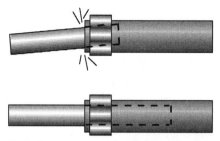

8.3 If a boom section is extended all the way *(top)*, it won't be as strong as if it overlaps *(bottom)*

Good boom poles have plastic bushings inside them, to keep one section from hitting another. If an older pole makes noise when you move it, chances are the bushings have worn down. A strip of female Velcro—the loop part—usually has the right thickness and "give" to serve as a replacement.

When you're finished using a boom, wipe it down as you collapse it. This will keep dirt from working its way inside, where it can damage the clutch or bushings.

Boom handling

Holding a few pounds of metal and plastic over your head might seem trivial at first, but can get very heavy as the day wears on. Avoid holding the arms in a wide Y position (Figure 8.4); this puts a lot of the load on your upper arm muscles. Instead, stand like an "H" (Figure 8.5), with the arms as straight up as possible. (If you're moving the boom around, the outside

8.4 Extending your arms to the sides puts extra strain on your muscles . . .

8.5 . . . keeping your arms straight as possible lets bones and joints carry most of the weight.

arm will need to be slightly bent for control.) Gravity will force the weight straight down through your bones, instead of making you carry it with your shoulder muscles.

It may be tempting to hold the boom like a flagpole at a parade (Figure 8.6), but this gives you less control over how the mic is aimed. Since the pole itself will be at an angle, it's likely that it'll cross into a corner of the shot.

If you don't need the full length of the pole to reach the actors, hold it a foot or so in toward the middle rather than at the very end. This way part of the boom will act as a counterweight, and you won't be stressing your wrists as much.

It takes a human model to demonstrate additional details, so we'll use Chris O'Donnell (not the model-turned-actor, but one of the best boom operators in the Boston area). Note, in Figure 8.7, how Chris keeps his inner arm (left, in this photo) straight and rigid. It's not directly overhead, because he doesn't need the height, but vertical enough that his bones provide most of the support. The outside arm is at the end of the boom, slightly bent so it can move easily. This gives control without being tiring.

8.6 Don't hold the boom like a flagpole

Chris is tall, so for some shots he can hold the boom at chest level (Figure 8.8). This position is less tiring than overhead. In fact, many boom operators bring an apple box or step ladder to get some extra height, no matter how tall they are. But the strategy is still the same: he keeps the inside arm rigid, bearing most of the weight straight down; his outside arm does the steering.

Check the position of the hands in Figure 8.8 as well. The inner hand is under the boom rather than wrapped around it, and acts as a pivot. The outer hand is wrapped around the *top* of the boom, because the other hand's pivoting action makes this end push up.

In both photos, you can see how Chris holds the cable tightly at the end of the boom instead of letting it flop. Cable management is important, because a section of wire hitting the pole will make noise. That's also why there are a couple of loops at his belt: he can move the boom suddenly, and the loops prevent cable from dropping or rubbing against the floor.

The wire is looped around the pole in these photos, a common practice outside of L. A. Some boom designs let you run wires inside the pole, which seems to be the preferred Hollywood

8.7 Chris O'Donnell shows how to hold a boom properly, overhead . . .

8.8 and at chest level

method. It doesn't make any difference which you choose, so long as the cable is kept tight and can't swing or bounce when you move the boom. If you're using inside wiring, wrap a couple of turns of cable around your finger where it exits the boom, so you can keep tension on the wire to stop it from swinging around inside.

You also have to secure the cable at the mic end, both to keep it taught and to provide a strain relief that protects the connector. Figure 8.9 shows the end of Chris' boom, with a couple of hairballs doing that job. Common practice, here in New England, is to mount the Ponytailers with "balls in back," facing the rear end of the mic. This way, you can glance at the entrance to the windscreen and see which way the mic, inside, is pointed. (You can also use tape to secure the cable.) If the cable is inside the pole, add a small loop of wire at the mic end; it protects the mic and connector if something snags the wire between takes.

8.9 Hairballs in use. Not only do they keep things neat; they also let you know that this mic is pointing down.

Two more tips

Booming requires strength and agility. You can build up the arm muscles necessary with pull-ups and overhead weight presses. You can strengthen your hands and fingers—just as important—with squeeze balls.

It also requires skill and talent, and frequently luck. Even the most experienced operators occasionally get into trouble with noises. If at all possible and you're dealing with just a single actor, run a lav on a second track. Or actively mix multiple lavs for that track. Just don't mix lavs and boom together; that limits your options in postproduction.

Using Lavalieres

A lav works by being close to the source of sound—the actor's mouth—so that the inverse square law (Chapter 2) assures a clean pickup with very little room reverb or natural noises. For dramatic dialog, this may end up being *too* clean. Don't try to compensate by moving the mic farther down the actor's body; all you'll gain is extra clothing noise. Instead, use a second mic for room ambience. Point a shotgun away from the actor or put a boundary mic on the floor near a wall. If you can, record it to a separate channel and mix them in post; otherwise, just mix a tiny bit of the room mic in with the lav.

Types of Lavs

The first lavalieres, in the early days of television, used dynamic elements and were so big and heavy they actually had to be worn on a lanyard around the neck—hence the name. (Louise de La Vallière, a girlfriend of Louis XIV, liked to suspend pendants from a gold chain around her neck. Never thought you'd find that in a book about digital sound, did you?)

Today, lavs almost always use electret condenser elements (Chapter 7), and they range in size from about a third of an inch diameter by half an inch long, to smaller than the head of a match. While the smallest mics are easier to conceal, as the element gets smaller it intercepts fewer moving air molecules. This generates less voltage, and electronic noise from the mic's preamplifier becomes more significant. As a general rule, smaller mics generate more self-noise, but today's mic manufacturers have learned how to make even tiny mics quiet enough for video tracks.

The preamps are powered by a small battery in the XLR connector, phantom voltage on the audio line, or a special multi-pin connection to a wireless transmitter. The internal batteries are usually good for at least a day or two's worth of shooting; when they get weak, you'll start to hear distortion or extra hiss. If you've got a source of phantom power, it's more reliable for wired lavs and you won't need to bother the talent for battery changes. Batteries in a wireless transmitter don't last more than a few hours.

If you're buying a lav to use with a wireless, specify what kind of transmitter you have. The connectors are different. If possible, get an adapter that'll let you use a standard XLR connector as well, for times when interference forces you to switch to a wired lav.

Lavs are sometimes described as having "reach," with some being better than others for distance miking. Actually, the main difference between them is how much noise their preamps make—quieter ones can be amplified more, so you record more details of the scene—and how evenly they pick up different frequencies. A mic with more bass is often considered a close-up mic and can be appropriate on a spokesperson or demonstrator who's talking directly to camera. Mics with less bass are better matched to the sound of boom mics and can be intercut more easily in dramatic scenes. Some lavs have a "presence" peak around 3 kHz to pick out the voice better when an actor turns slightly away. A few deliberately boost all the high frequencies to compensate for the muffling effect of clothing. While either of these characteristics can be desirable on their own, they make matching with other mics more difficult.

Almost all lavs are designed as omnidirectional, but when you place them on an actor or on a wall of the set one side of them is blocked. Some lavs have their element pointing towards the top of a cylindrical case, while others point toward the side. This makes no difference in the pickup pattern, though it does influence the shape and thickness of the mic. All lavs have a pattern of holes or a grill either on the top or side where the sound enters; be careful not to block it when mounting the mic.

A few directional lavalieres are available. They're difficult to hide in clothing because they have to be precisely pointed, and because the tape used to mount a hidden mic blocks the holes that make them directional. However, they can be handy as plant mics.

Mounting Lavalieres

Decide whether the mic can be visible in the shot. A lot of times there's no need to hide a mic, either because the talent is obviously a spokesperson or because a shot is wide enough that a tiny dot on the lapel won't be noticeable. It's always easier, and always sounds better, to have the mic outside the clothing. Sometimes, all you need to do is wrap some paper tape around the mic and clip, and color it with a felt-tip pen to match wardrobe.

The smallest lavs are about an eighth of an inch in diameter. They look like a blob of glue on the end of a particularly skinny mic cable. (Don't believe a mic can be that small? Figure 8.10 shows me holding a Countryman B-6, one of my favorites. Despite its tinyness, it sounds just like my Sony ECM-55, the full-size lav in Figure 8.11.)

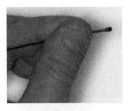

8.10 That blob on the end of the wire is really a mic . . . and my hands aren't particularly big.

Mics that small can peek above the collar, or be poked through a buttonhole or between the weave of a loose sweater, and secured from the back with tape. The mics come in colors, or with colored caps. If you choose a color that's close to the wardrobe or skin, the normal bleed of a video camera will blur out the mic. It will be invisible in all but the tightest shots . . . and extreme close-ups concentrate on the face, not on the collar or buttonhole.

Clip-on lavs

Lavs come with a variety of mounting clips and tie tacks to make the sound operator's job easier. Choose an appropriate one for the clothing, and you're almost all set.

The mic should be as close to the mouth as possible. A shirt collar or high up on a jacket lapel is always preferable to the middle of a necktie. If talent's head will be turning during the shot, choose the side that'll be favored—usually the side facing the interviewer or camera.

If the mic comes with a foam windscreen, you may want to use it to prevent popped Ps. You'll seldom need to use the wire mesh windscreen supplied with some mics, except in windy exteriors.

Don't let the wire dangle from the lavaliere. You need to provide some kind of strain relief. If the mic is wired to the camera, accidentally pulling on the cable can unmount the mic, or even damage it. Even if the cable just goes a few feet to a transmitter in the talent's pocket, the strain relief will protect the mic from cable-borne noises. If you're using a clip, loop the wire up through the clip and into the clothing (Figure 8.11A). Then grab it from behind with the clip's teeth (Figure 8.11B) to hold the loop in place.

An alternate mounting method, for mics that'll be on clothing, is the "vampire" clip. Instead of alligator teeth, it has two short pins that can be stuck through an inner layer of cloth. They cost about $10 at film sound suppliers. If you're using one or a tie-tack mount, make a loop of wire as a strain relief and hold the loop in place with tape. It will be similar to the strain relief shown in Figure 8.12.

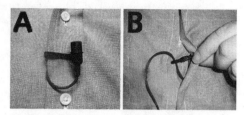

8.11 Loop a lav's cable up through the clip *(A)*. Inside the shirt *(B)*, grab the cable with the clip's teeth.

Hidden lavs

Lavs are commonly hidden between layers of clothing, high up on the chest or under a collar. The preferred mounting method is to take two pieces of one-inch tape and fold them into triangles, like folding a flag, with the sticky sides out. Put these half-inch sticky triangles on both sides of the mic, and stick the mic to the inner layer of clothing with one. Loop the cable below the mic as a strain relief, with a piece of tape or thread to hold the loop loosely enough that there's some play if you tug on the wire. Tape the cable down below the loop. Figure 8.12 shows the completed assembly.

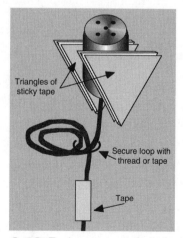

Triangles of sticky tape

Secure loop with thread or tape

Tape

8.12 Taping a concealed mic in place

Then press the top layer of clothing onto the other sticky triangle, holding it in place so it can't rub against the mic.

If talent is wearing only one layer of clothing and you have to mount the mic directly to skin, use nonallergenic surgical paper tape. Wipe the skin with an alcohol prep pad first to remove grease and perspiration. The tape and pads are available at drugstores.

You can use similar mounting methods to hide a mic under long hair, the bill of a hat, inside a woolen cap, or even—with a very small mic—on an eyeglass frame. One favorite trick is to hollow out a fountain pen and cut a hole in the top, then place the mic inside. A shirt pocket can be a reasonable place for a lav, and you don't have to worry about clothing noises. You'll have to make a small hole in the pocket for the wire, but presumably your video has some budget to repair wardrobe.

Hair mics can be secured with spirit gum, used by makeup people to attach mustaches. They usually don't need a windscreen, even outdoors—the hair itself acts as a screen. Mount them as low on the scalp as possible. If the hair is worn long, just under the ear can be a good place. Bangs will let you mount a mic on the forehead.

Body-hugging T-shirts or other very tight clothing presents a special problem, in that you don't want the lump of a microphone or its cable to show. A couple of suggestions:

- Use a miniature lav like the one in Figure 8.10. Tape or vampire-clip it right behind the collar, which is usually thicker cloth than the rest of the T-shirt. Then run the cable around the collar and down the back.

- Wrap two layers of an elastic bandage around the talent's chest. Put the mic between them, with its element just sticking out, in the depression in the middle of the breastbone.

Cable termination

If talent is wearing a wireless transmitter, hide the transmitter somewhere on their body and you're done. Observe the precautions about wireless antennas in the next section.

A wired connection is more reliable, so cable is usually run down a pants leg. Don't let the mic's XLR connector dangle! This puts extra strain on the thin mic cable, and if the character has to move around during a shot, the connector will make noise hitting the floor. Instead, loop the excess cable and secure the connector inside the pants. You can use a rubber band and safety pin to attach it to the inside cuff, or an ace bandage or ankle warmer to wrap it to the talent's leg.

As the talent moves around, an assistant crouched at the side of the set can pull up, or let out, cable slack.

If the character will be seated, you can run the wire out the back of their shirt or under their jacket. Stuff the XLR connector into a back pocket and secure it with a rubber band and safety pin.

Between takes, all the talent will have to do is reach up and unplug. Then they'll be free to roam around without you having to unrig them.

Coverage and multiple lavs

If two performers are going to be very close together, miking just one of them may be sufficient. In fact, wedding videographers frequently mic just the groom or minister (the bride would never stand for anyone messing with her gown). This picks up the entire ceremony.

If the performers are going to be apart for some of the scene, you'll need to mic them separately. But don't just combine their mics together; this increases noise pickup. Use a mixer and actively bring up just the person who's speaking at the time, or route each mic to a separate channel on the recorder and take just the active one while you're editing.

If performers are on separate mics and then come together for intimate dialog, each mic will pick up both voices and the effect can be muddy if both mics are mixed. Instead, use just one of their mics until they separate again.

In very noisy environments—particularly if the noise is mostly low-frequency—putting two identical lavs on the same actor can sometimes help control things. Mount one as closely as possible to the mouth, and the other at least a few feet away. Inverse-square will mean that both mics pick up about the same amount of noise, but the close one gets a lot more voice than the distant one. Invert the polarity of the distant mic, and its signal will cancel part of the close mic's noise when you mix them together. Monitor as you adjust the two mic levels, to hear when things are at their quietest.

Newscasters frequently wear dual lavs on their lapel or tie, and some alligator-clip mounts are designed to take two mics at once. This redundancy is insurance against failure during live broadcasts, not—as some people claim—to so that polarity inversion can be used. (The mics are so close together than they pick up the same mix of noise and voice.) Only one of those mics is used at a time.

Avoiding Noise in Lavalieres

All other things being equal, a lav is usually electrically noisier than a shotgun. This is a function of the smaller element, and there's nothing you can do about it. If you turn the mixer or preamp all the way up, you may hear some hissing. Fortunately, a lav is almost always closer to the sound source than a shotgun; it picks up more sound pressure, so you don't need to raise the volume control as high.

Mechanical noise is a bigger problem, but easy to control. If you've mounted the mic properly, there shouldn't be any clothing rubbing directly against it. Clothing can also rub against the mic's cable, and the noise will be transmitted up the wire. If this happens and the strain relief isn't enough to keep the mic from hearing it, tape the wire somewhere it'll be protected. Some mics have special fiber inserts in their cables so they don't transmit as much noise.

Clothing can also rub against itself, and the mic will pick up the rustling sound. It may take some detective work to isolate the exact area where the rubbing is taking place. Once you do, use triangles of tape to hold clothing in position. The anti-static solution sold for home clothes dryers can soften crinkly layers of clothing. If a shirt has been heavily starched, spray water on it near the microphone for some local destarching.

Coordinate clothing choices with the wardrobe department or talent. Cottons and woolens will always be quieter than synthetics or nylons. Corduroy should be avoided.

Planted Mics

Because they're so small, lavs are usually used as plant mics. But their higher self-noise means they have to be close to the sound source. If you can hide a full-size mic in the same place, you'll find it sounds better.

If you're planting a lav at a desk or table, hiding it in a pencil jar or flower pot may pick up echoes. Depending on how the talent sits while they're talking, their voices might be directed at the table surface and bounce back to the mic. If the mic is a third of the way between table and mouth, these reflections can be almost as loud as the direct sound. To avoid this, use a directional lav, or mount the mic to some surface that can block reflections (such as the hidden side of a telephone or a computer monitor).

Watch for hidden low-level noise sources when you're planting a mic. A computer monitor, for example, will radiate electronic hash while it's turned on. Electret lavs are usually immune to this, but a mic with a transformer will pick it up. A potted fern can be a good place to "plant" a mic, but its leaves will get noisy if there's a breeze.

The best way to pick up dialog in a car is to clip a cardioid mic to a sun visor or headliner just above the front window, for front passengers. Rear passengers can be covered with a second mic attached to the back of the front seat, though if the road and car is quiet the front visor mic might be able to cover them. As an alternative mounting, place a hypercardioid under the dash, sticking up between two passengers. If only one person is talking, you can use a short shotgun there.

Avoid using body mics in car shots. Shoulder belts can rub against them, making noise. Also, since they're so close to the mouth, they miss the characteristic boxy acoustics of a car.

Controlling Wind Noise

An electronic filter can reduce the rumbling noise of a very light wind—the kind that would hardly ruffle a flag—but anything else requires a mechanical solution as well.

Shotgun mics should always have a windscreen because the holes that make them directional also pick up wind noise. Even swinging back and forth on a boom can create enough wind to be a problem. Low-cost foam windscreens that cover the entire mic should be adequate for interiors unless the boom is moving quickly, and on wind-free days may be usable for closely miked handheld interviews outdoors.

If there's any wind outdoors, or you're whipping the boom around indoors, you'll need more protection than a foam windscreen can provide. Hard windscreens, consisting of a wire or open plastic frame surrounded by fine mesh, work by creating a low-turbulence area around the mic and can be very effective. They're often called *zeppelins* because of their shape. For extra protection, a layer of furry cloth can be wrapped around the windscreen; it makes the assembly look like a small animal, but it does cut down on noise. If you're using a zeppelin, a foam windscreen on the mic itself may also help. However, there must be at least a half inch of airspace between the windscreen and the interior of the zeppelin for it to work properly.

The tiny foam windscreens that come with lavalieres can reduce popped Ps, but don't provide any protection against outdoor wind. A metal mesh windscreen designed for the mic can help, using the same principle as the zeppelin on larger mics. If you don't have one of them available, try using a combination of these sound recordists' tricks:

- Pull the foam tip off a video head-cleaning swab. It's often just the right size to fit over a lav.

- With the swab in place over the mic, wrap a couple of layers of cheesecloth around it.

- Snip the fingertip off a child's woolen glove (remove the child first), and fit it over the cheesecloth for extra protection. This also gives you the opportunity to choose a glove color that will match the talent's overcoat, so you can leave the mic outside their clothing without it being too obvious. Putting the mic under a heavy overcoat protects it from wind, but cuts the voice down too much.

If you're shooting in a howling wind-storm, the noise *will* get into the mic. The most you can expect from a windscreen and filter here is to reduce low-frequency sounds that can interfere with the recording. Get the mic as close to the speaker's mouth as possible, or wait for calmer weather.

> **Nothing can control airplane noise.** If there's a plane flying overhead, some of its noise will be picked up. It might not be enough to obscure dialog *in that shot*, but when you edit to it from a different take, there'll be a distracting shift in the background sound.
>
> If you're planning to edit what you shoot, wait until the plane passes.

Using Wireless

Don't let the name confuse you. A "wireless mic" is actually two different systems: a microphone to turn sound into electricity, and a radio link to get the mic's signal back to the camera. Many videographers concentrate their efforts on making sure the mic can't be seen. But to get a consistently good soundtrack, you also have to pay attention to the wireless part.

Wireless used to be a fairly scary way to do things, with battery-hogging transmitters and receivers that were prone to interference. But new technologies have made even low-cost wireless systems a lot more reliable. That's good, because there are some times you just can't use a wire, for example:

- Wide camera angles and some lighting situations can force the boom too far from the actor for successful pickup. You have to use a lav. If the shot is wide enough that we see the floor, or the talent has to do fast moves, a mic cable won't be practical.

- Actors often turn from the camera and deliver a single line into a doorway, open window, or some other spot you can't reach with a boom. But plug a PZM or small cardioid mic into a wireless transmitter, and you've got a plant mic that can be hidden on the set for just that line.

- You can also plug a boom mic into the transmitter. Wireless booming—sometimes with a separate wireless return, so the operator can check placement and hear cues from the mixer—combines the sound quality of a large condenser mic with the flexibility of radio.

- Blocking can make other kinds of pickup impossible. If the talent will be walking from one room to another or around bulky set objects, a dangling cable from a wired lav will get in the way.

- Booming often isn't possible at event or documentary shoots. A wireless rig on a competitor at a sporting event, or on the groom at a wedding, can capture sounds that would be lost otherwise.

- If a location has a lot of video or computer wiring, or is near a radio or TV transmitter, interference can be radiated into mic cables. In these circumstances, a wireless connection may sound better than a wired one!

Multiple wireless mics, or a wireless on one character while a boom follows another, is often the only way to record complex dialog where the actors are moving around. They can also give the actors flexibility to ad-lib and overlap: if the mics are recorded to separate tracks, important lines can be brought up in postproduction. While there are a few multi-channel receivers available, they're not the highest quality. Use multiple systems, tuned to different frequencies, instead. You can rent "quad boxes", multi-mic systems that combine four receivers into a lunchbox-sized pack, with circuits to share the antennas and power supply.

While wireless gives you exceptional flexibility, it has its own drawbacks. Good sound quality and reliable transmission isn't possible unless you adjust the transmitter and place the antennas properly. In some situations, you can do everything right and still suffer horrible interference. But if you want to do wireless right, the biggest drawback is the cost.

Buying Wireless

Wireless is one of the areas where there's a direct relationship between how much you spend and how reliable the system will be. The high frequencies require precision design and components, and that doesn't come cheap. Budget systems, costing two to three hundred dollars, might be adequate for your production. But if you're unhappy with the results, know that professional systems—at three to four times the price—really are significantly better at getting a signal from one place to another. At least, all of this equipment is available from rental houses so you can try before committing.

Hollywood sound recordists pay as much as $5,000 for a top quality wireless transmitter and receiver like the Audio Ltd TXU series—and that's without the microphone. What they're buying is reliability and the ability to squeeze a signal through difficult circumstances, but mostly they're paying for the sound: when used properly, these units sound almost as good as a mic cable. Lectrosonics has a number of wireless systems for about half the price that are almost as good. These are the rigs to use if you're shooting 35mm film for theatrical release.

A new alternative is digital wireless. It *does* sound as good as a wire, and has the advantages of letting the receiver control the transmitter, the ability to string up multiple receivers to cover a large area (the receivers constantly poll each other to select the best signal), and AES/EBU output. As of this writing, only two companies make digital wireless; the rigs cost around $3,500 and don't have the reach of a top-quality analog system. Both reach and price should improve, as manufacturers bring this technology to the prosumer market.

If professionals pay that that kind of money to achieve the sound quality of a $30 mic cable, what can a videographer expect from a system costing much less? Sony, AKG, Sennheiser, Shure, and Audio-Technica sell wireless combos in the thousand-dollar range, including microphone, that are good enough for television production. Azden, Nady, and Samson offer combos in the $300–500 range that are fine for corporate and event productions. What you're giving up is how natural the voices sound: as price goes down, bandwidth and dynamic range shrink, making dialog seem more "canned." If your goal is an educational or sales video that will be played through small TV speakers, the difference isn't critical.

If you want to hear these differences for yourself (or don't like the idea of paying more for a mic than you paid for the camera), consider renting. Larger rental companies will have a variety of brands to choose from, and they'll help you choose frequencies that will avoid interference at your shooting location.

Whether buying or renting, there are a few features you should definitely look for. They add to the cost, but are worth the investment:

Ultra-high frequency

Originally, wireless mics ran in the upper part of the VHF TV band, using standard broadcast channels 7 through 13. At the time it was very difficult to build small, reliable equipment for frequencies higher than that. TV channels were used—even if a local station broadcast on the same channel—because wireless mics could squeeze into the hole between conventional television's separate audio and video signals. But that loophole in the spectrum is closing. A lot of other services also use VHF frequencies, so interference was often a problem on that band.

Fortunately, modern circuits can easily handle the UHF range above TV channel 14. It costs a little more to build equipment for that part of the spectrum, but it's less crowded up there—for now—and each channel can support more individual wireless signals. The higher frequency means that manufacturers can use broader audio channels for better fidelity. UHF uses a smaller antenna, so it's easier to wire the actors, mount a receiver on the camera, or build special directional antennas for difficult pickups.

The disadvantage of UHF is that the signal is more fragile: it can bounce off light stands and girders in the walls, and even be absorbed by cast and crew on the set. There's no danger to the humans involved, but if things or people move around during a take you might hear sudden dropouts.

The DTV Squeeze   Even if you're not shooting anything more sophisticated than a VHS wedding album, America's move to digital broadcast television will affect you.

The FCC has mandated that local stations turn digital within the next few years (Congress has been granting extensions). Unfortunately, digital TV uses an entire 6 MHz channel—either for a single HDTV broadcast, or for two separate standard-definition signals. Audio and video are part of a single data stream, and there's no hole between them where a wireless mic can sneak through. Even if a channel is nominally vacant where you're shooting, a nearby city's high-powered DTV can overpower your battery-operated rig. The competition is worse than you might think, because existing VHF TV stations have to move to new UHF channels to in order to have enough bandwidth for DTV. (At the same time, they're staying on VHF to serve analog viewers.) In the greater Boston area alone, 16 new digital UHFs are coming on line. The FCC keeps a city-by-city list of the new channels at http://www.fcc.gov/oet/dtv/start/dtv2-69.txt.

The best solution is to be flexible, particularly if you travel to multiple locations. Get wireless equipment that can support a number of different channels. If you know where you'll be shooting, check with your dealer or rental company to make sure the equipment you choose will be usable. Scanners with laptop software are available that can automatically search for blank channels.

Diversity reception

UHF's tendency to bounce off metal objects can present a problem when using wireless. Figure 8.13 shows how it could arise, even on a very simple set. One dashed line represents the main signal path between an actor's transmitter and the camera's receiver. But note the bent path—a signal bouncing off a nearby light—which is almost as strong. Depending on the distances involved, the bounced signal may reinforce or partially cancel the main one. If anything moves, including the actor, these distances change and so does the cancellation effect. It will also change if the righthand crew member steps forward and absorbs some of the signal. The other dashed paths start to show how complicated it can get at a shoot: if anyone moves, the signal may fade in or out.

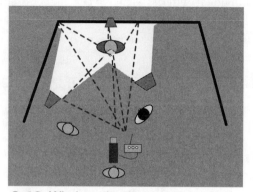

8.13 Wireless signals can reflect off metal objects, and the pattern changes when anything moves

In this case, diversity truly is strength. Diversity receivers actually have two spaced antennas with separate radio-frequency circuits. They constantly compare signals and use whichever antenna is getting the best one. Because real-world paths are so random, it's highly unlikely both will be fading at the same time. Both VHF and UHF systems can use diversity reception, but UHF's higher frequencies mean the antennas don't have to be spaced as far apart and the receivers can be smaller. Digital wireless systems, which operate in the UHF range, include diversity and also have the polling option described above.

Frequency agility

Until recently, wireless equipment used fixed frequencies. Transmitters were controlled by stable crystal oscillators. Receivers used similar crystals along with carefully tuned resonant circuits. Changing the frequency required a trip to the service shop, but the spectrum was less crowded in those days so the trip was seldom necessary.

Then things got busy. More feature and corporate crews started using wireless, often requiring frequencies for multiple mics. Media events started attracting news crews from around the country, and a city's wireless-mic population would swell by the hundreds overnight. While chapters of the Society of Broadcast Engineers have tried to bring some sanity to local usage, they only step in when there's a news event with herds of live reporters. There's no official traffic cop and the FCC doesn't assign spectrum to individual producers. Wireless collisions became common, where other voices would mysteriously drift into a shot.

Just like an agile athlete, frequency-agile wireless rigs are flexible and can change direction quickly. Instead of crystals, they have precisely controlled oscillators that can be set to several different operating frequencies. Good ones let you select among a few dozen, and the best offer more than a hundred frequencies spread over a number of UHF channels. They're a lifesaver if you're shooting near other crews. When DTV reaches your city, they may be the only wireless mics that remain useful.

Limiting and companding

All wireless mics should include some form of limiter. It saves very loud sounds from being totally lost, at the cost of some distortion, and prevents the transmitter from interfering with adjacent frequencies. The limiter is preceded by a volume control, so the transmitter can be adjusted for a particular mic and acting style. If it's not adjusted properly, either there'll be too much electronic noise or the limiter will be constantly on, distorting the dialog.

Higher priced wireless rigs also use *companding*, a system that uses a volume compressor on the transmitter, precisely matched to an expander at the receiver. This yields more dynamic range with less noise, for a better overall track.

Physical form

Wireless transmitters designed for dialog usually take the form of small body packs, slightly smaller than a wallet. There's a connector for the mic to plug into, which also provides power for the mic's internal preamp. Professional systems may be supplied without microphones; users usually order their favorites from other manufacturers, customized to plug into the transmitter. Low-cost systems often come with low-quality generic lavaliere mics, which are sometimes wired directly into the transmitter.

Transmitters can also be built into small metal cans with full-size XLR jacks, as *plug-on transmitters*. These are handy for plugging onto the end of a shotgun or the end of a boom cable, or for connecting to a standard mic for hiding on the set. Hand-held wireless mics, with transmitters built into their bodies, are designed for stage vocal performance and rarely used in film or video.

Wireless receivers used to be fairly large boxes, but have shrunk to cigarette-pack size. Those with diversity reception tend to be slightly larger, to accommodate the extra circuits and spacing between antennas, but can still be small enough to mount on a camera. As of this writing, digital receivers are larger than analog, about the size of a thick paperback novel.

Reach

Depending on its design, a wireless transmitter may radiate between 10–250 milliwatts of electrical power. But while that number lets you predict how fast the battery will wear down, it doesn't say much about how well the system will perform in the field. Some of the best professional systems radiate less than 100 mW. You can usually ignore a manufacturer's "range" specification, particularly if it's linked to a boast about power. The actual usable distance also depends on the quality of the receiver, the frequency, reflective and absorbing surfaces on the set, and how you place the antennas. That's why it's important to learn how to use a wireless properly.

Pre-emphasis

Wireless systems boost high frequencies before transmitting, and correspondingly reduce both highs and picked-up noise in the receiver. This means that loud high frequencies may distort, even when the transmitter's volume is set properly.

Experienced operators check wireless system quality with the "key test": they jangle their car keys in front of the microphone, and listen to how clean the received signal is. In a very good system, it'll sound something like keys. In a poorer one, there's so much pre-emphasis that you get mostly hash and static. But a system can fail the key test and still be usable for non-critical productions, since dialog is mostly lower frequencies.

Using a Wireless

Hiding a mic on an actor is only half the battle. You also have to adjust the transmitter, and rig it and its antenna properly.

Volume adjustment

Most transmitters have a small volume adjustment screw with a LED or meter to indicate when the limiter is activated. After the mic is in place, ask the actor to deliver a few lines in the voice they'll be using. Adjust the volume so the limiter just starts to turn on at the loudest part of their speech. If that results in too soft a signal at your camera, turn up the receiver's volume control or add some extra gain in a mixing board. Cranking up the transmitter won't make things any louder; it'll just add more distortion.

Transmitter and antenna rigging

Transmitters usually have belt clips so you can hide them on an actor's back, if they're wearing a jacket or won't be turning away from the camera. A jacket or pants pocket can also work, though it might require cutting a small hole in the cloth for the cables. If you want pockets without the pants, audio supply houses sell little pouches with elastic or velcro straps. These can be used to hide the transmitter at belt, thigh or ankle level. In a pinch, you can tuck a transmitter into a dancers'-style ankle warmer or wrap it to a leg with an elastic bandage.

The mic cable absorbs radiation and should be kept as far away from the antenna wire as possible. In extreme situations, putting those wires together can feed some of the radio energy back into the system and cause bad distortion.

VHF transmitters have long wire antennas that should be extended in a fairly straight line. While you can dress an antenna into the actor's waistband, it's often better to let it hang down inside a dress or pants leg. A long rubber band, tied and taped to the end of the antenna and then safety-pinned to a stocking, can keep the antenna straight while providing some strain relief and flexibility. Some recordists assemble custom antenna stretchers for this purpose, with a small alligator clip and a length of elastic ribbon. The clip pulls on the end of the antenna, and the ribbon is tied around the leg.

UHF antennas are short and stiff, making them much easier to rig. Just try to keep them away from the mic cable. If a UHF antenna sticks out so much that it shows when the actor turns, use some paper tape to attach it to the costume where it'll be out of sight. It's always better to attach antennas to wardrobe than place them directly against an actor's skin. People absorb radio waves. Perspiration makes the situation worse. A wireless transmitter's miniscule power isn't a health hazard, but it's so tiny you can't afford to squander any. If a lot of signal is being absorbed by the actor, there won't be enough to guarantee quiet pickup at the receiver.

Some transmitters don't appear to have an antenna at all. They actually use the mic cable as an antenna (a few extra components keep the radio signal from interfering with the audio). This limits your options: while the antenna wire should be straight, the mic wire often has to take a winding path from mic to transmitter. If you're stuck with this kind of system, use long loops in the mic cable instead of abrupt turns. Never coil the wire to eliminate slack.

Receiver placement

Reception is always best when the transmitter and receiver have a line-of-sight path and are close together. Mounting a receiver on the camera can satisfy the former, but a long shot may keep the units too far apart. This gets worse if there are things around that reflect or absorb radio waves. In most cases, you'll get a more consistent pickup by taking the receiver off of the camera so you can put it on the floor, just out of camera range. Or mount the receiver high up on a ladder or grip stand near the talent. Higher is better, because it usually provides a good line-of-sight path without too many reflections. If the actor is moving around, have a production assistant carry the receiver—keeping their body away from the antenna—just out of camera range.

A single antenna on a non-diversity receiver should be oriented the same direction as the transmitting one: for example, if the transmitting antenna runs down the leg of a standing actor, the receiving one should also be vertical. Single antennas work best when they're parallel to each other. If you're using a diversity receiver, angling the two antennas 90° can help you compensate for reflected signals. Try it with one antenna horizontal and the other vertical, or the two in a V configuration.

Low-cost receivers often have short cables with unbalanced mini-plug outputs, designed to plug directly into a prosumer camera. Extending these cables can lead to noise and hum problems. If you want to move one of these units closer, plug it into a nearby mixer. Then run a balanced cable from the mixer's output to a transformer-coupled adapter (Chapter 9). Of course, the cost of mixer and adapter may be more than you saved by choosing a cheap wireless.

Professional-quality UHF receivers usually use removable short metal or rubber antennas with standard radio connectors. These can be unplugged and replaced with more powerful antennas for better pickup.

When Wireless Goes Bad

If you follow the tips in this section, and are in a location without too much interference, a wireless rig will give you decent pickup most of the time. But because they're more complex than a simple piece of wire, things can go wrong.

If audio starts sounding funny in any way at all, check the batteries first. Depending on the model and the shooting situation, weak batteries will result in distortion, low volume, intermittent interference, noise, or other gremlins. Since you can't predict which symptom will appear, change the transmitter battery whenever you hear any problem with a system that previously worked. If that doesn't help, change the receiver battery as well. Always use high-quality, fresh alkaline or lithium batteries.

If it's not the batteries, look for user errors. Even audio professionals have been caught by receiver output levels that don't match the camera, mics that have come unplugged, or actors who've fiddled with transmitter controls. Then look for radio-frequency problems: many receivers have a meter to let you check the signal strength. If it's suddenly dropped and you know all the batteries are good, check to see if a mic cable has gotten wrapped around an antenna, a large reflecting object has moved near the set, or a performer's wardrobe has gotten wet.

Occasionally, two wireless won't work properly where one will. If you're using multiple systems for different characters, make sure they're on different frequencies. But also be aware that each *receiver* radiates a tiny signal of its own, which can interfere with other receivers nearby: try separating the units a few feet.

While some mics are rated as water-resistant, all of them rely on very tiny amounts of static electricity to turn varying air pressure into voltage. Excessive humidity, as well as downright dunking, can interfere with this. Moisture around the transmitting or receiving antenna will also cause problems. Most transmitters and receivers can survive normal on-set banging around, but physical shock can damage the crystal or knock fragile tuned circuits out of alignment.

Watch out for anything that can generate interference on the set—neon lights, electronic dimmers, generators, even coils of powered cable. Video cameras, recorders, and monitors can also generate local interference that can be reduced by moving away from them. Cell phones don't work at the same frequencies as wireless mics, but nearby cellphone antenna installations—often found on the tops of office buildings—may be powerful enough to harm a wireless signal anyway.

And always bring a backup wired connection, whether it's another mic or an adapter to use the wireless rig's mic with a standard cable. Sometimes the voodoo doesn't work.

A wireless alternative

Some situations are just not conducive to wireless use, because of interference, large amounts of metal in the building, or large distances between performer and camera. In that case, a portable MiniDisc recorder can provide a bail-out. These can fit in a performer's pocket, and—when used properly—provide excellent sound for dialog. Since the recording isn't on the videotape, it's essential to provide some form of sync reference so you can put things back together in your NLE; there are tips in the next chapter.

You may have to train the performer to start and stop the recorder. Some units revert to automatic level control each time you stop them. If you're using manual volume control, it may be better to pause instead of stop between takes.

Tiny MiniDisc recorders are often sensitive to shock, both while they're recording and for about ten seconds after stopping or pausing (because they're still writing a table of contents). This can result in drop-outs, or a loss of identification marks between takes. Normal walking usually isn't enough to cause a problem, but running or other sudden movements may destroy a recording.

Room Tone

Every acoustic space has its own sound. This isn't just a combination of air conditioners, distant traffic, and other machinery coming through the windows, but also how the size and shape of the room itself modify these sounds. We're almost never aware of this sound, but if it goes away—perhaps because a line of dialog has to be opened up to accommodate a cutaway—we can tell that it's missing.

It's common practice in features, after all the shooting at a location is done but before equipment is struck, to record a minute of "room tone:" just the sound of the room itself, with the same general mic placement and volume settings as were used for dialog. Then in post, if a production track has to be muted or replaced with a studio version, the room tone is mixed in for acoustic continuity. Room tone is also used to replace on-set noises, or to smooth over edits between takes.

The practice is often ignored in video production. Because video sound is edited less precisely than film, broadcast through noisy channels, and played back at low volumes in home systems, it's thought that room tone won't be missed. Obviously, I don't agree. If you're doing an intense dramatic video, record tone. You'll need it.

On the other hand, if you're doing a fast-paced dialog sequence or a commercial, it may be possible to skip recording any separate room tone. A good sound editor, using a modern workstation, can usually pull enough tone from between words or at the heads and tails of takes to satisfy any dialog fixes in this kind of video.

Production Recording

You know what kind of mic to use. You know where to put it to capture subtleties in the voice. You know how to carry its signal over a cable or wireless. So, now that you've got that good mic signal, *what do you do with it?*

The answer might not be obvious.

Getting Audio Into a Camera

Okay, you're actually getting audio into a recorder. But these days, the recorder is integrated with the camera, which records sync audio along with the video.

Professional cameras will have balanced mic inputs on XLR connectors, with separate level controls and switchable limiters. Connecting them to a high-quality microphone should be simply a matter of plug-and-play. If you're in that situation, skip to the next section and learn how to set the camera's controls for best results. If you want to use multiple mics with that camera, read about mixers later in this chapter.

Prosumer cameras usually have mini-jack unbalanced inputs. Because they're unbalanced, long mic cables can be prone to noise pickup. The mini-jack usually has a DC voltage on it, to power the preamplifier of a consumer-level electret mic (and a few specialty prosumer units, such as the Ambient Tinymike). This isn't phantom power and won't power a pro mic. In fact, if it's connected directly to some pro mics with a simple XLR-to-mini cable, it can cause distortion.

The most common way to deal with all these issues is a balancing adapter with XLR inputs. You can also use a mixer or external preamp for this purpose, and gain other advantages as well. If you're using a mixer or preamp, it's likely you won't need a separate balancing adapter.

Balancing Adapters

Transformer adapters

This is either a small metal box that screws into the camera's tripod socket (and has its own socket on the bottom), or a beltpack that can be worn or taped to a tripod leg, with a cord that plugs into camera's mic input jack. It contains transformers to balance the mic inputs, and individual volume controls. Most also have switches to combine the mics to a single channel, and a line-level input. At least one model also includes a phantom power supply, which provides 48 volts for the microphone from a 9-volt battery. The adapters let you use balanced cables and microphones, which are virtually

9.1 A typical under-camera transformer adapter, with added circuitry for phantom power

immune to wiring noise. Non-powered ones cost between $170–225; phantom power adds about $50. Figure 9.1 shows the BeachTek DX6A, an under-camera model with phantom.

There are two philosophies used in building these adapters. Most of the BeachTek units are designed for the footprints and grounding schemes of specific line of cameras. Studio 1 Productions' adapters have switches to adjust their grounding, and can be used with any camera or MiniDisc recorder. Either approach can give you good sound. The BeachTeks are a little bit easier to use, but might not work if you upgrade cameras. (Their DX6A has switchable grounding and is more flexible.) While older Studio 1s are designed for under-camera use, their more recent units are designed as belt-packs with long flexible cords.

Adapter caveats   Some belt-pack adapters aren't balanced, and just contain a volume control, DC-blocking capacitor, and XLR jack. This defeats the noise-immunity of balanced wiring. You may be able to get by with unbalanced wiring for short cable runs, but for best results, look for the word "transformer" in the specifications.

Some adapters have a balanced mini-jack for line level signals, matching a few wireless receivers, but not the normal configuration for mini-jacks. Because of the way they're wired, if you plug in a normal mono mini-plug (from a mixer, or other wireless models) and the jack's ring conductor doesn't connect properly, the bass suffers horribly. This can happen with a lot of mini-plug cables because of a slight difference in plug sizes, which normally doesn't affect their use. If you plug in a normal stereo mini-plug (from a CD player, for example) and the ring connects properly, phase problems can erase most of your audio.

- For best results with stereo and most mono sources, ignore the mini-jack on the adapter and plug right into the camera.

- If you're using a wireless receiver with balanced mini-plug output, use the adapter. Or plug directly into the camera, but discard one channel's audio in post (it'll be out of phase with the other). Check the receiver's specs to see if it's balanced—some popular Sennheiser units are—or just look at the plug: balanced ones have two insulating rings, like a miniature version of the three-conductor phone plug in Chapter 4.

Listen to the signal through the camera, on good headphones, to verify the connection is working properly.

Active adapters

Canon builds electronic XLR adapters that mount on the top or back of specific cameras. Instead of a transformer, they use op-amps to balance the mic inputs. The circuits are powered from a special jack on the camera, or by contacts on the adapter's hot shoe mount.

Electronic balancing is perfectly acceptable, and found on many studio mixers and professional cameras. These adapters have slightly better frequency response, but slightly more noise, compared to transformer-based units. But the differences are too small to worry about.

Mixers and preamps

If you're using a unit with XLR mic jacks, you can assume it has transformers or op-amps built in and the inputs are balanced. While their outputs are typically balanced as well, if the cable connecting it to the camera is reasonably short, you won't need one of the adapters discussed previously. A simple adapter unbalanced adapter, discussed in the following, is all you'll need for a mini-jack camera connection. If you want to use a mixer or preamp with the RCA connections on a Canon XL1, use the attenuator described later in this chapter.

Unbalanced Adapters

You can get low-cost XLR-to-mini cables, designed for use with prosumer cameras, at video supply houses. These contain capacitors to block the DC voltage, which otherwise could cause distortion in some microphones. But they defeat the mic's balanced wiring, which can increase noise pickup through the cable. So use these adapters only if the mic cable will be kept short, or if you're feeding the camera from a nearby mixer mic-level outputs. If you're using a mixer with line-level outputs, use one of the attenuators described later.

Build your own

If you're willing to do a little soldering, you can make a cable adapter for a few dollars' worth of parts. You'll need a female XLR connector for the mic (Radio Shack #274-011), a mini-plug to match your camera (#274-284), and a few feet of 2-conductor shielded wire (#278-514). The secret is a small electrolytic capacitor (like the 220 microfarad, 16 volt #272-956) to stop the recorder's polarizing voltage from causing distortion in the mic. The capacitor rating isn't critical—anything over about 100 μf and 6 volts should be adequate—and you'll find smaller units at electronics suppliers. The Shack's capacitor is just small

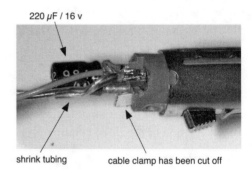

220 μF / 16 v

shrink tubing   cable clamp has been cut off

9.2 A small capacitor, hidden in the XLR connector, blocks DC voltage in this adapter.

enough to squeeze inside the XLR shell, though you may have to break off a piece of the cable clamp to make it fit (Figure 9.2).

Figure 9.3 shows how it's wired. The capacitor's polarity is critical: a white arrow indicates the negative side, which must go to the XLR. Also note how the cable shield is left unconnected at the mini-plug: insulate it with tape or shrink-tubing to prevent shorts.

The circuit shown connects one mic to both channels of the camera. If you want stereo, wire two XLRs with capacitors the same way. Connect both shields and black wires together at the mini-

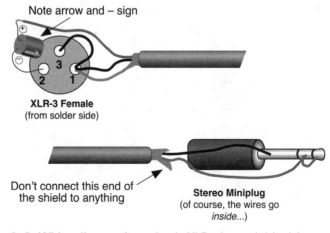

Note arrow and – sign

XLR-3 Female
(from solder side)

Don't connect this end of the shield to anything

Stereo Miniplug
(of course, the wires go inside...)

9.3 Wiring diagram for a simple XLR mic to mini-jack input adapter.

plug, and wire them like the diagram. But connect the red wire from one capacitor to the plug's tip, and the other to its ring.

The circuit works with most dynamic and condenser mics . . . and you can use it with a MiniDisc recorder as well. But remember: this isn't a balancing adapter, and doesn't give you the noise-immunity of balanced wiring. Don't expect things to sound great if there's more than a dozen feet of cable between mic and camera.

You can also get molded metal XLR-to-mini adapters for a couple of dollars at electronics chain stores. These don't block the DC voltage, don't provide balancing, may give you only one chan-nel of signal, and their weight can stress a mini-jack. They shouldn't be used.

About mini-jacks

Mini-plugs are physically and electrically fragile. If there's a strain on the cable—even from the weight of an XLR connector—they'll unplug. If they're plugged and unplugged too many times, their springs weaken and the connection becomes noisy. I have no idea why any manufacturer would think such a cheap component belongs in a four-thousand-dollar camera, but you have to live with the little devils:

- Secure cable plugs with a rubber band wrapped around the plug and camera, or with a piece of gaffer tape.

- Provide strain relief for the weight of a cord-mounted XLR connector by taping it to the camera or tripod.

- If you're using a camera-mounted balancing adapter, attach it to the camera before plug-ging in. If you're using a belt-pack, provide some strain relief and *don't walk away from the camera while you're plugged in.*

- If you anticipate plugging and unplugging a lot, get a short extension cable, tape it to the camera, and leave it plugged in all the time. Wear out the extension cable instead of the camera.

Avoiding Noise

Neither balanced nor unbalanced wiring is absolutely noise-proof. Mic signals are fragile, and cables can pick up radiated junk. For best results, use a balanced mic (virtually any mic with an XLR connector), Star-Quad (Chapter 4), and a balancing adapter or XLR inputs at the camera. You can use ordinary 2-conductor shielded XLR extensions instead, but the noise advantage is worth the few extra dollars Star-Quad adds to a cable's cost.

To chase down noise sources, wear good isolating headphones and turn up the volume. Listen for buzzes, hums, and clicks. You may also hear hiss, but that's probably coming from the camera itself; there are tips in the next section for keeping it at a minimum.

The worst electronic buzzes often come from electronic lamp dimmers. They convert relatively quiet 60 Hz AC power into a spiky mess with harmonics all over the audio band, which is then transmitted by the high current wiring from dimmer to lamp. If there are dimmers for the room lights where you're shooting, turn them fully up or off to eliminate the noise. If you're using dimmers to control set lighting, either throw them away and use lower-wattage bulbs or neutral-density gels, or get noise-free *autoformer* or *Variac* dimmers. Variacs are available from theatrical suppliers or electronics repair suppliers (they're also used to diagnose problems in TV sets). One that'll handle a thousand-watt light costs about $100, or rents for about $12 per day.

Noise is also radiated by power and video cables. Run mic cables at least a couple of feet away from them. If a mic and power cable have to cross, do it at a right angle for the least amount of noise.

Clicks are caused by high-current devices being turned on, causing a spike that radiates through the power lines in the walls. Elevator and HVAC motors are prime causes, but some unbalanced circuits will pick up noise from motors as small as a vacuum cleaner. Some high-power motors can also cause buzzing if they're not in perfect condition. The best solution is to use Star-Quad balanced hookups, and keep cables away from the walls.

Impedance

When I first got into this business, Ohm's Law (Chapter 4) was an important consideration when connecting a microphone. Dynamic and ribbon mics generated very little power, and much of it could be lost to noise or distortion if they were plugged into the wrong impedance. So microphones and inputs were standardized at various impedances: 250 Ω and 500 Ω for professional ones that plugged into a transformer-based input, and around 10 kΩ for consumer ones that fed a vacuum tube directly. These impedances were critical, and every sound engineer knew them.

But modern cameras have input impedances ranging from 500 Ω to 2 kΩ, and mic outputs can be as low as 100 Ω, causing a few videographers to go nuts trying to match them together. Obsessing over impedance isn't really necessary. These days, impedance matching is critical in only a few situations. Ohm's Law hasn't been repealed, but it's not enforced the way it was when I was younger.

It may be that videographers fixate on impedance because it's one of the few specifications prosumer manufacturers reveal. Frequency response, distortion, and directivity specs are a lot more important . . . but you get that kind of data only from the pro manufacturers.

Remember, the medieval microphones I dealt with back then were driven by audio power. Today just about every mic runs on batteries or phantom power. Modern inputs can listen to a signal's voltage while ignoring its wattage. Perfect power transfers aren't critical. But The Law still applies to some mic connections.

- Most mics at a video shoot are transformerless electrets. Their tiny built-in amplifiers are happy feeding a wide range of input impedances, as long as the input has significantly higher impedance then the mic itself. A typical "500 Ω" mic may have an actual output of 200 Ω, and will work fine with inputs between 500 Ω and 5 kΩ. Transformer-based camera adapters have input impedances close to 500Ω, and op-amp XLR inputs are usually around 2 kΩ . . . so if you're using this kind of setup, everything should be fine.

- Likewise, don't worry about mini-jack camera inputs when using consumer electret microphones. The camera spec might be "high impedance" and the mic might be rated "low," but the actual impedances and voltages will be similar to XLR setups. As this implies, you can plug most XLR mics directly into a mini-jack input (using an unbalanced adapter), without worrying about a transformer box. You'll lose the advantages of balanced wiring, but impedances and levels should be fine.

Bottom line: most of the mics and recorders you'll come across already know how to play nicely together . . . at least as far as impedance is concerned. There are only a few special cases where ohms and watts become critical.

- Most hand-held performance and interview microphones are dynamic, and impedance can be important to them. They work best with transformer inputs, or with medium-to-low impedance transformerless ones. Either way, you'll need more gain than with electret mics. Ribbon mics, while rare at shoots, are great for voice-over recording. Their impedances are similar to dynamics.

- Externally-polarized condenser mics, found on feature film sets and high-end studios and usually costing in the $1,000 range, often have internal transformers. An exact match isn't necessary, because the output power isn't generated by air molecules, but the range of usable input impedances isn't as great as with an electret. Anything over 1 kΩ may result in problems. They work best with a transformer input, or transformerless equipment designed for pro use.

An ancient impedance myth

Back when I first learned this stuff, low impedance usually meant high quality. This was particularly true of mics. Pro mics used dynamic or ribbon elements and were designed for 250 Ω or 500 Ω transformer connections. Consumer mics used much cheaper crystal or ceramic elements, which didn't sound as good, but at 10 kΩ–30 kΩ could be plugged directly into tube circuits.

On top of that, the capacitance of long mic cables acts as a selective resistor, lowering its resistance as the frequency gets higher. If the signal impedance is low, this resistance is negligible. But if the impedance is high, it can act as a short . . . gobbling up high notes, and making crystal or ceramic mics sound even worse.

But the basis for these distinctions aren't true any more. Today's toy walkie-talkies and $500 shotguns both use electret elements, operating at about the same low to middle impedance. There are major differences in sound quality between them, but it's not because of how many ohms are listed on the spec sheet.

Camera Settings

There are actually two different challenges here: first, adjusting the camera for the best possible sound; then, making good artistic judgements about dialog levels. That first one is by far the greater challenge. Unfortunately, camera manuals aren't much help. Most seem to be written by the marketing department (or at best, a video specialist), and are remarkably free of useful audio information.

The advice in this section is based on solid engineering, actual measurements of camera audio sections, field experience, and trying to help clients who couldn't understand why the tracks they brought me sounded so bad. I can't guarantee it's best for every camera and shooting situation, but in most cases using popular cameras, it will give you the cleanest recordings.

Sample Rate and Bit Depth

DV audio is almost always set to 48 kHz sample rate and 16-bit words. That's the standard for every format from MiniDV to Digital Betacam. In theory, it's capable of better-than-CD quality. But unless you're using professional equipment and digital audio connections, it often falls far short.

Some prosumer cameras can also record with 32 kHz sample rate and 12-bit words. It's not a good choice. The low sample rate increases the chance for aliasing distortion. The fewer bits result in a 24 dB higher noise floor. Don't use this mode.

While 32 kHz, 12-bit mode can let you record additional tracks at the shoot or add narration or music to existing tapes, there are better ways to accomplish both. Multiple tracks can be captured in separate recorders, discussed in the following. Narration and music should be added in a computer, not the camera.

Volume Setting

The challenge in any recording is to be loud enough that the signal isn't polluted by noise, yet not so loud that parts of it distort. Digital recording can be less forgiving than analog in this regard, because its distortion is less tolerable. DV cameras are even more critical because their electronic noise can be high.

ALC

You'd think the answer would be to use Automatic Level Control, a feature on most prosumer cameras. These circuits constantly adjust the volume to get the best recording. But they're not very smart. If the dialog pauses for a while, they'll turn up the volume looking for something else to record. As they do, any environmental or electronic background noise is boosted. As soon as dialog resumes, they lower the volume. When you play back the tape, you can hear noise rushing up during the pauses. When you cut two shots together, there may be an abrupt jump in noise level.

Automatic Level Controls should be turned off for any professional shooting. Some cameras turn ALC back on whenever you power up or change the tape or battery, so keep checking to make sure things have stayed the way you set them. Low-end cameras might not have any manual level control at all.

There are rumors that a few low-cost cameras let you turn off ALC with a hidden, undocumented menu command. If there is such a command, the best place to find out about it is from other users, at a bulletin board like the Camera Forum in DV.com's Communities section.

If ALC can't be defeated, at least make sure you're sending the camera an appropriate level, that the signal path is very clean, and that the mic is close enough to the subject that background noise isn't significant.

ALC circuits usually look at the average level from both inputs combined, and adjust both channels the same amount. This is necessary for stereo recording. If you're using only one mic, route it to both inputs. Otherwise, the circuit may set the recording level too high.

Limiting, which protects the recording from sudden very loud peaks, is often available on professional cameras. While it's similar to ALC, it's faster and only triggers on the loudest sounds. When things are properly set up, it doesn't affect most of the dialog. If you have this feature, leave it on.

Defeating ALC

If you're using a single microphone in a stereo camera with ALC, you may be able to block ALC by injecting a mid-range tone, louder than dialog, on the second channel. This will give you a track that's slightly softer than ideal. When you boost it in postproduction, you'll also bring up camera noise.

Another way to defeat ALC is to feed the camera so soft a signal that the automatic circuit is at the maximum volume at all times. Some people turn down the volume controls on balancing adapters to achieve this. But with most cameras—particularly the consumer-level ones that have non-defeatable ALC—this isn't a good idea. As they apply more amplification to the input, hiss and distortion increase dramatically.

I often get asked whether you could defeat ALC by mixing a loud, very low- or high- frequency tone with the mic signal, and filtering it out in postproduction. The ALC would see the constant, loud signal and set itself accordingly. This isn't a good idea in practice. Low frequencies may make ALC pump in time with them; even they don't, they'll modulate the dialog and cause a tremolo that can't be filtered out. Loud high frequencies, in almost every prosumer camera, have serious problems with aliasing distortion. When added to the harmonic distortion in these cameras, a single high frequency can produce multiple tones, well within dialog range.

In theory, you could use an expander (Chapter 16) as an "anti-ALC." But most cameras apply ALC non-linearly, and the time it takes their circuits to react or reset is completely unpredictable. Companding—the symmetrical compression and expansion used to control noise in wireless mics—is a reasonable approach when done right. But the circuits have to be matched precisely. Trying it ad-hoc, with a random ALC and expander software, results in strange volume jumps and other anomalies.

Mic noise reduction   A couple of cameras, including Sony's popular DSR PD-150, have a MIC NR setting in their audio menu. This is a simple noise gate that turns the input off when it falls below a certain level, to control hiss from inferior mics or very low level environmental noise. Unfortunately, it *breathes*; hiss and room reverb stay on for a split second after the signal goes away, making a little "puff" sound as the gate shuts down. It has nothing to do with noise generated by the camera itself.

Avoid using this feature. You can do a better job in post, with the advantage of undo-ability if you don't like the sound.

Camcorder Audio Quality

The DV revolution changed the face of filmmaking. Anybody with skill, a few thousand dollars, and a computer can make a film that looks good enough for network broadcast. Electronic discounters sell cameras with decent video and reasonable optics, at prices a committed hobbyist can afford.

Paradoxically, it's had a bad effect on sound.

Economics suggests this isn't likely to change. Since these cameras are aimed at mass market discount sales, they have to be built on a tight budget. A few extra dollars cost per unit can make a serious difference in profit. Manufacturers believe people pay the most attention to picture when buying a camera—they're probably right—so sound quality is inevitably compromised. In fact, a couple of today's popular models have worse sound than earlier, less expensive versions.

This isn't just grousing by an audio curmudgeon. Go to Sony's pro broadcast and production equipment Web site (to take just one example) and you can see what they consider important. At http://bpgprod.sel.sony.com, they brag about frequency response, harmonic distortion, and noise—things that indicate how well a circuit will sound—but only for their audio equipment. When you look for audio specs on the PD150, all you'll find is "16 bit, 48 kHz sampling." This says as much about sound quality as "NTSC video" tells you about the CCDs or lenses. Even Sony's PR department couldn't give me deeper technical details, when I asked officially on behalf of *DV* magazine.

So I decided to gather my own. With the magazine's sponsorship, my son Dan—also an audio engineer—and I gathered some popular DV cameras and hooked them up to lab test equipment. We published our findings in late 2002. This section of the book includes specific numbers, as we measured them, and interprets the result. It also suggests ways we developed, using those numbers and test equipment, to get the best sound possible.

Newer cameras will be available by the time you read this, and audio quality does seem to be slowly improving. We hope to be able to check representative new cameras as they're released. For more up-to-date information, check DV.com or the DV Reader's section of my own Web site, www.dplay.com. Between rentals, shipping, and our time, testing gets expensive; I can't promise we'll have checked the model you're interested in. Even so, the ways we found to get decent sound from the current crop of cameras will probably be valid for generations to come.

How we did it, and what the numbers mean

> ⚠️ **Warning**
> This section is technical. I've included it so readers (and manufacturers) will understand our level of objectivity, and be able to replicate the results. If it gets a little too spec-happy for you, skip down to "The Results" section or "Summary and Suggestions."

We were looking at three things: noise, distortion, and frequency response. All our tests fed calibrated signals to the cameras' analog inputs. Their outputs were connected, via FireWire, to a computer with AES/EBU outputs. We used a studio-quality digital to analog converter to feed signals back to the test equipment. This way, we knew we were measuring just the camera input circuits, and their analog outputs wouldn't be a factor.

We made our measurements in a well-maintained Amber 3501 distortion test set and a new Terrasonde ATB+ multifunction audio analyzer. We also used an oscilloscope to look at distortion products. Bypassing the camera, our setup had 0.01% THD+N, 83 dB s/n below −12 dBFS, and was within 0.25 dB from 20 Hz–20 kHz . . . almost an order of magnitude better than the devices we were testing.

For mic-level testing, we generated signals at −35 dBu, about what you'd expect from a hot mic close to the subject, and turned MIC ATT on if the camera had that function. We also tested at −50 dBu, representing other common mics, and at line level (−10 dBV for most cameras; +4 dBu for the DSR570). Cameras were set to 48 kHz, 16-bit sampling.

Noise The *signal-to-noise ratio* (s/n) is a measurement, in decibels, of how much hiss and other electronic junk a circuit adds to a recording. A higher s/n means less noise and a cleaner track.

9.4 Dan gets ready to start measuring some cameras.

Signal-to-noise can't be measured without a reference level for the signal. In analog, this is usually 0 VU, even though momentary peaks frequently exceed that level. But in digital, zero is an absolute limit. Inputs that exceed it get horribly distorted. Most MiniDV manufacturers recommend an average level of −12 dBFS for dialog, with the rest reserved as headroom for a safety margin; we also used that level. This means our numbers can be compared to traditional analog equipment. We fed a signal to each camera and adjusted the volume for −12 dBFS on its meter. Then we measured the output, removed the signal, and measured the output again. The difference between those measurements is s/n.

Dynamic range, often quoted as an alternative to s/n, includes the headroom. In analog circuits, it's meaningful only if you know how much distortion was present. But in digital, it's a simple sum: s/n + headroom = dynamic range. Our test setup, with 83 dB s/n below −12 dBFS, had 95 dB dynamic range. That's within a decibel of the theoretical maximum for 16-bit sound.

This kind of performance is almost never achieved outside of labs and top recording studios. If you're shooting for theatrical release or heavily-processed broadcast, 60 dB s/n below −12 dBFS is desirable. Corporate and event videographers can get by with 45 dB s/n or so, if the voices don't have much dynamic range; more is needed if there are volume swings.

Distortion   When an audio circuit's output has tones that weren't in the input, that's *distortion*. Back in analog days, this usually took the form of extra harmonics at musically-related frequencies. Digital aliasing distortion is uglier and non-musical. Distortion analyzers measure everything that's not part of the input signal—analog-style harmonics, digital aliasing, and random noise—and call the measurement THD+N (Total Harmonic Distortion + Noise). It's expressed as a percentage of the output. We tested THD+N using a 1 kHz signal.

The THD+N measurement can also reveal noise that's otherwise hidden by noise gates. Since the gate is on during a THD+N measurement, the noise shows up as increased distortion. Distortion and noise are also related in a circuit design, and designers can trade one for the other to a limited extent. So if you see a camera with particularly good ratings in one regard, make sure the other hasn't been compromised.

A THD+N of 1% used to be acceptable in pro analog recording. These days, 0.1% is considered reasonable, and a lot of pro gear is better than 0.01%. But 1% is still adequate for dialog, particularly in a FireWire-connected editing situation where subsequent transfers won't add distortion.

Frequency response   There's a lot of myth about this measurement. In fact, what's often quoted isn't a measurement at all: just specifying the frequency limits doesn't tell you much at all. For response to be meaningful, you also have to know how the output level varies from one end of the band to another. A specification of 20 Hz–20 kHz ± 2 dB is considered reasonably high fidelity. Without the "±2 dB" part, it's just marketing hype.

Frequency response is often plotted on a graph. That can be revealing for speakers and microphones, which can have uneven response throughout the band. But digital recorders usually don't have much variation in the middle of the band; they just fall off drastically at the extremes. Instead of including a graph for each camera, we've graphed typical ones in the summary. But we've noted, in the individual descriptions, where the output fell 2 dB from its value at 1 kHz. For dialog, 2 dB points at 100 Hz and 15 kHz are considered very good. If a camera's high frequency response fell considerably short of that, we also noted how far down it was at 15 kHz. For music, wider response is usually necessary.

The Results

Signal/noise ratios are relative to –12 dBFS, the recommended operating level of most prosumer cameras. We turned MIC ATT on for the –35 dBu signals—it really does improve the sound—but had to use the normal mic position to get a proper level from the –50 dBu signals. To level the playing field, we used balanced inputs for all mic signals. Volume controls were kept near their midpoints for most measurements.

Just about every camera had wider response through the headphone output than via FireWire, suggesting it's connected before the analog-to-digital converter.

Even if you have a different model camera, read the section describing the Canon XL1. It contains explanations that apply to all the equipment we tested.

Canon XL1 We tested the XL1 with a variety of configurations, including Canon's rear-mounting MA100 electronic balancing adapter, and an under-camera BeachTek transformer adapter. For line level signals, we used the camera's rear RCA jacks rather than the BeachTek mini-jack, because it's a purer path. We discovered that those inputs seem to work best with a non-standard, but easily-achieved –30 dBV. We didn't test the more recent XL1S, but did look at an even newer unit, Canon's GL2.

Table 9.1   Canon XL1 audio performance

Input configuration	Canon MA100		BeachTek DXA-4c		Audio 1 (RCA)
Input level	–35 dBu	–50 dBu	–35 dBu	–50 dBu	–30 dBV
THD+N	0.3%	1.2%	0.24%	2.5%	0.23%
S/N	54 dB	41 dB	54 dB	50 dB	61 dB

Frequency response was down 2 dB at 80 Hz and 12 kHz through the MA100, and down 2 dB at 90 Hz and 10 kHz through the DXA-4. These differences are insignificant for dialog recording. The MA100 was down 5 dB at 15 kHz.

We found moderate aliasing distortion, something that's controlled by using oversampling in pro equipment. The XL1 added multiple tones between –25 and –30 dB for signals in the 500 Hz–10 kHz range, and single tones –20 dB for signals 12 kHz and up. This tells us the camera doesn't use oversampling, which also explains the high-frequency loss. It also suggests there's some additional harmonic distortion for signals above 1 kHz.

Where you set the volume knob can have a strong effect on noise. So can the nature of the balancing adapter: while electronic ones have better response than transformers, they're also noisier. With the MA100, there was more than 20 dB noise difference between minimum and maximum volume setting, and noise increased fairly linearly as you raised the control. Using the BeachTek with a low-level signal, there was about 16 dB more noise as the volume control moved from 0 to 100%, most of it occurring when the setting was above 50%. With MIC ATT turned on, there was a 5 dB noise difference in the first 50%, and only 1 dB additional noise as you approached 100%. We suspect Canon used lots of negative feedback with the mic attenuator, a good thing. MIC ATT is not available when using the MA100.

Canon GL2   While the GL2 is a lower-cost camera than the XL1, it's also a newer design. We suspect that some of its performance improvements are also seen in the XL1S. We tested the GL2 with Canon's MA300 active XLR adapter.

Table 9.2   Canon GL2 audio performance

Input level	–35 dBu	–50 dBu
THD+N	0.5%	4%
S/N	69 dB	60 dB

The relatively high distortion for low output mics—the worst we measured in any camera—is offset by the high signal-to-noise ratio. Canon probably used a little circuit trickery to trade one for the other. The performance with medium output mics was considerably better.

Response was down 2 dB at 90 Hz and 9 kHz, and down 7 dB at 15 kHz. Aliasing was somewhat better than the XL1, at –30 dB worst case. Both these factors suggest more modern and conservative filter design, though oversampling doesn't seem to be used.

JVC GY-DV300U   JVC was the only manufacturer who disclosed even partial specs on their Web site: a frequency response of 20 Hz–20 kHz. Their manual quotes a response of 50 Hz–20 kHz, but since both sets of numbers are meaningless without a decibel deviation, feel free to take your pick.

Table 9.3   JVC DV300 audio performance

Input level	–35 dBu	–50 dBu
THD+N	0.2%	0.15%
S/N	66 dB	65 dB

We were able to achieve the latter range within 4 dB—impressive for any prosumer camera—so there's no reason for JVC not to publish the full story.

One other spec turned out to be important, if you record with Automatic Level Control. That's the mic input level, which is specified at –55 dBu, slightly lower than most mics used in DV. This camera's ALC works fine at that volume. But it distorts with a hot mic signal of –35 dBu. We don't recommend ALC for dialog, but if your situation requires it and you're using a DV300, you'll probably need an external attenuator. On the other hand, the manual volume control lets you use higher level mics with no problem: The camera has no line input setting.

Response was down 2 dB at 67 Hz and 14 kHz, –3 dB at 50 Hz and 16 kHz, and –4 dB at 20 kHz. Aliasing distortion was similar to the XL1 under 12.5 kHz, though the DV300's extended high-end response brought with it more aliasing at very high frequencies.

Sony DSRPD150 Sony's original PD150 acquired a reputation for poor s/n. Eventually Sony developed a fix, which was built into cameras made after July 2000 and can be retrofitted onto older units. We used a recent camera, checking the serial number with Sony to verify that it had the latest circuits.

Table 9.4   Sony PD150 audio performance

Input level	−35 dBu	−50 dBu	LINE
THD+N	0.3%	0.5%	0.3%
S/N	58 dB	52 dB	58 dB

We did our tests with the MIC NR menu setting both on and off. It didn't seem to make much difference. As near as we were able to determine—Sony's press representative couldn't put us in touch with anyone who could explain how it worked—it's a simple noise gate in an early stage of the preamp.

Response was down 2 dB at 160 Hz and 9 kHz, and −5 dB at 15 kHz. Aliasing was similar to the XL1. The volume control was responsible for 1 dB of s/n change between 0% and 50% for low-level mics, with 8 dB more as it approached 100%. Mid- and line-level signals had no change in s/n with the volume control up to 50%, and got 5 dB noisier above 50%.

One warning with this camera: although it accepts line-level signals at its XLR inputs, it can't handle +4 dBu, the standard for that kind of connection. It works best with an input of −10 dBV, typically found on RCA line outputs. If you're using it with a professional mixer or preamp, you'll need an attenuator (described at the end of the next section).

Sony DSR570WSL This professional camera has 2/3-inch CCDs, can record widescreen images, and can be used either with CCU-based studio setups or as a field camcorder. It costs about four times as much as a PD150. As you'd expect, its audio performance was also higher end.

Table 9.5   Sony DSR570 audio performance

Input level	−35 dBu	−50 dBu	LINE
THD+N	0.1%	0.15%	0.1%
S/N	73 dB	60 dB	76 dB

While Sony recommends −20 dBFS nominal operating level—the usual standard for broadcast—we took our readings at −12 dBFS so the results could be compared to other cameras.

Frequency response was down 2 dB at 50 Hz and 15 kHz. Aliasing was single tones around −30 dB worst case, considerably better than the prosumer cameras.

Tascam DA-P1 portable DAT recorder   For comparison, we also tested two audio-only recorders. Tascam's non-timecode DA-P1 is often suggested as an alternative to in-camera recording. While it's a 1994 design and not up to current pro audio standards, it's still an improvement over the DV cameras.

These figures were from the DA-P1's digital output. Signal-to-noise was 14 dB worse through the analog outputs. That's an important consider-

Table 9.6   Tascam DA-P1 DAT recorder performance

Input level	–35 dBu	–50 dBu	LINE +4 dBu (XLR)	LINE –10 dBV (RCA)
THD+N	0.6%	0.6%	0.6%	0.6%
S/N	81 dB	70 dB	79 dB	77 dB

ation, if you're comparing a FireWire connected DV camera to a DAT re-digitized through an analog input. Not only will the analog output be noisier; you'll also get noise from the sound card or input pod.

Frequency response was down 2 dB at 20 Hz and 20 kHz using 48 kHz sampling, through both analog and digital outputs. Aliasing was –20 dB worst case, not bad performance considering the extended response.

Sony MZR-37 pocket MiniDisc   This consumer toy cost me less than $250 at Circuit City in 1999 and is no longer avilable. But its performance was a surprise.

These figures were measured using the MiniDisc's analog line output. We were able to get 3 dB better s/n, and cut distortion down to 0.02%, by recording a disc in the MZR-37 but playing it in a deck with digital outputs.

Table 9.7   Sony MZR-37 pocket MiniDisc performance

Input Level	–35 dBu	–50 dBu	–10 dBV
THD+N	0.05%	0.05%	0.05%
S/N	72 dB	72 dB	80 dB

Response was down 2 dB at 20 Hz and 16 kHz. Aliasing was comparable to the prosumer cameras.

Summary and Suggestions

Figures 9.5–9.8 compare the cameras and recorders in four areas: THD+N, s/n, effect of volume control on noise, and frequency response. We didn't plot every camera's frequency response, but the omitted ones were similar. With this data and a little electronic common sense, we can make recommendations for getting the best sound from any prosumer camera.

1. Use as little gain from the camera's internal preamp as possible.

In most cameras, you can't avoid the preamp entirely. But by keeping MIC ATT turned on, and the volume control at 50% or below, you can lower circuit noise to a minimum. Many of the electret mics used in DV production have enough output to work this way, when used at a proper miking distance.

Some mid-priced Audio-Technica shotgun mics have too low an output to be used effectively in most cameras. You'll need a preamp or mixer (later in this chapter), but using one means you won't need a separate XLR adapter. Make sure it's calibrated so that 0 VU on the preamp or mixer's LED meter matches –12 dBFS on the camera. This may require an attenuator. Sennheiser shotgun mics have higher output, and if you're using them properly for dialog, no extra preamp should be needed.

In the XL1, you apparently *can* avoid the internal preamp by using the RCA inputs with an external preamp or mixer. You'll need an attenuator for this as well, to lower the standard +4 dBu output to about –30 dBV.

In-line XLR attenuators are available from broadcast suppliers, and some DV dealers offer custom cables with that function built in. There's information about building your own at the end of the next section.

2. Keep automatic level controls and any microphone noise reduction option turned off.

While ALC is sometimes claimed to reduce electronic noise, it also raises apparent background noise in most miking situations. The MIC NR setting on the PD150 had very little effect. Both background and electronic noise can be effectively controlled in post, if you kept the mic close to the subject. Noise reduction algorithms work best on tracks with very little echo and a good ratio of dialog to background.

3. Be very careful of recording levels.

The recommended –12 dBFS prosumer recording level doesn't leave much margin for error. Sudden loud noises can cause digital distortion, which can't be fixed in post. But if you record much softer than that, parts of dialog will be very close to the noise floor. So it's essential, with these cameras, that you set levels carefully and monitor them during the shot.

One professional trick is to split a single mic so it's recorded on both camera channels, but with one channel set about 6 dB lower than the other. Use the hotter channel, with less noise, most of the time. But switch to the quieter one if things get close to distortion.

4. Don't sweat the aliasing, in most situations.

The aliasing distortion in most of these cameras would be unacceptable in current-generation audio equipment; it's the kind of digital grunge that made sophisticated listeners reject early CDs. Fortunately, human speech (and many forms of acoustic music) isn't very strong in the frequencies that trigger aliasing.

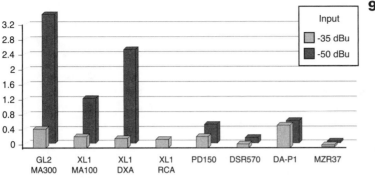

9.5 THD+N, a measure of sound purity, for the tested cameras and recorders. Shorter bars are better. The light gray bars all indicate reasonable quality when used with a medium output mic or an external preamp. The three tall dark gray bars probably represent cases where the manufacturer traded distortion for noise at very low mic levels.

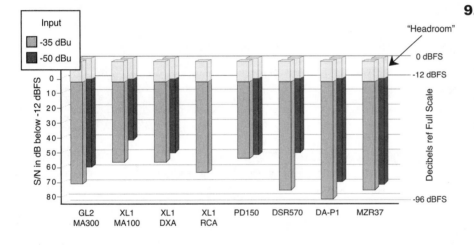

9.6 Signal to noise, a measure of hiss and other junk. Longer bars are better. Despite various rumors, the PD150 noise was similar to the original XL1, when using XLR inputs. We expect the newer XL1S' performance is closer to that of the GL2.

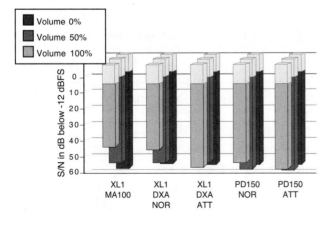

9.7 Typical effects of volume control position on signal to noise. Longer bars are better. Read the individual camera measurements for some implications.

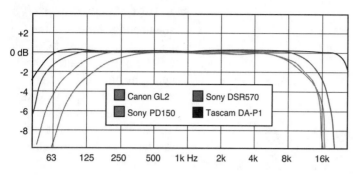

9.8 Frequency response for two typical prosumer cameras, a professional camera, and a portable DAT recorder. All four are adequate for dialog, but the DAT recorder is obviously better for music. Other frequency specs are in the text.

5. Monitor with headphones while you're shooting, but play back important takes as well.

Most cameras apparently have their headphone jacks connected before the analog-to-digital conversion circuit. While you record, headphones can tell you if levels stayed appropriate and let you spot mic or cable problems. But you'll have to play back to make sure there weren't problems with the digitizing or tape.

6. Consider a separate recorder for theatrical or music-oriented projects.

The previous tips will give you a track good enough for most broadcast and documentary projects. But using a separate recorder—what filmmakers call *double system*—can give you a much better track. While most portable digital recorders lack timecode, the decks themselves are inherently speed-stable. There are tips for syncing double-system at the end of this chapter.

You'll get the best double-system results if you transfer the recording into your editor digitally. If your NLE doesn't have digital inputs, it may be worth having a sound studio convert the field recordings to files and deliver them on CD-ROM.

A sense of perspective   The audio performance in prosumer cameras is far from perfect, when compared to even low cost digital audio equipment. But it's not too far from what filmmakers considered reasonable a few years ago. When you consider the average recorder condition, speed, and tape stock of most field recordings during analog days, and add the audio deterioration caused by multiple generations of magnetic stock during the postproduction process, the measured results would be similar . . . or even much worse, in 16mm production.

Analog film sound didn't suffer aliasing distortion and handled overloads more gracefully than digital, but it was plagued by *wow* and *flutter*: constant, audible speed variations that can't happen in digital recording.

A sort of disclaimer   We tested just one of each of these models, and it's possible that we got a lemon. But it's unlikely. This kind of equipment tends to be consistent—either it works as designed, or it doesn't work at all—and our test units came from well-maintained rental and private collections. Manufacturers who feel they got short shrift are welcome to submit other units for analysis. I'll post corrections on my Web site (www.dplay.com/dv) if our tests show that they're significantly different.

BBC-modified VX2000s

Shortly after the PD150 came out, the BBC investigated it for documentary use. They're sticklers for sound quality, and found the camera to be lacking. But they came up with a clever alternative: buying cheaper Sony VX2000s—essentially, the same camera without XLR connectors and missing a few other professional features—and modifying them in BBC shops to completely bypass the internal preamp. Then they commissioned Glensound, a high-quality broadcast electronics manufacturer in Kent, to develop an external unit with better specs.

The Glensound preamp, GSTN1, looks like an under-camera transformer adapter and is used the same way. But it contains a high-quality preamp, designed specifically to work with the modified VX2000. It costs £258 (about $400 when I wrote this), from www.glensound.co.uk. They can give you contact information for the modification; when I checked, the Beeb would modify anybody's VX2000 for £150 (about $225). With shipping from and to the U.S., the whole process might cost just under $825. So if you're contemplating buying a PD150 just for its XLR capability, a VX2000 handled this way will get you better sound for less.

Of course, there are other differences between the cameras. Also, the modified VX2000 can't be restored to the factory configuration, and will have to travel with the Glensound box forever.

To the best of my knowledge, nobody in the U.S. is performing this modification (I asked one manufacturer of appropriate preamps to consider it as a package deal, and they refused). And it's not available for other cameras.

Adjusting the Volume

Shooting a dialog track that will be edited requires consistency, from shot to shot and from scene to scene. Otherwise the edited video will be full of distracting acoustic jump cuts. These take a long time to correct at the mix.

A character's dialog level, as read on the record level meter, should stay consistent throughout a scene. Of course the volume may change if they shout or whisper, or if they're walking away from the scene, but that's related to what the character does on camera. We shouldn't be aware of any changes in their volume when you move the boom, or switch from boom to lav, because without any visual reference the shift becomes distracting. Since the electrical output of a mic varies both with the element type and distance from the speaker, the bottom line is you have to adjust the recording level when changing mics. It may even be necessary while booming.

Not all characters have to be at the same volume level. Differences in personality, or in their intensity during a scene, may mean that one voice is louder than another. But they should be fairly close—within 4 or 5 dB—or else the scene will be difficult to mix.

If you're using just one or two mics, it's easiest to route them directly to the camera. Set them for appropriate volume (dialog should come up to –12 dBFS most of the time) and record with a constant level. Be aware that a character's volume will change if a boom operator can't hold a steady distance because of inexperience or how the scene is blocked and lit. You'll have to compensate while you're editing. If you have to raise part of a track by any significant amount, you'll also increase the noise—both because of camera noise in the clip, and because of errors caused by 16-bit processing in most NLEs.

It's better to keep subtly adjusting the volume while the scene is being shot, so the characters stay constant. It can be inconvenient or even impossible to do this with a camera's volume controls while shooting. The best solution is a separate preamp or mixer, even if it's being used only as a remote volume control and not actually mixing anything together. And, of course, you'll need someone with good ears and a steady hand to operate it at the shoot.

If you're using more than two mics and don't have a good multi-track recorder, you must use a mixer. (Some cameras can record four simultaneous audio channels, but they sacrifice quality when they do. It's best to forget the manufacturer even provides this mode.)

Mixers and Preamps

The only serious functional difference between a mixer or preamp is mixing—combining multiple audio signals into a single channel. Otherwise, both can work as preamps to boost a mics to line level, which results in better performance with almost all cameras. Both almost always have balanced XLR inputs, eliminating the need for a separate balancing adapter if the unit is fairly close to the camera.

Preamps

Mic preamps designed for video use are small and rugged, and can be worn on the belt, slung over a shoulder, or fastened to the tripod (the Glensound preamp for the VX2000, described in the previous section, mounts under the camera). They're battery powered, provide 48 volt phantom for the mic, and usually have other specialized functions including:

- Switchable filtering to eliminate low-frequency rumbles and some wind noise. Most filtering should be put off until the more relaxed (and undoable) atmosphere of post. But wind and rumble filtering should be done in the field, because these frequencies can distort dialog in the recorder.

- Switchable limiters.

- LED metering.

- Headphone outputs.

- Transformer-coupled inputs and outputs. The input transformer provides the best cable noise rejection with the lowest self-noise. The output one lets you run long cables to the camera (if it has balanced inputs), and prevents the possibility of noisy ground loops between preamp and camera.

Preamp output is almost always +4 dBu balanced (a few may use an obsolete +8 dBm standard). Unless you're plugging into a fully professional camera like the DSR570 described earlier, you'll need one of the attenuators described in a few pages.

Field preamps are high-quality, specialized equipment, usually costing around $350 per channel. Preamps designed for music recording may cost less, but generally lack features and ruggedness. Some music preamps cost a lot more—into the thousands—but that kind of quality and specialized sound is lost in dialog recording.

Basic Mixer

Mixers let you combine multiple mics into a single camera channel. In most multi-mic dialog setups, you have to constantly move the faders. Only one mic should be feeding a recorder channel at a time. Otherwise, room noise and reverb can build up. If two people are speaking simultaneously and going to the same track, both faders should be lowered slightly.

Small tabletop mixers, designed primarily for home music recording, can be used for this purpose. They lack features found in field preamps, aren't very rugged, and usually require AC power. Their specs are rarely as good as a field preamp, either. But they're certainly good enough for dialog, and if you can put up with the inconveniences can be a great bargain. Acceptable models, with two or four mic inputs, are often on sale at music chains for around $100. The Mackie 1202 4-mic model, which sounds good enough for feature films, is only about $400.

On the positive side, most of these mixers have large knobs or slide controls that make it easy to make fine adjustments during a take. They also often have equalization controls, which should be set to neutral and ignored. Seriously, put gaffer tape over them, so you're not tempted to equalize in the field. They're designed for music recording, and are too broad for dialog and at the wrong frequencies. It's always better to leave equalization decisions for the calmer atmosphere, tighter controls, and better monitoring of postproduction. A bad decision in the field may be impossible to correct.

If a mixer or mic has a bass cut switch, you may be able to use it to cut wind noise and rumble.

If you're mixing between a boom and lav or plant mics, there will probably be some difference in their sound. Don't equalize the primary mic, but it's okay to use a little bit of equalization on the others—no more than 3 or 4 dB—to make them match. Of course, that's only if you're experienced with equalizing dialog, know the frequencies involved, and have very good headphones. And note what you've done on the script or sound log, so it can be undone if necessary in post.

Most tabletop mixers have small knobs near their XLR connectors to adjust each input's sensitivity. Be diligent about setting these to avoid noise and distortion. The general procedure is to set each of the volume controls to a preset point (usually marked with a zero or U), point the mic at a typical source from a typical distance, and adjust the sensitivity so the mixer's meter comes up to just above 0 VU.

Field Mixer

These units combine the ruggedness (and often, the high audio quality) of a field preamp with mixing capabilities. They have features designed specifically for film and video production, including most of the ones found on a field preamp.

These mixers typically have three or four inputs; in stereo mixers they're switchable between left or right output or both. They also usually include a tone generator and built-in mic for identifying takes. While their size makes them portable—they're typically worn over the shoulder—it also dictates small knobs that may be difficult to use smoothly during dramatic dialog. Depending on features, prices range from about $350 for the three-input Marenius MM-3100 mono mixer, to between two and four thousand dollars for units used in feature film production.

Many field mixers have *preamp gain* controls. They work similarly to MIC ATT on a camera: set them for the lowest gain that lets you get a good reading on the unit's meters. Unlike the volume controls in cameras, a mixer's control will stay quiet until you reach the very top of its range.

Connecting to the Camera

Field mixer outputs are usually switchable between mic and line level. If your camera can handle the signal, a line-level signal will give you a better recording. But be careful: prosumer cameras (and the PD150) consider line level to be −10 dBV. Most mixer and preamp outputs are +4 dBu, and will cause distortion. You'll need an attenuator. Don't try to reduce a mixer or preamp's output to by turning down its volume control; this just adds noise.

Some cameras accept only mic level, but you probably shouldn't use the mic output on a mixer. That's because most mixers are built with a mic level of −50 dBu. A signal this soft gets noisy in DV cameras. Instead, use an attenuator to knock the mixer's line level output down to −35 dBu, and use the camera's MIC ATT setting. You might also need a capacitor to block DC voltage on the mic input, similar to the one in Figure 9.1.

You can also use a transformer adapter, described in the front of this chapter, to connect a mixer or preamp to a camera. Its volume controls function like an attenuator.

Attenuators

These devices, also called *pads*, are simple resistor networks that lower the level of an audio signal. At the same time, they can connect a balanced source to an unbalanced input—though without the noise immunity of true balancing.

Attenuators are available pre-built in XLR male/female barrels, or as cables, for between $30–$50 at broadcast suppliers. Many of the cable ones also include blocking capacitors.

Or you can build your own for a few dollars. There are three circuits for this, depending on how the equipment is balanced. The value of the resistors in each is determined by how many decibels of attenuation you need. Resistors don't have to be fancy: 1/4-watt 1% film resistors, available on special order from Radio Shack (5 for $1), are perfectly fine. Or use 1/8-watt 1% film resistors from an electronics supplier. It won't make any difference in sound quality.

I've specified resistor values that Radio Shack sells, because they're easiest to get. This meant making some small compromises in the pads' designs, and they're not precise to the decibel. But they'll get a signal down to a level that your camera can record well. If you can't find resistors of these exact values, a few percent difference won't matter. The drawings show mono attenuators, but you can double them for a stereo mini-jack input: connect the output of one (marked "to pin or tip" in the drawing) to the mini-plug's tip for the left channel, the other to the mini-plug's ring, and both grounds (from pin 1 on the XLR) to the sleeve.

If you're connecting an electronically-balanced output (most tabletop mixers) to an unbalanced mini-jack or RCA input, wire it like Figure 9.9. The two resistors marked R1 should each be 200 Ω, and R2 750 Ω, to drop professional +4 dBu line level to consumer −10 dBV line. To drop pro line level to −35 dBu for a

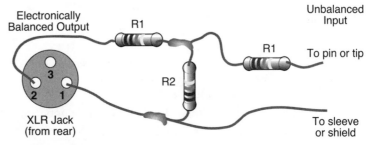

9.9 Use this circuit to plug a +4 dBu electronically-balanced output into a prosumer camera. There are two resistors marked R1 because they have the same value; see text for details.

camera MIC ATT input, R1 is 590 Ω and R2 is 20 Ω. If you can't find a 20 Ω resistor, use two 10 Ω in series or two 39 Ω in parallel. If you're using the RCA inputs on an XL1 and want a −30 dBV signal, R1 is 511 Ω and R2 is 75 Ω (or two 150 Ω in parallel).

If you're connecting to a mini-jack input, the jack probably carries DC power for a microphone. Add a capacitor like the 220 microfarad, 16 volt (Radio Shack #272-956), used in the mic adapter earlier in this chapter. Connect it between the output R1 and the mini-plug, with positive (+) side pointing towards the mini-plug.

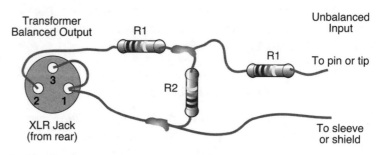

If the mixer or preamp has transformer-balanced outputs (most, but not all, field units), use the circuit in Figure 9.10. To go from +4 dBu to –10 dBV, all three resistors are 332 Ω. To bring +4 dBu down to –35 dBu, R1 is 590 Ω and R2 is 25 Ω. If you can't find at

9.10 Use this circuit with transformer-balanced outputs

25 Ω resistor, use two 49 Ω in parallel. Use the capacitor described in the previous paragraph for mini-jack mic inputs. To get –30 dBV for an XL1, R1 is 560 Ω (or two 1.1 kΩ in parallel) and R2 is 38 Ω (150 Ω and 51 Ω in parallel).

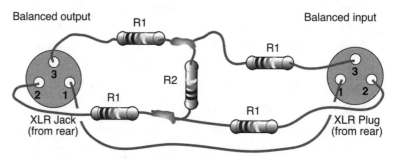

Figure 9.11 shows the circuit for an XLR-to-XLR balanced attenuator. It can be built into an empty male/female barrel, available from broadcast suppliers, but may be more convenient in a cable long enough to go from preamp to cam-era. To drop a +4 dBu

9.11 This circuit provides attenuation while keeping the signal balanced

signal to –10 dBV balanced (for PD150 line inputs), the four R1s are 200 Ω; R2 is 249 Ω. To drop it to –35 dBu mic level, R1 is 301 Ω, and R2 is 15 Ω. It's important, in this circuit, that all four R1s be exactly the same value.

XLR-to-XLR attenuators can be used with long balanced cables. The attenuator should be at the camera, not the mixer. If you're building a cable version, put the resistors in the male end. This keeps the signal at line level for most of the run, for better noise immunity.

Aligning the mixer's meters

Whether the mixer or preamp has VU meters with moving needles or a row of LEDs to indicate output level, it's set up as an analog VU meter. Almost all MiniDV camera meters are set up to read digital dBFS. The two scales are not the same. Furthermore, what the camera records is influenced by its volume control, something the preamp or mixer has no knowledge of. So you can't expect a mixer's meter to have anything to do with the camera's, until you've calibrated things.

The best procedure is to feed the camera some test dialog. First, adjust the mixer controls so that most of the peaks reach zero VU on the mixer's meter.

Then turn the camera's automatic level control *on*. Note how the camera's meters respond to dialog: this is what the manufacturer calibrated the automatic controls to and is probably the best recording level for that camera. For most cameras, it'll be −12 dBFS. Once you've got a feel for what the camera's meters do with ALC on, turn it off. Adjust the camera's manual controls for a similar meter reading. Note that you haven't touched the external mixer's controls at all during this paragraph.

From this point on, you should be able to rely on the mixer's meters. But check the camera's meters during the take. A meter designed for music recording can miss quick changes in dialog levels.

The previous procedure is best done with actual dialog, while the actors are rehearsing or with a friend talking at a constant level, rather than with a lineup tone. The relative response of analog and digital meters to tone is different from the way they respond to voice. Professionals use tone, but understand the differences involved.

Meter-less cameras?   You need an objective way to measure the recording volume. Unfortunately, a few consumer cameras don't have a level meter at all. This is doubly unfortunate, since those are usually the cameras with the poorest quality audio, having only a narrow range where they can record effectively at all.

Studio 1 Productions used to make an accessory LED VU meter that was driven by the headphone jack and mounted on top of the camera. It had its own headphone jack, so you could continue to hear what you're shooting. At $200, it was an expensive solution—particularly considering that it was needed most on the cheapest cameras. But it worked, and you may be able to find one.

A more precise and possibly cheaper solution is to take your laptop to the shoot, and connect it to the camera via FireWire. Start up any NLE or audio software with good metering, select FireWire audio, and you're set.

Headphone Amplifiers

If you're using a mixer or most preamps, you can use it to drive headphones for the boom and mix operators. But if you're plugging a mic directly into most cameras, you may need a separate amplifier. That's because small cameras seldom have enough headphone output to drive a set for the director and one for the boom operator.

One possibility is to skip the director's phones. But that raises the possibility of the director buying a take with subtleties in the performance that weren't heard at the camera position.

Headphone amplifiers, fed by the camera's headphone output and designed for three or more separate sets of phones, are a good solution. AC powered units, intended for recording studios but usable in the field, cost about $150 at music stores. Rugged battery-powered ones, designed specifically for film and video, cost about $300 at broadcast suppliers. All will have separate volume controls for each output.

Or the boom operator can use a *bridging amplifier*. This is a belt-pack unit that passes a microphone signal through without affecting it, while tapping off some audio to drive a battery-powered headphone amp. About $350 at broadcast suppliers . . . though if you're considering this route, it makes more sense to give the boom operator a belt-pack mic preamp with headphone output, and send a line-level signal to the camera.

No matter how you drive the boom op's phones, somebody must be listening to the camera's headphone output: either the videographer, director, or mixer. Otherwise, bad connections (and user errors) will never be spotted.

Double System

Often, videographers consider buying a separate DAT or MiniDisc recorder because they're unsatisfied with the sound from their camcorder. The technique is known as *double system*, and is the standard for features using actual photographic film. (Features shot on HDTV sometimes record in the camera, as a time- and money-saving step.)

It can be a waste of money for prosumer video, particularly if you haven't yet tried the steps in this chapter. A balancing adapter, mixer or preamp can produce usable broadcast, corporate, and event tracks with most of the mics and cameras available today. That's how a lot of television is shot, even when there's a professional sound crew.

Occasionally, videographers consider using double system because they're dissatisfied with a camera-mounted mic. That's definitely a waste of money. Put the mic where it belongs, first. Then decide if the camera's sound isn't adequate.

But for projects where dialog quality is critical, such as features that'll be projected in a theater, double system has definite advantages. As this chapter reveals, even relatively low-cost audio recorders do a better job than most prosumer and low-end professional cameras. Double system can also be an alternative to wireless miking, using a pocket MiniDisc recorder on the talent.

Double-system comes at a cost. It requires operations that are unnecessary with in-camera recording: syncing and logging. It's also less convenient, particularly when the recorder is hidden on an actor. In that last case, you're also vulnerable to mishaps that mute or distort the sound . . . but don't get spotted, until you listen to a playback of the entire take.

Syncing Double System

Syncing is actually two separate functions. You have to make sure audio and video start at exactly the same time, and you have to keep both running at exactly the same speed.

Timecode

In the professional world, the first chore is handled by SMPTE timecode (Chapter 12). Identical code is recorded on the videotape, and in a timecode-equipped DAT or hard disk recorder. On playback, the audio deck looks at code coming from the video player, winds its tape to a matching location, then adjusts its speed until the two match exactly. Once the audio is synchronized, the deck turns speed control over to *house sync*—a color video signal distributed to every device in the facility—that drives both the audio and video players.

Timecode can be used in some decks to keep the entire take in sync, with no house sync. But that's a holdover from analog days, and isn't a good idea with digital audio. A DAT playback can be disrupted by tiny speed changes that wouldn't be noticeable on an analog recorder. If a facility doesn't have house sync, the DAT deck's internal crystal will usually give better speed control than timecode.

Timecode is also used at most film shoots. An electronic slate with large LED readouts and an internal timecode generator is synchronized with the audio recorder's timecode generator. At the start of each take, the slate is photographed (and its code may also be burned into the edge of the film).

The DAT recorders used in this system cost more than some professional DV cameras. That money buys extremely high audio quality, built-in mixers, and other production-oriented features as well as timecode capability. Producers use timecode because it's a tremendous time-saver. But you can sync double system without timecode . . . Hollywood did for decades.

Non-timecode speed stability

Modern digital audio recorders have reliable internal crystals that keep their speed stable, often within one frame for as much as half an hour. Similar crystals are used in video cameras. Since speed variations in either audio or video affect sync, you have to consider the possibility of two crystals slipping in opposite directions. Even so, expect a well-maintained setup to stay within a frame for at least 15 minutes. If a single shot will last longer than that, you may need a recorder that can lock to blackburst or video reference from the camera. Or shoot some *B-roll*: shots that belong to the scene but don't show lips moving, such as an interview subject's moving hands or a reaction from an audience member. When sync drifts too far, cut away to the B-roll for a moment while you add or delete a few frames in the master shot to match audio again.

You can expect this kind of speed stability with recent models of DAT, MiniDisc, and portable CD recorders. Equipment more than ten years old probably has less accurate crystals. Analog cassette or open-reel tape recorders—even most professional ones—don't run at a constant speed and can't be used for lipsync. The Nagra portable open-reel recorder, a standard in film production for decades, used a special *pilot* track to control its speed.

Film speed   Modern professional film cameras have internal crystals and run at a constant speed when properly maintained. If film is transferred to videotape properly, the scanner is locked to the same reference as the videotape. We have to deal with pull-down (Chapter 12), but film sync is painless . . . in the professional arena.

Older cameras with battery or spring motors are notoriously unstable. The only way to achieve sync with them is to have a small pilot generator, inside the camera, constantly monitor the running speed. The pilot output must be recorded on a separate track of the audio tape during the shoot. Usually a sync cable attaches the camera to the recorder for this purpose.

If you plan on using an older camera, check with the facility that will be transferring film to tape before you shoot. They'll have precise specifications for the pilot recording. You'll probably save money by recording audio as analog, on a rented Nagra. There are no procedures for using pilot tracks digitally, and the transfer house will be right to charge a premium for that service.

If you're going to be using an older camera and transferring the film to video yourself, by pointing a camera at a projected image, forget about lipsync. Don't even count on replacing dialog later, since you won't have a reference track. This is a good time to think about telling the story in voice-overs, and reverse angles where we can't see the speaker's lips.

A few older cameras had large AC motors that would synchronize to the power line. These are as stable as modern crystal-equipped cameras, don't need a pilot, and will work with digital audio recordings.

Achieving lipsync without timecode

The easiest way to get sound and picture moving together is to record identical tracks on both. Feed the recorder's audio output to the camera, and record it along with picture. Once everything's in your computer, slide the separate audio track until it matches the videotape's. You can do this visually by matching waveforms in an NLE's timeline, then checking sync by playing them together. When they're matched, you shouldn't hear an echo. Once they're in sync, delete the video's track and lock the remaining audio to picture.

This is a little harder to do when you can't feed the same signal to both recorders. A camera-mounted mic will hear much more echo and noise than a properly-positioned boom or lav, and visual matching will be more difficult. Camera distances can delay the video's track by more than a frame across a large room. If you can't run a cable, consider using a low-cost wireless rig between the recorder's output and the camera. Noise hits, distortion, and dropouts that would be unacceptable in finished audio won't harm a reference track.

Or use a traditional film slate. That's one of those hinged boards with diagonal lines, which you clap together right before the director yells, "Action!". Shoot the slate in close-up, and make sure the mic is no more than a few feet from it. Then look at the shot in your NLE's clip window. Find the first frame where the top of the slate is closed (it'll be blurred in the frames immediately before) and drop a marker. Then, on the timeline, match the start of the clapping sound to that marker. A lot of videographers like to record an additional *tail-slate* at the end of the take, as insurance. If audio is in sync at the start of a scene and has drifted by the end, you'll know there's a speed problem. But with a tail-slate, you can measure how far the end has drifted, and adjust the audio or video clip speed to compensate.

Sound can also be matched to picture without any reference at all. This is time-consuming for professionals, and can be almost impossible for the beginner. There are some tips in Chapter 13.

Logging

The other responsibility when using double-system is keeping track of everything. That's why Hollywood slates have the scene and take number written on them, and an assistant director calls out the same information so it's recorded on the tape. At the same time, a camera assistant notes that information in a camera log, and the sound mixer writes it on a sound report. Those papers accompany the film and tape throughout their life. Small pads for sound reports are available at film sound dealers. Or use a small notebook, and jot down the scene and take, the program number or counter location on your recorder, and any notes that may be helpful about noises or other unusual conditions. Write down the kind of mic you're using and approximate mic distance, if you think dialog replacement might be needed. If the shoot involves multiple media—more than one DAT, MiniDisc, DV tape, or audio CD—number everything and log which recordings belong to each videotape.

Logging each shot isn't as important at spontaneous events, where you might be able to identify audio recordings by their content. But it's crucial when producing a dramatized film, since different takes of a scene will have the same words. It's also essential if there won't be reference audio on video or film.

Using DATs

DAT stands for Digital Audio Tape. It's actually short for R-DAT (the R stood for Rotary, but all digital tape is rotary these days). The tapes are about the same size as a MiniDV cassette, though with a slightly different shape. The standard recording format is 16 bit with 44.1 kHz or 48 kHz sampling, though a few decks support a low-quality 32 kHz mode. No data compression is used in the normal modes, and a good DAT recorder will sound as good as a CD.

While highly capable timecode DATs are used in feature production, Tascam's DA-P1 portable has become the standard for MiniDV double system. (It's also the only decent non-timecode portable on the market.) It has switchable limiters, phantom power, a large meter and volume knobs, and runs on battery or AC power. The unit weighs 3 pounds and can be worn over the shoulder while recording.

DAT has good enough specifications that you can record at the pro standard of –20 dBFS, if you're using a high-output mic or line-level source and will be transferring to NLE digitally. This extra headroom can protect you from distortion at dynamic performances and breaking events. Good DAT recorders don't have ALC; you have to set the volume manually. But you can do it with the tape paused and still fine-tune while rolling, something that's virtually impossible with camera volume controls.

Even non-timecode DATs record a continuous running time (in minutes and seconds) that can be used to locate takes. They also have up to 99 Program Numbers, similar to tracks on a CD. You can drop these numbers while recording, have the recorder add one each time you press record, or have it add one whenever new audio starts out of silence.

DATs, like DV, rely on a continuous control track that's recorded along with the signal. When you finish a take, let the tape roll for a few seconds longer so that there's control track to start the next take. After you play back or when inserting a partially-recorded tape, use the deck's End Search function to find the end of the control track. If the control track is disrupted, you can still record and play. But the end search and running time display won't work properly.

DAT care   The most likely place for a DAT to suffer damage is at the very start of a cassette, because of the stress of having the tape automatically pulled out and wound around the head. Record ten or fifteen seconds of silence or tone at the head of a tape, before starting a take; that'll reduce the possibility of tape damage hurting something important. Rewind the tape completely before removing it from the player.

Like MiniDV tapes, DATs should be kept in their boxes when not in the recorder. Even though both kinds of cassettes have a hinged door and sliding bottom to protect the tape, the data tracks are tiny and the internal head drum spins very fast. Dirt, in the wrong place, can cause dropouts or even damage the recorder.

Occasionally, you'll come across a new DAT tape where the protective shell is partially open. This isn't a problem. Gently press the two white buttons on the sides of the cassette, and you can slide the lower part of the shell back up.

If you're shooting in a warm and humid location, make sure your DAT tapes and recorder are fully acclimated to the weather before attempting to load or use a tape. If either one is cold, condensation can form on the tape drum inside the recorder. Tape sticks to the moisture and can wind multiple layers around the drum. Not only will you lose anything that's recorded; you'll probably also be stuck with an expensive repair.

This situation can happen when equipment is stored in an air-conditioned space and then taken outdoors. Allow at least half an hour outdoors for temperatures to settle before using the recorder. You may be able to speed up the process with a hair dryer on a low setting. Don't let high heat soften plastic parts in the recorder or the tape's shell.

A similar situation can happen in very cold weather, if you bring equipment that's been outdoors into a warm, humid room. Again, allow time for the temperature to equalize.

Professional DAT decks have an indicator to warn when there's moisture inside, but most consumer-level ones don't. MiniDV tape is subject to the same problem, and a few cameras have a moisture indicator.

MiniDisc

This technology got off to a rough start, with early versions having serious audio quality issues. But the standard keeps on being refined, and these days there's nothing "Mickey Mouse" about MiniDisc's sound.

The disc itself lives in a thin plastic cassette about 2-1/2 inch square. Like a computer floppy disk, it has a metal shutter that slides to one side when it's in use. But MiniDiscs use light as well as magnetism. A tiny laser heats a spot on the disc during recording, softening it so a magnetic head can ripple the surface slightly. During playback, the laser's power is reduced. It bounces light off the surface, and the ripples are read as data. The result is a medium that's reusable like a floppy disk, but is as robust as a CD.

Unfortunately, MiniDiscs don't have the data capacity of CDs. In order to hold an hour of stereo—considered the minimum for consumer media—audio must be compressed. Early MiniDisc *ATRAC* compression was distorted and noisy. But newer versions of the algorithm are fine for most purposes, and sound better than high-bitrate MP3s. The compression also supports a mono mode with two hours of high-quality recording.

MiniDiscs can't sound as pure as DAT or CD, but decent consumer-level units have better audio than most MiniDV cameras. Of course, a lot depends on how you use them:

- The electronics—particularly in miniature units—can be a limiting factor. If possible, use a higher-quality player for transfers into your editing system. Ideally, you should connect to the NLE digitally. Relatively low-cost home MiniDisc players often have a Toslink output for this.

- ATRAC's effects are cumulative: a MiniDisc copy of another MiniDisc will sound much worse than the original. Transfer directly to a non-compressed medium for editing and mixing. If your final track will be used in a compressed format other than ATRAC, such as MPEG-based Web audio, you'll probably be okay.

- Know the system's limitations. ATRAC has a hard time with very loud, high frequencies. This seldom occurs in video production, but consider another medium for recording brass quintets or electronic music.

- Operations are very sensitive to physical shock. Even if your system has a "shockproof" buffer memory, recording can be interrupted if you shake the unit around while it's working. It takes several seconds to update the disc's index after you press Stop, and this is also a delicate process. Hold things still until the LCD display returns to normal.

- Learn what your recorder's automatic level control sounds like, and how to turn it off. This may be a two-handed procedure that has to be repeated each time you press Record. Using Pause instead of Stop between takes will keep some units in manual level mode.

"Mini" isn't just a marketing term. Figure 9.12 shows a complete stereo rig in my left hand. The recorder is the Sony MZ-R37 measured earlier in this chapter, held so I can work the record and pause buttons with my thumb. The mic is their MS908, a stereo unit designed for on-camera use—you know what I think of *that* idea—but very nice for recording ambiences. This size also makes MiniDisc a useful alternative to wireless transmit-

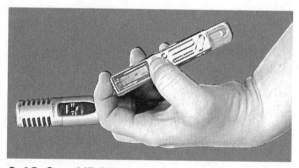

9.12 Sony MZ-R37 stereo rig.

ters. You trade the inconvenience of double system (and of teaching talent or a nervous groom how to turn the recorder on) for higher audio quality and freedom from interference.

MiniDisc doesn't have to be miniature. Marantz and HHB make full-size portables with XLR inputs and other professional features. Broadcasters and theatrical sound producers frequently have large rack-mount units that take full advantage of the medium's editing and instant-cueing capability. The format is used in Hollywood for playback as well. Because its speed is stable, performers can dance or lipsync to it for music videos. Its fast cueing and easy-to-edit track markers make it flexible in the field. If you're shooting to a playback, plug the player's line output into your camera as a reference.

The best place to learn more about this medium, and find honest reviews of new models, is www.minidisc.org.

CD Recorders

Marantz makes a portable recorder that uses ordinary CD-ROM and CD-Rewritable blanks, and produces discs that can be read in any modern CD player or computer. It has field-worthy professional features, including phantom powered XLR mic inputs, switchable high-pass filter, and a limiter. It also features oversampling, as any professional equipment should, to eliminate aliasing distortion and extend the frequency response. Its specifications are studio-quality.

The unit is about the size and weight of a small dictionary, and runs on AC power or 12-volt battery (using the same connection as professional cameras). But it's not as rugged as other field equipment, and it has to rest on a vibration-free, level surface when recording. Marantz calls it "transportable" rather than portable.

Still, at under $900 for the recorder and using media that costs 50¢ for an hour of storage, it may be the most cost-effective way to get quality double-system sound. You just have to respect its physical limitations.

Computer

You might already own a good location recorder. If you have a modern laptop computer with USB or FireWire connections, you can give it decent-quality audio inputs at a reasonable price. One of the best units, SoundDevices' stereo USBPre, has phantom power, headphone outputs, and is fully field-worthy. It costs $700, but much lower-priced units are on the market and the category is growing.

Computer reliability is an issue with these systems. Unlike the specialized computers embedded in DAT or MiniDisc recorders, laptops *do* crash. But if you've configured the system properly and aren't trying to do anything else with the computer, it should be stable.

Consider storage and file transfer issues as well. Digital audio at DV standards requires about 12 megabytes per stereo minute, and a fast hard drive. If your laptop and NLE are network-capable, you can transfer files via 100Base-T Ethernet. Otherwise, you may need to add some form of removable media, such as a CD-ROM burner or Zip drive.

Or bring a large FireWire-equipped hard disk to the shoot, and plug it into your laptop. When you're done, plug it into the NLE tower and start editing. You'll have instant access, with no time wasted transferring files. Macintosh laptops include a function that turns the whole computer into a FireWire drive. Record on the Mac while you're shooting. Then, when you're ready to edit, hold down the T key while restarting. Connect a FireWire cable between laptop and tower, and its files will show up on the NLE's desktop. You'll probably want to transfer them to the tower's hard drive for convenience, but it'll be at FireWire speeds.

Multi-track Recording

Robert Altman pioneered a shooting style where performers were free to ad-lib and step on each other's lines. Each principal wore a lav, but there was no attempt to mix them at the shoot. Instead, they were all recorded separately on multi-track tape. The director made decisions about which lines to concentrate on while he was editing.

I don't recommend trying this with a DV camera in four-channel mode; that setting sacrifices quality too much. But you can get four tracks by using both the camera's normal stereo mode and a double-system recorder.

Or use a multi-track digital recorder, common in music and audio post studios. These 8-track units are rack-mount devices but small enough to carry to the shoot. They have line-level inputs, so you'll need separate mixer outputs or preamplifiers for each track. Multiple units can be synchronized for as many recording channels as you need.

Make sure you'll have a matching player available at post. There are two different formats. Tascam DA-88 (also known as DTRS) is the standard format for film and video production. Alesis ADAT is more typically found in music studios. Their sound quality is equivalent, but the recording methods aren't compatible. Both systems let you sync multiple units for more tracks.

NLEs typically have only two audio inputs. This can be a problem with multiple tracks because you'll have to digitize them in pairs and—unless you have timecode—sync them manually. It's unlikely that the sync between any two pairs will be accurate enough to let you mix them together. Tiny errors, too small to affect lipsync, can create a hollow or echoey sound if the mics were in the same acoustic space. But you can switch freely among the stereo pairs, picking up some actors' lines and muting others.

As an alternative, record multi-track in the field but connect each track to a mixer when you're digitizing. Then you can fade between mics while they're still in sync, and create a mono dialog mix. If characters will overlap, route them to separate channels in a stereo pair; this will let you refine the mix in post. If you ever change your mind and want to hear what some other character said, it's no problem to go back to the original multi-track tape.

9.13 Recording eight simultaneous tracks at a shoot. The Mobile IO interface is being powered by the laptop.

You can also record multi-track in a computer, using FireWire interfaces designed for music recording. Mark of the Unicorn makes an 8-track rack-mount unit for about $800. It has only two mic inputs, but you can add preamps to the other six line-level inputs. You'll also need multi-track software in your laptop. Metric Halo offers a more advanced, field-worthy interface designed specifically for Mac laptops. Their Mobile IO (Figure 9.13) costs $1,500, records eight simultaneous tracks from microphones or line-level sources, and tucks neatly under the computer with a meter panel showing in front.

Chapter 10

Recording Voice-Overs, ADR, and Effects

Rose's Rules:

✔ Compared to sound at the shoot, the technology for a voice-only recording is a piece of cake.

✔ It's much easier to get a good performance when all the actor has to worry about is voice. But the skills that make you a good videographer won't help: you have to know how to ask for a take that *sounds* good.

✔ There are no rules for recording sound effects, only suggestions. If a sound fits, use it.

The Voice-over

My wife, Carla, used to do a lot of voice-over work. Since she's good with dialects and part Swede, she was booked as the Scandinavian spokesperson in a radio commercial series for Howard Johnson Motels. But the session didn't go well: the director kept telling her to "sound more Swedish." She poured on the accent, and finally started substituting authentic Swedish words, but nothing satisfied the director.

The problem was her hair! While Carla is statuesque, she's not a blonde. The producer couldn't look at this tall brunette and hear a Swede. So the engineer (not me) moved her to a far corner of the studio, where the director wouldn't see her. Once he was able to concentrate on her voice, he bought the next take.

The point isn't that some directors are stupid, but that too many people in this business learn to listen with their eyes. The visual skills that make you a good videographer or editor aren't of any value in a voice-over session. With no cameras to worry about, the technique of miking a voice recording is totally different than miking dialog. And the things you say to make an actor appear convincing on a set are usually ineffective when all you have to work with is their voice—that's why Hollywood uses dialog coaches in addition to directors.

But there is a body of easily learned techniques, mostly developed in radio, that will help you do a better job of recording and directing a narrator. Start by thinking about the voice-over process as two different jobs: You can be the recording engineer, or you can be the director. You can even learn to do both at the same time, but only if you approach them separately.

I've organized this part of the chapter to help you do both jobs with a minimum of schizophrenia: even though you'll have to perform the tasks simultaneously, engineering topics are discussed first, and directorial issues later. If you're working with an engineer with a lot of voice-over or ADR experience—major production cities have studios that specialize in this stuff instead of music—you're set. If you've found a narrator on the web, there's a good chance they have their own studio and will engineer themselves while you direct. In either case, skip to the Directing section.

Engineering a Voice Recording

Videographers often wear many hats (or headphones) in their work, and it's entirely possible that you'll have to function as both engineer and director. But even if you're working in a studio with a staff engineer, you owe it to your project to understand the technical side of things. Part of the reason for this is to keep an eye on the engineer: if their primary experience is in music recording, they might be approaching a voice session the wrong way.

If you're going to do the engineering yourself, brush up on your audio skills before the session. Do some practice recordings with a colleague, until the button-pushing part becomes second nature. That way you'll be able to concentrate on directing when the high-priced talent shows up.

Session Planning

There's a lot of preparation to making a good recording, and you should start long before inviting that colleague in for the practice session. You have to make sure the recording space is suitable for a voice-over; you have to verify you've got the right kind of equipment; and you have to provide the nontechnical accessories that make a session go smoother.

The best way to find out if a room will work for voice-over or dialog replacement is to walk around in it and listen for noise and echoes. A voice-over exists in limbo. There should be no sense of a physical space between the narrator and the viewer. Any reverberation can destroy that illusion of intimacy. If you're replacing dialog, you'll need to use electronic reverb, fine-tuned to match the original location. Echoes from the recording room will just get in the way. Most quiet music studios are too reverberant for either voice-over or dialog replacement.

As you walk, face a far wall and make a loud vocal sound that suddenly stops—I prefer to open my throat and go "UCK!" like a seal barking—and then listen for how the sound is reflected back to you. If you don't hear much of anything, the room will work well. If you do hear an echo but it's short and has the same timbre as your test sound, you're probably still okay. But if the echo rings for a while, or sounds filtered or hollow, look for someplace else to record. Do this echo test with a vocal sound, rather than by clapping your hands, because it'll tell you more about how the room responds to voice frequencies. You should also turn around to bark in different directions. Some rooms sound bad when you face one wall, but a lot better if you face a different wall or a far corner.

Once you've determined that a room is basically suitable, keep walking around until you find the position in the room that sounds best. If you do hear some echoes in a room that's otherwise ideal, all is not lost. There are some suggestions for improving room acoustics in Chapter 7.

Once you find that ideal position, stand quietly and listen. If you hear traffic or other loud noises, the room obviously isn't going to be usable. But more subtle rumbles and hiss can also affect a recording. Low-frequency sounds can come from bad fluorescent fixtures—easily fixed by turning off the light—or be transmitted across the building's structure from air-conditioning or elevator machinery. Voice-over recording usually has more bass than dialog recording (boom mics aren't very sensitive to extreme lows), so a rumble that would be tolerable at a location shoot can be a problem for the voice-over.

The high-pass filter built into many professional microphones and mixers can help reduce these rumbles. If a low-frequency sound is extreme, try the double-microphone technique in Figure 10.1.

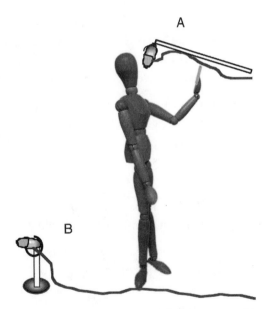

Microphone A picks up both the announcer and the rumble. Microphone B, facing away from the announcer, picks up mostly rumble. By inverting the phase of B, you can mix in a negative version of the rumble to cancel itself out. (The easiest way to invert the phase is an adapter that exchanges pins 2 and 3 of a balanced mic's XLR connector.) A couple of warnings: This technique only works on low frequencies, where the wavelength is long enough that both microphones hear the same part of the wave. And it can be tricky to balance the two microphones, so you might want to set

10.1 Using two mics to pick up room rumble

this up long before the talent arrives. Adding a bass boost and a high-cut filter to mic B can help.

High-frequency hisses are usually the result of air vents or computer fans. You can quiet a vent by prying off its grill; most of the noise comes from turbulence around the vanes that direct air around the room. But if an equipment fan can't be turned off, you'll have to get as far away from it as possible. Fortunately, high-pitched sounds are easily controlled by sound blankets.

Make a sound check

It makes sense to gather and test all your equipment long before the session, so you can fix anything that's not up to snuff. If you're like most videographers, you might have to hunt for the right kind of microphone:

- The lavaliere mic that's so useful during a shoot is of little value for voice-overs. These mics are often omnidirectional and pick up more of the room's echoes than are desirable. If you absolutely have to use one, don't pin it to the announcer's chest. Suspend it a few inches above, and slightly to the side, of the announcer's mouth. And put in a fresh battery.

- Mid- or large cardioid mics are usually the best choice in a studio. They can be aimed to avoid echoes bouncing off the control room glass or script stand—yes, that's a very real problem. But cardioids are more subject to popped Ps, so you may have to experiment to find the best position. A silk screen can be placed in front of the mic to reduce popping. It works both by slowing down the blast of air and by spiking the talent so they don't get too close to the mic.

- A short shotgun or hypercardioid mic can give you the most flexibility in a less-than-perfect studio. Place one 6 or 7 inches from the announcer's mouth, and it'll be far enough away to avoid popping but still manage to reject any residual room echoes.

- Condenser mics are almost always a better voice-over choice than dynamic ones. While radio engineers and stage performers love dynamics for their ruggedness, these mics lack the crispness and overall tonal balance that can make a voice-over track stand out. Large dynamics specifically designed for voice-over, such as the ElectroVoice RE-27 and Shure SM-7, are an exception.

- Ribbon mics can give you a very smooth sound, more natural than a condenser, but require quiet and sensitive preamps. A prosumer mixer might not be workable.

- Dialog replacement sessions should use the same kind of mics as the original dialog, in about the same position. If you're not sure, put a lav on the talent's lapel, and a short shotgun or hypercardioid about two feet in front, pointing towards the mouth from just above the head.

There's a lot about microphone types in Chapter 7.

You should also hunt for a microphone stand with the flexibility to let you place the mic in its best position. It's usually a bad idea to put the mic directly in front of the performer's mouth (example A in Figure 10.2); not only is this position more prone to popping and other mouth noises, it also gets in the way of reading the script. Above and slightly to the side (example B) is better, and moving the mic a few inches up or down from this position can help you avoid sibilance. A short shotgun (example C, shown without its windscreen) can be placed even higher. A mic stand with a short boom arm will give you the most flexibility.

The best recording equipment—particularly if you're trying to both direct and engineer at the same time—is whatever will let you put off decisions as long as possible. You want to be able to concentrate on the performance, not on a bunch of dials.

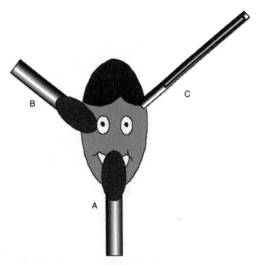

10.2 Three different voice-over mic positions. Avoid A.

- If you've got a DAT, MiniDisc, or CD recorder available and a way to get its recordings into your NLE cleanly, record to it. It's easier than recording in a computer, more reliable, and you'll be able to put every take on the shelf for future revisions.

- If not, but you've got a good sound card or other audio input, record in your NLE. Each take should be a separate file. This is a little more work, because you'll have to enter and keep track of file names, but keeps you from losing everything if a file gets corrupted. Follow the level-setting tips in Chapter 12.

- If you don't have a good recorder or a good audio input on your computer, record into your camera. Use a good external mic, and follow the tips in Chapter 9. Then transfer the bought takes into your computer via FireWire.

- There is no point to recording a voice on analog tape, even with the best open-reel studio recorders. Blank analog tape is expensive, and doesn't sound as good as digital. Some music producers like the distortion that analog adds, but it fights intelligibility on spoken word.

The best recording chain for a professional announcer is a microphone, a simple preamplifier (perhaps with a bass rolloff switch) or mixer, and a DAT recorder. If the announcer is less than professional and doesn't control projection very well, a limiter can help rescue otherwise marginal takes. If a limiter seems to add noise or distortion, turn down the preamp's volume control. Make sure any automatic level control is turned off.

Don't try to equalize or compress while you're recording. These processes are irreversible. It's best to put processing decisions off until the final mix, since music and dialog can affect how you process the voice-over. Professional engineers regularly break this rule and apply all sorts of processing to the original recording. But unless you've had lots of experience with this kind of equipment, it's better to work with the safety net of an absolutely clean original track.

A simpler recording chain will also help you make a cleaner recording, by avoiding extra circuitry that can contribute hum or noise. Enlist a colleague to help test your chain. Have them read a script and adjust the recording level for their voice, but then have them stop while you record about 30 seconds of silence at those settings. Play back, and when you get to the silent part, turn the monitors as loud as you can. If you hear hum or hiss, pause the tape. If the noise continues even when the tape stops, it's probably in the monitor. If the noise pauses with the tape, you've got problems in the recording equipment. Turn the monitor volume back down, halfway between its normal position and maximum. Decide if you can live with the noise at that elevated volume, because by the time you've finished processing and mixing, it may be that loud. If not, get your equipment checked before investing in a voice-over session. Don't expect noise-removal software to solve the problem; all it can do with this kind of noise is make it less annoying.

You can monitor the recording via headphones, or with speakers in another room. Don't forget a monitor for the talent. Professional announcers need to hear themselves in high-quality headphones, so they can adjust their own performances. Closed-ear headphones are essential if they'll be working to music or other cues, to keep the cueing sound from getting into their microphone. But these headphones tend to be big and heavy. Lightweight full-size headphones that rest gently against the ear, like the ones shown in Figure 10.4, are more comfortable; use them when there won't be simultaneous cues. At the least, provide a pair of top-quality portable CD headphones, such as Radio Shack's Pro-35 ($40).

Don't be surprised if you see a performer take off one side of the headphones and cup their hand to an ear, just like old-time radio announcers did. Some very good contemporary narrators use the same trick, so they can catch tiny nuances that don't make it through the limited response of a headphone.

Those tiny IFB earpieces used by on-camera announcers and newscasters are also comfortable, but don't sound good enough to give an announcer useful feedback. A few DAT recorders have *confidence heads*, which let you monitor a playback of the signal while it's being recorded, to check for tape problems. This introduces a delay. If you're monitoring this way, make sure the announcer has a nondelayed signal for their headphones. And provide a way to adjust their monitoring volume separately from your own. Electronics stores sell in-line volume controls for small headphones, and they can be a handy—if sometimes fragile—convenience.

You may need one other piece of equipment that's often overlooked in temporary recording situations: If you and the talent are going to be in separate rooms, make sure there's a way to communicate with them. Professional consoles often have a talkback system built in, but the simple mixers found in most video-editing suites don't. If nothing else is available, a cheap battery-operated intercom makes a good emergency talkback.

Nonelectronic essentials

Some other equipment can also make a big difference in the quality of a voice-over recording:

- A tall stool, if the script is more than a page or so. A good announcer will almost always prefer to stand—or at least, lean—while they work. If they're sitting in a low chair, they can't control breathing as well.

- A proper script stand. Folding music stands aren't tall enough for standing announcers, forcing them to look down as they read and constricting their throats. You need something tall enough to put the script at eye level. Also, you need a stand that won't echo. The talent's mouth, microphone, and stand are all very close together, and reflections from the stand can cause hollowness in the recorded sound. A partial solution is to put a piece of carpet over the stand. Even better is a piece of fiberglass acoustic tile. You can improvise a totally non-echo stand from a lighting flag and clothespins.

One elegant solution appears in Figure 10.3. It consists of an ordinary mic stand, a gooseneck mic adapter, and a large clip from a stationery store. It's very easy for the talent to adjust for the best reading position. Make sure there's a solid table or counter nearby, so the talent can write down those inevitable script changes.

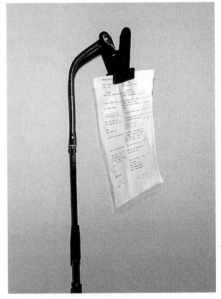

10.3 This versatile script stand is hardly there at all.

- Plenty of nonglare light. If you're using overhead lights, make sure the microphone (or talent's head) doesn't cast a shadow on the script. Some narrators prefer clip-on lights that can be attached directly to the script stand.

- Water. While ice-cold water is refreshing, it tightens the throat. Room-temperature is better. Water is particularly important during periods of low humidity: as the body loses moisture along with the breath, saliva in the mouth will thicken up and can cause snapping or crackling during consonants.

The Recording Session

If you've done the right preparation, engineering chores at the session itself will be fairly simple. This lets you concentrate on directing the performance.

Before you begin, record about 10 seconds of the microphone or a test tone and then play it back. This not only verifies that the equipment is working, it also keeps you from losing something important to the kind of tape damage that's most likely at the head of the roll.

When the talent first walks up to the microphone, stay near them and ask them to read a little of the script. Every performer stands slightly differently while they're working, and this is the best time to fine-tune the microphone placement. Then go to your equipment and have them read a little more so you can adjust the recording level. Even if you've found the ideal level, you may want to keep one hand on the volume control during the first few takes. Inexperienced performers tend to read a little louder when they know it's for real.

Once you're ready to record, you have only a couple of ongoing responsibilities as engineer:

- Keep track of takes and take numbers, and write them down on the script. If you don't have a slate mic in your setup, slate into the talkback system; the talent's mic will pick it up. Slating isn't necessary if you're recording into a computer with separate files for each take.

- Keep an ear open for problems that can build up during the session, and be ready to stop the session to fix them. As the narrator's mouth dries out, you might hear clicks and snaps in their voice; stop and give water. If they've moved too close to the microphone and are starting to pop, reposition the mic (or spike them by moving the script stand). If a mic battery starts getting weak and you hear distortion, replace it. It's difficult—if not impossible—to fix any of these problems during post.

- You may want to time the takes with a stopwatch. This is an art in itself: train yourself to start the watch immediately on the first syllable, and not to stop it until the final syllable is finished sounding. Don't use a watch that beeps.

After the final take, play back a little bit to verify that the recorder is still working.

Recording Narration to Picture

Recording to picture makes things a lot more complicated, both for you and the performer. Since it's so easy to move voice tracks around in an NLE, it may make more sense to record to precise timings with a stopwatch instead. For scenes where the talent has to understand a visual rhythm or emotion, play it once and then let them perform. If you absolutely must record to picture:

- Give the talent a monitor that's near their script, so they don't have to keep refocusing. The best solution is a small LCD monitor on the script stand itself (Figure 10.4). A conventional CRT's glass will reflect the voice, so make sure it's on the dead side of the microphone. Listen carefully to make sure the monitor isn't adding a whistle or hum that's getting picked up by the mic.

- Give them some other form of cue along with the picture, such as a series of beeps right before they're to start, or let them hear the dialog track immediately before their line. Very few performers can concentrate on both a written script and an on-screen image, and if they have to switch their concentration suddenly, they'll probably come in late.

- Don't obsess about timing. If a perfect take overlaps the next shot by a few seconds, you can probably fix it in the editing.

10.4 If talent has to see video, it's best to use a small LCD monitor on the script stand

Timecode isn't as helpful as you might expect for this kind of recording. Unless you have an elaborate automatic logging system, you'll have to repeat the master video's timecode with each take. This confuses the edit controller or DAT recorder's chase circuitry, and the long preroll you'll need for each new timecode pass will just slow down the session.

The easiest way to synchronize multiple narration takes that have been recorded against picture is to start with some kind of reference audio—dialog, a scratch track, or a beep before the scene—on the videotape. With each take, dub the reference to one channel of your recorder and record the narrator on the other. After the recording is done, dub both the selected take and its reference back into your editor. Slide the stereo pair around in your editor until the two references match, and then you can delete the reference.

Dialog Replacement

If dialog recorded at the shoot isn't usable, you have to replace it. This is not an option to consider lightly. Even in Hollywood, where ADR (automated dialog replacement) or *looping* (from the original, nonautomated loops of picture and soundtrack that were used) is common, it's frequently done poorly and stands out in the film. On the other hand, Marlon Brando used to love looping as an opportunity to perfect his performance. Rumor has it that's why he mumbled so much in the original takes.

There are two engineering considerations for ADR. You have to match the sound of the original recording, and you have to cue the talent in a way they'll find helpful.

Matching the sound

To match the original recording, you'll need to use a microphone that's similar to the original principal mic, at the same distance and angle that was used at the shoot. This is the most critical aspect of making an ADR session work properly. The kind of close-miking that's used for voice-over recording is wrong for ADR, and tracks recorded that way are very difficult to match with production dialog.

You'll also need to use some psychology: A voice-over studio shouldn't have any noticeable echo, but the natural room reverb at the original shoot helped the actors hear their own voices. When they get into the studio, if they don't hear at least some echo, they'll tend to push their voices harder to compensate. Even if they capture the mood perfectly, the voice won't match because the projection will be different.

On the other hand, if the studio has too much echo you won't be able to match the original reverb at the location. Real rooms add unpredictable coloration to a sound, and it's unlikely that a studio's echo will be anything close to the reverb you picked up in the field. Technically, the best way to match is to record ADR with as little echo as possible, and then use a good digital reverberator to simulate the original room.

One solution is to build a voice-recording room that's highly absorbent along three walls, and slightly reflective in the front. Face the actor toward the front of the room, and position a cardioid or shotgun mic—whatever was used at the shoot—so its dead side is toward the reflective wall. Another is to record in a totally dead room, but mix a tiny amount of reverb along with the talent's voice in their headphones. Either of these solutions raises the ante for the recording facility: it must have a room built for this kind of recording, a console that can apply reverb to one set of headphones but not to the main monitor or recorder, and a reverb unit that can simulate small rooms (most music-studio reverbs have much too big a sound).

Of course, you can also match the original room's acoustics by recording ADR lines in the original location. If the scene was shot at an in-house studio or the location is still accessible, this will be the easiest and cheapest solution.

ADR techniques

First, identify which lines need to be replaced and separate them by character. Actors' skills (and patience) for ADR vary; it might take one person a long time to do their lines, while someone else can breeze through theirs. There's no point to making one actor repeat a successful delivery while their partner blows take after take. So even if a scene has multiple characters, you'll be recording them in separate sessions.

The lines should be broken into short units, ideally no more than a sentence or two at a time. It's a lot faster to match lip sync on two short speeches than a single long one.

There are two principal ways to record ADR, leading to occasional debates among sound recordists about which is best. If you've got the ability to use either one, leave the choice up to the actor.

If you're also the picture editor, you have some options that aren't available to us lowly sound people. If a scene needs massive dialog replacement, you can recut it to favor long shots where lipsync isn't as noticeable. ADR won't have to be as precise.

Or provide cutaways and reaction shots during longer speeches. This way there'll be some places to make tiny off-camera voice edits; these can restore sync to a line that "almost makes it."

The traditional method is to make picture dominant. Start a visual streamer right before the line starts. Originally, this was done by drawing or scribing diagonally across a few dozen frames of a copy of the film itself, creating a line that marched across the screen from left to right. These days, streamers are generated electronically and added to a video playback. The actor listens to a playback of the original line a few times to get comfortable with the delivery, then watches picture. As the streamer reaches the right side of the screen, the actor reads the line while watching mouth movements. Keep repeating until the sound seems to be in sync with picture. The advantages to this method are that the actor can feel freer to experiment with the delivery and doesn't have to wear headphones.

A modern alternative is to make sound dominant. Generate an audio streamer of three short beeps exactly one second apart. Put it on a separate track, exactly one second before the start of the line on a production dialog track. Set this audio track to play in a loop, and feed it to the headphones. The actor hears the rhythmic repetition of beeps and line, and within a few passes will be able to speak along with it. Keep repeating until actor and playback are in unison. The advantage to this method is that it can be faster with performers who aren't used to looping, and since it isn't necessary to concentrate on picture—video playback is optional—the actor can be looking at a script instead.

In both methods, it's important to establish a rhythm. Make sure that recueing the sound or picture is fast and always takes the same amount of time. If your system isn't equipped for loop play, make multiple copies of the streamer and original material on the timeline of an NLE or audio workstation.

As soon as you've got a successful take, mark it and move on to the next line. You can record the new version with the looped timecode from the original, or with new continuous timecode while you keep track of the offset, but the easiest way is to dub the original dialog on one track while you record the new performance on the other. After the session, take the last take of each line and slide it so the reference exactly matches the original uncut dialog. Then delete both the original track and the reference, leaving just the replacement.

The new track will sound drier than the original, since it doesn't have any room reverb (unless you recorded it at the original location). You can add temporary reverb to make the scene more realistic while you're editing, but don't commit to it until you've had a chance to compare original and new tracks on a good monitoring system.

Don't obsess over ADR. If many of the critical consonant movements are in sync, it's probably good enough. Modern audio workstations and multi-track audio editors give you a lot of flexibility to make tiny tweaks in the recording, or change the timing of individual words without affecting pitch.

Directing the Voice-over

I was watching TV with my son, many years ago when he was in the "What does daddy do at work?" stage. A commercial came on for a superhero action figure, with a voice-over suggesting:

Narr: Imagine you can make him fly.

"Daddy's job," I explained, "is to have him say those same words as

Narr: Imagine! You can make him fly!

While most professional narrators will deliver a credible reading on their own, you can't just settle for a pretty sound. You know the project's goals better than they do, you know what has to be conveyed, and you probably know a lot more about the subject. So be ready to add dramatic director or dialog coach to all the other hats you wear.

Casting and Talent Unions

It goes without saying that you can't direct a narration until you've hired someone to read your script. Otherwise, well . . . it goes without saying.

The right narrator can be as crucial to a project's success as the writing and visualizations. A lot of information—and subtle emotional information about your project and company—will be conveyed by this voice alone. Don't make casting a last-minute decision. Expect to spend some time, money, or both selecting an appropriate narrator. The golden triangle of production applies here, too: you can get a world-class narrator easily, if you're paying union rates; or you can look a little harder and find someone good who's less than scale; or you can save both time and money and get a voice that damages your project.

"The Union" is either AFTRA (American Federation of Television and Radio Artists) or SAG (Screen Actors' Guild), both operating in the United States only. Traditionally AFTRA handled videotape and SAG confined itself to film. New technologies have blurred the lines, and SAG is trying to assert control over things like CD-ROMs.

Their contracts and rates are virtually identical for voice-overs, but their pension plans are slightly different, so I leave it up to the actors to decide which union they'd rather be paid through.

AFTRA is in New York at (212) 532-0800, SAG is in LA at (213) 954-1600, but don't call either until you've finished reading this section. Their Web sites are www.aftra.org and www.sag.org.

Defining the voice

First, ask yourself the basics: Why are you making this video? What's the primary message you're trying to convey, who's going to see it, and why are they paying attention? Then read through the script, aloud. You'll start to hear what kind of a voice you want, so you can make a list of appropriate adjectives like *light, serious, hip, warm, cultured.* (Even *neutral* can be appropriate, though it's more often a symptom of lazy casting.) Think also about whether you want a man or a woman—the answer shouldn't be automatic.

Now that you know who you're looking for, you can start the search:

- Call other producers. Most are willing to share their discoveries. If you hear a radio or TV spot you liked, ask the station which agency supplied it and call their casting director.

- If you're recording in a studio, ask for their recommendations. Many studios have cassettes or CDs with a selection of their favorite local performers and can send you a copy.

- If you're in a big city, call the talent agents. They have composite tapes also and will send them at no charge to any legitimate producer.

- If you're not in a big city but have a strong regional theater company, find out if they have any visiting players who do narration at home. Theater and voice-over skills are totally different, but many full-time actors are good at both.

- If you're paying scale and have signed a union contract, call the union and ask for their talent guide or directories. Bear in mind that the unions make absolutely no representation about the talents of their members, so you can find union turkeys as easily as nonunion ones. In many cities, union members have gotten together and produced composite CDs so you can actually evaluate their voices and skills.

- Call the local producers' association, broadcast association, or MCA-I and ask for advice.

- Look on the Web. Some announcers have pages advertising their services, complete with downloadable or streaming demos. Set your favorite search engine for "narrator," and you'll get pages of links. If the voice you like isn't in your city, don't worry: professionals are used to being directed by phone, and can point you to a studio near them that has the proper equipment. Many web-based announcers have their own facilities.

- As a last resort, call a casting company. While a few are good, a lot are visually oriented and don't understand voice-overs. They'll charge you to record a number of actors and models reading your material, but their choices and direction may be totally random.

Evaluating a demo

The only way to choose a voice is by listening to a demo. If a voice actor doesn't have downloadable demos on a Web site, ask them to mail you their cassette or CD. Be suspicious if they don't have one, and offer to send you a single recent reading instead. This probably means they haven't done enough work to be comfortable in a studio. When you first listen, make sure there's some variation between pieces. Every voice changes slightly from day to day, and every studio and director have a slightly different sound. If the different selections all sound the same, the actor probably threw it together in one long session—again, an indicator of inexperience.

Now consider four specific things:

1. Naturalness

It takes both talent and experience to read a script and still be conversational. Even the most gifted beginner can tighten up when recording; under stress, throat muscles involuntarily constrict.

> **It's a Catch-22**
>
> An actor won't get good until they've done a lot of work. They won't get a lot of work until they're good. If you're unsure of your own directing chops, go with the experienced actors—they'll help you a lot. But if you've got skill and patience, you might find a very talented novice who'll do a good job and work for less than the going rate.

That changes the sound, and while audiences won't know why, they'll feel uncomfortable in sympathy.

2. Technical chops

Breath control is critical. Sentence endings should have as much support as beginnings, and emphasis should be done by pacing and pitch rather than volume. The energy must be consistent, so you can edit one take to the next. And there's certainly a craft to saying "magnetohydrodynamic" or "norepinephrine" the way your audience expects.

3. A professional attitude

Professionals understand they've been hired to convey a message, not to display their beautiful voices. They know this video isn't about them.

4. Finally, the pipes

Voice quality isn't as important as these other characteristics, and many of the best narrators just sound like ordinary people.

Union? Nonunion?

The talent unions do not control production. Nobody will bust your kneecaps if you hire a non-union actor. Rather, they're associations of working professionals who've agreed to work only with producers who honor their contract. You're free to cast anyone you want, but actors may refuse to work for you if you're not on the union's list, or if the cast also includes non-union performers. There has to be a "signatory producer of record" involved—it can be you, the recording studio or production company, or a casting agent. The signatory will have you sign a release guaranteeing contract provisions for this particular production, but this doesn't obligate you for any other production.

If your budget is really tight, you might be tempted to cast by asking colleagues to try a reading. Even if they'll work for free, it's a false economy. An amateur can waste money on studio and editing time, add a layer of cheesiness to your beautiful visuals, and make your audience wonder why you've wasted their time. College radio experience 10 years ago, weekend membership in a community theater, or even a bustling career as a stand-up comic doesn't equip someone to read a narration.

However, you can find good actors who'll work for less than scale. Many cities don't have a union local, and the narrators there charge whatever they want. Rates usually settle at about 75% of scale. Radio station production directors are usually underpaid, often moonlight, and may have the versatility to read your script without sounding like a disk jockey. The Internet, ISDN hookups between studios, and overnight couriers have broadened the competition, and many good performers will negotiate rates . . . particularly if the project will be shown to a closed audience, or in a city where they're not normally heard.

You'll find a large pool of nonunion talent in large production cities, but these are often the ones who can't compete with the pros. Some performers in midsized markets manage to play it both ways, working through the union for broadcast jobs but nonunion for corporate pieces. They tend to charge scale for their work, but don't require any of the union's extra payments (see the following section).

On the other hand, a union performer can be a real bargain. Actors like to work. Many voice-over stars with serious credentials, who charge a premium for commercials or network narrations, will do corporate projects or closed-audience videos for scale if they have the time.

Union rates

Scale for corporate voice-overs is based on two factors: how long the performer is in the studio, and whether the video will be kept in-house or shown to a larger audience (such as a trade show or point-of-purchase display). In 2002, base scale was $346 for a one-hour session of an in-house video; about $40 more for videos that'll be shown to the general public. Rates typically increase just under 5% a year.

Union scale for commercials is based on a myriad of factors including the length of time on the air, the number of cities it'll be shown in, which cable networks are involved (if any), and even whether the airtime is being purchased from a regional network or all the individual stations in the region. (Networks are cheaper.) Minimum base scale is $375 for the recording . . . and then anywhere from a few dollars to thousands for the usage.

But that's just the base scale. Most performers are represented by agents, who tack on their 10% and may demand more than scale for busy performers doing commercials. Then there's the union itself: it insists that the performer become your employee for the duration of the session, making you responsible for payroll and unemployment taxes. And of course the union gets its own cut to support their health and pension funds. Figure another 28% for taxes and pension. And the total has to be received by the union within 12 working days of the session, or else serious penalties kick in.

Keeping all the math and procedures correct is no job for an amateur. Most producers who use union talent also employ paymasters, who take care of the whole nasty mess, become the employer of record, and rent you the talent for a mere 10% more. This also lets the paymaster assume the liability for unemployment insurance, so your company's rates don't go up if you neglect to hire that actor the next week. Paymasters are franchised and regulated by the union. If you're using a studio or production company's contract to avoid becoming a signatory yourself, they'll probably charge you an additional 10% for the handling and their need to make prompt payment.

Fun, huh?

The only discount is when an actor has formed a separate "For Services Of" corporation for tax or liability reasons. You'll still need a paymaster, but the actors' F/S/O corporation assumes Social Security and other payroll taxes.

Planning Ahead

Successful directing starts long before the talent shows up. At least three days before the session, figure out how the reading should sound.

Sit at your desk and read the whole script, aloud and in full voice. Listen carefully to yourself. Do the sentences work for the ear? Is it obvious which words should be stressed, and is there a natural pattern that emphasizes them? Does it sound conversational? Make a note of any sentences that are hard to interpret, or don't make sense to your ear.

Then fix them. This can be as easy as adding a couple of extra commas or dashes to break the sentence up. Or it might require a change that has to be approved higher up, which is why you're doing this preparation long before the recording.

Deciding what to stress

There are two ways to decide what to emphasize in a sentence. You can say it a few different ways and see which sounds best, but that wastes time and can lead to monotony (as exemplified by Ted Baxter, the newscaster on the classic Mary Tyler Moore show). Or you can use some applied information theory.

Assume that the most important part of the sentence is that which conveys the most information. Information is directly related to unpredictability, so the most important words are the ones your audience hasn't heard before. Imagine a script:

```
Narr:    Joe Blow has served our district for nineteen years. Joe Blow is
   honest, smart, and competent. Vote for Joe Blow!
```

It's certainly appropriate to stress the first mention of Joe's name. But if you stress the other two times, it'll just sound boring. You're throwing a lot of the commercial's information-carrying ability away.

In the second sentence, try stressing the adjectives instead. They're the newest information (though hardly unexpected in a political spot). In the third sentence, stress the verb—that's the command to action and the newest thought. Besides, by this time the viewers already know Joe's name. They won't remember it any better, or be more convinced to vote for the guy, just because you said his name stronger.

Don't make the radio-announcer mistake of stressing the conjunction. "Joe Blow is honest, smart, *and* competent" merely implies that the "and" part is unusual, and these three characteristics are seldom found in the same politician. This might be technically true, but that's a subject for a different book.

Stress enhancement techniques

Professionals use lots of different ways to emphasize a word in a sentence, and saying it louder is the worst of them. Changing the volume suddenly just makes things harder to record. Instead, they'll do the following:

- S-l-o-w the word down. This is particularly effective on client names, which may be more unfamiliar than other words. In fact, I'll often slow down the name with my workstation's time expansion feature, if the talent hasn't already done it for me.

- Raise the pitch slightly. Every sentence has an inflection pattern, but if you suddenly jump above the expected pitch, you'll call attention to the word. It's as effective as making the word louder, without the technical problems.

- Pause slightly before the word. It doesn't have to be a noticeable pause; just . . . break the rhythm slightly. I sometimes manually insert a one-frame or half-frame pause before important words.

Try these techniques aloud at your desk, and listen to the result. Your coworkers may think you're crazy, but you'll become a better director.

Prepare the announcer

As soon as you've got a final script, and ideally a couple of days before the session, note any technical words or jargon. Prepare a pronunciation guide, including which acronyms should be spelled out (such as *N. L. E.*) and which are pronounced as words (such as *Simp-Tee* timecode). Some narrators prefer the guide as a cassette tape or CD; others as a page they can keep referring to. Print out a clean copy of the script, in at least 12-point double-spaced type and using upper- and lowercase. Send the guide and the script to the narrator. If you're planning to e-mail it, make absolutely sure they can handle the file format. If you're sending them a pronunciation guide as MP3, it helps to zip the file and remove the .mp3 extension from its name. Some ISPs seem to randomly trash e-mail with .mp3 attachments, possibly to placate record companies. Web-savvy talent may have an ftp site where you can drop off files.

The announcer might not choose to mark up or even read the entire script, and most assuredly won't memorize it, but at least they'll have a chance to get prepared and familiarize themselves with any difficult terms. Most professionals are very good at glancing at a script and figuring out how to cope with the trouble spots.

If you're not going to have an approved script until the day of the session, send the talent a preliminary version and the pronunciation guide. But let them know how many changes to expect, or what areas are likely to be revised.

If you're using an outside studio, this is also a good time to get them prepared. Make sure the engineer knows how many people you'll be recording at a time and how many extra bodies to expect in the control room. If you're bringing reference audio- or videotapes, make sure the studio will have the equipment to play that format. Verify how you want the narration delivered—every take or just the approved ones; what kind of tape/disc/removable drive you prefer and whether it should be in a specific file format; and how you want any sync marks or timecode. If possible, talk to the engineer who'll be doing the job instead of the studio's traffic manager. Believe me, these messages can get mighty garbled on the way from office to studio.

With good preparation, everything will be ready at the appointed time. The point is saving money: Actors and studios charge the same per hour whether they're performing, watching you phone someone to interpret a complex part of the script, or waiting for an engineer to fetch a cassette deck or extra headset.

> **Budgeting tip:** for long narration or commercial voice-over sessions, each extra body in the control room can add an hour of studio time. For the most efficient sessions, invite only the talent, engineer, director, and one client representative or content expert if necessary. Each additional person with an opinion will slow things down.

Script preparation

The day before the session, find the person who has ultimate approval over the project and make them initial a copy of the script. Remind them that changes will be expensive.

Then read through the final script and break it down, just as you would for a video shoot. Be sure you know where the logical breaks and emotional changes occur. This way, you can decide how the session should flow:

- Multiple takes of the full script might be appropriate for short narrations or when you need emotional continuity.

- Multiple takes of one- or two-page segments can help the actors develop their own characteristic interpretation.

- Recording straight through, but stopping immediately for corrections and pickups, is most efficient for long narrations and anonymous narrators.

Besides, a script breakdown can save you hundreds of dollars in talent fees. If you can separate the characters and schedule them out of sequence, you won't be paying actors to sit around while you record other parts.

At the Session

Now you're ready to have some fun. Radiate two things in the studio: a positive attitude about the project, and unambiguous directions.

I've seen sessions destroyed by a director complaining about the client, budget, or last-minute changes. It might make you feel good to vent those frustrations, but it also tells the talent you don't need their best work on this project. If you can't say anything nice, say something noncommittal that sounds good . . . but don't ever say nothing. The actors and engineer depend on you for specific instructions.

This should start before the tape rolls. Make sure everyone understands what you're looking for, and be ready for actors' questions about meaning or pronunciation. Listen carefully when the engineer is setting levels. If you need a different projection or energy level from the performer, this is the time to speak up. Pay attention to the technical aspects as well; if you don't like what you hear, fix it now before you commit to a setup. The wrong mic position, equalization, gating, or compression will be impossible to repair without re-recording.

As soon as everything's ready, start rolling. There's nothing to be gained from rehearsing an entire voice-over. If characters have to interact dramatically—something that almost never happens in a voice-over—it may be worth rehearsing a couple of key sequences around a conference table. That lets you set the rhythm and emotional development. Otherwise, send them into the studio and start the session.

The Narrators Speak

The best people to tell you how to direct are the performers themselves. So I spoke to two of PBS's busiest: Don Wescott has voiced more than 75 *Nova* episodes, as well as most of the promos for *Mystery, American Experience*, and *Masterpiece Theater*. Wendie Sakakeeny was *Nova's* first female voice and has done almost as many episodes as Don, along with narrations for *National Geographic* and many Fortune 500 companies. Even if you don't watch public television, you've heard both of them in thousands of commercials.

Don: The more you can tell me about the project, the better. It's great to know the audience and who you're trying to appeal to, as well as what's going on in the pictures.

Wendie: But don't waste our time with a whole lot of background information. It doesn't matter how many versions you've done before, or the history of each source in the video. Tell us the attitude and tone and who's going to see it, and then let us do our jobs. What we certainly don't need is for you to read the entire script, paragraph by paragraph.

Don: One guy gave me a 20-minute read . . . in a monotone. He read the entire script. That's crazy. If you have to do a line read, save it for the lines we've read wrong. But definitely give us constant feedback. I love to hear back, "I like this, I don't like that, speed up here, breathe here . . ." The more talkative a director, the better. You have to tell us what's good as well as what's bad.

Wendie: It's important to establish *how* you're going to give direction, and what you expect for retakes. If we make a mistake, let us finish the sentence but don't go on for several paragraphs. Catch us while we're still in the same frame of mind. Also, are you going to slate everything, or just pause? Do you want us to pick up whole paragraphs or just the previous sentence?

Don: There should be just one director. The fewer people in the control room, the better. The best sessions are just the performer, the producer, and the engineer.

Wendie: But make sure the producer is empowered to make changes if something doesn't work. The worst sessions are when the script is written by a committee, and nobody is available to answer questions about it.

Don: You want to be a good director? Come fully prepared and maintain an open flow of communications during the session. And know how to say it yourself.

Tape is cheap, and CD-ROM is even cheaper. Even the first take—with all its mispronunciations and bad timing—might yield some perfect phrases or a replacement syllable when you later discover a problem in the selected take. Record everything. Erase nothing. If you're so strapped that you absolutely must recycle tape stock, wait until after the project is mixed.

How to talk to an actor

There's a fine line between giving your performers sufficient feedback, and being a blabbermouth on the talkback. You have to let them know what to change, and it's always good to tell them what you liked. The key is keeping your directions meaningful. "That was real good, could you do another?" doesn't give the talent much to go on, no matter how many words you say it in.

Most actors will give a better performance if you tell them what you want fixed ("I need more of a sense of pride when you get to *serving our community*") and let them work out the details, rather than tell them exactly how to do it. But if you don't hear what you want on the next take, get more specific ("Slow down on those three words, and stress *community* a little"). If all else fails, give a line read: say it exactly the way you want to hear it, and let them mimic you.

Announcers, as opposed to actors, usually prefer line reads, but only if you as director can read the line properly. You might *think* you're delivering an Oscar-worthy performance, but if the announcer hears a string of monotonous syllables, that's what you'll get back. Improve your line reads by practicing some of the techniques in the section on stress patterns (page 216) and by getting feedback from colleagues.

While you should be decisive, you don't have to be a martinet. If you make a mistake, say so—and be prepared to accept the blame. The most effective direction I've ever heard is "You did exactly what I asked for. But I guess it's not quite what I want." This also invites the performer to help you find a better solution. Directing isn't a zero-sum game, and you don't win any points by making the person in the booth look bad.

When a session goes wrong, directing can turn into an adversarial process or worse. There is a particularly hilarious tape of an Orson Welles voice-over session for a line of frozen foods that has been circulating for years (I got my copy from an older engineer in 1972). The famous actor/director tries to read inept ad agency copy, puts up with a committee of bad directors, and finally blows his stack. You can hear it at www.dplay.com/audio/Orsonplay.htm (the upper-case O is important) . . . or navigate there from my web site's Humor section.

Keep track of things

Slate every take verbally. It doesn't have to be more than a simple "Take 4." This simplifies editing, and lets the talent know you're recording. If you're using a DAT, MiniDisc, or CD recorder, you can save cueing time later by using the Program or Track number as the take number. If you're recording to videotape, have someone note the timecode for each verbal take number. In many studios, the engineer will do the slating. You can concentrate on listening and making notes.

Take lots of notes. Once you hear a great reading for a particular line, write its take number on the script next to the line—even if the rest of the take wasn't very good. You're covered if the talent never reads it that way again, and you'll save lots of time by not having to search for those golden moments.

Notes on a voice-over session should be more comprehensive than a script log from a shoot. Don't just write down that a whole take was good or bad; give yourself enough details to know which phrases particularly impressed you. Then you'll be able to find them immediately while editing, instead of having to play back the entire session again for evaluation. Figure 10.5 shows my notes as I made them during a typical voice-over session. You can see how I've already marked which words will come from which takes. It's not very neat; but, boy, is it efficient.

Besides, once your script is covered with these numbers, you know you've gotten everything you need. Sign the actors' contracts and you're done.

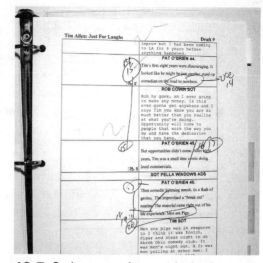

10.5 Script notes after a typical voice-over session

Directing Children

Two factors conspire to add an element of unpredictability to sessions with young children, but if you're aware of them, you'll at least be able to maintain a small element of control:

- The child has to be cooperative.

- The parent—or whoever brought the child to the session—has to be relaxed and willing to let you do your job.

The biggest factor in the child's ability to cooperate is how alert and awake they are. Children have limited attention spans, so plan short sessions (under 10 minutes, if possible) with lots of interaction between you and the child.

One of my favorite props when working with the three- to seven-year-old set is a small stuffed tiger. When the child first shows up for the session, I ask—with complete seriousness—if they'll take care of my tiger for me. I hand them the toy and give the two a minute or so to get acquainted. Then I lead the child (who's still holding the tiger) into the booth and sit them on a chair.

A chair is essential. Otherwise the child will be all over the booth and a different distance from the mic for each line. A short shotgun is usually the best mic to use, since kids generally don't have much projection. The shotgun's lack of bass isn't a problem with young voices.

When we're ready to record I put the tiger on the mic (Figure 10.6), giving the child a familiar face to talk to. This keeps their mouth focused in the right direction, without them having to sit rigidly (or even be aware this was the goal). Since the animal is soft, it doesn't cause reflections into the mic. Just be careful not to block the holes that give the mic directionality.

10.6 A tiger perched on a short shotgun, ready to record a child

Then I sit down across from them, and we have a conversation. Being in the booth with them always seems to result in a better performance than directing via talkback. If I can't structure the material as an ad-lib interview, I break their part down to individual lines. We do two or three takes of each with immediate verbal rewards and specific directions, and then move onto the next line. If they need loosening up, we play a game: I say the line, and they immediately repeat, in as many silly ways as I can. Of course, one or two of those 'silly' ways are the readings I'm looking for.

Kids are distracted by other kids. If you can, don't have more than one in the recording area at a time. Younger children will start paying attention to their compatriots. Older boys—10 years or so and up—start playing to each other and often turn into wise guys. Once one goes, the whole crowd is lost.

Parents should be told what to expect, and be warned that it's unlikely they'll be in the room during the session. Ask them *not* to rehearse the lines; the whole reason you're using children is for their natural, spontaneous performance. (Don't even tell a parent what the lines will be like. They want their children to do an impressive job and may be tempted to do some rehearsing, even though you've asked them not to.) Do ask the parents to make sure the child is fed and rested.

Also, tell parents that it's no problem for them to arrive a little late. Trying to get any kid somewhere unfamiliar at a precise time can produce anxiety for both parent and child. The alternative—arriving too early and then waiting in the car or building lobby—just builds suspense.

Recording Sound Effects

The best time to record prop noises may be during the shoot itself. Throw an extra mic next to the noisy object, if necessary, and fade it up in time for the sound. The result will match the room's acoustics and be perfectly in sync.

A lot of times this may not be possible because the effect mic would be in the shot, because the sound conflicts with dialog, or because the location is just too noisy. In the first two cases, simply record prop sounds right after the take. Everybody's eager to move on to the next setup, but a minute now can save you an hour in postproduction. Scream "room tone" (previous chapter) and everybody will stand still while you record 30 seconds of background sound. Then say "just a second, folks" and make the prop noises.

If you can't record prop noises at the shoot, you'll probably have to foley.

Foley

Today's sound libraries on CD and Internet are remarkably comprehensive—there are collections full of footsteps, and others with nothing but solenoids and switches—and audio workstations let you adjust their sync at the touch of a button. We cover library effects in Chapter 15.

But it's often faster to create the little sounds in real time. Footsteps, clothing rustles, and pen-on-paper effects are prime candidates for what sound editors call *foley* sessions. The name honors Jack Foley, a Hollywood second-unit director and sound genius in the 1940s. The process is fairly simple: play back the picture, mimic what the actors do on screen, and record the result in sync. A good foley artist can watch a scene once, gather props, and record a fairly accurate imitation in a single take. But effective foley is more than just "going through the motions." Professionals have developed tricks over the years to make their foleys more effective, and many of them can be used in your productions.

Proper foley requires a setup similar to ADR, where recording is in sync with picture playback. You can also do what's sometimes called *digital foley*, recording the effects without picture, matching them later in an editing system or audio workstation.

Deciding what to ignore

It's a lot of fun to play with a bunch of noisemakers in the studio, but unless you've got a Hollywood budget and a full set of props, it's usually better to use prerecorded effects rather than foley. Business videos and local television don't need the kind of precision required for the big screen. Production dialog tracks may already have appropriate sounds that just need to be isolated and equalized.

It also helps to add the background sounds before recording foley. A lot of times you'll find a bang or a footstep in the background that can be slid to match the on-screen action. Not only does this save a lot of recording time; it saves tracks and makes mixing easier.

You might also save time by adding the music before a foley session. Hollywood sound editors like to give directors a lot of choices, so they'll create foleys for every little movement. Most never make it to the final mix. Productions with more limited budgets—including a lot of network shows—don't even worry about some foley when there's music playing.

Just the fx

Foley effects should be recorded as cleanly as possible, without any echoes or background noises. Echoes get in the way when you're editing and seldom fit the on-screen environment. Unless a studio is designed for voice recording, it's probably too reverberant to do a good job without lots of blankets or other sound absorbers (Chapter 7).

Small effects are usually recorded best with a short shotgun mic, fairly close to the sound. Larger effects like footsteps need a bit more perspective, with a less directional mic, to keep a constant level. Roll off low frequencies below 90 Hz or so—many mics have a switch that does this—to eliminate the proximity bass boost and match the way the boom was used in production.

Usually foley is recorded in mono, since it'll be panned to the action when the show is mixed. Stereo just wastes tracks and invites phase errors. If you're foleying a main character's movements, keep it in the center with their dialog.

Record as loud as you can. Even small sounds like pencil taps should be recorded at a high volume. This makes it easier to add equalization at the mix and reduces system noise buildup.

Finding appropriate foley props

You'll want to gather a lot of toys—er, professional foley props—to do the job right. The most important is probably a suitcase full of old clothes and papers. Cotton, silk, and wool sound different, so have at least one item of each. A large jacket is usually the most versatile object of clothing, since you can put it on easily for a full sequence as well as rub or rustle it to simulate individual actions. Underwear is seldom necessary (as a sound prop).

Throw in stuff to write with. Newspaper, note paper, cardboard, and fax paper all rattle differently. Pencil, ballpoint, and felt-tip pens have their own sound. Even the suitcase will be useful. You can creak the snaps, hinges, and leather flaps as everything from a briefcase to a pocketbook.

Stock your studio with a couple of different kinds of telephones. Old-fashioned black ones with mechanical bells have a distinctive resonance that you don't find in the modern plastic ones. And don't forget the phonebook: gaffer-tape a big city directory so the pages don't rattle, and throw it on the floor for an instant falling body. (Some people like to slam their arms against a table for falling bodies because it's easier to get the timing right. But it's just as easy to adjust the timing in software. I prefer to reserve the use of my forearms as falling or jumping animals.)

Experiment with different ways to hold each prop. The same coffee cup can have three different sounds depending on whether you hold it by its handle, wrap your fingers around it, or grab it from the top. Even pens and pencils will have a different sound depending on how you hold them.

Foley footsteps

You'll also want pairs of hard- and soft-soled shoes. Unless the script calls for spike heels, the difference between men's and women's shoes is often just a question of walking style, equalization, and gating (see Chapter 16 for how to apply these processes). For best results, wear shorts when walking.

Of course, you'll also need someplace to walk. Many Hollywood studios have *foley pits*—sections of studio floor equipped with sand, gravel, tile, and even waterproof pans for mud and puddles. Each surface has a unique sound. Chances are your building's management would object if you just threw this junk on the floor, but you can still have appropriate walking surfaces:

- If your studio is carpeted, try putting the microphone very close to the floor while you walk. With a little equalization, carpet can be a very convincing grass lawn.

- Of course, if your studio is carpeted, you won't be able to make convincing hardwood or concrete footsteps. It doesn't take much carpentry to build a walk board (see

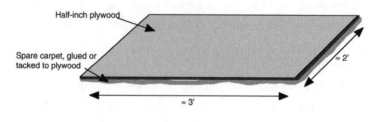

10.7 A walk board for carpeted studios

Figure 10.7) for carpeted studios. Take a piece of half-inch plywood, and glue or tack a few carpet strips on the bottom. The strips keep the wood from sliding around and make the floor sound more solid. Scatter some sand on the plywood, or change the equalization and echo, to get the sound of other surfaces.

- Use something more rigid, such as particle board or doubled plywood, for stairs. The airspace (Figure 10.8) adds an extra hollowness. To "walk" upstairs, use your full weight and scrape the front of your foot slightly against the top edge. For downstairs, eliminate the scraping and land heavily on your heels. If your studio has

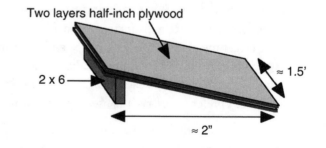
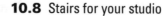

10.8 Stairs for your studio

hardwood or linoleum floors, put some weather-stripping or old rubber tire along the bottom of the 2×6 so the stairs don't creep around.

- A slab of marble or slate from a home supply store can be everything from sidewalks to office lobbies.

- If you don't want to spread gravel around your studio floor, put it in a large canvas or burlap bag. Seal the bag, lay it flat, and go for a walk.

Don't forget, you can also walk with your hands. Fill a large plastic dishpan with sand or gravel—or, to be kinder on your hands, use cornflakes or semisoft cat food—and punch your way across the scene. Close miking, equalization, and a little compression will make the sound bigger.

A supermarket of effects

You'll find a lot of sounds at your local grocery store. As you cruise the aisles, listen for the following:

- *Corn starch*. Look for the small rectangular box. Squeeze the front and back together for perfect footsteps in snow.

- *Dry cat food*. Its shape and consistency make it sound like gravel scraping.

- *Cookie sheets*. Some folks like to rattle them for a classic thunder effect, but I prefer the thunder in a good CD library. On the other hand, they're great for banging; depending on how you hold the sheets and damp their vibrations, they can be anything from the side of a submarine to the hood of a car.

- *Mason jars*. Remove the rubber ring, and you can scrape the glass top against the jar for anything from a mechanical scrape to an ancient stone tomb door. Legend has it that the Martian ships' hatches in Orson Welles's classic *War of the Worlds* broadcast were close-miked mayonnaise jars . . . but only when opened in the proper acoustic of the studio's tile bathroom.

- *Cabbage*. I like to make bodies fall by dropping phone books. But for a really gory fall, slam a head of cabbage against the table.

The art of manual effects owes much to the sound geniuses who brought radio dramas to life in the 1930s and '40s. Today we use digital libraries, workstations, and effects processors, but if you want to learn about the basics, read Robert Mott's *Radio Live! Television Live!: Those Golden Days When Horses Were Coconuts* (2000, McFarland, ISBN 0786408162). It's available through my Web site at www.dplay.com/dv/books.html. And listen to everything.

Recording Ambiences

A continuous track of a separately recorded background, mixed under an entire scene, can smooth out individual edits and lend a sense of reality. Sometimes it may be the only way to simulate reality. Consider a sequence that takes place in a restaurant or busy office. You'll want the extras to be as quiet as possible while you're shooting so you can concentrate on getting good (and editable) dialog tracks. Chances are, they'll mime their luncheon conversations or phone calls. But in the final mix, we have to hear the crowd's voices as well as the clatter of silverware or the office's telephones and printers. In fact, we should hear more than just the on-screen crowd; the assumption is there are other people just out of camera view, making the same kinds of noise.

Since we're hearing a lot more background sounds than we can see sources for on camera, sync becomes a nonissue. If prop sounds from the principal characters match up with their actions, the whole scene appears to be in sync. This means you don't have to worry about recording ambiences at the shoot. You can grab *any* similar restaurant, office, or whatever and it'll sound right. In fact, using background sound is often the only way to achieve the effect of a large busy room with only a few extras and a small shooting stage.

Finding background locations

Look through the script and make a list of different locations that will need sound, including places where there should be active crowds, places with characteristic mechanical sounds (such as generating stations or airplane interiors), and exterior long shots where you're using lavs that won't pick up the natural environment.

You may find it's easiest to get some of the backgrounds from library CDs (Chapter 15). A $75 background CD can include clean recordings of all the environments you need, along with a license to use them in all of your productions. If you're planning to do the final mix at a sound studio, check with the studio's manager; most have large libraries they'll let you dip into for free or a nominal fee.

For backgrounds that won't come from a library, expand your list to include details about the sizes and shapes of the areas and what kind of activities take place in them. This is much better than just listing the areas by name and will keep you from making scouting mistakes. For example, something called "hotel lobby" can be busy or calm; vaulted or low-ceilinged; stark or with lots of furniture; or be next to a restaurant or swimming pool. When you're scouting places to record, look for the characteristics rather than just a building that matches the original name. Your local post office or library can make a better hotel lobby recording than the Holiday Inn down the street.

This can also help prevent you from getting stuck with ambiences that aren't usable. Supermarkets and hotel lobbies usually have music coming from their public address systems. Even if you can identify and license the cuts being played (background music services sometimes use production music libraries), you won't be able to edit it or change the mix. Find a retail operation that doesn't use music, such as a hardware or computer store. If you want to add music to it, use some of the tricks in Chapter 16 to give library cuts an authentic public-address texture that's still mixable and controllable.

Recording backgrounds

I've found that building managers usually won't care if you record backgrounds, so long as you're unobtrusive and the building or its occupants aren't identifiable. In most public spaces, the best strategy is to walk in with a small recorder and mic, make the recording you need, and get out. The only time I've ever been stopped was in a casino, where they have strict rules about electronic equipment.

Omnidirectional mics work nicely for mono recordings and are unobtrusive. Clip a lav to your jacket and carry a small DAT or MiniDisc recorder in a shoulder bag. Even a high-quality cassette recorder will do a good job, since sync isn't an issue. Try to stay perfectly still while you record, so you don't pick up clothing noises. Record for at least a minute if there aren't many spoken voices. If there are voices, record a lot longer; you'll want to do some editing, and any looping to extend a background to fit a scene will become apparent as the voices repeat. If you're sure of your equipment, there's no need to monitor the recording (it's easy enough to go back and repeat a recording that didn't turn out well). But if you must monitor, use Walkman-type phones and pretend you're listening to music.

Since you're not worrying about picking up dialog or distinct sounds, you can use what you learned in Chapter 2 to change the acoustics around the mic and effectively modify the room where you're recording backgrounds. Is a luncheonette during a slow hour still too noisy to be the sophisticated restaurant you need? Hold the mic close to the bench where you're sitting; the back of the bench will mute sounds from that direction, and the padded cushions will absorb high frequencies from the other. Need an office lobby to be noisier and more echoey? Hold the mic close to the floor, or near the building directory or some other area that attracts footsteps.

Stereo backgrounds can add life to a production. If you think stereo is necessary, be aware of possible mono compatibility issues if you're aiming for broadcast, Web, or VHS release. The best mics for that are set up as m/s stereo (Chapter 7), such as the unobtrusive Sony MS-908 shown with a MiniDisc recorder at the end of Chapter 9. You can also get reasonable non-compatible stereo backgrounds with a lav clipped to each shoulder—your head provides separation—or by wearing a binaural mic (they look like headphones, and use the shape of the head and ear to help define the sound field). It may be just as effective to record mono. Gather enough material that you can put different sections of it on separate tracks. Use two sections that were at least 30 seconds apart, panning one somewhat to the left and the other somewhat to the right. Add a little stereo reverb to create a sense of environment.

Vocal Sound Effects

Back in the pretape days, when radio commercials were recorded to vinyl in a single take, a New York sound effects artist was asked to bring some puppy barks to a pet food session. He played through his trunk full of dog recordings at the rehearsal, and nothing satisfied the producer. But when the big moment came, the bark was perfect. Afterward, the producer asked: "What did you do? Change the speed? Equalize? Play two barks at once?" The effects artist walked up to a nearby mic, screwed his mouth sideways, and went "wralf!".

Even with today's immense CD libraries, vocal sounds are used both for convenience and to create unique effects. Learning how to make and manipulate these silly noises can teach you a lot about the human voice and effects design in general . . . and besides, it's a fun topic to end a long chapter.

Vocal sounds are either voiced or unvoiced, depending on whether they're pure breath or if the vocal chords are used. (There's an exhaustive discussion of how vocal sounds are produced in Chapter 13.) Unvoiced noises are more useful as effects because it's easy to turn them into mechanical sounds. Voiced sounds are usually limited to organic things like monsters or insects.

If you work very closely to the microphone, you can also use high-pressure sounds like the plosive /p/ to generate distortion, which makes the sound richer. But you have to be very close, almost touching the mic with your lips. Electret condenser units tend to break up with an ugly crackling sound under these circumstances, so you'll be better off with a mid-priced dynamic.

A few things that can help:

- Use an omnidirectional mic, and put a handkerchief over it to protect from pops.

- Try to find a mic with a built-in windscreen, so you can get closer to the diaphragm.

- Look for a mic with low sensitivity, so you can use more air pressure without overloading the preamplifier.

- Practice by listening to a playback, comparing yourself to sound effects recordings or live sounds. You can't do this with headphones in real time because bone conduction means you'll hear your voice differently than the mic does.

Mouth–sound processing

There's a lot more about editing and processing sound effects later in this book, but some processes apply specifically to vocal effects. Once you've got them recorded, you have to dehumanize them. The first step is to delete any mouth noises, breaths, and handling sounds. Leave some silence between sounds and at the end of the file, so there's someplace for an echo to go. Then listen through for additional cues that the sound came from a human mouth rather than something inhuman—sometimes you'll hear little clicks of saliva or errant voicings in an unvoiced sound—and edit those out. Now you're ready to play.

The first step is to change the pitch. If your program has an option to Preserve Duration when changing the pitch, turn it off. The Clip Speed setting in an NLE can also be used for this. Once a voice gets more than an octave away from its original pitch, the resonances are changed enough that it doesn't sound human any more. Try some radical shifts: at four octaves down, an /s/ sounds like a scraping rock. Try playing with Pitch Bending, a function in many audio-only programs: An /s/ that rapidly drops from very high to very low makes a good laser gun. A tiny slice from the middle of a /z/, at one-third normal pitch, becomes a frog's "ribbit."

Then mess with the envelope. Mechanical sounds usually start abruptly, but human sounds build up over time. Delete the start of one of your noises to give it an abrupt beginning, or use your program's Envelope window to simulate some of the natural envelopes in Chapter 2.

To simulate a machine, collect a variety of short pitch-shifted unvoiced sounds. Edit them together, copy them all, and paste them as multiple loops. This rhythmic repetition can then be pitch-bent to make the machine start up or slow down. Add some flanging for a nice rotary motion.

Equalization helps turn a vocal sound into something less than human. Try dips around 1.75 kHz for unvoiced sounds, and around 300 Hz for the voiced ones, before you start playing with the ends of the band. Machine sounds frequently benefit from a few sharp peaks between 500 Hz and 1.5 kHz.

Many of the microphone techniques for creating vocal sound effects were developed by Wes Harrison, an entertainer who has built a career of mouth sounds and comedy as "Mr. Sound Effects." He started in the mid-1950s as many of the explosions in MGM's classic *Tom and Jerry* cartoons, and he was both the baby seal and the storm in Disney's *20,000 Leagues Under the Sea*. As of this writing, almost 50 years later, he's still going strong. You can hear him in night-clubs around the world. And he's still hilarious, with a comic style reminiscent of Red Skelton at his prime (but using noises instead of physical shtick). If you're lucky enough to catch his act, it'll be both professional education and entertainment. There's a short segment of his work, from his self-produced album, on this book's CD (Track 38).

Section IV

Postproduction

✔ There's a writer/producer I work with, who loves every part of the production except the very last step: saying the project is done. His preference would be to tweak projects endlessly in postproduction, in a search for creative perfection. Unfortunately, his clients and investors can't wait that long. He once told me, "A video is never finished. It's just taken away."

✔ This last section of the book is about getting the best audio in the least amount of postproduction time, so you can use whatever's left—before they take the project away—for additional creative tweaking.

The whole idea of "postproduction" originated in the glory days of Hollywood, where tasks were broken up so studios could crank out dozens of films simultaneously. Films were shot—that's *production*—and then edited and mixed in *post*production; then they were released from the assembly line.

These days post is anything you do after you've struck the set and may include insert shots, new recording, computer-generated images, and a lot of other content creation. For some documentaries and commercials, the whole project is done with stock footage and computers; there's no production; only post postproduction.

Overview and Tricks

The world is linear. Noon always comes one minute after 11:59 AM. Productions are linear as well. Even interactive CDs and DVDs are built out of essentially linear sequences. Humans can't handle nonlinear time, so the very idea of nonlinear editing is an oxymoron.

The terms "linear" and "nonlinear" actually refer to the timeline that a production is built on, and how much control we have over it. It has nothing to do with whether a production is analog or digital.

But the decision to use linear or nonlinear editing can have important implications for how sound is handled.

Linear Editing

In linear editing, the timeline is inviolate. It starts at the head of the production, runs for the duration of the project, and then stops. You can copy things onto the timeline or erase things from it, but you can't change the timing of the line itself.

If you're editing video in a linear online session, the timeline is the master tape. Scenes are assembled by copying camera shots from a playback deck to the desired place on the master. Usually they're copied sequentially—shot 1, then shot 2—but there's no technical reason you can't copy them out of order, leave a hole for some shots to be put in later (Figure S.1), or insert new video over an existing sequence. Dissolves and other effects are performed in real time and recorded on the master tape along with the images. Since the program is built onto the master tape, there's no rendering process; as soon as the last edit is complete, the job is done.

The problem is that once something is on a linear timeline, it can't be moved. You can erase or record over a scene, but you can't nudge it a couple of frames without re-recording it. If everything in a show is perfect except the third shot is four frames too long, you can't cut out just those frames. You have to re-record the next shot four frames earlier, and—unless you care to stretch something—you also have to re-record everything after it.

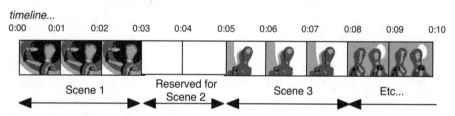

S.1 A linear-edit timeline can be assembled out of sequence.

In linear audio for video, the timeline is usually a multitrack tape locked to the video master by timecode, but sometimes it's multiple audio tracks on the master video itself. Sounds are recorded on tracks as both audio and video are played, but—as with linear video—you can't change the timing of an element without re-recording it.

When all the tracks are assembled the way they should be, they're mixed onto a final master.

Nonlinear Editing

Nonlinear editing revolutionized video production in the late 1980s, but it added only one new concept: the ability to pick up and move whole pieces of previously assembled timeline. It was a crucial difference.

In nonlinear video editing, all of the images are stored in a computer, usually on hard disk (though other random-access media can be used). As far as the computer's concerned, the timeline is really just a database: a list describing what part of its storage will be played back at any moment. When you move scenes around, the nonlinear editor—usually called an NLE—merely rearranges the database (Figures S.2 and S.3). Only a few bytes of data are involved, so this appears to happen instantly.

When the program is finished, complex effects are created by combining data from different places on the hard disk; then all the images are retrieved according to the database and either shown in real time and recorded to videotape, or copied onto one large file.

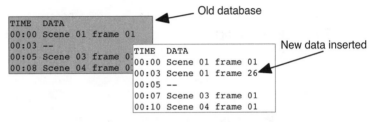

S.2 Nonlinear editing is really just database management . . .

At the deepest software level, many nonlinear systems can be thought of as just incredibly fast linear database editors. The databases themselves can even be linear: when you insert or rearrange a scene, the system copies part of the data list from hard drive to temporary storage, rearranges it, and then "dubs" it back.

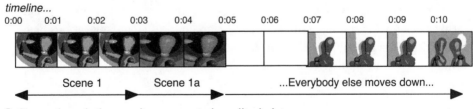
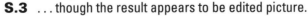

S.3 . . . though the result appears to be edited picture.

Nonlinear audio editing works just about the same way, with multiple databases—one for each track—relating to sounds stored on hard disk. Since audio editing isn't frame-based and can be more precise than video, the counting system is more elaborate. Sophisticated systems keep track of individual samples (see Chapter 3). Effects such as reverb or compression can either be created during the editing process and stored elsewhere on the disk, or be noted in the database and applied on final playback.

Linear versus Nonlinear for Video Editing

The primary advantages of linear video editing are speed and simplicity. There's no time wasted on digitizing, file transfers, or rendering, so a long program with just a few edits can be put together in little more than the length of the show itself. The equipment is simple: all you need is one or more playback decks, a video recorder, and some way to control the decks and select the signal. The concept is even simpler—cue both decks and press Play on one while you press Record on the other[1]—even though it may take a lifetime to master the art involved.

The primary disadvantage of linear editing *used to be* loss of quality. Each time an analog tape is copied, it picks up distortion and noise (see Chapter 3). But digital videotape and signal chains don't suffer from this. These days, the disadvantages of linear editing are the equipment cost and the time it takes to cue and record each individual edit.

Linear editing may be faster or slower than nonlinear.

- Linear wastes very little time on "overhead." There's no need to preload video, render, or dub the final project to a master tape.

- But the edits themselves take place in real time, plus a few seconds for cueing and locking.

- If a program is long and doesn't have many edits, linear editing will be faster. But if it's short and has complex sequences, nonlinear will be faster.

The primary advantages to nonlinear video editing are that it's easy to make changes to a sequence, and that the equipment can be small and inexpensive—all you need is a video recorder and a computer. On the other hand, nonlinear systems have steep learning curves and are subject to setup and configuration troubles. Unless you're already an expert or very lucky, or purchase a turnkey system and training seminars, you'll find yourself facing mysterious blank frames, loss of lip sync, or other troubles—and you might not be able to tell whether it's your fault, the software's, or some incompatibility in the system.

Implications for Audio

You have to pay more attention to audio during a linear editing session than during a nonlinear one. If the sound quality doesn't match across a cut, it may be almost impossible to correct it after the program is done. Unless you have an automated mixer linked to the video editor, cross-

---

1. Okay, that's just the concept. To do this for real also involves preroll, synchronization, vertical-interval switching, and things like that, but an editing computer usually takes care of this dirty work.

fades have to be done in real time by moving faders while you're watching the picture. Equalization and other corrections have to be applied on the fly, and you can't go back to change them without redoing the edit.

To handle sound properly in a linear edit, you absolutely must have good audio monitors and the time to pay attention to them. You also need a clean audio path, with good wiring and a high-quality mixer. If there's a sound problem and you can't fix it immediately, you may have to live with it forever. On the other hand, you can hear as soon as something goes wrong. And the most common audio problem with nonlinear editing—lost sync—almost never happens in a linear editing suite.

Nonlinear editing gives you more flexibility, but this can be a double-edged sword. While you've got the freedom to put off audio decisions during the visual editing process, this often translates to a carelessness about sound. There's a tendency for visually oriented producers to consider a project done when the pictures are finished, and blast through the audio mix without paying attention. Since most NLEs don't let you hear all of the audio effects at full quality until they're rendered in final form, you can miss problems that would be quickly spotted in a linear edit session.

To make things worse, NLEs are often supplied with miniature monitors and set up in rooms with bad acoustics. The next chapter discusses some of ways to help this, but with many NLE setups, you couldn't do a good mix if you wanted to!

On the other hand, audio elements don't need to be copied or changed during the nonlinear process. There are fewer ways for their quality to be accidentally compromised. You have to get sounds accurately into the computer when you start the project (see Chapter 12); but once you've done that, you don't have to worry about them until it's time to concentrate on the track.

This means you can put off critical mix decisions until you have a chance to think about them, and you can move these decisions to a different editing station . . . or to a separate facility with good monitoring and control equipment.

Audio Options Beyond the NLE

Video-editing software is designed to manipulate pictures, and its audio capabilities—even on the big-name systems—are often minimal. You can add expensive processing plug-ins, but you'll still be limited by the NLE's software. Fortunately, audio and video are kept as separate files within the computer. Edited or raw elements can be exported in standard formats, on CD-ROM or audio CDs, without losing any quality. They can be processed or mixed elsewhere, and then get married back to the picture.

All this means you've got lots of choices for how to manipulate audio in a nonlinear environment.

Edit and mix within the NLE

This approach usually restricts you to editing on frame lines, which may be too far apart for precise audio edits. It also can limit what mixing and processing tools are available, though many of the plug-ins that work with mainstream audio applications are also usable—with certain limits—in the video software. On the other hand, staying inside the NLE is fast and simple, and you don't need to learn a new program.

Edit in the NLE's computer, but with a separate audio program

This choice gives you a lot more audio-editing power. It's also cheaper than buying a dedicated system: good audio-only software costs just a few hundred dollars and can share plug-in processors with the NLE. Since both the audio editor and the NLE will be using the same drives, only a single set of files is necessary, and you don't have to worry about networking. However, both these kinds of programs demand processing power and a lot of RAM, so it might not be possible to use them simultaneously. And using a separate audio program does nothing to solve problems you may have with the monitors and acoustic environment in your work space.

Edit/Mix in a digital audio workstation

Software publishers like to call their sound programs digital audio workstations (DAWs), but the "workstation" part suggests there should be specialized hardware as well. Dedicated controllers, with jog/shuttle wheels and fullsize mixing faders, are available for audio programs like ProTools and Digital Performer. This is essential, since a mouse won't let you do the constant rebalancing between voice, music, and effects that are essential in a good video mix. High-end DAWs like professional versions of ProTools (it's a silly concept, but you can get an amateur version of Pro-Tools) also use dedicated, multiple digital signal processor (DSP) chips to do complex processing in real time. The very best systems even have dedicated towers, running specialized operating systems that are essentially crash-proof.

Most professional DAWs can share file formats and removable drives with an NLE. In large facilities, audio- and video-editing systems are often networked together and communicate using Ethernet to a central server.

But the biggest advantage to working in a DAW may have nothing to do with the hardware or software. Because they're expensive and can have a fairly steep learning curve, they're usually installed in rooms with good monitoring facilities and maintained by people who understand audio.

Organizing Postproduction Audio

Polish the video first. It's silly to try to fine-tune a soundtrack if the picture isn't finished. Audio moves in continuous sweeps rather than individual images, so trivial picture edits may require large segments of track to be rebuilt. Audio edits can also help smooth over abrupt picture cuts.

However, don't put off *thinking* about the soundtrack until after the picture is done . . . by then, it's too late to do a good job. There's a definite order to approaching the job, if you want the best track with the least amount of bother:

1. Decide which sequences will be driven by nonsync audio, and make sure you have the necessary elements (music for montages, voice-over, and so on).

2. Edit the picture, along with its dialog or any nonsync audio that drives it. If you can't edit the sound smoothly, put the audio across alternating tracks and provide *handles*—a few seconds of extra sound at the in- and out-points

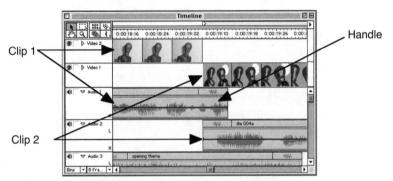

S.4 A handle extends sync audio past the picture edit.

(Figure S.4). These can be used later for correcting sound problems and fixing transitions.

3. Drop in any sounds that are necessary for plot development, such as phone bells, explosions, and off-camera dialog. Do this before committing to a final edit because you might have to extend or shorten a scene to accommodate the sound. Don't obsess about sounds that aren't perfect; it's okay to use what you have as a placeholder and plan to change it later.

4. Get the necessary approvals for the video, make any required changes, and lock the picture. Make sure everyone involved understands that from now on, any picture changes that affect timing—even by one frame—will also affect the cost or complexity of the track.

5. Fine-tune the audio elements. There's also a definite order that makes this more efficient (See "Audio Priorities" on page 241.).

6. Mix the track and get *it* approved.

7. Finish the job: layback the track to videotape, or import it back to the nonlinear editor for final rendering.

Titles and other visual effects can be added at the same time the sound is being finished, if they won't have any effect on sync. Obviously, visual effects that are linked to sounds—explosions, flames, or a laser whoosh as the title is revealed—must be in place before the final mix.

Dealing with Nonsync Audio

It's important to have voice-overs and music available before you start cutting, because they influence how the picture is edited. But it's not important to have the same ones you'll use in the final mix.

Scratch tracks

Many producers prefer not to record the voice-over of a long project until the picture is fully cut, because any script changes may require another recording session. Sometimes you don't even know what has to be changed until the picture is edited.

But without a narration track, it's difficult to cut the picture. You have to guess how long each line will take, and edit in a sterile environment with no audio reference. This is extra work both for the video editor and for some poor narrator who will then have to read each line to an arbitrary timing.

Instead, record a temporary narration track in your own voice. Quality isn't important—you can use a cheap multimedia mic, and record right at your editing station. What *is* important is that you speak slowly and meaningfully, simulating the pace you'll want from the professional narrator. You can edit precisely to the scratch track; when you place key images and titles to fit against your own reading, chances are they'll still line up against the high-priced talent's version.

Besides, if your client approves a project hearing your amateur narration, think of how blown away they'll be when they hear a professional doing the job.

Temporary music

Hollywood editors often use a "temp track," borrowing a piece of a pop song or even one of the studio's other film scores, and cut montages and other music-driven sequences to it. When the final score is created, the composer can use the temp as a guide for tempo and feel. Occasionally a director falls so much in love with the temporary music that they buy the rights to it and use it in the finished film.

If you're dealing with lower-than-Hollywood budgets, however, It's probably not a good idea to borrow existing copyrighted music to use this way. If someone falls in love with the piece, you'll have to tell them they can't afford the rights to use it (copyright law doesn't forgive an infringement just because someone made a mistake). Besides, it's easy to get so used to hearing a particular piece of music that nothing else—no matter how good—will sound right.

Instead, use a rough version of the actual music you're planning to use. If the video is going to have an original score, get the composer to throw together a demo of the scene's music. If you're buying library music, select the pieces for that scene before you start editing. Don't worry about the roughness of a demo or problems with specific aspects of the library cut; you can fine-tune after the picture is edited. In the meantime, you'll have the right feel and rhythm to cut against, and you won't have to worry about client disappointment in the final mix.

Audio Priorities

Once the picture is cut, it's most efficient to approach the remaining audio operations in a definite order:

1. Clean up the dialog first. It tells the story. Take advantage of cutaways and extreme wide shots to smooth out a performance or fit in an alternate performance.

2. Edit the narration second. It explains what we're seeing. If you've been using a scratch narration track, now's the time to replace it with the real thing. Chapter 13 has some tips on both narration and dialog editing.

3. Replace any plot-critical effects that need fixing. Ignore smaller sync effects for now; you might not need to waste time on them after the music and ambiences are in place.

4. Insert the music. If you're using library cuts, trim them to length. It doesn't take much effort or musical talent to stretch or shorten a piece of music seamlessly (Chapter 14 teaches you how).

5. Add background ambiences. Don't do this until you've added the music. In a lot of video projects—even big-budget network dramas—music can take the place of ambience.

6. Add whatever smaller sync effects seem to be missing. A lot of times, you'll find that a random noise from an ambience track can be nudged a few frames to take the place of a sync effect.

7. Mix.

8. Dub to the final medium. This may be a videotape or timecode DAT, or a file to be imported back to the NLE or DVD mastering system.

Mixing and Editing are Separate Functions

Modern DAWs can handle editing and mixing almost simultaneously. You can start mixing a sequence, notice a dialog glitch or misplaced effect and fix it immediately, and then continue mixing where you left off. You can also begin mixing a scene, decide that you don't like one particular cross-fade or level, rewind to where the problem began, and start mixing again. The system will join the various parts of the mix seamlessly. These are great conveniences . . . but only if you don't take advantage of them too often.

While the computer lets you develop a mix in pieces, it's not a good idea from a human point of view. Audio develops over time. Your viewers will watch the scene as a continuous whole, and it's almost always best to mix it the same way. There's more about mixing in Chapter 17.

Chapter 11

Postproduction Hardware

Rose's Rules:

✔ The tools you use in video editing affect the technical quality of your track.[1] Any damage you do here will be difficult or expensive to fix later.

✔ When you set up an edit system, it's often more important to pay attention to detail than to spend a lot of money.

✔ The most important audio equipment you can own is the monitor amplifier and speakers. If these aren't right, you won't be able to get the best performance out of anything else.

---

1. There's only one exception: if you're importing dialog to an NLE via FireWire or other digital wiring, getting all other audio from files or ripped CDs, and will be exporting individual edited tracks as files to mix elsewhere.

Nonlinear editing systems never exist in a vacuum. They need other equipment to be usable. You'll want a set of reliable audio monitors, at least. If you're also going to use this system for input and output—that is, if you're not going to be getting all of your elements as preformatted files, and deliver in a computer format—you'll also need video and audio decks, routing and control equipment, and audio wiring. Even the simplest installation requires attention because how you handle signals will make a difference in what your finished track sounds like.

Monitoring

The quality of your monitoring system doesn't directly influence anything in your soundtrack. Signals don't pass through your speaker or amplifier on their way to the viewer. But your monitors are the most important piece of audio equipment you can own. That's because signals pass through them on the way to your brain, where they affect every decision you make.

Before you go out to buy new or better monitors, take a look around your editing room: the environment where you work can have as much of an influence on the sound as the speakers themselves.

Editing Room Acoustics: When Good Speakers Go Bad

You're ready to edit your magnum opus. You put up color bars and adjust the monitor so everything is a mellow shade of rose pink or a shocking green. Then you smear grease on the picture tube, splash some white paint around it, and—just for good measure—adjust a strong light so it glares off the screen (Figure 11.1).

11.1 It's just a cartoon, folks . . . but some people mix with the aural equivalent.

Maybe that's not how you work on pictures, but I've seen a lot of editing rooms where they do exactly that to the track. Badly positioned speakers—in some cases, they don't even face the operator—interact with the room's walls. The combination actually blurs the sound. Speakers are chosen because they sound flattering in this blurred environment, rather than because they reveal the truth.

It's not hard to set up a good listening environment. It just requires a little thought and some elementary physics.

As you learned in Chapter 2, the echoes in a room can interfere with a sound in ways that aren't immediately obvious. You don't hear it as an echo, but you do hear cancellations and reinforcements of different pitches in the sound, affecting its color or timbre. And this effect can change drastically, depending on where you are in the room. In many desktop editing environments, the highs you hear directly in front of the video monitor can be different from what a client hears two feet away.

You cannot fix this with an equalizer, even if you care only about a single listening position. That's because the problem can be drastically different at frequencies that are too close together for an equalizer to pick out, and it varies with the distances between speaker, wall, and listener—moving your head six inches can change what you hear. It's even influenced by room temperature.

Soft and hard

The best solution is careful edit-room design. By calculating how different wavelengths will cancel or reinforce, you can plan the room dimensions to smooth out the sound. If you're building a new studio from scratch, pick up a book on acoustics and learn how simple changes in the floor plan can make tremendous differences to the sound. (I'd recommend those by F. Alton Everst, such as *Sound Studio Construction on a Budget*. They're understandable and relatively non-mathematical. You can buy them at a discount through my Web site, at www.dplay.com/dv/books.html.)

But if it's too late to move the walls—or, if for some reason, the building's owners disapprove—you can still use some rule-of-thumb acoustic science to correct a bad-sounding room. Go back to the second part of Chapter 7, and read some of the ways to improve the sound at a location. Substitute your editing position for the microphone, and the monitor speakers for the actors, and the same techniques will work in the editing suite.

Homemade sound eater

Luxury postproduction facilities have posh treatments and careful acoustic design. But the non-linear editing suites in television stations, corporate environments, and kitchen-table production companies tend to be random rooms with bare walls. Absorption is almost always needed to make these rooms sound good.

You can buy studio-quality absorbers and diffusers from acoustic consultants for a hefty price. Or you can build reasonably efficient fiberglass absorbers for very little money, using only minimal carpentry skills. The key is to use the right kind of fiberglass. Owens-Corning #703 is a semirigid yellow board designed for sound and is much denser than the pink fluffy stuff sold as home insulation. A carton of 80 square feet, in 2-foot-by-4-foot panels two inches thick, costs under $75 at hardware superstores, acoustic suppliers, or ceiling contractors in most big cities.

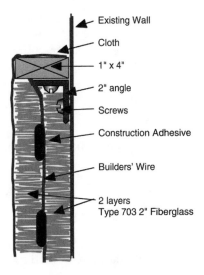

Existing Wall
Cloth
1" x 4"
2" angle
Screws
Construction Adhesive
Builders' Wire
2 layers
Type 703 2" Fiberglass

11.2 Basic, low-cost wall-mounted absorber.

Figure 11.2 shows the basic construction. The overall size isn't critical, but try to cover about half of the total area in a stripe from a couple of feet below ear level to a couple of feet above (if you're seated, that's around 2–6 feet from the floor), on any wall that's causing problems. The worst offenders are usually the wall directly behind your editing position, and the side walls from a few feet in front of you to a few feet behind. Tiny scraps of fiberglass can fly around during construction, so wear long sleeves as you do the following:

1. Build a rectangular frame out of 1-inch-by-4-inch pine, cut to fit the wall area. The finished panels won't weigh much, so you can attach the frame to the wall with a couple of small angle brackets and not leave too much damage if you have to move.

2. (Optional) Nail a couple of flat strips of rough 1-inch-by-2-inch furring strip (also called *strapping*) to the wall, across the length of the frame. This will space the panels out from the wall, trapping sound better. But you can skip this step if you don't want to mess the walls up.

3. Lay a piece of #703 inside, cut to fit the frame. Friction should hold it in place while you work. Secure the fiberglass with a few lengths of galvanized builders' wire stapled to the inside of the frame.

4. Stick another layer of #703 on top of the first piece. A few dabs of construction adhesive will keep it from sliding around.

5. Cover the whole thing with decorative cloth, burlap, or even brightly printed bed sheets. In commercial buildings, you'll probably need flame-retardant cloth, available from upholstery suppliers for a few dollars a yard more than the stuff that burns.

One-by-four pine is less than four inches wide—it's one of those ancient lumberyard traditions—so four inches of fiberglass will be slightly thicker than the frame. The furring strip, if you used it, will add about 7/8 inch. If you don't like the way this bulges the cloth, use wood cut to an exact width. If you want a more professional appearance, replace the top layer and cloth with wedge-shaped foam tiles (available from audiovisual suppliers). The foam wedges don't absorb much better than the fiberglass does, but they look good, and their shape provides some diffusion at high frequencies.

Adding more diffusion to a room is even easier: a few shelves filled with random-size books or tape boxes will do an excellent job.

The nearfield solution

The other way to conquer room acoustics relies on the inverse-square law: if a sound has to travel twice as far, it becomes four times softer. Make the distance from speaker-to-ear significantly less than the distance from speaker-to-wall-to-ear, and the echoes will be relatively less important.

That's the secret behind *nearfield monitors*, the square boxes you often see perched on top of the console in recording studios. These speakers are very close to the engineers' ears, so the engineer hears a lot more of them than of the reflections off distant walls. Nearfields have only a couple of problems:

- By definition, only a small area can be within the "near" field. So the monitors are effective in only one place. Unless you all sit very closely together, the producer, editor, and client will hear something totally different.

- It's next to impossible to get a good sound out of a box that's small enough to fit on the top of a console. Typical cube and small bookshelf speakers are notorious for distortion and limited bandwidth.

One high-tech solution is to integrate smallish speakers with a precisely calibrated amplifier. But it takes a lot of engineering and expensive components to do this right, and the professional versions that actually sound good can cost a few thousand dollars per pair, much more than equivalent full-size monitors. More modestly priced speaker/amplifier combos—those for many hundred dollars—are often full of compromises that cause uneven response at various frequencies, and distortion at both ends of the band. Speakers like this aren't suitable for professional mixing. Low-cost amplified "multimedia" speakers, costing as much as $200 a pair, may offer pleasing sounds for gaming or listening to MP3s—but can lead to awful video mixes, which may be nothing like what your viewers will hear.

Choosing Monitor Speakers

If you're going to be mixing with your NLE setup, you need good speakers. These aren't necessarily speakers that "sound good." Most people are partial to speakers with too much bass and a missing midrange because it's flattering to a lot of popular music. Many manufacturers deliberately build their speakers this way. But speakers like this will cause you to make bad decisions in the mix.

Fortunately, there are strategies you can adopt to help find speakers you can rely on . . . even if you're not blessed with golden ears.

The theoretical case against small speakers

Some people claim you should always mix on tiny speakers because they represent a worst-case scenario: if a track can make it there, it can make it anywhere. But if you think about what those speakers are really telling you, you'll realize they can't be relied on at all. Figure 11.3 shows the frequency distribution of a typical voice (black) and music (gray) track, as measured in Waves' PAZ psychoacoustic analysis plug-in. The relative heights show

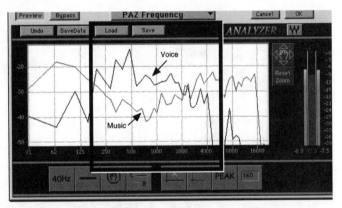

11.3 A small speaker can give you the wrong idea about voice/music proportions.

how much energy is in either track at any frequency. I've drawn the black box to indicate the accurate range of a typical desktop monitor—between approximately 200–7,000 Hz.

If you only look inside the box, you'll think the voice is louder than the music. Play this mix on a speaker that sounds like this, and you'll think it's fine. But if you look outside the box—or hear the mix played on a better loudspeaker—you'll discover there's much more overall energy to the music. The voice would get lost on a good system—and you'd never know it on this speaker.

Even if your viewers don't have the best of speakers in their sets, this track is likely to find its way through a number of compressors and other level-control devices before it gets to them. Every time the music hits a loud note, these processors will squash the entire mix down—even if the note is in a range that small speakers would ignore. (TV stations use multiband processors to reduce this problem, but many of them also pass the signal through wide-band compressors with the same unfortunate effect. Cable networks, Internet broadcasters, and DVD-authoring stations usually have just the wide-band units.)

It's fine to check a mix on small speakers, but making primary mix decisions on them misplaces the track's priorities: you're sacrificing how voices will be heard on better sets, to favor how music is heard on poorer ones. Video is a dialog-driven medium. If anything is at risk, it should be the music.

The real-world case against small speakers

So far we've dealt with small speakers in the abstract. But once you get to real-world examples, the problem isn't just lost highs and lows—it's also what the speaker does to the middle. Good full-size monitor speakers are accurate over their entire range. Mixes you do on them will sound right on any other good monitor and will at least be predictable on most tiny monitors. But bad speakers are random; corrections that improve the sound on one may make it a lot worse on another.

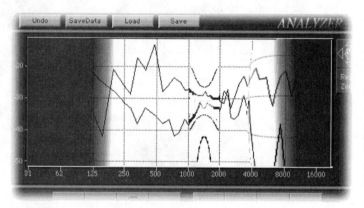

11.4 One popular small monitor is this uneven with the frequencies it *can* handle.

For example, there's a small powered monitor that's been popular for years. It looks professional, even has XLR connectors, and is often bundled with expensive dedicated nonlinear editors. It doesn't sound professional. A speaker-designer friend of mine tested them with lab equipment, and I used what he discovered to retouch our frequency-analysis plot. The result is Figure 11.4 . . . not that Waves' PAZ will ever look like this on your screen, but it does accurately depict how these speakers distort the sound balance.

The high and low ends disappear in the figure because they also do in the speaker. While the manufacturer claims a low-frequency limit of 80 Hz, things are very quiet down there. In reality, the bass starts to fall off drastically at 150 Hz and is essentially too soft to be useful by 100 Hz. The opposite happens to the highs: to reach a claimed 13 kHz cutoff, they apply a gigantic boost at 8 kHz . . . so these speakers tempt you to turn the midhighs much lower than is appropriate! To top it all off, there's a major dip between 1–2 kHz—probably to make pop music sound better on them. Nobody could do an accurate mix with this kind of frequency response. Worse, all that equalization adds significant distortion.

A different multimedia speaker is often bundled with dual-processor towers, high-end video cards, and expensive NLE software. It consists of multiple 1-inch diameter speakers in a narrow stick, designed to sit on either side of your monitors. This arrangement is even worse: along with the uneven response caused by intentional equalization, the frequency response changes depending on where your head is. That's because the length of the path from each speaker to your ear will be different, causing random cancellations and reinforcements (Chapter 2).

Subwoofers

Those stick-like speaker systems come with a subwoofer, another approach that doesn't work for video mixing. It's similar to the "satellite" systems sold by respected speaker companies for unobtrusive home or restaurant music listening. Bass notes aren't very directional and don't get affected as much by room reverberation, so a system like this can give you great flexibility in how it's mounted. But the thumping bass it provides doesn't tell you what a track will sound like on television. Almost all of these systems split the band in the middle of critical speech frequencies—exactly where most well-designed small speakers are most sensitive—and distort or lose signal where you need the most accuracy. They're great for background music—and useless for critical listening. The only time they're appropriate is if you know the viewer will also be using identical speakers—which might be the case in an interactive kiosk—and the track will never be played anywhere else.

Subwoofers, in and of themselves, are not the problem. Theatrical surround-sound systems use them effectively, but they also use full-size speakers for the main channels. This way, the subs can concentrate on much lower frequencies than those in satellite systems. Critical sound in a theatrical surround system is carried by full-range, properly located speakers, and the subwoofer is used just to enhance bass notes.

You might conclude from the previous that I think computer-store multimedia speakers—either stand-alone ones, or those with subwoofers—are horrible for mixing video. You'd be right.

How about headphones? Headphones can be helpful when editing, because they block out distractions and let you hear details of the dialog. But they're *too* detailed for mixing. Even ones with accurate sound will lead to a mix that's too subtle. You'll probably make sound effects or music too soft to compete with dialog, and subsidiary voices too soft to work with principal ones. Unless you're sure the audience will be listening with headphones, don't mix with them.

Choosing full-size speakers

If you want to know what you're mixing, you need full-size monitors. Your best source is a broadcast or studio supplier, or a high-end audio dealer, rather than an electronics chain or music store.

Read the specs: It's a dead giveaway when a manufacturer brags about a speaker's frequency range, but doesn't say how much the sensitivity varies within that range. Watch out for specifications on speakers with built-in amplifiers; some quote impressive numbers and even supply a frequency-response graph, but they note in tiny type that these ratings apply only to the amp.

On the other hand, you can trust your muscles. Try to lift the speaker. Professional speakers use much heavier components, both for rigidity and to generate stronger magnetic fields. If an amplifier is built in, it'll have a large power transformer.

Train your ears to know when a speaker is doing a good job (this will also help you do better mixes). Enlist the aid of a friendly studio engineer, and listen to a good program mix in a studio. The narration should sound natural and close-up, with the consonants perfectly clear. The music should have a sheen or high-end sparkle. Listen for a full bass sound, but don't be swept away by deep bass that gets thrown away in the broadcast process. Get familiar with the relative ratio of voice to music sound on this mix. Then have the engineer make a copy of it on CD.

Go to a dealer where you can audition different speaker systems simultaneously. Pick two stereo speaker pairs, adjust them to the same volume, and switch back and forth while you listen to that CD. Start with the best two pairs the dealer has to offer, and work your way down in quality (or price) until you notice that the disc doesn't sound like it did in the studio any more. Go back up one notch—that's the speaker for you. (If the speaker you choose is out of your budget, don't feel bad. It merely means that you've got better hearing than somebody in your financial league has a right to expect. Settle for the best speakers you can afford, and try to stay aware of what's missing in them.)

Be wary of dealers who won't let you switch between speakers, don't have a way to let you match the volume of two different systems (the speaker that's louder almost always sounds better), or won't let you play your own CD. Relying on well-known manufacturers can help, but it's not infallible; one of the biggest names forbids its dealers from demonstrating their products alongside any competing ones. It's scary, but they sell a lot of speakers to people who don't know any better, and can't hear equivalent but cheaper competitors for comparison.

Speaker setup

Once you've got the speakers, mount them rigidly—loose mounting can absorb bass notes. The tweeters should point toward your listening position and be about at ear level, because high frequencies are the most directional. There shouldn't be anything between the entire speaker and the listener; a computer monitor, part of a tower, or even a CD player can reflect high frequencies away from you.

One of the best arrangements for speakers is an equilateral triangle, slightly above ear

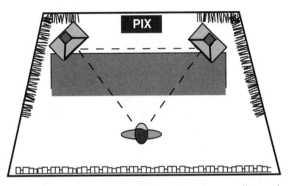

11.5 Speakers and you should form an equilateral triangle.

level and pointed down, as shown in Figure 11.5. That control room also uses absorption around the front and sides, has a bookshelf diffuser on the back, and uses another technique—splaying the side walls so echoes don't build up between them.

Choosing an Amplifier

Don't skimp on the size of the amplifier, either. Professional ported-design loudspeakers might need only 10 watts per channel for average speech-level mixing (acoustic suspension designs are more power-hungry), but that's just the average. Peak requirements are many times higher, and an amp that can't handle the load will sometimes generate a form of distortion that actually damages the speaker elements. Fifty clean watts is an absolute minimum per channel.

Building a good amp is a lot easier than building a good speaker, and higher-end amps from consumer-electronics stores can be perfectly adequate for driving your professional speakers—the only major differences between a top hi-fi amp and a studio one are ruggedness and reliability. Again, weight is a good guide: a decent amplifier needs a good power supply, and, in consumer amps, that always means a heavy power transformer. (Some music mixers prefer the sound of vacuum tube amplifiers. These will be even heavier because of their output transformers. However, tubes present absolutely no advantage—and a lot of disadvantages—in a digital video mixing suite.)

If you're buying the amp at a consumer retailer, it may come with a built-in FM tuner. This isn't a problem in itself, but check to make sure the FM sound doesn't leak through when you're using one of the line inputs. Other features to check:

- The stereo image should stay rock-stable as you raise or lower the volume control, and not drift from side to side. A cheap volume control won't have its channels matched properly across the entire range, and that can fool you into making bad balancing decisions in your mix. It also suggests the manufacturer might have cheapened things elsewhere as well.

- Tone controls are worthless on a monitor amp. All they'll do is stop you from hearing what's really in your mix. Since a consumer amp inevitably comes with tone controls, look for a switch to defeat them—or at least a detent to keep their knobs set to a neutral position.

- "Extended bass," "Hyper-bass," and even "Loudness" are tone controls in disguise. They won't do you any good. If an amp comes with these features, make sure you keep them turned off.

Room equalization

Some professional studios have installed equalizers in their monitor amplifiers to boost or cut specific frequencies and smooth out the speaker's performance. Don't even think about trying this with the tone controls in a consumer amp. Their action is much too broad for this and will do more harm than good. In fact, I'd recommend against doing it under any circumstances. Unless you've got very good speakers and carefully tuned acoustics, the necessary correction will add its own distortion—even if you're using a high-quality equalizer. And you can't do this kind of tuning by guesswork. You need precise test equipment and training to use it properly.

"Digital" amplifiers

Some monitor amplifiers and amp/speaker combinations come with digital inputs and connect to your editor via USB or a digital audio cable. All this does is move the digital-to-analog conversion circuit from inside your computer's tower to inside the amp. While a computer's audio output might not reach the highest specifications for critical listening, the circuits used today are more than adequate for monitoring and mixing when used with a good analog amp and speakers. There's nothing inherently wrong with the idea of a digital input in a monitor system,

> **The easy way out.** Smoothing out the acoustics and buying a high-quality amp and speakers can be expensive. It may be more efficient to just keep the multimedia speakers that came bundled with your NLE—they're good enough for editing—and then rent time in a well-equipped sound studio when it's time to mix.

but it adds to the cost and limits your selection. Don't bother with it, unless your NLE doesn't have an analog audio output.

A useful gadget: mono test switch

One feature that's seldom found on consumer amplifiers, and almost essential for accurate video mixing, is a mono test switch. It combines the left and right channels electrically so you can hear if there are any phase errors that will affect mono compatibility. This is essential for broadcast,

Internet, or VHS projects. Even though stereo TVs and VHS decks are common, a lot of cheap dual-speaker color TVs skip the stereo circuits to save money, and VHS decks become mono when you use the antenna connection instead of dedicated audio outputs. Lots of people put stereo speakers around their computer monitor, but just as many rely on a single speaker in the tower.

You can't take mono compatibility for granted; bad wiring, asymmetrical processors, and some "three-dimensional" effects can make a good stereo track sound awful in mono. A few stereo music synthesizers completely disappear when their channels are combined.

It's easy to build a mono/stereo test switch. This gadget sends both channels to one speaker, silencing the other. It can also simultaneously lower the volume, so you'll get a better idea of how a mix will sound at typical listener levels.

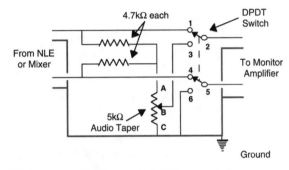

You can see how it works by following the schematic in Figure 11.6. The left and right outputs of your NLE or mixer are combined through the two 4.7 kΩ (4,700 ohms) 1/2-watt or 1/8-watt carbon resis-

11.6 A simple adapter to add the controls most hi-fi amps leave off.

tors; Radio Shack #271-1330s are fine. These keep the individual outputs from drawing current from each other. They also cause a tiny loss of stereo separation through the monitors, but, with most equipment, it won't be noticeable. (The resistors are the right value for modern NLEs and prosumer audio gear, but not for tubed or transformer-coupled equipment; if you've got that stuff, you probably already have sophisticated monitor controls.) The 5 kΩ audio-taper potentiometer (#271-1720) lets you preset a lower volume for mono listening. The switch is a light-duty double-pole, double-throw toggle (#275-636). With the switch up, the amplifier sees the stereo outputs of the computer; with it down, one side of the amp sees the mono sum, and the other is grounded to stay silent.

The easiest way to deal with input and output cables is to buy 6-foot shielded audio cords with appropriate connectors for your equipment; probably these will be phono plugs for the amplifier and either phono or 1/4-inch phone plugs for the mixer or NLE's sound card. Once you're sure the cords are right for getting a signal into your amp, cut them in half and separate the inner conductor from the outer grounding shield. Cut off an extra few inches to use as hookup wire, unless you have some other light-gauge wire sitting around from a telephone or toy train project. Use shrink-tubing to insulate the resistor leads. For best results, build the circuit in a metal box and also connect the ground point to the box; this provides shielding as well as a solid mounting surface for the switch and volume control.

This circuit isn't complicated to build, but it does require soldering. (There aren't any hazardous voltages, so it's a good project for the beginner. If the very idea of soldering sends hot metal flashes down your spine, enlist a local high school hacker to build the circuit for you. Or buy the parts and pay a TV repair shop to assemble it.) The gray lines in the schematic represent the cable shields; it's important that these all be connected to each other as well as to the volume control and switch. The ground connection is optional, but may reduce noise if you tie it to a grounding screw on the amplifier. The bold letters and numbers refer to specific terminals on the switch and control, identified in Figure 11.7.

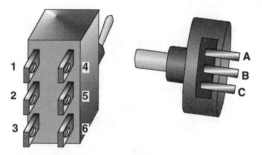

11.7 Connection key for Figure 11.6.

All of the parts are available from electronics stores, and the whole thing should cost less than $15 plus any labor charges for assembling it. I used Radio Shack part numbers because there's probably a store within a mile of where you're reading this book. They can also sell you a soldering kit with instructions, #64-2802, if you want to try building it yourself.

Plug one side into your computer's or mixer's line outputs, and the other into a monitor amplifier. With the switch in one position, you'll hear stereo. To check compatibility, flip the switch to the other side and make sure every element still sounds right. To check the mix balance, turn down the volume control until you barely hear the sound. In a well-mixed track, you should still be able to follow the dialog even when it's too soft to catch all the music and sound effects.

Computer Input/Output

Many videographers are using FireWire to transfer audio and video digitally between camera and NLE. This is the cleanest way to get dialog into a computer, or to lay a finished mix back to DV tape. They use the generic headphone or line-level analog audio outputs of their computer while editing and mixing. While these outputs aren't up to current pro-audio standards, they're adequate for monitoring all but the most demanding theatrical mix.

If the only other sound sources in your production are already digitized as files, or are audio CD tracks *ripped* (converted to audio files) in the CD-ROM drive, you don't need any other input or output equipment.

But many projects need to add sound from microphones, MiniDisc, and DAT during postproduction. You could use your camera to digitize these signals and turn them into FireWire, but MiniDV camera audio doesn't live up to the quality of these other media. See Chapter 9 for the full story, along with some tips for making the most of a camera's audio-input circuit.

A low-cost Media Converter box with both analog and FireWire connections is going to be just as bad. These devices are not built to any higher audio standards than the worst MiniDV cameras we measured. If you're using one with an older digital camera that has only analog outputs, the problem is even worse: distortion, noise, and poor frequency response will be doubled, once at the original shoot and once when re-digitizing. For best results, use a good video-capture card and one of the audio-input solutions in the rest of this section.

Sound Cards

You can add high-quality audio inputs and outputs to any PCI-equipped Windows or Macintosh tower, by using a third-party sound card. These usually have multi-pin connectors and breakout cables or pods with a variety of audio connectors. Some also add MIDI and other functions (such as SCSI or FireWire).

There are two levels of quality here. Cards intended for amateur musicians and gamers are sold through computer stores. They're designed for that market, with functions such as built-in MIDI synthesizers and pseudo-surround effects to enhance gaming. But their basic audio specifications are fairly poor. Brand name is no guarantee of quality—one very-well-known name sells their cards to system integrators for less than $15 each in quantities of 20 or more. The system might specify their brand, but the quality will be as bad as the worst generic card. Even higher-priced cards from that same manufacturer can hurt your sound: the money goes for gaming and multimedia features, not for better analog circuits. Some of these cards have s/pdif inputs. Unless you use them with an external analog-to-digital converter, or connect a DAT or MiniDisc directly to the digital input, you'll get poor quality.

Professional-level sound cards are sold through broadcast and audio dealers. They don't have to be expensive. M-Audio (www.m-audio.com) and others make cards with good analog circuits and converters for around $200. These have prosumer –10 dBV unbalanced line-level connections as well as s/pdif. More professional cards, with +4 dBu balanced connections and AES/EBU digital audio, are in the $500 range. Professional PC-card-based units with similar connections but designed for laptops cost about the same.

As with so many other pieces of hardware in this book, you can learn a lot about relative quality by comparing what kind of specs a manufacturer brags about. M-Audio's web site describes their 2496 card, mentioned previously, as having a dynamic range of 104.0 dB when going digital to analog, and 100.4 dB for analog to digital. They specify that the measurement is A-weighted, a standard that reveals more electronic noise than others. While this dynamic range can be achieved only with 24-bit recording, the numbers indicate excellent analog circuits that won't compromise 16-bit recording. M-Audio also quotes <0.002% THD+N, and a frequency response of 22 Hz–22 kHz ± .04 dB.

Compare this information with what you'll find at the site of one of the best-known cards sold through computer stores. Their top unit—which they claim is for the "professional home studio"—lists a dynamic range, period. No measurement standard; no distortion figure; no frequency response.

No matter what kind of sound card you're using, it's not a good idea to run mic-level signals into it. There's too much interference on the motherboard of a computer near its PCI slots, and a low-voltage mic signal can get polluted unless the card manufacturer was very careful about shielding. Add an external mixer or preamp, and send line level to the card.

USB Input Devices

For even better noise performance, you can move all of the analog circuitry out of your computer. Use an external input/output box with a USB connection. High-quality ones from pro audio manufacturers start around $350, and include balanced mic as well as unbalanced line and s/pdif. Balanced lines or ultra-high-quality mic preamps add about $300.

While there might not be a financial advantage to using an external USB converter, there's certainly an operational one. Installation is usually plug-and-play, though a driver might be needed. You can swap the converter to a laptop or upgraded tower easily. Many units offer other functions, including full-size faders for mixing and transport controls, and come with bundled multitrack audio software.

If all you need is a clean transfer from DAT or MiniDisc, you can get s/pdif to USB converters for as little as $100. This is a hot category, with new products constantly being introduced. Check with a broadcast supplier or large chain music store.

Multitrack FireWire Interface

If you need more than two simultaneous channels, you can use one of the interfaces described at the end of Chapter 9. You'll also need multitrack audio software; these boxes can't handle more than two channels at a time from an NLE.

The Mixer

Despite their name, mixers aren't used just for combining multiple tracks in a postproduction suite. More often, they're used to select and control individual signals, adjusting the volume and possibly adding equalization before they're digitized into the editor. In fact, unless your NLE has multiple-track outputs, you probably won't use the mixer for mixing at all; you'll do that operation in software.

The ability to manipulate a signal when you're digitizing is both a blessing and a curse. You can boost levels and reduce noise or add crispness quickly with analog controls, to take advantage of the widest digital range once the signal is in the computer. But if you're going to tweak a track before you digitize, you need some way to repeat those tweaks exactly if you have to redigitize part of a scene. You also need a way to assure that good recordings aren't harmed by inadvertent tweaking.

The problem is that most analog mixers are ambiguous. You can't set the volume or equalization to precise levels, and you can't take the equalizers out of the circuit when you don't want them. Low-cost mixers, with small controls and sparse calibrations on the panel, are almost impossible to set the same way twice. They can also have problems with signals leaking from channels that appear to be turned off, adding tiny amounts of noise or feedback into your tracks.

Midpriced digital mixers avoid these problems by letting you display and set volume and equalizer settings numerically, and by storing your most common setups for instant recall. A few come with software that lets you store settings in your computer. Most of them also include other processing, including compression, noise gates, and reverberation (Chapter 16). They often include digital as well as analog inputs and outputs, so you can avoid the potential distortion of another conversion. These mixers are mass-produced for the home-music market, bringing their price down to under a thousand dollars. If one has sufficient inputs and outputs, you won't need a patchbay, so it might be the only piece of audio control and processing equipment you need.

Many mixers provide line-level monitor outputs, which are a convenient way to hook up your amplifier and speakers without disrupting the main connection to your NLE's input. But even if they don't, the headphone outputs are often clean enough and the right voltage to feed an external monitor amp. Check the manual (or just try it, making sure the amplifier's volume is turned all the way down when you first make the connection).

Mixer alternatives

If you're mixing within your NLE but still want some control over levels and equalization while digitizing, consider a stand-alone equalizer instead. These provide finer control than the basic equalizer knobs on a mixer and are calibrated for easier resetting. A parametric equalizer—with knobs to control tuning as well as frequency—will let you hone in on offending noises without affecting too much else in the track. Hook up the equalizer through a patchbay, so you can bypass it when you want an absolutely clean connection. Processors, including equalizers, are discussed in Chapter 16.

Audio Sources and Recorders

While a lot of your track will probably consist of dialog recorded in the camera, and then imported into an NLE from the camera or a separate video deck, you may also want additional equipment to play back nonsync elements such as music, sound effects, and narration.

Then again, maybe you won't. Chances are your NLE already has a provision for importing stock music and effects from audio CDs, and most sound studios and freelance suppliers can now provide narration and original music on audio CD, or as files on CD-ROM and removable hard drives. So consider all the equipment in this section optional.

CD players

Library music and sound effects are distributed on audio CDs, the same format as you'd play in a home stereo. These discs are readable in the CD-ROM drives supplied with virtually every computer, and software to convert the sounds to standard WAV or AIFF files either came with your system or can be downloaded for free from the Internet. These programs deal with sound as data, so the quality doesn't get degraded by converting it to analog and back, and they can import a long selection in less time than it would take to play it as audio. If you need only a few sounds from CD and don't have a sample-rate-conversion problem, you can use your computer's disc drive and save the cost of a separate player. On the other hand, unless your production is at a 44.1 kHz sample rate—the standard rate for audio CDs—the software will have to manipulate the data so it plays properly at the new rate. With some NLEs, this can take extra time and add noise and distortion.

There may be other advantages to using a separate CD player with audio outputs and re-recording into your NLE. It's faster to find specific sounds with a player, because discs load more quickly and the dedicated controls make cueing easier. You don't need to leave your editing software and launch another program to make the translation. Some ripper software doesn't let you select just part of a CD track or preview its sound, forcing you to turn an entire track into a large file to extract one small sound—or to discover you had chosen the wrong track. Reasonably priced professional CD players also offer features that may be impossible or require extra processing steps with a CD-ROM drive, including varispeed to change the tempo and timbre of a sound, the ability to cue directly to index points within properly encoded CD tracks, and—though I'm not sure why you'd want them—DJ-style scratching effects.

The best way to record audio from a stand-alone CD player is to use its digital outputs. Professional players come with s/pdif interfaces, which can plug directly into a properly equipped sound card. Good home players have Toslink outputs, but Toslink to s/pdif adapters cost less than $100. When you re-record audio through one of these connections, the signal isn't affected by noise or analog-conversion distortion. However, if you're using a digital connection, you may have to forgo varispeed or scratch effects; these change the sample rate to a nonstandard value, and most low-cost digital input devices can't deal with that at all. If your production isn't at 44.1 kHz sample rate, you'll be facing the same conversion issues as with a CD-ROM drive.

You can avoid the sample-rate problem by using the player's analog outputs. Most players have very high-quality output converters, so the limiting factors will be your analog wiring—which should be as direct as possible—and the quality of your analog inputs. With good equipment, neither of these should present a problem.

You can also use a portable battery-operated CD player to import audio. Look for a unit with a line-level output on the back (many of them have one for connection to a hi-fi system), so you can avoid distortion and variations caused by the headphone amplifier and volume control. While the output converters on a portable player may not be as good as those on a studio deck, running the portable on batteries instead of its AC adapter will completely eliminate power-line hum. If your studio is plagued with ground loops, this may be the cleanest analog connection.

DAT, MiniDisc, and MDM

When I wrote the first edition of this book three years ago, DAT tape was the only standard for interchange among audio studios. Narrations and original music were always supplied in this format and post audio facilities expected you to bring nonsync elements recorded this way. Timecode DAT, recorded on units costing many thousands of dollars, are still the standard for professional video and film sound. If you're working in this environment and have timecode on your other equipment, you'll need one of these decks.

But for the MiniDV filmmaker, timecode DAT is now overkill. Professional studios and narrators or composers with their own facilities can give you material as files on CD-ROM or as audio CDs. They can even e-mail pieces as MP3 files, or put them up on a Web site. In my studio, we regularly send full-resolution, 16-bit 48 kHz stereo mixes to video post houses via FTP. Of course, that's just for short-form projects like commercials, since 48 kHz stereo generates more than 11 MB of data per minute. But we've gone from handling hundreds of timecode DATs a month to a couple of dozen.

If you're using a portable DAT deck for field recording, it probably has s/pdif outputs. You can use the same deck to transfer digitally into a properly equipped computer. But if you're doing a lot of winding and cueing, a full-size non-timecode will be better. Units costing around $1100 have direct access to individual tracks, shuttle wheels, and high-quality analog and digital outputs. They also can stand up to heavy tape winding better than the portables.

MiniDisc combines the recording flexibility of DAT with the random access of a CD or hard drive, and may seem like an ideal medium for postproduction. However, it was introduced under a cloud—early units incorporated a somewhat nasty-sounding lossy compression algorithm, and even modern ones still use some form of data reduction—and never achieved the professional acceptance of DAT. But MiniDV filmmakers are using the medium as an alternative to noisy in-camera recording (see Chapter 9). If you work this way, there's a definite advantage to transferring the disc into your computer digitally. Full-size portables have s/pdif or AES/EBU outputs; HHB's Portadisc also has a USB jack for realtime transfers without a separate adapter. If you're using one of the smaller recorders with analog-only outputs, you'll get much better sound by investing in a home MiniDisc player and using its s/pdif or Toslink output.

MDMs (modular digital multitracks) are used extensively in music studios for original recording and in high-end audio post facilities for interchange, but seldom find their way into an NLE setup. There are two competing and noninterchangeable formats, Alesis ADAT (used in music) and Tascam DTRS/DA-8 (almost universal in postproduction), so check with the client or other studios you'll be working with before specifying one or the other.

Analog audio media

Audio cassettes are still considered a handy, low-cost way to distribute music demos or voices for auditions, though they're quickly being replaced by audio CDs burned in a computer. But even the best analog cassettes don't have the quality or speed accuracy to be used with video.

Quarter-inch (and wider) audio tape is often used in music production to add "analog warmth"—a particular, pleasing form of distortion—but high-quality analog recorders are too unwieldy and expensive for video work, and the distortion builds up quickly over multiple generations. A few Hollywood features are still mixed with analog recordings on film-style perforated stock, but this is for economic reasons—studios may prefer to use equipment that's already paid for—rather than any technical advantage. MDMs, DVDs, and removable hard drives are the norm in professional film today.

Some historic documentary sounds, effects, and music may be available only on analog vinyl disks. If you have to play them, check with local studios and radio stations to find some way to transfer their sound to digital. (I still keep a turntable and preamp in the basement, wrapped in plastic, for just such occasions. I haven't unwrapped it in more than a decade.)

The best strategy with any of these analog media is to transfer to digital as soon as possible. Don't try to correct problems at this stage, unless they're being introduced by the playback mechanism—a badly maintained analog tape recorder will add hiss and lose high frequencies, and dirt or dust on a vinyl record can add noise. These problems can permanently damage your source material, so have them fixed before you continue with the transfer. Once the sound is in the digital domain, you can experiment with noise-reduction software and equalization and still be able to undo the effects.

Synthesizers and samplers

If you're a skilled musician, you might want to add music-making equipment to your NLE system. The technical requirements for this are documented in tons of books and magazines. They also tend to be somewhat different from the requirements for postproduction, so it might be more efficient to build separate setups and let two people play at the same time. Even if you're not making music, a small synthesizer can be helpful in the postproduction studio for laser zaps and other electronic effects.

Some library music is distributed as MIDI files, a compact data format that describes when and how to play individual notes in a song. But unless you have a full MIDI studio (and know how to produce and mix music), it's not of much use in sophisticated video production. Low-level synthesizers that play MIDI through a computer's sound card have limited sound quality. Software-based synthesizers that take over a whole computer are better, but require some music-production chops to use properly.

Samplers—RAM-based digital audio recorders, with exceptional flexibility to warp the sound quality during playback—are often used in sound design. Both software-based ones and hardware samplers can be helpful in the postproduction suite for sound-effects manipulation—if you know how to work them.

Other Handy Gear

Software and hardware-based processors—such things as equalizers, compressors, and reverbs—are discussed in Chapter 16. But there are some other gadgets that can help you assure a good soundtrack.

Meters

The on-screen meters in most nonlinear editors range from deceptive to worthless. It takes computing power to make a digital meter that matches broadcast standards, but many programmers seem reluctant even to put calibrations on their nonstandard meters. Figure 11.8 shows the minimalist record-level indicator in one very-popular video-editing program; using it as a meaningful guide for setting levels is almost impossible (but see the tips at the end of this chapter).

11.8 The record-level meter in one popular program hardly tells you anything.

A proper meter should indicate both the peak level—bursts of sound that can overload a digital circuit, causing crackling noises—and the average level that a listener hears. It should also be calibrated in meaningful units—in a digital studio, that is decibels below full scale (see Chapter 3). Some programs have on-screen meters that are properly calibrated and indicate peak and average levels as different colors (Figure 11.9); but if your software doesn't, it's worth investing in an accessory external meter.

To be absolutely accurate, a digital meter should be connected to a digital audio signal—that way, no analog circuitry can have an effect on it. But meters like this are built to precise specifications and are expensive. A good compromise is an LED meter with analog inputs; you can get one that displays both peak and

11.9 A good software meter indicates peak and average levels.

average levels for under $200 at broadcast suppliers. Connect it directly to a sound card's constant-level output, so there aren't any volume controls between the signal you're recording and the meter. (If your software or sound card driver has an output level control, leave it at the nominal 0 dB or 100% position.)

It's difficult to find a good mechanical meter these days—the kind with a swinging needle. To measure volume properly, a VU meter must have precise ballistics and electrical characteristics. These things have gotten so expensive that even large recording studio consoles don't have them any more. The cheap voltage meters sold as accessories for editing suites don't have the right response to audio waveforms and are too bouncy to use as a reliable indicator while mixing.

Spectrum analyzer

A close cousin to the level meter is the spectrum analyzer, which displays the relative level of each frequency in a signal. Figure 11.3 showed one software version that can be called up to analyze a file. To be truly useful, though, a spectrum analyzer should be available while you're mixing—and the software version ties up computing cycles and screen space.

High-quality hardware spectrum analyzers, with rows of LEDs that measure the level at every third of an octave, cost many thousands of dollars. Lower-cost accurate analyzers, with just a couple of LEDs for each frequency, are designed for calibrating PA systems and aren't useful for mixing.

But even a less-than-perfect spectrum analyzer can be handy. Once you've learned to correlate what you hear through good monitors with what you see on the analyzer, you've got a way to verify that what you think you're hearing is really there. I used to keep an octave-band analyzer in my studio (Figure 11.10), wired up to the monitor circuit, so I

11.10 A $100 hi-fi spectrum analyzer used to sit on top of an expensive timecode DAT deck in my studio.

can glance at it when I suspect fatigue or a head cold is plugging up my ears. This analyzer, part

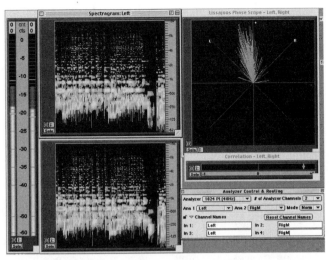

11.11 These days, I use a sophisticated software suite for measurements, SpectraFoo.

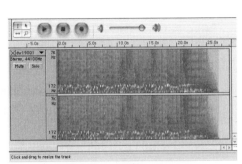

11.12 Audacity's spectrum analyzer isn't fancy, but it's free.

of a graphic equalizer sold for home stereos, cost less than $100 at a close-out sale. You may be able find similar units at yard sales or online auctions.

These days I use a software suite that includes precisely calibrated meters, *spectragrams* for each channel (they plot both frequency and volume over time), and stereo-management tools (Figure 11.11). It also includes oscilloscopes and other meters that aren't in the screenshot. The suite, SpectraFoo (www.spectrafoo.com) requires a fast, dedicated Macintosh and works best with a digital input card.

If you're willing to wait until after a mix to check for spectral problems, you probably already have a non-realtime spectrum analyzer. Look in your audio software. Or pick up a copy of Audacity (Figure 11.12), an open-sourced freeware audio editor for Mac, Windows, and Linux.

Tone oscillator

Even though a lineup tone isn't strictly necessary for digital videotape—the digits themselves provide an unambiguous reference—it's still essential for making the digital-to-analog leap in a dub house or broadcast station. A steady tone is also necessary for calibrating equipment, checking stereo balance, and assuring that every device in a mixed analog/digital signal chain is operating at its best level.

You can get a miniature test oscillator, built into an XLR plug, that uses phantom power and puts out a microphone-level signal. The units cost under $75 and are sold for checking PA systems in the field, but can be plugged into a mixer for postproduction use. More flexible units with line-level outputs and a variety of test signals are available for under a few hundred dollars. One or the other should be a part of any professional studio.

A less flexible, but zero-cost alternative is on Tracks 12–14 of this book's CD. I've recorded one minute of a 1 kHz tone at –20 dBFS (network standard), –12 dBFS (analog "zero" equivalent for miniDV), and 0 dBFS (for digital testing). If you transfer the tracks as files directly into your editing software, the levels should be accurate enough to use at the head of your digitally output tapes. You can also play them through a standard CD player as an analog lineup tone.

Phone patch

Sometimes you need to play a library cut or dialog edit to a distant client just for content approval, without needing the quality of a file transfer or overnight courier. You could hold a telephone handset up to a speaker, but the results are hardly professional. You can buy a telephone coupler for a few hundred dollars. Or you can build this $10 version, which sounds just as good (and also lets you record a telephone signal through a line-level input). It's based on a circuit you used to be able to rent from the phone company—back when there was only one phone company to deal with—and under ideal circumstances can sound as good as the connections at radio call-in shows.

The coupler doesn't work into digital phone wiring. But chances are your phones are analog, even if your sophisticated office system includes voice mail and call-forwarding. To find out, turn a phone over and look for a "Ringer Equivalent Number" (REN) value printed on a label; if you see one, the phone wiring is analog. (Sometimes the REN label is hidden under a snap-on mounting bracket, so look carefully.) If you don't see an REN, you can still use the coupler with one of the $50 handset modem adapters sold for business travel—but it's hardly worth the effort, since most of those adapters already have an equivalent circuit built in.

The circuit diagram is laughably simple, with only two components (Figure 11.13). A 1:1 600 Ω transformer isolates the computer and phone system from each other, while still letting audio pass through. Radio Shack's tiny version (part #273-1374) isn't exactly high fidelity, but its quality does match that of a

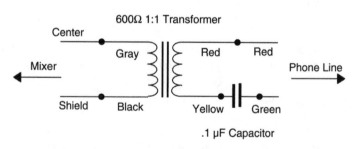

11.13 Easy-to-build telephone coupler. The color codes refer to specified Radio Shack parts.

telephone line. A 0.1 μF (microfarad) capacitor (#272-1069) protects the transformer from the constant voltage that's always on a phone line, and keeps the coupler from interfering with normal dialing and hanging up. If you're getting parts from a more comprehensive supplier than Radio Shack, look for a capacitor with a 100-volt rating; it'll last longer. The only other parts you need are a wire that connects to your telephone line and a cable to plug into your mixer's line-level or headphone output.

This circuit is so easy to build that I threw one together on a piece of scrap cardboard (Figure 11.14), using cellophane tape and paper clips. The thick black wire on the left comes from the computer's or mixer's line output. Find a cable with an appropriate plug, cut off one end, and use a knife or cutting pliers to pull off the outer covering. You'll see a metal shield—braided or twisted wires, or a foil wrapper—around a single insulated conductor. Separate the shield from the inner wire and twist it together, and then strip back some of the insulation from the end of the inner wire (or buy a #42-2370 cable, which has a phono plug and is already prepared for use). The gray telephone wire on the right is a #279-310, which has a standard modular plug on the other end and can plug into any analog telephone jack. You can also plug this into the "data port" on some telephones. Or use any two-conductor low-voltage wire, and connect to the red and green wires inside the phone jack on your wall.

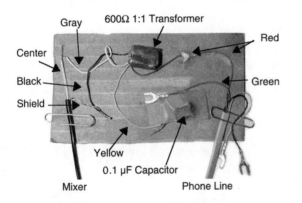

Follow the color codes in the photo and schematic, and connect the components by twisting their wires tightly together (soldering isn't necessary). Make sure the connections are secured so they don't touch each other, and be sure to cover the wires on the telephone side of the circuit with tape so nobody accidentally touches them. When the phone rings, these carry as much as 125 volts. It's low current, but can give you quite a tickle.

11.14 No soldering required. You can build this telephone coupler with paper clips and cellophane tape.

To use the coupler, just plug it into a sound source and a telephone jack. You'll need a regular phone on the same line to dial and monitor the call; the easiest way to hook them both up is to plug a Y-connector (#279-357) into the wall and then plug both the phone and the coupler into it. Raise the source's volume until it just starts to distort in your phone's handset, then back it off a little. It's okay to leave the coupler connected between calls, but be aware that anything going through your mixer will also be transmitted into the conversations going on.

If you want to use this coupler to record a telephone conversation, simply plug it into a mixer's line-level input. Your local voice will be some 20 dB louder than the distant caller's, a characteristic of any analog phone system. If you're recording an interview, keep your phone muted during the responses so breaths and other local noises don't overwhelm the distant voice. To record a conversation, you'll need to keep a quick hand on the level control. Or get a true "hybrid" circuit, which balances and nulls out your voice from the phone line. It's too complicated to describe here, but you can buy one for about $500.

Moving Signals Around the Editing Suite

The simplest audio setup for NLEs is a straight digital connection—FireWire, AES/EBU, or s/pdif—between the VTR and the editor. You can import audio, edit and possibly mix it within the editing system, and put the finished track back on videotape without compromising the signal in any way. Hang a monitor amplifier and speakers on the editor's analog outputs, and you're ready to go (Figure 11.15).

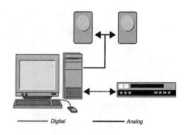

11.15 Simple NLE audio wiring with a digital VTR.

It's possible your setup will be this simple. If so, congratulations. Skip the rest of this chapter and start editing.

But if your NLE has only analog inputs and outputs, things get complicated very quickly. You can run a wire from VTR output to editor input for digitizing, and from editor output to monitor to hear what you're doing; but once the job is edited, you'll have to rearrange things to get the signal from NLE back to tape and from tape to monitor. If you add additional sources such as a DAT or CD player, the complexity grows geometrically. You need some way to choose which signal gets digitized, to dub between media, and to connect the monitor to the right output for each different function (Figure 11.16).

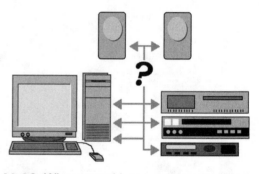

11.16 When you add more equipment, things stop being simple.

There are three different ways to deal with this web of connections:

- You can reach behind the equipment when you want to change signal routing, find the right cords, and plug them into the right jacks for the current task. Aside from being inconvenient and confusing—you have to remember how things are wired before you can use them—this puts extra stress on the equipment's connectors and can lead to early failure.

- You can use a routing device, which can be as simple as a low-cost patchbay or switch, or as complex as a microprocessor-based router, to handle the connections for you. Aside from protecting the equipment's connectors, this makes the whole process more straightforward. You don't have to do any reaching, and you can glance at the patchbay or switch to see how things are set up at any moment.

- You can wire everything to a mixer, which then serves as your central audio control. This gives you other options for manipulating the sound, but may also subject your sound to unwanted changes.

The best solution—and the one applied in almost every professional studio—is to use both a patchbay and a mixer. The patchbay supplies flexibility and direct connections when you don't want the sound changed, and the mixer gives you control when you do.

The Patchbay

Audio has been routed with plugs and jacks since the earliest days of the telephone, and a patchbay with dangling cords seems to be a required element in every photo of a recording studio or broadcasting plant. There's a reason: patchbays make it easy to control where the signals go.

In its most basic form, a patchbay is simply a means to extend the jacks from the back panels of your equipment and group them in one convenient place. Even low-cost ones (under $100 for a 48-point bay) use rugged 1/4-inch balanced phone jacks, which last longer and provide a better connection than the miniature or phono jacks on your equipment. Many brands have jacks on both their front and rear panels, so you don't need to do any soldering to install them; just get cables with appropriate connectors for your equipment on one end and a 1/4-inch plug on the other, plug them into the back of the patchbay, and forget about them. If your equipment has balanced inputs and outputs (Chapter 4), use two-conductor shielded cables with tip/ring/sleeve plugs to preserve the benefits of balancing. If some of your equipment is unbalanced, use standard two-conductor cables for it. In most situations, the balanced jacks in the patchbay will find the right conductors, and you won't need separate adapters. Keep unbalanced cables as short as possible to avoid noise pickup.

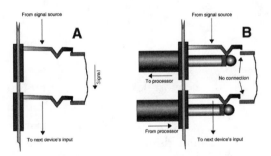

Most preassembled patchbays have switchable "normals"—circuit paths that are activated when no cord is plugged in. Figure 11.17 shows how they work.

11.17 Normaled jacks provide a connection even when nothing's plugged in.

The contacts in a normaled jack are slightly bent. When there's no plug inserted (Figure 11.17A), they make contact with a separate jumper that routes the signal someplace else. If that happens to be another normaled jack, as drawn, it's called a "full normaled" patchbay. When you plug in a patchcord (Figure 11.17B), the contact is pushed away from the jumper. Signal goes to the plug, but nowhere else. Balanced patchbays will have dual contacts and jumpers in the same jack—one for each conductor in the cable—and both are activated by the plug at the same time.

A patchbay can also be "half normaled." Imagine if the top jack in the drawing didn't have a jumper, and there was a wire from its main contact directly to the jumper in the lower jack. You could plug into the top jack to tap the signal coming from the source device, but it would still also be connected through the patchbay to the next device. But in that same arrangement, if you plugged into the lower jack, you'd break the normal connection and substitute just what's on the plug.

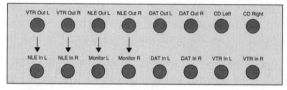

11.18 A basic NLE patchbay.

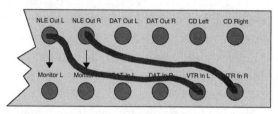

11.19 With two patchcords, you're ready to lay the finished project back to tape.

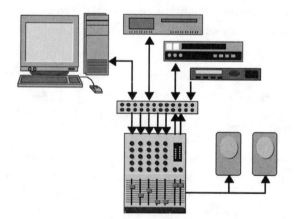

11.18 The most flexible—and professional—configuration uses patchbay and mixer together.

Common practice in sound studios is to put signal sources along the top row of a patch bay and destinations along the bottom. A patchbay in a small nonlinear editing suite might be organized like Figure 11.18. The arrows on the first four sets of jacks indicate a half-normal connection.

Since the VTR is normaled to the NLE inputs, and the NLE's outputs are normaled to the monitors, you can digitize and edit without using any patchcords. When it's time to dump the finished project back to tape, you'd add two cords (Figure 11.19). The normals to the monitor amp aren't interrupted, so you can still hear the NLE's output. If you want, you could plug two more cords from the VTR's outputs to the monitor inputs and check the signal going to tape; this would break the normaled connection between NLE output and monitor.

The most flexible configuration is to use a mixer and a patchbay. Connect each source in your studio to a separate mixer input through a normaled jack pair, the mixer's outputs to your NLE's inputs, and the mixer's monitor or headphone outputs to your amplifier (Figure 11.18). For most operations, all you'll have to do is raise the appropriate faders (leave all of the others down to reduce noise); when you want the cleanest signal or special routing, just grab some patchcords.

Switchers and Routers

While it's possible to route digital audio through an analog patchbay, it's not recommended. Ordinary patchbays aren't designed to handle the high frequencies of serial digital audio, and the connectors can cause high-frequency reflections that make it harder for your gear to interpret the valid signal. Special patchbays are designed for AES/EBU wiring, and broadcast-video patchbays do a decent job with s/pdif, but both these types are expensive solutions.

A few companies make electronic AES/EBU switchers. These route any input to any output—usually in an 8×8 or a 16×16 matrix—with additional buffering so that a signal can be sent to more than one device. Since they're driven by microprocessors, complex setups can be recalled quickly. Some of them also include reclocking and sample-rate conversion. While these routers are also expensive solutions—prices start around $1,000—they're the only efficient way to handle signals in a complex, all-digital facility.

Less-expensive switchers are also available for both digital and analog audio. The simplest of them are just mechanical switches in a box, but can be practical when you just need to select one of a few sources for an input. More elaborate ones can switch audio, video, and machine control simultaneously and are handy when your suite includes more than one video source.

Wiring the Postproduction Suite

The best, highest-quality way to wire your equipment together is to use digital connections for everything except the monitor circuit. Get appropriate cable for the high-frequency digital signal (see Chapter 4), and, if you have a lot of gear, use a digital mixer or routing switcher.

If you have to use analog connections, the best plan is to stick with balanced wiring (also in Chapter 4, along with some suggestions for when you have to mix balanced and unbalanced equipment). If everything in your facility is unbalanced, there's no point to using balancing adapters. But there is a way to reduce noise in unbalanced setups, if you're willing to do some soldering:

1. Use the same kind of two-conductor shielded cable as you would for balanced wiring.
2. Connect the "hot" conductor—usually white—to the center pin of the phono or phone plug at each end, or to pin 2 of an unbalanced XLR.
3. Connect the other conductor to the sleeve of a phone plug, outer shell of a phono plug, or to pin 1 of an unbalanced XLR.

4. Now here's the trick: connect the cable's outer braided or foil shield to the sleeve, shell, or pin 1 *at one end only* (Figure 11.19). Use shrink-wrap or electrical tape to make sure the shield doesn't touch anything at the other end.

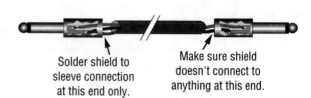

Solder shield to sleeve connection at this end only.

Make sure shield doesn't connect to anything at this end.

11.19 You can reduce noise in unbalanced circuits by connecting the shield at one end only (shown here with phone plugs).

5. Be consistent about which end of the shield gets connected: always connect the end at your patchbay and leave the equipment end floating, or always connect the end at the equipment and leave the patchbay end floating.

Only do this with two-conductor shielded wire, and with a definite ground connection through one of those wires. If you leave the shield disconnected with one-conductor shielded wire, you may get horrible hum.

Practical ground-loop elimination

In Chapter 4 we talked about how a ground loop can form and produce hum or noise in a circuit, and how balanced wiring can eliminate almost all of the problem. Unfortunately, much of the equipment in the prosumer realm is unbalanced and not immune to ground-loop noise. It's also difficult to chase down loops, since equipment may be interconnected with video, machine control, Ethernet, and MIDI as well as audio cables and power-line grounds—and any of these can form an extra ground path. Finding and fixing a ground loop can be more voodoo than science.

Sometimes you can reduce the effect of a ground loop by tempting the circuit with an even better ground. Heavy-gauge wire has very little electrical resistance, so if you provide a ground path using thick wires, it can divert some of the ground-loop current from being carried on the signal wires. Get some heavy-gauge wire and run lengths of it from one piece of equipment to another—on audio equipment, there's usually a back-panel screw marked "ground" specifically for this connection; on computers, connect to the outer metal shell of a rear-panel jack. A good wire for this purpose is 8- or 10-gauge electricians' type TW wire, available for a few cents a foot at building-supply stores, or automotive primary wire, which is slightly more expensive but also more flexible. You should hear the hum go down as soon as you make the connection. (You might also hear it increase, which means you're just making the ground loop worse. Like I said, sometimes it's voodoo.)

If you can't find an exposed ground connection on a piece of equipment, *don't* go rooting around inside the cabinet. You might find dangerous voltages instead.

If you can't get rid of a noise-producing extra ground in a power or control cable (or even figure out which cable is the culprit), you can often reduce ground loops in unbalanced equipment by breaking the ground path that takes place across the audio cable:

- Sometimes, just cutting the shield connection can help. Turn down the speakers; then pull a phono plug partway out, so its shell isn't contacting the jack, if your equpment has phono plugs, make up a special test cable where the sleeve isn't connected. Turn up the speakers *slowly*. Sometimes this fixes the problem, but other times it makes it much worse.

- You can isolate audio circuits completely by using a transformer. Small stereo-isolation transformers, prewired to phono jacks, are available at automobile sound dealers. Radio Shack's version (#270-054) costs about $15. If one of these fixes the problem but the transformer isn't good enough—you'll notice a slight decrease at the extreme high and low frequencies—you can get a higher-quality unit from a broadcast- or video-supply company.

One special hum case occurs when a VTR or monitor is connected to cable television as well as to a computer or audio equipment. The cable company's wiring is connected to the power-line ground in a lot of different places and is a hotbed of ground loops (which don't matter to the high-frequency television signal). But once you complete the circuit to a piece of grounded audio equipment, hum develops. It won't go away when you turn off the VTR, but should disappear if you disconnect the television cable.

If you're hearing this kind of hum, you can make a television frequency isolation transformer for under $10. Get a couple of 75 Ω to 300 Ω antenna transformers—one each of Radio Shack #15-1140 and #15-1523 work well for this—and connect them back-to-back at their screw terminals (Figure 11.20). Then insert the whole assembly in series with the TV cable, making sure that

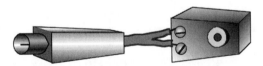

11.20 Connect two antenna transformers back-to-back to break cable TV ground loops.

nothing shorts the cable's shield from one side of the transformer to the other. If the hum doesn't stop, you may have gotten "autoformers" instead of true transformers. Check with an ohmmeter; there should be very high resistance between the screw terminals and either coaxial connection.

This cheap fix may pick up snow or other video junk in marginal conditions, but it won't degrade the audio. If the hum disappears but other problems appear, get a better-quality transformer at a high-end stereo store.

Wiring monitor speakers

Hi-fi enthusiasts claim great benefits to using special braided or oxygen-free cables between the amplifier and speakers. The physics behind these claims is doubtful. Ordinary 18-gauge "zip cord"—the stuff table lamps are wired with, available at any hardware or electronics store—should be sufficient for almost any speaker wiring chore in a digital video studio. If speaker cables are going to be longer than 10 feet or so, you might want to bump up to 16-gauge zip cord, also commonly available.

Two considerations are important when wiring between a speaker and amplifier, particularly if they have individual screw or pressure terminals.

- Electrical phase must stay consistent, or else it will be difficult to get a good idea of the bass notes in your mix. One screw or terminal at each speaker, and on each channel of the amp, will be marked with a + sign or special color. One conductor in the cable will be copper color, or marked with a stripe or ribs in the insulation. Use these identifications to make sure both speakers in a stereo pair are wired exactly the same way. The code doesn't matter—for example, you may choose to connect + on the amp, to the striped conductor in the cable, to the red screw on the speaker—but it has to be the same for the left and right channels.

- The fine copper wires that make up each conductor in the cable can become unwrapped, and a tiny stray wire may bridge two terminals and cause a short. This may damage or blow a fuse inside the amplifier. If possible, tin the wires with a soldering iron to keep them together, or use a high-quality crimp-on lug. If not, be very careful that every strand of wire is held in place by the screw or binding post.

Mixing −10 dBV and +4 dBu Equipment

Even the most professionally wired postproduction suite may have some unbalanced −10 dBV equipment (see Chapter 4), and NLE setups are apt to have a lot of it. Prosumer VTRs, CD players, musical equipment, and sound cards are likely to operate at the lower interconnect voltage. Consumer-grade monitor amplifiers may be totally professional in every respect except their input circuits.

There's no reason the two standards can't coexist in the same facility. Small buffer amplifiers, costing $50–75 per channel, are available at broadcast- and video-supply houses. They take a −10 dBV unbalanced signal and provide both amplification and balancing, turning it into +4 dBu balanced. If your facility uses balanced wiring, they can be mounted right at the CD player or other low-level source to give you noise immunity as well as a voltage boost. If you need to integrate a high-level balanced input (such as on a broadcast VTR) into an unbalanced system, it's probably easiest to mount the booster right at the deck and consider it just another prosumer device.

If you have just a few low-level unbalanced inputs (such as a prosumer VTR) in an otherwise balanced environment, it's best to use similar buffers or transformers at the decks to turn them into balanced inputs. This way, all the cabling remains balanced, and you won't be facing sudden changes in the grounding scheme when you patch into them.

If you have just a few high-level balanced sources in an unbalanced setup, things are even easier: you can build a simple resistive adapter for a few dollars. Instructions are in Chapter 9, in the section about attenuators. Use the circuit in Figure 9.9 on page 187, and its first set of resistor values (R1 is 200 Ω, and R2 is 750 Ω). You'll lose the benefits of balancing at the professional devices, but it's no real loss since you're not using it anywhere else in the room. You may find it more flexible to build a variable version of this circuit using a 5 kΩ trimmer or variable resistor: Just substitute the three terminals on the trimmer for the three resistor connection points in the circuit, with the middle trimmer terminal going to the pin of the −10 device. Set it once for a proper level, then ignore it.

If the balanced source is a classic piece of studio equipment, it may have transformer outputs. In that case, use the circuit in Figure 9.10 on page 188, and make all three resistors 332 Ω.

Impedance matching

Modern postproduction equipment is voltage-driven, and not subject to the impedance-matching rules that plagued us in the days of tubes and transformers, and are still valid for dynamic and ribbon mics. In general, you don't have to worry about matching "high" or "low" impedance.

- Soundcards, MiniDV decks, and most other unbalanced line-level equipment usually have outputs around 500Ω, and inputs between 5 kΩ and 50 kΩ. The wide output-to-input ratio means you can feed multiple deck inputs from a single output with simple Y-adapters. The highest input impedances can also pick up buzzing and other noises from electrical wiring; if this happens, try putting a 4.7 kΩ resistor in parallel with the input.

- Balanced NLE breakout boxes, mixers, and most high-end decks with XLR connectors follow the same impedance rules as unbalanced ones, even though they operate at about four times the audio voltage.

- Some of the high-end processing equipment in music studios has both input and output transformers. In most cases, these work fine with the impedances found in transformerless balanced equipment. Occasionally, a 600 Ω output transformer can produce extra highs and hiss when connected to 5k Ω or higher input. Put a 680 Ω resistor in parallel, and the sound will smooth out.

There are only a few exceptions:

- Classic passive equalizers, like the blue-panel Pultecs that now fetch classic-car prices, are very sensitive to input and output impedance. If you're lucky enough to have some of this gear, treat it to transformers on both sides.

- The connection between amplifier and speaker should be matched for a lot of reasons. But Ohm's Law also comes into play when choosing the cable; a high resistance, at these very low impedances, can cause serious signal loss. That's why extra-thick speaker cables are used in pro installations.

- Digital audio signals require matched impedances, but not because of Ohm's Law. These signals operate at such high frequencies that the wrong impedance will send data echoes back down the line, possibly disrupting the signal. Even the wire has to be matched for impedance. AES/EBU digital audio (usually on XLR connectors) needs 110 Ω cable and inputs; s/pdif digital audio (RCA or BNC connectors) uses 75 Ω.

Nonaudio Wiring

The digital video-editing suite is a complicated place, and some signals that have nothing to do with audio can still have an effect on your sound.

Digital sync

Digital audio is almost always handled in serial form: a string of ones and zeros is taken as a group, to represent one 16-bit (or higher) digital word. For this to work properly, the equipment has to agree how to find the start of each word—because if it can't, unpre dicta blethin gscan happ ento yourso und (like that). Each digital stream is self-clocking—a piece of equipment can look at it and determine where the word should start. But in a complicated facility, many audio signals may be moving simultaneously. If they don't all start their words at exactly the same time, the equipment won't know how to translate them. And audio/video equipment such as digital VTRs have the added burden of keeping the picture and sound words starting together, so they can be recorded or processed predictably.

Word clock

In sound studios, digital audio is often synchronized by routing a separate audio sync signal. This "word clock" is wired like video, using 75 Ω cable and BNC connectors. One device is designated as the master clock, and every other piece of equipment is set to sync its own internal circuits to it. The advantage is predictable operation, particularly when multiple audio signals have to be mixed together. Many digital mixers don't need word clock and will buffer each input's data until all the timings match—but this adds another processing step, and another chance for the signal to get degraded.

Video sync

Equipment designed to handle audio in a video environment, such as professional DAWs and timecode DAT recorders, often gives you the option of synchronizing both their internal timing and their digital words to a video signal. This is the same blackburst, video sync, or "house black" that you should be distributing to your VTR and NLE already; all you have to do is extend it to the additional inputs. It's better than timecode for keeping the internal timing of DATs and DAWs in step, since it's more precise and not subject to audible variations.

Most audio equipment that can handle a video sync signal also provides a separate, synchronized word-clock output. So you can use a blackburst generator for all your video equipment, route its signal to a convenient DAW or DAT recorder, and then distribute synchronized word clock to the audio devices that don't accept video sync. This will keep all the timings accurate and assure the cleanest digital audio processing. You might not even have the choice whether to do this: some digital video devices won't accept digital audio unless it's also locked to blackburst.

Timecode

Even though it's not as good as video sync for controlling internal timing, SMPTE timecode is the standard for tracking individual frames of audio- and videotapes, and making sure shots and sounds start when they should. Its data format and standards are discussed in the next chapter, but it also has an implication on edit-suite wiring.

SMPTE code is usually distributed as an unbalanced, audiolike signal. Its 1-volt square wave, right in the middle of the audible band, has harmonics that can leak into any nearby audio cables. The result is a constant chirping, very much like the sound of a fax transmission.

For best results, keep SMPTE cables far from audio ones. Don't run the two kinds of signals through the same patchbay. SMPTE is so likely to cause interference that it can even distort itself; if you run two different timecode signals on the dual shielded cables used for stereo wiring, the resulting cross-talk may make both unreadable.

Timecode information can also be carried over FireWire and RS-422 machine control wires. This kind of code can't radiate into audio cables in normal situations. Don't worry about it.

Chapter 12

Levels and Digitizing

Rose's Rules:

✔ Getting a clean signal into your NLE isn't as easy as just hitting the "Capture" button. There are a lot of places where things can go wrong, and some of the damage doesn't show up until it's time to mix.

✔ On the other hand, it's easy (and cheap) to diagnose and fix these problems. Once you do, they tend to stay fixed, and, after that, your digitizing should go smoothly.

✔ SMPTE timecode generally isn't used in MiniDV production. But if a project is headed for broadcast or a professional post suite, you have to know what timecode is all about.

✔ You can use a computer to create a track for 16mm and 35mm film projects, if you stay aware of some non-intuitive timing issues.

Someday we'll all speak the same language. Eventually digital video cameras, editing systems, broadcast facilities, and possibly even feature-film studios and video games will share the same file systems. Getting sound or picture from one unit to another will be as simple as popping in a DVD or data cartridge, or logging onto a network.

You can do this now to a limited extent with audio. A studio or composer can send you narration or music on removable media, ready to run on your NLE. They can leave it for you at an ftp site or password-protected web page. After you've edited, you can send elements to an outside mix facility the same way.

But for most nonlinear production, you're going to have to transfer at least some of the sound from camera tape or audio medium to computer file, and then from NLE back to videotape. You have to make sure that nothing gets lost in the process. If your only transfers are to and from a camera or deck via FireWire, this is fairly simple. If you're using non-computer forms of digital audio, or analog connections, there are a few extra steps to take.

Digital Audio Transfers

When Digitizing Isn't

Editors often use the term "digitizing" to refer to bringing sound or pictures into NLE, but if you're transferring via FireWire or a digital audio link, digitizing doesn't really happen. The signal already exists as ones and zeros. It's merely going from serial data on tape, to a data stream on a wire, into a RAM buffer, and finally to one or more files on a hard drive.

If the file's sample rate and bit depth matches that of the data stream, and you're not making any intentional changes to the sound, this nondigitizing *capture* process should be completely transparent. Unless there's a timing problem somewhere along the line, the computer won't do anything that can affect the sound. On the other hand, you may need to turn sound at one sample rate or bit depth into a file with different specifications. This can add distortion and noise if done improperly.

In virtually every case, transferring sound digitally works better than using analog wiring. Each analog/digital conversion—even with the best equipment—adds distortion and can make the sound duller. If a digital signal needs equalization or volume changes, it's better to keep it in the computer and use software . . . even if you have a good analog processor available. On the other hand, there's nothing wrong with taking a signal from the computer digitally, running it through digital processors, and then sending it back. That operation is done frequently in professional audio postproduction.

This all-digital bias isn't the case in music production, where a certain amount of analog *warmth* may be preferred. Music mixers will run their computer-based creations through an analog processor or a generation of analog tape because of the pleasing distortion it can impart. But with the multiple generations of processing necessary for dialog-driven video, clarity is a lot more important than warmth.

- If your system gives you the option of straight digital transfer—camera or deck to NLE via digital wiring, with no analog in between—use it.

- Years ago, there could be advantages to using analog connections to transfer digital media in certain situations. Today, this is almost never true.

FireWire and other data transfers

The computer industry is way ahead of audio. If you're sending audio over a connection designed for computing, such as FireWire, things will be relatively foolproof and work well. Or, when they don't work, diagnosing the problem can be easy.

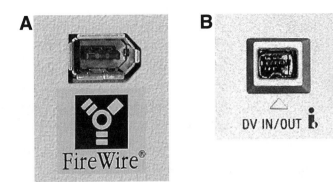

12.1 FireWire connectors.

FireWire is a high-speed data connection standard used for digital video with audio, multichannel audio, and computer peripherals such as hard drives and CD burners. In most devices, it appears on a 6-pin jack (Figure 12.1A); cameras and other video devices usually put it on a 4-pin jack to save space (Figure 12.1B). Only four of the conductors are used to carry data, so a simple adapter cable is all that's needed to connect one to the other. The other two wires are used to power a few non-video devices.

FireWire was developed by Apple. While they made the specification public, they charged for the use of the name and the Y-shaped logo in Figure 12.1. Sony adopted the same spec, but avoided licensing fees by calling their version i.Link and using an *i*-shaped logo. The Institute of Electrical and Electronics Engineers, an international standard-setting organization, adopted it as IEEE 1394. Some filmmakers just call it the DV connection. All of these things refer to the same standard. In mid-2002, Apple made the original name and logo free to use on any equipment that complies.

FireWire is hot-swappable, and usually plug-and-play. Get an appropriate cable, plug it into camera and computer, and a few moments later the camera is available to the system. FireWire standards call for a maximum cable length of about 15 feet, but that's to carry a full 400 megabits per second (MBPS) of data. DV uses only 100 MBPS, so longer cables can be successful. (Despite the data capacity of FireWire, DV transfers can't be faster than realtime; the transports and heads aren't quick enough.)

While FireWire devices are immediately recognized at the system level, most NLE software scans for the camera only on start-up. Plug in the camera, turn it on, and make sure it's in VTR mode before launching the program. NLEs can often control the camera's transport as well, and some perform automatic batch transfers. Since FireWire shows up at the system level, you can use a FireWire-connected camera as a source for recording in many audio-only programs as well. While FireWire can carry low-resolution four-channel sound from cameras that support 12-bit recording, most audio or video programs will record only two channels at a time. Select the appropriate pair in software before you capture or record.

FireWire connectors look something like the USB ones used for keyboards and other desktop peripherals, and the wiring scheme is similar, but they're not compatible.

FireWire caveats   While FireWire is usually plug-and-play, some gremlins can sneak in.

- Some third-party cards can have problems that cause loss of sync. This doesn't seem to be an issue with computers whose FireWire connectors are on the motherboard (all recent Macs and some Windows machines).

- Obsolete FireWire drivers can also cause loss of sync, as well as periodic clicking or drop-outs. Check the card's manufacturer and Apple or Microsoft for updates.

- Dropped video frames can show up as a loss of audio sync, because they're hard to notice unless there's fast motion in the picture. Check the capture report for lost frames, and follow your NLE manufacturer's tips for reducing the number.

- While FireWire handles audio as data, your computer treats the incoming signal as sound. If the system-level record or input volume control isn't set to 0 dB, it may try to adjust the volume, increasing noise or distortion. (As you recall from Chapter 2, 0 dB is a ratio of 1:1—often, the midpoint on a computer's volume control—and not tech-speak for "zero volume.")

- A few cameras use a slightly-nonstandard sample rate. It's close enough to 48 kHz to sound okay, but can result in tracks that gradually slip out of sync over long transfers. You could fix this problem with an analog transfer—the computer would redigitize at the proper rate—but you'd lose all the advantages of a digital transfer. It's better to tolerate the slowly drifting sync as long as you can, and then use a visual cutaway or find a pause in the track and trim a few frames to restore sync.

- Most MiniDV cameras don't lock the audio frames to video ones. This usually isn't a problem, but may cause trouble when dubbing to a more professional format. Your NLE might have a setting to restore the lock; or you might have to dub audio via analog. Since high-end video decks have decent analog circuits, this won't compromise quality when done properly.

USB transfers   One MiniDisc recorder (HHB's Portadisc) has a USB data output, which can be plugged directly into a computer or through a hub. It shows up in your computer as a system-level sound source, and can be selected in audio programs or NLEs. Like FireWire, transfers take place in realtime: you can't select a MiniDisc track and drag it to your desktop the way you would with USB removable media.

Low-cost adapters are available to convert s/pdif digital audio to USB. They're useful for transferring from other MiniDisc decks, DATs, and digital mixers or processors. But using them puts you in the world of digital audio, rather than computer data, where there's more to worry about.

Transferring with Digital Audio

Even though an all-digital transfer won't introduce noise or distortion, it can still have problems. These generally present themselves as periodic clicking in the track, a low-level hiss that comes and goes with the signal, occasional dropouts, or sometimes a flutter or roughness to the high frequencies,. They're often the result of impatience or deadline pressures causing operator errors, rather than a fundamental failure in the equipment. Digital audio is *almost* plug-and-play. But there are some things you have to pay attention to.

The following rules apply to *any* digital audio you might be moving around your edit setup. Follow them when connecting digital mixers and processors, as well as when you're feeding a digital source to a computer input.

Use the right cable   Generic hi-fi cables have the right connectors for s/pdif, but can cause dropouts when used for digital connections. Modem cables look like they should be able to handle multitrack audio in TDIF format, but can damage the recorder. If you're not sure you've got the right kind of wire, check the manufacturer's instructions and Chapter 4 of this book.

Choose an appropriate sync source   Digital inputs rely on serial data, so they need synchronization to find the start of each word. Consumer gear synchronizes automatically to the input, so this may not be an issue. But professional equipment often gives you a choice of synchronizing to the input, a separate audio or video sync source (see Chapter 11), or internal crystal. Some gear supports only external sync with certain inputs.

If your facility is wired with video or word-clock sync, use it whenever possible to prevent problems. You'll have to specify the sample rate or video format for it to work properly. Some digital audio systems require you to set the sync source in two different places—at the internal clock, and at the input module—and will have problems if these settings disagree (it's bad software design, but you may have to live with it).

If you have to dub from a nonsynchronizable source such as a CD player or portable DAT, you may have a choice: set the computer to sync from its input, or look for a setting to *reclock* (resynchronize) the input. Either will usually work. If the source has an unstable crystal, using the input as a sync source will often be cleaner. But if the source is intentionally out-of-spec—for example, if you've varispeeded a CD, forcing its sample rate to something other than 44.1 kHz—you *must* reclock the signal. If you don't, the effect of varispeeding will disappear when you play the transferred file at the normal rate!

Plan for as few sample-rate conversions as possible   It's probable that you'll have to change the sample rate of one source signal or another during production. CDs and MiniDiscs run at 44.1 kHz. DATs can be 44.1 kHz or 48 kHz. Digital videotape is usually 48 kHz, but may be

32 kHz. Internet and multimedia audio might come through at 32 kHz or 22.050 kHz. Productions that involve 16mm or 35mm film usually require a 0.1% sample-rate correction (more about this later). But you can't mix the production—or in most cases, even edit it—until all the rates match.

Most NLEs will not do a good job of previewing, and will take extra time rendering their final output, unless every clip on the timeline matches the project's sample rate.

A little planning here can make a world of difference. Figure out what your final sample rate has to be. If you're going to digital video or DVD, 48 kHz will be necessary. If you're mixing for CD-ROM or analog video, use 44.1 kHz. Set your NLE to this rate, and convert any nonmatching digital signals as you transfer them. This can eliminate extra processing later on. For best results, do the conversions in a good audio program: modern software converts at extremely high frequencies, and does a better job than converting in an NLE.

When doing analog production, it makes sense to run tapes at their highest possible quality and not dub to the final format until the master is done. But in digital production, there's no generation loss—and absolutely no advantage to preserving a higher sample rate than the finished media.

If you're creating audio for mixed sample rates—for example, if a mix will be released on digital video (48 kHz) and audio CD (44.1 kHz)—it may be advantageous to work at the higher rate. But think things through before deciding. If the video is being broadcast only on analog TV, nothing above 15 kHz will be transmitted—so it makes more sense to work at 44.1 kHz, giving the higher-quality CD the advantage of fewer conversions.

There is a small benefit to setting your production to the lowest sample rate that will satisfy every eventual use: lower rates use less file space and can be processed by the computer faster. While the difference between 48–44.1 kHz is only about 8%—any savings there will be buried by the much greater storage and processing requirements for video—the difference between 48–32 kHz is one-third! If your converters can do a good job at that rate and you're sure you'll never need anything above 15 kHz, storage and processing savings can be significant in a long program.

Keep the bit depth as high as possible   The minimum for professional production is 16-bit audio. Using 24 bits is better, because it gives you greater margin for error and lower noise. It's often used in film and professional music production. But it's not available in cameras or double-system recorders within the reach of most DV filmmakers.

You may find 12-bit audio adequate for recording noisy events, but it shouldn't be used during production or editing. And 8-bit audio is all but obsolete.

Low bit-depth problems *are* cumulative over multiple generations. Keep your signal at the highest possible number of bits at all times. If your mixing software supports 24-bit audio, use that setting and save the mix in that format, even if you're starting with 16-bit clips. You'll get lower noise, which means you can mix at a slightly lower level to avoid distortion. If you've shot 12-bit audio in the field—and you'd better have a darned good reason for using that lower-quality setting—your NLE will convert it to 16-bit before saving. No quality is lost with this upward conversion, but none is gained either.

Eventually you may have to convert a mix from 24-bit back to 16-bit to fit on a video or CD format. When you do, be sure your software's Dither option (Chapter 3) is turned on. If possible, keep a high-bit version of the file so you don't pick up extra noise if you have to make changes.

Normally, don't normalize until the mix is done   *Normalizing* is the automatic process of scanning a file, finding the loudest sample, and then amplifying the entire file so its maximum level reaches a preset peak. It's useful in some situations, but almost never for production tracks. That's because each clip of a scene will be amplified a different amount, depending on the loudest dialog in the clip. This changes the background level from clip to clip, making a smooth mix almost impossible.

If you have to amplify because a scene was shot too softly, use a Gain or Amplify function instead, and apply the same amount to a copy of every clip. Most audio programs can do this as a batch process. Then check each of the new clips to make sure none of them reach 0 dBFS; if they do, go back to the originals and apply less gain.

After a project is mixed, you may want to normalize the entire track so it plays as loudly as possible. But use a program that lets you choose the maximum level. 0 dBFS—the default in many programs—is too loud for most hardware to handle. If your project is destined for computer media, normalize to about –2 dBFS as a safety margin. If it'll be broadcast from digital tape, –10 dBFS is the standard maximum level (though some local stations will accept –2 dBFS MiniDV tapes, if properly marked).

There's a myth that normalization is necessary to get the best results from MP3 and other psychoacoustic compression (Chapter 3). Strictly speaking, it isn't: the algorithm breaks the incoming audio into short chunks, normalizes each before encoding, and then applies a matching gain reduction on playback. Pre-normalizing the files won't make any difference to how the system performs. Many people play MP3 files on the street or in their cars, so making the source material louder can help it compete with background noise. The same holds true for Web video. But DVD is often played in quiet surroundings. Even though it uses similar algorithms, tracks for this medium can be set to whatever level you think artistically appropriate.

Avoid data compression until the final step   You may need to run the final mix through QuickTime or other data compression for distribution. If so, keep an uncompressed version. These processes are not reversible—decoding the compressed audio always results in some data loss—so you'll need the original if you have to re-edit or compress with a different algorithm.

Besides, new processes are constantly being developed. Tomorrow's compression might be a lot cleaner, and you'll want to be able to take advantage of it without being stuck with yesterday's data loss.

Don't compress individual tracks, either. They'll just have to be decoded when you edit or mix—even if the software does this in the background, without telling you—and coding artifacts will build up when they're recompressed. Wait until you've got a mixed track, and then do the whole thing in a single pass.

Listen!   Whatever you do, keep an ear on what's actually coming out of your NLE or processor rather than on what's going in. If an element is being processed in software, play the whole thing back before proceeding. Most digital audio problems will show up on good monitors, if you just listen carefully, and can be undone if you catch them quickly enough.

Digital audio processors

If you need to tweak levels, equalization, or volume compression and you have a good outboard digital processor or mixer, it's acceptable (and certainly a time saver) to apply this correction while you're transferring from digital media. But keep things subtle; it's a lot easier to add additional processing later than to compensate if you go overboard now. Make sure the source, processor or mixer, and recorder or computer are at the same sample rate. Be sure to store the processor's settings so you can reapply them if you have to retransfer.

No matter how good your digital reverb is, don't apply this reverb during the initial transfer stage. If a track seems too dry to match the picture—perhaps because a radio mic was very close during a long shot—cherish its purity; tracks like this are the easiest to edit. Once the show is completely cut, and you've also got music and sound effects in place, you can add appropriate reverb.

Digitizing Analog Signals

Often, analog sources such as Betacam tapes or live mics have to be edited, or you're using digital sources like DAT or MiniDiscs, but your NLE isn't equipped for digital input. In these cases it's necessary to *digitize*, converting the analog signal to digital in the input circuits of the editing system. This introduces a whole new layer where things can go wrong.

The problem is that analog audio can't be controlled with the precision or simple user interface of digital transfers. Until a signal is turned into ones and zeros, your computer can't help. Using computer controls to compensate for badly-set analog equipment makes things even worse.

- The best way to avoid problems with digitizing is to not digitize at all. Connect digital sources like DAT or MiniDisc through an s/pdif adapter. Import CD audio from the computer's CD-ROM drive instead of playing the tracks on an analog-output player.

- Most recording studios, announcers, and composers can supply elements as files or audio CD. Use this option instead of redigitizing other media. Not only will the quality be higher; it's also faster to transfer a file than to redigitize a realtime playback.

It takes some thought to set up a system for digitizing well, but, once you've done the preliminary work, things will go smoothly. The place to start is with the analog circuits in your edit suite, before the signal ever gets to the NLE.

Gain-staging

Everything in your analog signal path has a finite dynamic range. There's only a narrow window between too soft—when the signal is mixed with hiss and other electronic noise—and too loud to handle without distortion. Each piece of equipment has a specific range where it gives you the best performance. Gain-staging is the process of fine-tuning the volume as it passes from one piece of equipment to another, so that the signals always stay in that range. (This also applies to digital signals, but their dynamic range is wider, and you don't have to worry about recalibrating at every step—once a signal is digital, its level stays the same, no matter what equipment or software you use. So unless you're writing audio processing software, gain-staging is usually thought of as an analog concern.)

Figure 12.2 shows how things can go wrong in a setup with preamp, equalizer, and compressor—but the same problems can occur in a setup with just a preamp and computer input, between the input and output circuits in a mixing board, or any other time a signal has to pass through multiple stages.

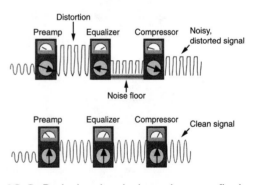

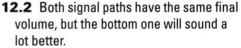

12.2 Both signal paths have the same final volume, but the bottom one will sound a lot better.

Although both signal paths in the figure yield the same volume at the end, the top signal is distorted and noisy . . . and won't sound good in a mix. The problem is that the preamp was set for too much gain in the top path. This forced it to a higher level than its own circuits could handle, causing distortion on its output. It also meant that the equalizer saw too much signal, so its volume had to be turned down. But it was turned down too far, forcing its output down to where part of the signal is obscured by electronic noise. The input to the compressor was then turned up to compensate, amplifying both signal and noise . . . and doing nothing about the distortion.

In the lower path, the preamp is set to a reasonable amount of gain. Its output is just right for the equalizer, which puts out the right amount of signal for the compressor. The result is a signal that's just as loud as the top path's, but a lot better sounding.

Unfortunately, the nice meters and large calibrated knobs I drew usually don't usually exist in real life. Many consumer and semipro devices don't have more than a flashing overload light. The only way to tell if equipment is working in its proper range is to test a lot of different levels.

Here's a general procedure, though it's worth checking individual product manuals, since specific equipment may have other alignment procedures.

1. Start with the first item in your signal chain. Apply a normal signal, from the playback of well-recorded original track.

2. Raise the equipment's input volume until the overload light starts flashing; then lower it until the light flashes only on occasional peaks—no more than once every couple of seconds. If analog equipment has a bouncing meter instead of a flashing light, consider one or two units above the zero point—where the meter scale turns red—as the equivalent. If the equipment has an output-level control, turn it to the midpoint or detent.

3. Now do the same thing with the next device in the chain. You should end up with its input-volume control around the midpoint. If you have to turn it up or down a lot, there's either a mismatch between equipment at –10 dBV and at +4 dBu, or you've gotten microphone- and line-level connections mixed up. If it's the former case, you'll need a buffer or pad (see Chapter 11). If it's the latter, fix the wiring—anything else you do will sacrifice quality.

After you're sure that levels are being handled properly before the signal gets to your computer, you can start to turn the analog signal into data on a file. There are two potential trouble spots here: the quality of the NLE's digitizing circuit, and how well the software's meters are calibrated. You can do something about both of them.

Getting Better Inputs

No matter how fast a processor chip is, or how many audio effects are supplied with the software, the ultimate limit on an NLE's sound is its analog circuits. Often, there's not much control over their quality. A lot of systems are sold by people who understand video and software, not sound. Some high-end NLEs have proprietary audio interfaces that were designed by independent contractors, and the manufacturer doesn't even know their basic specifications.[1] Software-only NLEs have to rely on the user's third-party sound-input device, which may not be particularly high quality.

Unfortunately, turning audio into digits is an exacting process, and it requires expensive components to do the job well. One good solution is to get a full-sized portable DAT or MiniDisc recorder. Use it at the shoot for double-system sound (Chapter 9), since the quality is so much better than most in-camera recordings. Transfer these tracks digitally into your NLE, using a USB adapter with s/pdif inputs. Then use just the portable's electronics, with the tape stopped but in level-setting mode, to digitize mics and line-level analog sources. Record them in the computer through the s/pdif to USB adapter. These portables also have reliable metering and large analog volume controls, something you won't find with most other computer-input devices.

You need only one external converter to improve both digitizing and final output: while you're recording or editing, put the converter on the NLE's input and monitor via the system's built-in analog output. When you're ready to mix or send the finished track to analog tape, switch the converter to the output and use it in digital-to-analog mode.

Calibrating an NLE's Meters

The record-level meters that came with your NLE software are probably inadequate (see Chapter 11), and will probably lead you to digitize at the wrong level. This is a major problem, because even though a digital system may have a theoretical 16-bit range, computer-input circuits sacrifice some of the range, and processing errors[2] can destroy even more. You can't afford to throw away any bits. This gets even more important if you're editing material for broadcast, where subsequent processing—either at an audio post facility or at the TV station—will emphasize any low-level noise and distortion.

Even if you've got a separate hardware meter, it won't be accurate unless it's connected digitally or you've calibrated it for your system. Fortunately, calibration can be easy. You don't need any additional hardware or technical knowledge, the procedure doesn't take very long, and it'll remain accurate until you change the system.

Before you do anything else, check the system-level input volume controls (Figure 12.3). These take priority over any settings you make in software. They should be in their neutral position (shown) and left there for any audio operation.

1. Start by setting the program's input volume control (if it has one) to its nominal position. This is usually the default value and may be marked as 0 dB or 50%; in most situations, it will result in the cleanest recording. You'll be making volume adjustments as you go along,

---

1. I've spent frustrating hours on the phone with product managers of a big-ticket editing system, trying to find out how their analog-to-digital circuit was calibrated. They offered to send me a schematic, but said nobody in-house could read it.

2. The NLE's, not yours. If it calculates fades or equalization using 16-bit math, there'll be inevitable errors caused by rounding off the lowest possible numbers.

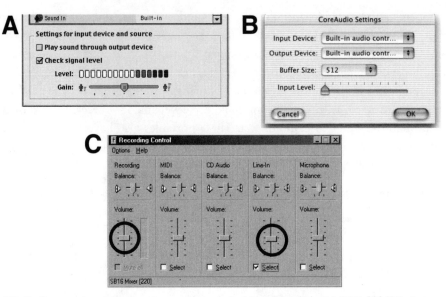

12.3 System-level input volume controls in Mac OS9 *(A)* and OSX *(B)*. Windows has two to worry about *(C)*.

but do them with an analog output volume control at the source. This is one case where analog is better than digital.

2. If your analog equipment doesn't have an output-volume control, or following this procedure makes you turn that control below about 30% of maximum, you'll need an accessory attenuator like the one described in the next section. Without it, you'll never be able to set the best digitizing level.

3. Find a well-recorded source tape. Play it and adjust the source's output (or accessory attenuator) so the recording meter swings into its red area only on occasional peaks. The red area might be marked 0 db, –6 dB, 80%, or some other message at the whim of the manufacturer, but it'll be at the top of the scale right below the overload indication.

4. Once you've adjusted the volume, record 10 or 15 seconds at that level and save the file. Use a name that'll help you remember the peak meter reading for that trial (see Figure 12.4). Now make two more recordings, one at a somewhat lower output level, and one somewhat higher. Note their peak readings also, and save them with appropriate names.

5. Open the three files and look at their waveforms. See which meter reading gave you the loudest recording without distortion; look for the file with the tallest waves that are still rounded (like Figure 12.4). If the waves reach the upper or lower boundary of the window or have flattened tops and bottoms (Figure 12.5), the recording was too loud.

6. It's unlikely that your results will match mine on the first set of recordings. So repeat the process, making finer and finer adjustments centered around the best meter reading from the previous trial. In a few minutes, you'll find the ideal reading. It doesn't matter what the

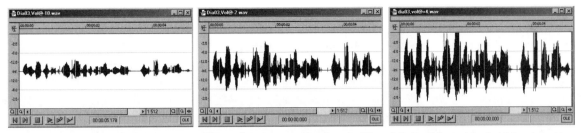

12.4 Save the file with a name that'll help you remember its level.

12.5 Good recording levels fill the screen without touching top or bottom.

12.6 When the digitizing level is too high, tops or bottoms of waves will be too loud for the window.

meter says in dB or percentage or arbitrary numbers, so long as you can repeat it. The next time you're digitizing, set the source's volume control so the meter reacts the same way. Dialog, narration, and different kinds of music can cause different meter responses, so you may want to repeat the calibration procedure with various audio sources.

Linear and "boosted" windows Some NLE software lets you view an audio clip with a built-in visual distortion that boosts lower volumes so you can see them better (Figure 12.7). This affects how the softer samples will appear, but won't change the sound or what you're looking for: the best recording level will be the one that fills the window without touching the edges.

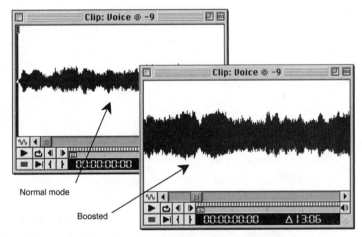

Normal mode

Boosted

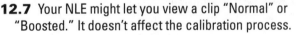

12.7 Your NLE might let you view a clip "Normal" or "Boosted." It doesn't affect the calibration process.

Accessory attenuator

If have to turn the source's output control very close to its lowest level to get a good recording, it's likely you'll be picking up extra noise from the source's output circuits. These usually follow the level control, so turning the knob all the way down has the same effect as bad gain-staging (as with the equalizer in the top of Figure 12.2). A better solution is to run the output device at its proper nominal volume, and insert an external volume control between its output and the digitizer's input.

For some reason, nobody makes such a helpful device. But you can build your own for about $5 using a single 5 kΩ audio-taper potentiometer (Radio Shack #271-1720) and appropriate connectors. Figure 12.8 shows how to wire it for balanced and unbalanced circuits, and Figure 12.9 identifies the connections as they'll appear on most brands of potentiometer. You must use soldered connections to avoid noise and may want to put the unit (or a pair of them for stereo) in a metal or plastic box with a large knob so it's easier to check and restore the settings. If that's too much work, get a local hacker to build it for you.

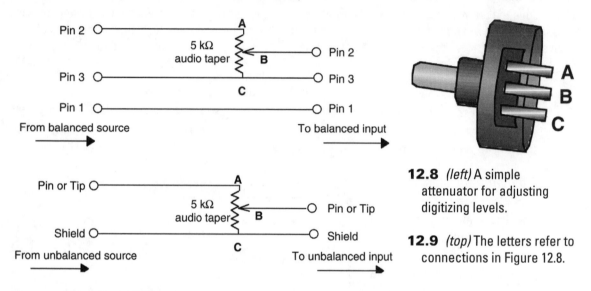

12.8 *(left)* A simple attenuator for adjusting digitizing levels.

12.9 *(top)* The letters refer to connections in Figure 12.8.

Diagnosing Problems

Bad digitizing levels can hide hum or noise in your audio chain. Once you've calibrated the system, digitize another test file at the correct volume. But this time, use a source tape that has some silence recorded on it as well as normal program material (unplug the mic, or turn the record-volume control down when you record this part). Play back the file and listen very carefully to the silent part. If there isn't any noise, your system is properly calibrated, and you're done.

If there is noise on the test file, digitize that source tape yet again. But this time, pause the source for a few seconds in the middle of the recording. Play back this file and listen to where you paused. If the noise stopped, it's on the source tape. You may be able to reduce it in software, but only at the cost of losing some of the desired sound. (Most "noise reduction" systems assume noise is most bothersome during pauses, and simply turn down the overall volume—or just the treble—when things get soft. But the noise is still there, lurking under the signal and ready to be emphasized by subsequent processors.) Some cameras generate a tiny amount of noise when the mic is unplugged. Others generate moderate amounts of noise at all times; read Chapter 9 for things you can do about it.

If the noise continues even when the source tape is stopped, it's being generated by the playback deck or digitizing hardware. Here are some steps for fixing it:

- Hiss is often a question of bad gain-staging.

- Hiss can also be caused by magnetized tape heads in an analog audio or video deck, or badly aligned analog equipment. You can get a demagnetizer with instructions at most electronics stores, but for anything else, you'll need the help of a technician.

- Random noises—snaps, crackles, and pops—are usually caused by loose connections or bad circuit components. Try cleaning the connectors (a rubber eraser works well, or you can get special cleaning fluids at electronics stores) or replacing the cables. If that doesn't help, it's time to take your equipment to the shop.

- Hum in desktop video setups is almost always the result of ground loops. See Chapter 11.

Once you've tracked down and fixed any noises or hum, make a final test recording at the ideal level you found, and look at its waveform. It's unlikely, but you may need to go through the calibration procedure again. Then relax, secure in the knowledge that your analog digitizing chain is properly set up.

Working with Very Low Sample Rates

If a project will end up only on the Internet or in a desktop learning situation, a 22 kHz sample rate may be adequate (and possibly desirable, because its smaller files make it easier to transmit or store). If you need very small voice files and compression schemes such as MP3 aren't supported by the playback medium, 11 kHz sampling may even be usable. (On some systems, these rates are actually 22.050 kHz and 11.025 kHz, as submultiples of the standard CD sample rate.)

These very low sample rates have little margin for error. Problems at the upper frequency ranges of a 44.1 kHz file, where there's very little musical information, are easily ignored. But those at the top of a 22 kHz file are immediately obvious in music, and those near the top of an 11 kHz file can cut into the intelligibility of a voice track. Two principles will keep you from getting into trouble.

The first rule is not to digitize at the final sample rate. Audio has to be filtered when it's digitized, to keep overly high frequencies from generating false data and accompanying themselves with whistles and squeaks. But the analog filters in most desktop systems aren't very flexible and can have serious problems when switched to low frequencies. Any filter, digital or analog, creates a distortion that gets worse as you approach its limit.

The solution is oversampling, discussed in Chapter 3. Professional equipment usually records in the megahertz range, with gentle analog filters, and then refilters in the digital domain as it divides the sample rate down. You might not have this option on a desktop system, but you can do the next best thing by recording at the highest frequency your sound card supports, and then converting in software. If you're working in an NLE, you'll need to keep the file at 44.1 kHz or 48 kHz while you edit and mix. Then downsample the output when you render it. If you're mixing in an audio program, you probably can run it at a lower sample rate. Convert the files before you start working to save storage space and processing time.

The second rule is to stay away from analog as much as possible. Each time you pass a signal through the analog inputs or outputs of a sound card, it goes back through those nasty filters. Unless you have significant oversampling, the high-frequency response will fall off rapidly. So if you have to leave the digital system to pass through an analog effect or mixer, keep the signal at a high sample rate while you do. Just downsample the final mix.

Metering and Lineup Tones

Audio-level meters do more than tell you how loud a mix is, or when you're digitizing at the right level. Used with a lineup tone, they provide repeatability: you can digitize part of a scene today, redigitize other parts of it next year, and all the audio should intercut perfectly. Meters and tone also assure consistency, so the dub house or broadcast station who gets your tapes will have some idea of what to expect for volume levels.

Experienced audio professionals usually take tones with a grain of salt. We use them to calibrate gain-staging, and are rigorous about providing accurate tones on tapes we send out. But we've all been burned by badly applied tones on tapes we get, so we verify levels against the actual program material before digitizing.

VU meters

The big Bakelite volume unit meter used to be a standard fixture on every piece of audio equipment. These were more than simple voltage meters; while they measured steady tones the way voltmeters did, they responded to quickly varying sounds very much like our ears do. Their ballistics were designed to smooth over very fast volume changes, so they correlated nicely with subjective loudness. They also drew current from the audio line, loading it down, and their rectifiers added a subtle but audible distortion to the signal.

So much for nostalgia. Today there are so few true VU meters being manufactured that they're too expensive to include in most equipment. If they were included, they'd need separate overload indicators since their damped movements can't catch the sudden peaks that cause digital problems.

Analog voltmeter

The things that *look like* VU meters (Figure 12.10) in modern analog gear are really simple voltmeters and don't have the same kind of calibrated dynamics. They're too fast to show you average levels, but can't respond quickly enough to short transients. On the other hand, they're accurate with steady signals and can be used for lineup tones. If you have a true VU meter and one of these voltmeters on the same signal, you'll notice that the VU is much easier to read because it's not jumping around as much. You'll also notice that if they're both calibrated to the same tone, sudden jumps to +1 on the VU meter might swing as high as +6 on the voltmeter.

12.10 The "VU" meters in most modern equipment are really low-cost voltmeters.

Peak reading meter

Both digital and analog distort when a signal is too loud. But analog distortion isn't noticeable on very fast peaks, while some digital gear will make a horrible crackling noise if a peak is much longer than a thousandth of a second—the first split second of a gunshot, for example. Even a fast-responding analog voltmeter can't display peaks this fast, so electronic circuits are added to capture the loudest reading and hold it for a few seconds. These circuits can also determine the average volume and generate a voltage that makes a lower-cost voltmeter behave like a proper VU meter. (Building one of these circuits and calibrating it with a specific voltmeter mechanism is still an expensive proposition, however, so you rarely find them outside of recording studios.)

Microprocessors can also measure peak and average voltage. Some audio programs put a relatively reliable combination meter on the computer screen, though the CPU might be too busy during actual recording to respond to very fast peaks. The most accurate hardware-based audio meters today have dedicated circuit boards with their own processor chips and display both peak and average level, either on a row of LEDs or superimposed on the video monitor. If the circuit is fed with an AES/EBU or s/pdif digital audio stream, the

12.11 A combination peak/average meter, calibrated for digital inputs.

meter is self-calibrating and absolutely reliable. Figure 12.11 shows one like that, available from Dorrough Electronics.

How Much is Zero?

Traditional VU meters were calibrated to 0 dBm—a precise standard—even though the circuits could handle a few decibels above that level with no trouble. So engineers got used to the idea of "headroom" and would run their equipment so that loud voices or music might exceed zero every few seconds. Lineup tones on the tape or over the network would still be calibrated to zero on the meter, but program peaks might hover around +3 VU.

But digital audio levels aren't measured in volts or dBm; they're expressed as a ratio below "all bits are turned on"—the loudest possible sound you can digitize, since there aren't any bits to show when a sound gets louder than that. The ratio is known as decibels below full scale (dBFS). This has led to a confusing state of affairs:

- Analog audio meters start at some negative number, around –40 VU, and then are calibrated through zero to a positive number (usually +3 or +6). Zero is the nominal operating level; lineup tones are set to match it, even though some peaks are expected to be louder than zero.

- But digital audio meters start at a negative number and top out at 0 dBFS. Peak levels have to be held below digital zero, and with a safety factor may be considerably lower. If you record a lineup tone at zero on a digital meter, and use that tone to set up an analog dub with tone equalling 0 VU, the actual track will be too soft.

- Since analog meters read up to +6 VU and digital ones up to 0 dBFS, it would seem logical to make the digital lineup tone precisely –6 dBFS. If you do this, and set the analog meter to zero on that –6 dBFS digital tone, the analog tape will agree with the digital one perfectly—*but only for steady tones*. Remember, analog meters show average levels and don't respond to instantaneous changes. Speech that looks perfectly good on the digital meter may only tickle the analog circuits at –18 VU if the meters are calibrated this way.

This is a very real problem, and often affects DV filmmakers the first time they send a tape out for broadcast or multiple VHS dubs. Unfortunately, there can't be a perfect solution. That's because the peak-to-average ratio depends on the program material. Live classical music or sporting events may have sudden peaks as high as 18 dB or more above the average level. But heavily processed pop music might have its peaks clamped to 2 dB above average.

While there can't be a one-size-fits-all solution for converting digital tones to analog ones, there are industry standards:

- Professional videotape and audio media intended for video or film (such as timecode DAT) have their tone at –20 dBFS. The loudest signal should never go above –10 dBFS for broadcast, or –2 dBFS for film.

- Prosumer videotape and other media such as MiniDisc have their tone at –12 dBFS. This is the standard mark on most MiniDV cameras and MiniDisc recorders. Peaks must never exceed –2 dBFS.

While the broadcast standard throws away almost a bit and a half of resolution, the signal-to-noise ratio in this kind of equipment is high enough that this isn't a problem. All professional film and video sound equipment is designed for this standard: –20 dBFS on the digital side equals +4 dBu on the balanced analog.

The prosumer standard has a much smaller safety zone, but picks up 8 dB better noise performance. Since MiniDV cameras have poor signal-to-noise ratios, this is important. But it means you have to be more careful when setting the original recording volume, since loud peaks might reach 0 dBFS and be irreparably distorted. Prosumer and consumer equipment usually relates –12 dBFS digital to –10 dBV unbalanced analog, though there are exceptions.

These standards are most important when communicating with the outside world. You can keep levels at the more convenient –12 dBFS average while editing and mixing on a prosumer NLE, and then lower the overall level to –20 dBFS average when dubbing to Digital Betacam.

Synchronization

This section is about the technical aspects of sync. There are pointers in Chapter 13 for manually fixing lipsync problems while you're editing.

While nonlinear editors have internal databases to keep multiple audio and video tracks in sync, you need a more standardized timing reference when you step out of that closed system. SMPTE timecode—developed by the Society of Motion Picture and Television Engineers, and first popularized as an editing and timing reference in the late 1970s—is the universal language to identify specific frames in a videotape. Analog and digital audio systems use it as well, to keep track of which sounds should play against those frames.

SMPTE code can also be used as a speed reference, by measuring the length of time from one frame to the next, but this usually isn't precise or stable enough for digital audio or even analog color video. Most systems use blackburst (see Chapter 11) to control the speed, once timecode has been applied to get the frames in sync. Better audio workstations give you a choice of what they'll do if timecode and blackburst aren't moving at the same speed: just report the error and continue relying on blackburst, resync so that timecode agrees, or stop cold and wait for operator intervention.

But if you're going to intervene, you have to understand what timecode is really doing . . .

Understanding Timecode

Prepare to be confused. Of all the techniques we use, SMTPE timecode is the most bewildering. What else can you expect of a system where 29 + 1 = 30 nine times out of ten, and 29 + 1 = 32 the tenth?

Timecode was invented to help video editing. Each frame gets a unique hour:minute:second:frame address, so you can assemble scenes more predictably. It also serves as a common reference to assure that sound, picture, and animation from different systems all fit together. The one thing it *doesn't* do is keep track of time. A minute of it won't precisely equal a minute on anyone's standard clock. An hour of the stuff might equal an hour on your wristwatch—or maybe it won't. And the last three sentences aren't true in Europe, Africa, or Australia!

Fortunately, all you need is logic—and a little bit of history—to become a master of time (code).

Once upon a time . . .

The problem started more than 50 years ago. Back in those black-and-white days, U.S. television scanned at 30 frames per second. This number was chosen both because it was easy to derive a sync signal from the 60 Hz power line that ran into every home, and because any hum introduced into the video circuits of early TVs would stay in sync with the picture and not roll around the screen.

When color TV was invented, more information had to be jammed into the picture to keep track of colors. But broadcasters didn't want to make this more complex signal incompatible with older sets because they'd lose viewers. So they stretched each frame a tiny bit longer—1/10th of a percent, to 29.97 fps[3]—and used the extra time to put in a color reference signal. The new frame rate was close enough to the older standard that monochrome viewers could adjust their sets to compensate. (If you're over 50, you probably remember having to jump up and trim the vertical hold knob whenever a TV station switched from monochrome to color.)

This 29.97 fps system worked fine until timecode was invented. You can see the problem in Figure 12.12. The top filmstrip represents 30 fps black and white video, with a digital wall clock beneath it. At the end of 29 frames, both the video and clock are ready to move on to a new second. But color TV (middle strip) is slightly slower, so it's still playing that 29th frame when it's time for a new second. The timecode numbers can't move until the frame is finished. This tiny error accumulates to the point that an hour's worth of timecode is more than an hour and three

---

3. It actually worked out to 29.97002997 fps. The difference between this number and the commonly accepted 29.27 fps can result in a one-frame error after about ten hours. Unless you're producing *War and Peace* with no commercial breaks, don't worry about it.

seconds long. A program that was produced to start at 1:00:00 timecode and end at 1:59:59 would actually finish a few seconds after two o'clock! (To think of it another way: The frame rate was slowed down 1/10th of a percent. An hour is 3,600 seconds, so slowing it down means 3,600 seconds times 0.1%, or 3.6 seconds.)

Broadcasters realized this timecode stuff could cause shows to bump into commercials, costing them money, and howled for a solution.

Dropframe

The broadcasters' solution was to periodically skip a few numbers. At the end of most minutes, the number jumps ahead by two. If your tape is parked at 00:01:59:29 (hours: minutes: seconds: frames) and you jog exactly one frame forward, you land on 00:02:00:02. Even though the format is called dropframe, no frames are ever dropped; instead, two numbers per minute are. The bottom strip in Figure 12.12 shows how it counts.

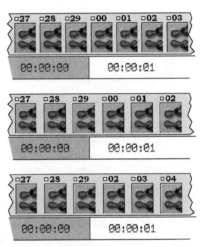

There are 60 minutes in an hour, so dropping two numbers per minute means 120 numbers will be dropped each hour. But the actual error caused by that 1/10th-percent slowdown was 3.6 seconds, or 108 frames. Now our timecode hour is 12 frames too short! So to fine-tune the process, six times an hour—once for every minute that ends in zero—counting reverts to normal. Park at 00:09:59:29 and jog one frame, and you land on

12.12 Dropframe is necessary because there aren't an even number of frames per second.

00:10:00:00. This puts back two numbers for every ten minutes, or—*ta-dah!*—12 frames an hour. When you do all this, an hour of dropframe timecode precisely equals an hour of the clock on the wall.

It works, but this crazy counting makes editing more complicated. The duration of a scene frequently doesn't equal the difference between its in-time and its out-time. Editing computers can handle this automatically, but human editors have a hard time getting around it. So television production in NTSC[4] countries uses two timecode formats:

- Nondropframe timecode counts continuously, so it's easier to use when running length isn't critical or for short projects. It's usually preferred in commercial postproduction and non-broadcast media.

---

4. NTSC really stands for National Television Standards Commission, though most broadcast engineers will say it means Never Twice the Same Color.

- Dropframe timecode is harder to count, but, on average, it agrees with the clock on the wall. It's preferred by broadcast producers and stations.

I once worked with a producer who insisted his projects were too important to use dropframe timecode. Every frame of his project was vital, and he didn't want any thrown away.

You know better.

Both dropframe and nondrop run at the same 29.97 fps rate, so tapes are interchangeable. You can produce your spot using nondrop, and TV stations won't turn it down (they may insist on dropframe for program masters, to make things easier in the control room). Well-designed editing systems even let you mix code formats in the same production.

Those crazy Americans

This nonsense applies only to NTSC countries—North and South America, and parts of industrialized Asia—where color video runs 29.97 fps. In the rest of the world-power lines are 50 Hz, so black-and-white TV evolved at 25 fps. This is slow enough that PAL and SECAM countries didn't have to stretch frames to accommodate color.

Audio programs and nonbroadcast computer systems sometimes use 30 fps timecode, since it's easier to count, and modern technology has no problem synchronizing it. By definition, 30 fps timecode has to be nondropframe . . . there's no point skipping numbers since it already matches the clock. You may see "30 fps dropframe" on editing equipment, but the name is the mistaken result of confusing frame rate with counting format. Table 12.1 summarizes the code formats.

Table 12.1   Code formats

Code Type	Frame Rate	Counting Format
24 fps	24 fps (film)	Count to 23, then 1 second 0 frames
25 fps	25 fps	Count to 24, then 1 second 0 frames
29.97 nondrop	29.97 fps	Count to 29, then 1 second 0 frames
29.97 dropframe	29.97 fps	Count to 29, then 1 second 2 frames . . . except once every 10 minutes, don't.
30 fps nondrop	30 fps	Count to 29, then 1 second 0 frames
30 fps dropframe	This rate and format combination seems silly, but some manufacturers support it anyway.	

Timecode Recording and Transmission

Timecode is usually carried as a biphase serial word around 2,400 Hz. The exact frequency depends on the frame rate, but it's always in the middle of the audio range. This way it can be recorded on one of an analog video deck's regular audio tracks, or on a specialized audio "address track" that includes circuitry to protect the code's square wave—one of the few times that a true digital signal is recorded as analog data. Since these tracks run parallel to the tape, instead of scanning diagonally like the picture, the code is called Longitudinal Timecode (LTC)—a term that also refers to that signal as it chirps through the studio wires as a digital serial stream.

LTC is rugged, can be read during fast wind, and is easy to deal with. But when it's carried as analog audio on a tape, it disappears when the tape is paused or shuttling slowly. So the same numbers are also frequently written as a series of white dots, as a digital code in the space between pictures. This Vertical Interval Timecode (VITC) lives with the video, so it can be read whenever the image is visible, but gets disrupted when the image is edited. It can also be carried over a studio's video wiring or transmitted on the air along with the picture.

Most professional analog video decks use both forms of code, choosing the most reliable at any given moment, and delivering the result as an LTC signal at the deck's output jack and—on request from the edit controller—over the deck's serial control wires. Most professional digital audio and video decks keep track of timecode as part of their other timing data, readable whether the tape is paused or playing, and deliver it the same way.

As far as the next piece of equipment is concerned, there's almost no difference between analog-recorded LTC, video-recorded VITC, or digitally recorded timecode.

Shuttling timecode

One anomaly makes LTC recorded on an audio track and LTC translated from VITC or digital data behave differently at slow speeds. Remember, timecode is transmitted as a serial word; you can't read it until a full word is sent, which takes exactly one frame. At play speed, this means the received code is always exactly one frame behind the picture that's playing. Editing systems compensate by adding a frame. This works even if the tape is shuttling at fractional speeds, since the audio track is slowed down the same amount.

But VITC and timecode from digital recorders continue to flash by once per frame, so LTC derived from it is constantly updating . . . even if the video is moving slower than a frame at a time. This means that if the picture is playing at half speed—one frame every 1/15th second—it's one frame late for the first 1/30th second, and then it catches up. At quarter speed, it's late for only the first frame in four. If a system tries to compensate for timecode delay when the picture is scanning at quarter speed, it'll be wrong 75% of the time. A few pieces of equipment can sort this out, based on how the numbers are counting, but the rest of them expect you to live with the error. Some give you the choice of generating timecode as analog- or digital-style, so you can set whether it has a constant or variable rate to accommodate the next piece of equipment.

Using timecode

Timecode, as a string of LTC data, isn't important until you want to synchronize two separate pieces of equipment or an audio tape with a video one. This seldom happens in the world of desktop production, but may be necessary when bringing material to a pro facility. Broadcasters frequently specify that commercials begin at exactly the start of a minute (00 seconds, 00 frames), and that programs start at exactly one hour. Audio or video post facilities prefer that your tapes have matching timecode, but can usually cope if you don't. Since most desktop filmmakers bring audio elements as CD-ROM, the issue is moot. With the exception of EBU Broadcast Wave format (supported only in high-end NLEs), files don't carry timecode information.

FireWire DV has its own timecode, and your NLE might be able to send it to a professional deck, where it can be converted to SMPTE. If you need to record a tape with timecode using LTC, many NLEs will let you attach a converter to the computer's serial port. Some NLEs can read an audio input as timecode, automatically placing a clip after it's been digitized. Since the NLE has only two inputs, this means the digitized clip can't have stereo audio.

Timecode can be used manually as well. If you're transferring a clip from one project to another, or from NLE to multitrack audio program, you can type its starting code as part of the filename. Plant a marker in the second timeline at that location, and you'll be able to snap the clip to it.

Syncing Film with Audio

A lot of projects are shot on traditional film but edited in a computer to get the best combination of image quality and editing flexibility. Since it's not practical to record sound on film the way it is with videotape, double-system is always used. In the professional arena, timecode is used for synchronization. But you can sync just as easily using a slate, as described in Chapter 9.

A slate can mark the start of a scene, but analog tape doesn't have sprockets like film or a control track like videotape or DATs. Before timecode was invented, speed control was a major issue in film sound. Analog tape is moved inside the recorder by pressing it against a spinning metal rod, and any slippage or tape stretch will change the speed. You could sync the front of a scene with a slate, but there was nothing to keep sound and film running at the same speed after that. A different scheme was necessary. This method is still used in some film schools and low-budget productions.

Pilot tones

High-quality portable analog recorders, particularly the Nagra III and pre-timecode IV series, used the *Neopilot* system for recording a 60-Hz sync signal on the tape. This *pilot* signal is generated by the camera, derived from wall current, or comes from a crystal in the recorder. On playback, the pilot is compared with an accurate 60 Hz source. If the tape has stretched or is slipping during playback, the pilot will be lower than 60 Hz and the playback deck's motor is sped up to compensate. If the tape slipped during recording, the pilot will be higher than 60 Hz, and the playback is slowed down. The result is an analog tape that plays back at exactly the same speed it was recorded. Its audio can then be transferred to a more stable digital medium for computer editing, or to magnetic stock with film-like perforations for conventional editing.

In Neopilot, the pilot doesn't get a track of its own. The entire width of the tape is devoted to a monaural audio track, for the highest possible quality. The pilot is recorded with a special tape head that superimposes two tracks on top of the audio. One of these tracks has its polarity inverted, so that when the top one is writing a positive signal, the bottom is writing a negative. When the tape is played back, a matching head decodes the pilot. Meanwhile, the main head reads the entire width of the tape and sees audio only. It's the tape equivalent of phantom power (Chapter 7)!

You may encounter a "Nagra tape" with location sound you want to use.

- Stereo pilot and timecode-based Nagras use a special timing track that can't even be detected on normal stereo analog tape decks. You won't hear them at all . . . but unless you have a properly equipped playback deck, there'll be no way to control the speed.

- Tapes from Neopilot mono Nagras—and there are a lot of them still in the field—will have a pronounced 60-Hz hum in each channel when played on a stereo deck. That's because only half the pilot signal is being detected, and the matched out-of-phase signal isn't there to cancel it. If you don't have proper playback equipment, you can't recover the speed information. But you can get rid of the hum: mix both tracks of the stereo deck together equally. When they're properly balanced, the hum will disappear (and the audio will also have less hiss).

Using film with digital audio

Digital recordings have inherently stable speed. If you're using them for film double-system and take the precautions in Chapter 9, sound and picture will play back at the same rate. If you then transfer the digital audio to a traditional sprocketed magnetic film (*mag*) recorder, you should be able to edit in a flatbed or on a sync block with no problem. But this method is largely obsolete, outside of film schools and very low-budget film production.

These days, it's more likely that sound (and possibly picture) will be edited digitally. That can raise some sync issues.

Editing film in an NLE Producers often transfer film to videotape for editing and eventual broadcast or distribution on VHS or DVD. But you can't just point a video camera at a film projection and expect good results. Film runs at 24 frames per second. Since NTSC cameras are

29.97 fps, they'd inevitably be catching some of the momentary black frames caused by the projector's shutter. The result would be a black *shutter bar* that rides up or down the screen.

Instead, film is transferred with a *3-2 pulldown*. This is a scheme that puts one film frame onto three whole video fields, and the next onto two (Figure 12.13). Since there are two fields in a single NTSC video frame, this makes it an almost perfect speed match for the video, and the black bars are never recorded. This isn't perceptible in most cases, since the film itself isn't slowed down. The only difference is that some film frames appear slightly slower in the video and others slightly faster. If there's really quick motion in the scene, a trained eye can pick it up. But most people never see the difference. This is how almost all the filmed features, dramas, and commercials you see on TV are processed.

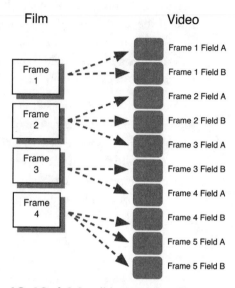

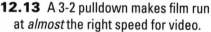

12.13 A 3-2 pulldown makes film run at *almost* the right speed for video.

The key phrase in the last paragraph is "an *almost* perfect speed match." It's not perfect, because of that same 29.97 fps issue that resulted in dropframe timecode. If the film were pulled down to a perfect 30 fps, we'd still see the shutter bars. So the film is slowed down 0.1% during the transfer. It really runs at 23.76 fps, which pulls down to 29.97 perfectly. Your film is turned into beautiful videotape (color correction is often added at this stage), ready for you to edit in an NLE.

Except for the sound. If you used double-system techniques with a digital recorder, it'll play back at precisely the right speed . . . or 0.1% faster than the picture. Since there are 1,800 frames in sixty seconds, by the end of a minute, the sound will be 1.8 frames early. There are three usual cures for this problem:

- In professional production, timecode DATs are synced with code on the film, but played back with their sample rate reduced 0.1%.[5] This slows the sound down. It's then dubbed through a sample-rate converter onto the video master. It may also be dubbed onto a *simulDat* with code that matches the videotape, for subsequent audio post use.

- On a desktop setup, you can use the pitch control in an audio program to make almost a perfect 0.1% speed reduction. It's unlikely that function will be calibrated in fractions of a percent, but a pitch change of –2 cents (there are 1200 cents in an octave) will result in a

---

5. Mathematicians will realize that 100.1% is not exactly the reciprocal of 99.9%. But like the earlier footnote about NTSC's frame rate not being precisely 29.97 fps, the tiny difference just doesn't matter.

slowdown that should keep the speed accurate for about five minutes. If the software allows a finer setting, −1.75 cents is better. Most programs have a Preserve Duration option when changing pitch. Turn it off: the goal here is to change the duration.

Unfortunately, the clip-speed control in an NLE isn't precise enough for this kind of fine-tuning.

- If your project uses a lot of fast cuts, ignore the problem. Sync each one separately. By the time sync has drifted enough to be noticeable, you'll be on to another scene.

While the 0.1% speed change and dropframe timecode are both necessary because of video's 29.97 fps frame rate, they're otherwise not related. You have to do the speed change anytime you're converting film to video, whether or not timecode is involved. You don't have to do the speed change when staying in the video domain, even if you're using dropframe.

None of the above applies to non-NTSC countries. There, video runs at 25 fps. 24 fps film is slowed down 4% during transfer. It makes a tiny difference to motion and pitch, but people accept it. Or the film is shot at 25 fps, costing a little bit more in stock and processing, and the problem goes away completely.

Editing traditional film sound in a computer   Some filmmakers prefer to edit with traditional techniques, using splices and optical effects, for eventual projection in a theater. But they want to cut sound in an NLE or multitrack audio program. So I'm often asked, "How can I use my desktop computer and low-cost software to make a track for the 15-minute, 16mm movie I've already cut as film?".

It can be done, but you'll need some luck. And you'll have to spend a few dollars even if you already own the software. Whether you're planning to release the project on film or videotape, the first step is to have a post house or TV station transfer the film to tape. The issue is synchronization, and you have to be sure the projector or film scanner and a timecode generator are both locked to a common blackburst. Even if you're planning to release on film, you can't skip this step or do the job yourself by pointing a camcorder at a screen. Home and school projectors don't have accurate-enough speed. You can, however, save a few dollars with a "one-light" transfer if picture quality isn't critical.

Since you're not cutting picture, you won't need NLE software except to capture the video as a file. Most audio programs can play back a video file while you're working. Or use an audio program that can sync to timecode from a VCR's audio track. Many relatively low-cost programs use MIDI timecode, and SMPTE-to-MIDI converters are available at music stores. Slow any sync audio elements down as described in the previous section, and then edit and mix until you're happy with the track.

But since your final output will be a composite film with optical or magnetic track, there's another step. The reference video you used building sound was, of course, slowed down 0.1% to eliminate shutter bars. You have to speed the mix up before it can be matched to the original film. You can do this by recording it in a timecode DAT recorder set for –0.1% pulldown, and then playing the DAT at normal speed while dubbing to optical or magnetic film. Film technicians might not have encountered this situation or have the right equipment, however, so check with the optical sound facility or film lab before making the final transfer.

Or use this shortcut: Edit individual tracks in a computer, and even do submixes if you want. Then transfer them all directly to mag film, and do some creative cutting on a flatbed editor before mixing film-style. Over the course of a 15-minute project, you'll have to delete about 21 frames to compensate for that 30 fps to NTSC pulldown . . . surely a piece of cake for someone who's spliced together an entire film.

Chapter 13

Editing Voices

Rose's Rules:

✔ Good dialog editing is transparent. The goal is to change the performance or even the meaning of spoken words, without ever sounding edited.

✔ You couldn't edit pictures without understanding how an actor's arms, legs, and faces move to express emotions or get things done. You can't edit their voices without knowing how the noises they make combine to express words.

Being a good video editor doesn't automatically make you a good dialog editor. The principles are different. But if you're good at cutting pictures, you already have one skill that's absolutely necessary for cutting sound: you pay attention to details. It just might not be obvious which details are important.

For example, one good trick for editing picture is to let on-screen movements bridge over a cut. If Sue reaches for a door at the end of scene 1a, scene 1b can be a close-up of her hand turning the knob. This continuous motion helps the viewer connect the scenes, so we see one action, even though it was shot in two takes.

Voice editing follows a different rule: you almost never want to edit across a continuous sound. If shot 1a's track ends with Sue saying, "I'm glad to se" and 2a begins with a different take of "e you, George"—that continuing /ee/ sound being the audio equivalent of when she reached for the doorknob—the audio edit will jump out at us. If I had to edit those two audio takes together, I'd cut on the /t/ in "to," the /s/ in "see," or even the tiny /d/ that starts the word "George."

This chapter is about finding those other editing points, and why they're better. These are the tricks a dialog editor learns—such as, did you know there's a /d/ in the front of "George"? Go ahead. Say the name aloud slowly. It starts with exactly the same tongue movement, producing exactly the same sound, as the /d/ as in "dog." The only difference is that in the man's name, it's followed by a buzzing /zh/ (like the one in "leisure"). The science behind this—how mouth movements and breath create individual specific sounds (phonemes), and how they blend

305

together into the words we recognize—is phonetics. It can be the handiest stuff for a dialog editor to know.

There's an official way to write these sounds. According to the International Phonetic Alphabet, the /ee/ sound in "see" should really be written /i/. The /t/, /s/, and /d/ symbols mean what you'd think, but the symbols for /zh/ and many other sounds don't even exist in normal typefaces because there are more phonemes than there are letters.

Unfortunately, the phonetic alphabet can look like hieroglyphics to the untrained (see Figure 13.1), so I'll use a simplified version in this book.

ðæts maɪ neɪm dʒeɪ

13.1 That's my name, Jay, in the International Phonetic Alphabet. Even if you can't read it, it's important to recognize that each character represents an individual sound. There are 15 separate, editable sounds in the four syllables of "that's my name, Jay."

In most of this chapter we'll use *dialog* to refer to any spoken words, whether it's conversations between on-camera actors, talking heads, location interviews, or voice-over. The editing techniques are the same. The only difference is that you've got more freedom when you don't have to worry about lipsync, so we'll use that as the basis for our examples.

The Right Tools for Editing Voice

Once you understand how voices should be edited, you can use these techniques for the rest of your career. The principles are absolutely portable, and they work because of how we listen, not because of special equipment or software. I use a DAW now because it's faster, but, years ago, I was cutting exactly the same way on 1/4-inch tape and 35mm magnetic film.

However, you should be aware there are easier environments to edit voice than most NLEs, which force you to edit on frame boundaries. A /t/ sound lasts less than a third of a frame, so one-frame resolution in a video program means you can't hone in on it accurately. Audio workstations and analog tape have essentially infinite resolution; you can cut from any place to any other place, regardless of frame boundaries. Even 35mm film sound is precise more than an NLE; you can cut from any set of perforations to any other, and there are four sets of perfs per frame, for an edit resolution of 1/96th of a second.

If you're going to be doing serious voice or music editing, I urge you to get a separate two-track audio-editing program to use along with your NLE. They speak the same file format, so you can move sounds between the two programs freely. Many of them also play video in sync, so you can watch a clip while you're editing. Even if your NLE has better than one-frame resolution—some let you nudge audio in- and out-points very precisely—it still probably forces you to treat each edit as two separate clips. This is much less efficient than audio programs, which treat sound as a continuous stream so you can cut and paste with word-processor ease. The time you'll save will offset the couple of hundred dollars an audio-editing program costs.

Scrubbing, jogging, and shuttling

Whether you're working in an audio program or an NLE, anything more sophisticated than basic paragraph-by-paragraph assembly requires the ability to mark edits while actually listening to the sounds at various speeds. Audio folks call the process "scrubbing." Editing programs may have two different scrub modes, roughly equivalent to shuttle and jog modes in an NLE's clip window. Normal tapelike scrubbing is similar to shuttling: the sound moves forwards or backwards, either at a constant rate or in response to a mouse being dragged or a knob being turned. As you speed up, the sound gets higher in pitch; as you slow down, the sound gets deeper, but it's easier to pick out separate phonemes because they're farther apart.

This is dynamic scrubbing

This is tape-like scrubbing.

13.2 Dynamic and tapelike scrubbing modes.

Most NLEs have a jog function, which advances the picture and audio one frame for each press of an arrow key. You hear 1/30th of a second's worth of audio at each jog. Audio programs aren't frame-based, so they use a different sort of jogging: *dynamic scrubbing*. As you move the mouse slowly across the audio, you hear short segments of sound—ranging in length from about a third of a frame to a half-second—continuously looping at normal speed. Since the sound is always played at its normal pitch, it's easier to recognize where vowels or musical notes change. Figure 13.2 is a graphic representation of these two modes. Dynamic scrubbing continuously repeats a short, moving loop so you can hear its natural pitch; tapelike scrubbing slows down each sound, but you can hear their precise beginnings and endings. Track 15 of the CD lets you hear the difference.

What, no scrub?   A few popular audio programs don't let you scrub in the waveform, and their tutorials insist that the only way to edit sound is by eye. Not only are they wrong about the basic premise, there's a workaround that's almost as good as scrubbing:

1. Select an area around where you think you're going to mark an edit point, of about half a second.
2. Activate the Loop Play command, so the area plays continuously.
3. Grab the left boundary of the loop, and slide it. The start of the loop will move to match, letting you hear more or less of the loop depending on how you moved it.

   With some programs, you'll have to Stop and re-start Loop Play for it to recognize the new boundary.

4. Move the loop boundary back and forth until it starts exactly at the sound where you want to edit. Drop a marker there.

It may seem like a lot of steps, but with practice—and one hand on the mouse and the other pressing keyboard commands—it becomes a fast way to find a precise edit point.

Editing I: Cutting in Silences

Nobody . . . talks . . . like . . . this. Speech is made of continuous sound, with constantly changing volume and pitches, punctuated by brief pauses when you breathe. Dub Track 16 of this book's CD into your editor—or read the preceding two sentences into a microphone—and look at it on a waveform or clip display. It'll probably look like Figure 13.3. Play through the clip, and notice how individual sounds line up with the display. Then save the clip: we'll be editing it a lot, and you'll want to keep coming back to this original version.

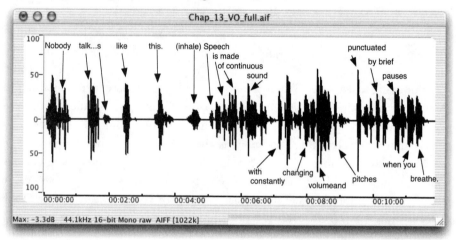

13.3 The first two sentences of this section.

I added callouts to make the picture easier to interpret. The hills and valleys represent where the track gets softer or louder.[1] Notice how some words share a broad hill ("volume and"), while other single-syllable words might have two separate hills of their own ("talks"). In the latter case, there's one loud burst for the /t/, a quieter stretch for /al/, a short pause while the tongue closes against the roof of the mouth, and then the louder friction of the /ks/.

If you wanted to edit between those takes, you could mark your cuts any time in the silences before each of the first four words or in the pauses after "sound" and "pitches." But you'd have to be careful if you marked the pause between the first and second sentences, because it's not really silence. That's where the announcer breathes. If you try to cut in the middle of that breath,

---

1. Read more about audio envelopes in Chapter 2.

you'll disturb its natural rise and fall—calling attention to the edit. You have to cut completely around it. Try it both ways, or listen to my version of that sloppy cut on Track 17 on the CD. (There's more about breath editing later in this chapter.)

The point is that it's very difficult to do a smooth edit in the middle of a continuous sound. Sustained vowels and long consonants (such as the /z/ in the middle of "pauses") are continuous, but so is room tone and the breath between words. In fact, it's the first rule of editing.

 Rule _____

Never cut away from the middle of one long sound into silence or into the middle of another.

But like every rule, there are exceptions. If you fool the ear into thinking that the first sound continued, you can get away with this kind of edit. We'll discuss how to do this with music in the next chapter. To do it when you're editing voice, you have to pay attention to how individual sounds start.

Editing II: Sounds with Hard Attacks

Notice how the left sides of some hills in Figure 13.3 are very steep. These are the beginnings of sounds that get suddenly loud: the /t/ at the start of "talks" and in the middle of "continuous," the /k/ at the start of "continuous," or the /p/ in "punctuated" or "pitches." One of the characteristics of sudden loud sounds is that they mask other, softer sounds that might be going on at the same time or immediately before it. So if you edit from a softer sound to a louder one, the loud sound distracts your ear from any discontinuities caused by the edit itself.

Figure 13.4 shows how sudden loud sounds can distract the ear in an actual edit. The left side of the figure is zoomed in so you can see how the waveform abruptly changes direction; this would normally cause a click. But because it's part of a cut from a softer sound to a much louder one, as you can see when the screen is zoomed out (right), nobody hears the problem.

Spelling errors?

There's no z in "pauses," and no k in "continuous" . . . so why are they written this way in the book?

Phonetics—even the simplified version in this book—depends on accurately hearing and depicting actual sounds. It has nothing to do with the letters in a word.

The s in the middle of "pauses" has a buzzing to it, just like the /z/ in "zoo." If you try saying it like the /s/ in "sue," you get a totally different word: "paw-sis." Try it. You'll find other cases where the letter s turns to /z/ at the end of "boys" and "eggs."

And why is the c in "continuous" written as /k/? It's certainly not the same sound as the c in "certainly," which would have to be written /s/. In fact, there's no character in phonetics for the letter c because it's always sounded like some other consonant.

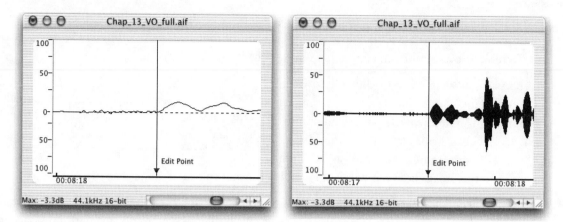

13.4 There's a jump in this edit (zoomed in on the left), but because the cut is to a louder sound, you'll never hear the problem.

This is the key to the second rule of editing:

 Rule _____

You can generally cut from any continuous soft sound into one with a hard attack.

_____

An Editing Exercise: Cutting Where There's No Pause

You can use that rule to change the material you just put into your NLE, deleting "continuous sound with" so it reads

```
Narr:    Speech is made of |constantly changing volume and pitches, punc-
     tuated by brief pauses when you breathe.
```

The | indicates where the cut should be.

1. Scrub forward in your editor until you hear the sharp /k/ sound at the beginning of "continuous," and make a mark.

2. Continue scrubbing to the /k/ at the beginning of "constantly," and make another mark.

3. If you're using an audio program, select between the two marks (Figure 13.5) and delete. You're done. If you're trying this in an NLE, make a duplicate copy of the clip; use the first mark as the out-point of the first clip, and the second mark as the in-point of the second, and slide them so they snap together (shown on two separate audio tracks in Figure 13.6 for clarity). Some NLEs let you use timeline tools, such as a razor blade, to separate clips into pieces without opening a separate window.

Play it back, and your edit should sound just like my version (Track 18 on the CD).

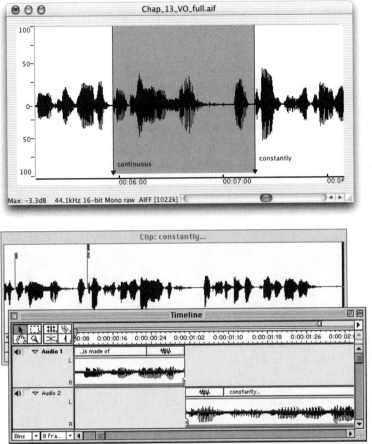

13.5 Marking the edit in an audio program, and selecting between the marks to delete.

13.6 Doing the same edit in an NLE means you have to join two partial clips together

In fact, we've cut away from one phoneme (the /k/ in "continuous") and into an identical phoneme in a different word (/k/ in "constantly"). If this were video editing, the equivalent—matching one action to another—would assure a smooth cut. The same rule holds for sound.

> **Rule**
> You can almost always cut away from the start of a sound in one word, and into the start of that same sound in another word.

But the cut-into-something-hard rule is more powerful. We could go from virtually anything to a hard sound, and it would be fine.

Here's proof (and a chance to practice another technique), cutting away from a /k/ and into a /p/:

```
Narr:     Speech is made of |pauses when you breathe.
```

1. Go ahead. Reload the original clip and mark the /k/ in "continuous."

2. Mark the /p/ in "pauses" for the other side of the edit. If you scrub slowly, you'll be able to hear precisely where the buzzing /v/ in "of" ends, then a tiny break, and then the start of the /p/.

3. Cut them together, and it should be as smooth as my version on Track 19 of the CD.

Practice a few times on other voice tracks, and you'll be ready for truly advanced voice editing.

Editing III: Hearing Phonemes

So far, you've made edits by finding and marking hard attacks. But speech is made up of sounds, not just sudden attacks. Once you learn to recognize individual phonemes and can find the beginning and end of them, you've got a lot more flexibility in how you edit.

An Even More Impressive Exercise

We'll start with a slightly more complicated edit, finding the boundary between /z/ and /m/ in "speech is made" so we can turn the line into

```
Narr:    Speech is |punctuated by brief pauses when you breathe.
```

1. Reload the clip, and start scrubbing from the front. You'll hear a recognizable /tch/ at the very end of "speech." At the end of it is the beginning of the word "is."

2. Keep scrubbing forward, and you'll hear a hissing or whistling—depending on how fast you're scrubbing—at the start of the /z/ that finishes "is." Scrub some more, very slowly, and stop as soon as that whistle ends. Mark it. That's the end of /z/ and the beginning of /m/ in "made."

3. Now mark the /p/ at the start of "punctuated"—just like you did in the previous exercise—and make the edit between them.

The result will sound like Track 20 on the CD. If it doesn't, you probably scrubbed a little bit too far after the end of the /z/. Undo and try again.

Fooling the Ear

If you can't find something hard to cut on, or identical sounds to cut between, you can sometimes fool the ear into thinking an edit is smoother than it really is:

• Cutting away from the start of one sound, and into the start of a *similar* sound, often works.

That's because in normal speech, the end of one sound is often influenced by the sound it's going into. The mouth has to get into the right shape for the next phoneme, and it starts moving slightly before the phoneme actually starts.

Try it yourself:

```
Narr:     Speech is made of continuous sound, with constantly changing
    volume and pitches |when you breathe.
```

1. Find the /s/ at the end of "pitches." Do this by playing or scrubbing until you hear the word "pitches" start, and then scrubbing very slowly. You'll notice the /tch/ in the middle of the "pitches," then the /i/, then a hiss as the /s/ starts. It's similar, but not identical, to the buzzing /z/. Continue slowly to the end of the hiss; that's the end of the phoneme. Mark it.

2. Move ahead a few seconds to the word "pauses." Mark the end of the final /z/, just like you did with the word "is."

3. Edit the two marks together. If it sounds a tiny bit awkward, you've probably left a brief pause after the /s/. Trim a tiny bit off that edit, and try again. Track 21 of the CD shows this edit with and without the pause, so you can hear the difference.

There's even a science to determining when sounds are similar. Read on:

Phonemes Come in Families

There are 46 phonemes in normal American English, but as an editor you really only need to know about a few categories of them: two kinds of consonants and two ways of making them, the vowels and a few special consonants that glide between vowels, and some common sounds that are really combinations of two others (such as the /d/ and /zh/ that make up the letter *j*).

Voiced and unvoiced consonants

You've probably noticed that /s/ (as at the end of "tots") and /z/ (at the end of "toys") have similar, but not identical, sounds. In fact, you form your lips and tongue exactly the same way to make them. The only difference is that /z/ has a buzzing from your vocal cords, while /s/ is made just by exhaling—your throat doesn't buzz at all. /z/ is called a voiced consonant; /s/ is unvoiced.

As an editor, it's important to know this distinction:

*   Unvoiced consonants have very little to identify who's speaking. Almost none of a specific character's voice is carried in these sounds. This means that except for matters of room acoustics or background noise, you can often substitute one actor's unvoiced consonant for the same consonant from a different actor. Believe it or not, you can take an /s/ from one of Sue's lines and put it in a similar word while George is talking, and it'll sound fine!

*   You can sometimes swap voiced and unvoiced consonants when you need to create new words. If George said "boy" when the script required "boys," but the only final *s* you have in his voice is from the word "tots," you might still be able to cut them together. The result will sound slightly foreign, "boysss" with a hissing ending, but may work in context. (You

can't use one of Sue's /z/ sounds for a George /s/, because voiced consonants include a lot of the sound of a particular person's voice.)

Other voiced/unvoiced pairs include

/v/	(as in "very")	/f/	(as in "ferry")
/zh/	("seizure")	/sh/	("sea shore")
/g/	("gut")	/k/	("cut")
/d/	("dip")	/t/	("tip")
/b/	("bark")	/p/	("park")
/th/	("then")	/th/	("thin")

This last pair is hard to notate without using the phonetic alphabet, because English makes no spelling distinction between them. The first would be notated as a lowercase *d* with a line through it (the first character in Figure 13.1), while the second is a Greek *theta* (θ—an O with a horizontal line through the middle).

Voiced/unvoiced pairs of consonants are very similar, and you can often edit between them, because the mouth makes an identical shape for them. But sounds also come in more general families, based on the physics of how they make noise, and knowing this can also help you find a place to edit.

Fricatives or friction consonants

The sounds /z/ and /s/, /v/ and /f/, /zh/ and /sh/, and the two /th/ sounds are all made by forcing air through a small opening formed by your tongue held close to some other part of your mouth. This air friction makes various hisses, whose high frequencies stand out when you scrub through a track slowly. Learn to identify this hiss (as when you found the end of the word "is"), and you'll be able to spot the start and end of these consonants quickly.

/h/ is also a fricative, but the mouth is held open and the friction happens between moving air and the sides of the throat. It also has a hissing sound, but a much quieter one.

Plosives or stop consonants

The sounds /b/, /p/, /g/, /k/, /d/, and /t/ are formed by letting air pressure build up and then releasing it quickly. Because of this burst of pressure, any plosive can cause a popping sound when it's delivered too close to the mic.

The only way to make a plosive is by shutting off the flow of breath momentarily, either by closing the lips (/b/) or by sealing the tongue against part of the roof of the mouth (/g/, /d/). This makes life easy for the dialog editor:

- When a plosive starts a syllable, there'll be a tiny pause before it. Listen for that silence, and you've found the exact beginning of the syllable. Some trained announcers start their voices buzzing before the pop of an initial /b/ or /g/; if you scrub slowly, you'll hear a frame or two of /m/ at the front of "boy." You can almost always cut this buzzing out without affecting the word.

- When a plosive ends a syllable, it actually has two parts: the closure, and then the release. Say the word "cat" slowly, and you'll hear two distinct sounds: /kaa/, then a brief pause and a short /tih/. If the same plosive consonant happens twice in a row (as between the words in "that Tom!"), you can almost always run them together (/thah tom/). Overly formal or nervous speakers will separate the two plosives (/thaht tom/); if you cut out one of the two sounds, the speaker will seem more relaxed.

Glottal and nasals

The sounds /h/, /n/, /m/, and the /ng/ at the end of "ring" are four completely different, long consonants. They can often be shortened by cutting out their middles, but they can't be substituted for anything else.

Vowels and intervowels

While there are five vowels in written English, there are a dozen in the spoken language. The important thing for an editor is learning to distinguish them because they can't be substituted for one another. For example, *a* is completely different in "cake," "cat," "tar," "tall," and "alone." If you're looking for an alternate syllable to fix a badly recorded word with an *a* in it, you can't just search for that letter in the script.

Vowels are, obviously, always voiced. They are always formed by buzzing the vocal cords and changing the resonant shapes of the mouth. They have no unvoiced equivalent.

The consonants /w/ and /y/ always appear with a vowel after them, and their very ends are modified by the vowel they're gliding into. If you need to fix a badly recorded /w/ in "whale," chances are the /w/ in "water" won't work well because the vowel is different.

The consonants /l/ and /r/ always appear with a vowel on one side, the other, or both. They're not influenced as much by the vowels next to them, but will be different depending on whether they're leading into one or following it.

Diphthongs or double phonemes

Some common sounds are always made of two phonemes joined together. Learn to listen for them because they give you twice as many editing options as single phonemes.

You can frequently isolate a single sound from a diphthong to use elsewhere. You can almost always cut from the middle of one diphthong to the middle of another, or to the start of a different sound.

There are two consonant diphthongs, /t sh/ (as in "church") and its cognate /d zh/ ("George"). There are five vowel diphthongs: /aah ih/ ("eye"), /aw ih/ ("toy"), /ah oo/ ("loud"), /ay ih/ ("aim"), and /oo uu/ ("open").

This is advanced stuff. Diphthongs in vowels are often hard to hear, but you really can edit them separately.

Intonation

Voiced sounds have pitch, and people vary this pitch as they speak to express emotions. As you get more into dialog editing, you'll be amazed how *little* attention you have to pay to this factor. If you're cutting between takes of the same copy, or changing words in a performance by a trained actor or narrator, the pitch will be remarkably consistent. Any slight variations you cause by editing will probably sound like natural intonation, particularly if the edit is smooth and the viewer is following the content. Wide variations will be immediately apparent, so you can undo the edit and try something else. One of the things you should try is a few percent of pitch manipulation or varispeed, if your editing system has this feature. A pitch shift—no more than 3% higher or lower—may be all you need to join two unfriendly phonemes.

Projection Levels

A performer's projection level affects more than how loud they are. As you raise your voice, the throat tightens, and the vocal buzz that forms voiced sounds loses some of its lower frequencies. At the same time, most trained speakers will also push their voices "into the mask," directing more energy to resonating cavities in the front of the face and adding high harmonics. You can't compensate for these timbral changes by simply adjusting volume. In most cases, you can't compensate for them at all, and editing between two takes of widely varying projection levels can be difficult.

The envelopes (Chapter 2) of individual words also frequently change as projection levels rise. The beginnings of individual words get stressed more, to separate them, than they'd be in normal speech.

If you must cut between two takes with different projection, keep the takes on two separate tracks as you move their phonemes around. Then experiment with volume and equalization to make them match. A little reverb on the softer track can also help. Once the sound matches, mix the two tracks to a single composite voice.

Editing IV: The Tricks

Breathless

Go back to Track 16 on the CD, the one you loaded at the start of this chapter, or look at Figure 13.3. There's a big puff of air in the middle. Most announcers will take a gigantic breath between paragraphs, and many loud, fast ones throughout the paragraph. These noises don't communicate anything other than "I'm reading from a script," and—unless you're trying for a comedy effect—should come out of voice-over tracks. Breaths in front of a take are easy to get rid of—just move the in-point a little later. But those catch-breaths during a read are more troublesome. While you can spot breaths on a waveform and hear them when you scrub, you can't just cut them out—that would pull the surrounding words too close together. You also can't just erase them or turn their volume down because that'll leave the words too far apart.

In general, a breath in a voice-over can almost always be replaced by a pause *two-thirds* its length. If it takes one second for the announcer to gasp, use 20 frames of silence instead. The result sounds cleaner, more energetic, and completely natural. This ratio has worked for me in thousands of projects with hundreds of different announcers. Even though I edit by ear—erasing the entire pause, playing the line in realtime, and tapping the Mark key where I think the next phrase should start—it almost always turns out to be two-thirds. I have no idea why the number is magic.

If you're starting with a clean voice-over recording and it will be used on a limited medium such as broadcast TV, or be mixed with music, you can replace breaths with digital silence. But if it'll be played at theatrical levels, use room tone; otherwise, the finished edit will sound choppy. On-camera breaths are trickier, since the two-thirds trick would destroy sync. Even replacing the whole breath with room tone may be a mistake: if we see the talent's mouth open, we should hear something.

Simply Shocking!

Amateur announcers and real-life interview subjects don't take the big breaths, but often do something worse: they unconsciously let their breath build up, then blast it out when they talk. It causes a little click if the phrase starts with a vowel. These *glottal shocks* are a natural result of nervousness in the throat, so we all get used to associating them with that condition. Your listeners won't know why, but they'll know your track is somehow hesitant and unconvincing.

Glottal shocks often follow long pauses, when a speaker is unsure and looking for "just the right word." If you try to shorten this pause but don't take care of the shock, your editing won't sound natural. It's easy to get rid of the pesky things, but only if you zoom in. Deleting about a hundredth of a second, at the start of a word, is usually enough to turn a speaker from nervous to confident.

Extensions

When cutting documentaries or testimonials, you frequently need to start or end a voice segment on a particular syllable, even though the speaker might have more to say before or after the clip. If they didn't pause exactly where you want to edit, even the most accurate edit will sound abrupt as they suddenly start or stop talking.

Add a little room tone or natural background noise, butted right up to the edit. This will make it sound as though the performer—and not your editing system—made the pause.

Snap, Crackle . . .

When the clock rolls 'round to winter, you can hear the announcers start ticking. You get annoying clicks and snaps in their voices, particularly when they're close-miked and saying sounds that require the tongue to touch the roof of the mouth (like /l/ or /k/). It's caused by central heating drying up their mouths. This thickens the saliva, which starts to stick and stretch and . . . well, the sound it makes is just as disgusting as the description.

Cutting out the snap can destroy the rhythm of the word. Erasing it—or replacing it with silence—can leave a noticeable hole.

But you can usually replace the snap with a tiny snippet of the vowel immediately before or after it. Locate a snap, select about the same length of audio right next to it— it'll be less than a frame—copy, and paste it over the snap. Depending on the program, you may need to use a Replace or Overdub function; you want the new sound to fit over the snap, rather than move the snap later.

Because the snaps are so fast, it's almost impossible to fix them in a frame-based NLE. Use an audio program. Or hand the announcer a glass of water, and re-record.

Speak with Forked Tongue

On the other hand, some voice tricks are easy in a multitrack environment like an NLE . One of the neatest is *mnemonic speech*, an effect invented by pioneer sound designer Tony Schwartz.

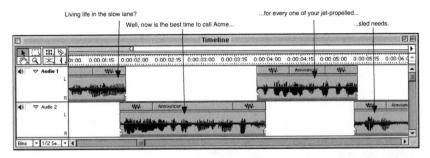

13.7 Mnemonic speech lets you hear two things in the same voice at the same time.

You've probably heard it in commercials: an announcer starts talking, and while he's finishing one phrase he's also starting the next. Two words, from the same voice, at the same time. If it's done well, you're not aware of an overlap, but you do get a sense of energy and urgency. (If it's done badly, you get a clichéd dragway ad.)

You can blast through mnemonic cutting quickly by setting markers in the track at the start of each phrase. Then break the clip at the markers, and move the individual sections onto alternate tracks. Finally, slide the sections so they overlap by a few frames. It's not necessary to fade at the start or end of each phrase—the natural flow of the voice will have the same effect as a cross-fade!

Figure 13.7 shows how the tracks will look in an NLE. Track 22 of the CD lets you hear them.

Editing V: Keeping Track of Sync

So far all of the voice editing we've talked about has been without pictures. Surprisingly, cutting sync dialog isn't very different. An NLE should take care of synchronization automatically; you can move and mark either sound or picture, and if the software knows the two belong together, they should both stay together. Two rules will keep you out of most trouble:

 Rule _____

As soon as you import or digitize synced audio and video, lock their tracks together in the software.

 Rule _____

Always keep a copy of the original, unedited take so you can check what proper sync is supposed to look like—or, when things get really bad, re-import them and start over.

Keeping things in sync in most audio-editing programs is a little trickier. Once you've loaded the audio/video file, the sound portion can be edited any way you want. If you do anything that changes its length—inserting or deleting sounds, or changing their tempo—sync will get lost. Minor changes shouldn't cause any trouble if you keep this in mind:

👉 *Rule*

To edit audio-for-video without affecting sync, stick with operations that don't affect overall length: use Replace rather than Insert, or Erase rather than Cut.

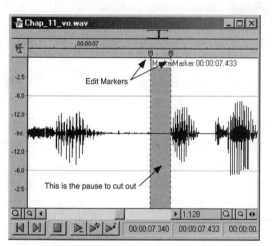

13.8 Cutting out the pause will slide everything after it.

It's just a tiny bit more work to delete specific sounds in a sync track, or close up the gaps between words, without affecting sync after the edit. Consider the original audio example from this chapter. If we wanted to shorten the silence between "continuous sound" and "with constantly," we could mark both sides of the silence and then cut between the marks (Figure 13.8). That, obviously, also moves the "punctuated by brief pauses" phrase and could cause us to lose sync.

But if we want to close up those two words without affecting the overall length, we just need to add a third mark at the start of the next phrase.

1. Select between the second and third mark—the phrase that immediately follows the desired edit (Figure 13.9).

2. Use the program's Copy function instead of Cut.

13.9 To preserve the sync of later elements, mark the next phrase, and move it earlier.

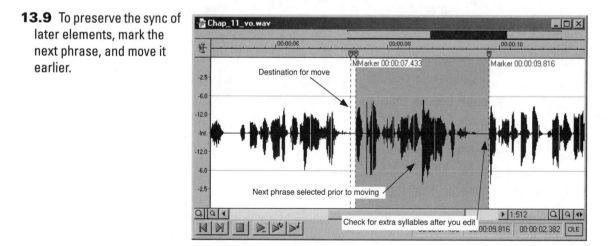

3. Locate to the first mark—the beginning of the edit—and use the program's Replace or Paste Over function. This moves the phrase closer to the one that preceded it, closing up the words.

4. Check the end of the newly replaced region. If there was a long pause after the section you moved, it'll probably be fine. But if there wasn't much of a pause, you may hear the last syllables of the moved section twice. Erase the extra, or paste some room tone over it.

Some audio programs simplify steps 2 and 3 with a single "move" command.

Parallel Track Operations

Sometimes, it's handy to move an audio element from one track to another without changing when it occurs. NLEs make this easy: you can use the Razor or similar tool to cut into the clip, and then move it to the next track while staying aligned to the frame line. If you want to do the same thing in an audio-only program or workstation, you may need to plant a marker at the edit, and use the same marker both as the start of a Cut operation and the destination for a Replace.

Track splitting

If two people have dialog during the same shot, they might get picked up slightly differently because of the mic angle. A little equalization on just one of the characters can help. Rather than switching the processor in and out as they exchange lines, you can split their lines onto different tracks (Figure 13.10). Then it's a simple matter to apply the equalization to the entire track during the mix. This is also handy for special effects if you want to deepen or add echo to just one voice.

Be careful, when adding the processing, that there isn't too obvious a jump in any background as they exchange lines. Making the cut very close to the start of the new line can help hide any jump.

13.10 Splitting dialog into multiple tracks so you can process them differently.

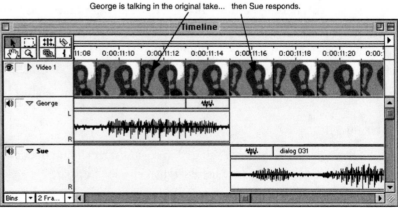

George is talking in the original take... then Sue responds.

Switching between mics

Use a similar technique if a scene has been shot with both boom and lav. Put each mic on its own track in sync with picture. When you want to avoid a noise on the primary mic (clothing rustles on the lav, or off-mic sounds on the boom), use the Razor or similar tool to make cuts on both tracks on either side of the noise. Remove the noisy section of the primary mic's track, and everything up to the noise on the secondary mic's track.

Continue through the scene this way. When you reach the end, throw away the last segment on the secondary mic's track. Then apply whatever reverberation is necessary to make the lav match the boom (Chapter 16), touch up the equalization on one or the other track, and they should play back as a perfect, noise-free whole.

Sync Problems

Lipsync sometimes drifts. Mouths will flap, but their sounds will be slightly earlier or later, making everything seem like a badly dubbed foreign film.

Sync problems are often the result of setup errors in the editing system, either at the board or interrupt level within the editing computer or because blackburst signals aren't being properly used (Chapter 11). Sometimes these manifest themselves as problems in a rendered output but not during preview, or during long playbacks but not short ones. There are as many possible causes as there are systems, so you'll need a technician or manufacturer's support line to diagnose and fix the problem. But once it's solved, it should stay solved.

Sometimes sync problems are the result of user errors, such as forgetting to lock tracks together or setting the wrong timecode or reference standard. Some NLEs make certain operations, such as L-cuts, difficult and prone to error. If sync seems unstable but you know the system is set up properly, check the manufacturer's FAQ or ask an editor who's experienced with your software.

If you're moving tracks from one program to another within the same computer, or exporting them as files to another computer but bringing them back before the final output, sync should stay accurate down to the sample level. The only times you'll encounter problems are if you're doing something that intentionally changes the file's length (editing it or changing the tempo), or a process adds or subtracts samples inadvertently (badly done sample-rate conversion, redigitizing, or reclocking real-time digital audio).

Knowing the cause doesn't help much, however, if you've already lost sync.

Fixing sync

Lipsync can be a strange thing. Before you start sliding things around, verify that they're really out. A few techniques are helpful when checking lipsync:

- Give yourself the advantage of a large picture monitor and smooth movement. It's hard to detect lipsync on a 240×320 pixel screen, and almost impossible to spot it at 15 fps. Speaker placement also makes a difference: a speaker next to the picture monitor will always sound like it's in better sync than one on the other side of the room.

- Shuttle audio and video at about half speed. This is fast enough that you can understand the sound, while being slow enough to spot lip movements in the picture.

- Look for plosives that build up sound behind the lips (/b/ or /p/). The first frame where the lips are parted should exactly match the first frame of sound.

- Try changing things and see if they get better or worse. Move the audio a frame earlier and watch the sequence. If that doesn't immediately look better, move it two frames later (so it's now one frame later than it originally was). If *that* doesn't help either, the problem isn't lipsync.

These same techniques can be used for fixing sync. Slide things until they're better, staying aware that sometimes a whole track may require correction, while, other times, only a few clips will be out. Some performances and shooting situations result in soft or difficult-to-spot lipsync. If a scene seems to be out of sync, but nothing you do makes it look any better, shrug and hope for the best.

👉 *Rule*

It's always better to err on the side of the track being a frame late, rather than a frame early. In the real world, it takes longer for sound to reach us than images.

Sometimes a track will start in sync, and then slowly drift farther and farther out. This is almost always because sound and picture are playing at slightly different rates, usually because of a setup error. Check the program's or equipment's settings.

If that doesn't fix it, go to the end of the program, and use some of the techniques above to see how far out of sync the track has gotten. Then convert the length of the program into frames. Take a calculator and divide the length of the program *plus* the error into the length of the program. Apply the result, as a percentage speed correction, to the track. This is a slightly Rube Goldberg-ish solution that doesn't address the original cause of the problem, but it works. And believe it or not, for a while, one of the biggest names in NLE software was proposing it on their Web site as a workaround for a known sync problem in their software!

A Final Exercise

Okay. You've read this chapter, you've practiced with the examples, and you've gotten pretty good at this voice-cutting stuff. Here's a challenge:

Track 23 of this book's CD is a famous sound bite from the last U.S. president of the twentieth century. Using that short bite as the only source—and nothing from anything else he ever said—turn it around so he admits the very thing he's denying here. The second part of the track can serve as a model.

Don't settle for just deleting the "not." If you swap a few phonemes, you can change the "have" to "had" . . . and "I did" to "I've." It's an impressive demonstration of editing prowess. (At least it was at a recent NAB Convention, when I did the entire job in about two minutes, in front of a live audience.)

Chapter 14

Working with Music

Was *The Jazz Singer* the first Hollywood movie with a musical score?

Not by a decade. Long before Al Jolson's 1927 hit, producers were shipping full scores for orchestras to play live during their blockbusters. And these were considerably more inventive than the tinny piano you might associate with *Perils of Pauline*. For example, the theme song that ran for decades on the popular *Amos 'n Andy* show was originally written for D. W. Griffith's 1915 epic, *Birth of a Nation*.

And if you think the idea of using pop music to cross-promote a movie is a new invention, you're off by more than three quarters of a century. Early Hollywood moguls commissioned sheet music and radio hits just to remind people of the names of their pictures. This gave us "Ramona" and "Jeannine, I Dream of Lilac Time"—pop standards that can still be found in catalogs—along with such monstrosities as "Woman Disputed, I Love You" and "Red Man, Why Are You Blue?"[1]

The point is, music has always been an essential part of moving pictures. And it can be just as important to your video.

Music can add the right seriousness, importance, or excitement to a presentation. It can tie a video together when the pictures don't match, or delineate sections when the topic changes. It can provide a driving rhythm for montages, or tug at the viewer's heart because . . . "we're a people

---

1. Let us review the preceding two paragraphs: a movie about a Jew in blackface, another movie glorifying the Klan, an overtly racist radio show that held the nation's attention for decades, and some random offensiveness against women and Native Americans. I hope we made a tiny amount of social progress during the century.

company." A grand theme, sweeping to a conclusion, can even let a suffering audience know a too-long corporate epic is about to end . . . so they should start paying attention again. No matter what kind of video you're producing, chances are you can find effective, interesting music for it without breaking your budget or the copyright laws.

Deciding What Music You'll Need

You don't need a musical education or any particular instrumental chops to use music effectively. Many films and TV series are scored by people who can't even read a note. What's needed is the ability to look at a script or roughcut, tell just what kind of music is needed, and then describe it in useful terms: your computer's keyboard is a lot more useful tool for this than a piano's.

A feature film's music director frequently hires someone else to write the themes, and many features even use the same production music libraries that are available for your video. If you want to use music effectively, you have to start thinking like a music director yourself. You can do it (even if your musical background is so limited you think MIDI is just French for midday). What's most important is your understanding of the emotional flow of the video. After that, it's just a question of listing the music and deciding where to get it.

Start with spotting notes, even for something as simple as a wedding album or the CEO's annual Message to the Troops. Read down the script or watch a roughcut, and note what kind of music you need along with the page or time where it belongs (Figure 14.1). Write down what the music is trying to convey (words like "inspirational," or "building to a limitless future" are more helpful than "music under"), and anything that strikes you about the orchestration, tempo, or style. If you don't know a precise musical term, don't worry. "Fast" or "sweet" communicate just as well as their Italian equivalents. You can also make notes by referring to musical groups, specific songs, classical forms, or anything else that serves as a specific reminder. Even "like the

Digital Playroom

Custom Productions: Focus, Focus, Focus

Music list v.2   *Times in mm:ss from offline*

TIME	CUE	DESCRIPTION
00:07	m001	*Industrial march.* Stock. Fanfares to approx :03 then under; hit at :15 ("uses of radio") then under again. Music slides up at :26 — sort of the opposite as the effect of a turntable slowing down. Can be done as DSP or use a gliss.
00:43	m002	*I want it all.* Original, almost reverential, orchestral, for BOSS' summary. Must cut into m003. 00:52 punctuate reverse angle: not overdone, just hold rhythm 00:57 after UNDERLING 1. Picks up again. Slight hit patriotic hymn under "every man, woman, child..." 01:03 hold after "want to buy". Keep rhythm, or just sustain chord 01:07 "Monday morning at 9" kicks off rhythm to bring into m003
01:09	m003	*Research montage.* Stock. Suggest orchestral rag... uptempo, offbeat, but mainstream orchestration to keep it businesslike. 02:05 out.
02:08	m004	*Tension and Resolve.* Original, through dialog. Keep the orch tone of m002

14.1 A music spotting list. This one is very specific, since some of the cues will be composed to fit.

stabbing in *Psycho*" is enough to get your point across. Include how long each piece will be on screen and any internal transitions.

This list is important even if you're the only one who'll be referring to it, or if you'll be pulling all the music yourself from a small library. Having it (or equivalent notes on the script itself) will save you a lot of time later.

Don't specify one long piece of music when two short ones will do. A composer of original music will usually work for a set fee based on how much music you need, not how many individual melodies there are. If you're getting music from a library, you've probably either paid buyout fees or will be purchasing a blanket license that covers the entire show. So it doesn't cost extra to change the music according to the dynamics of the video. Give the viewer a break from time to time—put in a different piece, or even silence. Twenty minutes of endlessly repeating music isn't interesting, even in elevators.

If you're listing multiple cues, indicate which should be related ("peaceful theme :45, based on earlier march #7") and which should sound different. Obviously, this will be a big help for a composer you hire. It also can be useful if you're getting stock music from a library, since some library cues are organized into suites of related themes.

Source Music

Source, or diegetic, music is part of the scene rather than the underscore (Chapter 5). But it's gathered during the scoring session and edited and mixed along with other music. So this is the time to also make notes on music that should be coming from on-screen performers or props like TV sets.

Sources of Music

Finding really great music isn't hard—all you need is time or money. Here are some ways to save both.

Original Music

The easiest (and most expensive) way to get music is to hire a composer. While John Williams[2] doesn't come cheap, you may find a Williams Wannabe at a local music school, recording studio, or over the Internet. There's been an explosion of low-cost, high-quality musical and digital recording equipment over the last two decades, and a skilled musician can turn out a fully professional score without a major investment in facilities or session players. Good original scores

---

2. Neither the Hollywood composer nor the English classical guitarist.

can now be had for anywhere from a couple of hundred to just under a thousand dollars per finished minute, depending on the level of production required. Episodic TV dramas are often done on a contract basis for under $10,000 per show.

A lot of composers maintain Web sites, and an Internet search for "original music" with "video" will turn up hundreds of qualified sites. Unfortunately, ownership of a Web site—even one with fancy graphics and a picture of a studio—is no guarantee of quality. Once you've found some likely candidates, you have to evaluate their work. Ask to hear some of their past scores, ideally both as excerpts from the finished videos that used their music and as the unmixed music tracks supplied to the producer. You want both so you can judge their musical and production abilities; If they don't have access to original score, it might be because they didn't create it.

There are four things to listen for when evaluating a music demo:

- Was it composed well? Is the music appealing, does it match the mood of the video, and does it stay interesting for its entire length? If a piece is supposed to be something other than electronic instruments, does it sound real? Making artificial strings or horns sound real requires serious composing and arranging skill—you have to know what those instruments *should* be playing—as well as good production.

- Was it produced well? Play it in stereo on good speakers. Hum and pops, badly tuned instruments, and a lack of clarity in the mix are signs of amateur production. This can indicate the composer doesn't have real-world experience or lacks the necessary equipment to do a good job for you. If the music wasn't produced at all—if the composer is providing self-playing MIDI files—you're going to be saddled with the chore of turning them into usable music. It can be expensive to do this well.

- Was it performed well? Music software makes it easy to fake an acceptable performance by fixing wrong notes, evening out the tempo or dynamics, and even adding an artificial "human" randomness. But there's a big difference between acceptable and good performances, particularly in how expressively a line is played. Listen particularly to solos. Do you get a sense of a personality in the performance? Or does it sound played by a machine?

- Is the style of music appropriate for your project? I put this last both because it's probably the easiest for you to evaluate—you know what you like—but also because it can be the least important. An experienced professional with good scoring chops can usually master a number of styles. I'm continually amazed at how flexible the composers I work with are.

Formerly Original Music

Stock music used to be a curse. When I started out, using a music library often meant you gave up quality to get economy and speed. Selections were heavily weighted toward small pop and dance bands because they were cheaper to produce, but that limited what could be written.

Orchestras were small, unrehearsed, and frequently out of tune. The few good cuts that did exist tended to be overused—I've judged business film festivals where three entries had the same theme song. It took a highly skilled music editor to blend a few different pieces into something that sounded new. But despite its limitations, stock music was often the only option. We had a library of over a thousand stock LPs in my studio, before the business changed entirely.

Digital recording, computers, and samplers[3] created the revolution. Composers could write and arrange full scores on their desktops, review and change what they'd written while listening to synthesized versions, and then walk into a studio and combine a few live players with better-quality synthesizers and sampled backup groups. Soon it wasn't even necessary to walk into a studio at all for some recordings; you could do the whole project in your living room. The over-flow of desktop composers raised the standard for all library music. Bigger libraries started to concentrate on fuller sounds and more of the acoustic or vocal textures that can't be synthesized.

At the same time, the explosion of media—all those cable channels and high-end videos—meant a lot more original music was being created. The composers often retained the right to sell remixed or generic versions of their works to a library after a period of exclusivity passed.

Bottom line: there's a ton of good, new stock music. A lot of what you can get today is excellent. You'll hear it in national commercials, network programs, and Hollywood features. There's also a lot more music to choose from. The biggest houses release as many as a dozen new CDs a month, and a Web search will turn up more than a hundred small libraries. (Many of the smallest libraries are one-person operations. Their work can suffer from the same limitations as low-end original scoring, so you should evaluate their libraries with the same criteria.)

What was formerly a major difference between library and original music—precise fit to the picture—isn't as big a consideration any more. Once you master the techniques of music editing, you'll be able to blend existing music tracks to fit picture as well as most of the classic Hollywood scores. Even if you're a musical klutz, you can learn to cut music smoothly and accurately using just desktop audio or NLE software. I'll teach you later in this chapter.

Contact information and reviews of many music libraries appear in the tutorials section of my Web site, at www.dplay.com.

Paying for library music

Publishers make their money by selling the same recording over and over. You can buy the rights to use it in your project for a tiny fraction of the cost of an equivalent original piece. Another producer might buy the same song tomorrow, but the selections are so wide these days, and there

---

3. Instruments that play recordings of acoustic instruments—even choirs—from their keyboards while remaining responsive to subtleties in the playing style. Kurzweil made the first successful studio version, in the mid-1980s.

are so many options for customizing music, that there's little chance a customer will recognize your corporate theme on a competitor's video.

Library music is sold two different ways. The rates depend both on how the publisher chooses to do business and how you plan to use the music, but they're surprisingly consistent within those two categories.

Needle-drop   The better libraries usually work on a needle-drop basis. The term comes from the original payment scheme, where a fee was charged each time a technician dropped the tone arm to dub from the record to a film for editing. A really good piece may be licensed thousands of times in its life, so publishers find it profitable to create quality product. Since CDs don't use needles, these are often called "laser drops" now.

Needle-drop libraries charge minimal prices for their CDs—$12–15 each—and will occasionally give or loan them to good customers. They make their money charging $75–90 per song for a business video, up to $1,000 or so for unlimited use in broadcast media and productions for sale. Rates can be negotiable, depending on your standing with the publisher, and you don't pay anything other than the disk fee until you decide to use a particular piece.

These libraries also offer "production blankets"—you can use their entire catalog, in as many snippets as you want—based on the total length of your project. A blanket for a 10-minute corporate video may cost about $350. It typically buys about half a dozen different pieces, but you can use hundreds if you want. Blanket licenses from larger publishers usually cost more because the music selection is wider. You can also buy annual blankets from some of the needle-drop libraries, covering all your productions for a prepaid fee. Prices vary widely, depending on the size of the library and what media you produce for.

When you use a needle-drop selection, you're responsible for reporting the usage—including details about the song, the project, and the medium—to the publisher. They'll supply you with forms or an online site for this purpose. Depending on your arrangement with them, they then send you an invoice or a license granting a nonexclusive right to use that music, forever, in that particular program.

Buyout   Many of the newer libraries sell their music on a buyout basis. You pay a relatively stiff price to purchase the CD, but have the right to use anything on it, in any of your productions. Disc prices vary but are usually between $60–160, with substantial discounts for multidisc sales. Essentially, you're investing that you will use the songs enough times to justify the cost. As with any investment, you can get burned; there is absolutely no correlation between price and quality. The incentive is for a publisher to turn out as many CDs as possible, and unscrupulous or undercapitalized ones will tend to pad their discs with multiple edited or extra-long looped versions of the same piece—things you can do just as easily (and much more efficiently) on an NLE. Quite a few buyout cuts sound like they were ad-libbed by a single keyboard player, over loops that *they* bought from a sampling library.[4] On the other hand, some buyout libraries are incredible bargains. If you do a lot of video and don't need Hollywood production quality, this may be the right choice.

I recommend that you never purchase a buyout CD from a library you haven't worked with before, until you've had a chance to evaluate the actual discs. A five-minute demo may sound impressive as a montage, but it could be hiding the fact that there's only five minutes of usable music in the entire library. Reputable music houses will provide evaluation copies, on short-term loan, to reputable producers.

Performing rights societies

Most library music is covered by ASCAP or BMI, the major organizations who see that composers get compensated when their music is played on radio or TV. This absolutely doesn't mean that a TV station's annual ASCAP or BMI fee lets you use their music in productions you create, even if the productions are promoting that station.[5] The societies keep track of how often each member's music is played on the air, so if you've been hired by a broadcaster, you

Digital Playroom

History Channel / "The Big Dig" (Tera Media) 48:00   JR# 4033

APPROX LENGTH	TITLE	COMPOSER	PUBLISHER
:30	Boston Patriots	Kelly Bryarly	Omnistyles (BMI)
1:00	Chiller	Steve Shapiro	Omnistyles (BMI)
1:30	Evening Concert	Mike Carubia	Franklin-Douglas (ASCAP)
3:30	Heritage Suite Finale	John Manchester	Franklin-Douglas (ASCAP)
1:30	Heritage Suite Opening	John Manchester	Franklin-Douglas (ASCAP)
2:30	Horse Country	John Manchester	Franklin-Douglas (ASCAP)
2:30	Killer Instinct	Brian Morris	Franklin-Douglas (ASCAP)
:45	Opec Summit	Derek Richards	Franklin-Douglas (ASCAP)
1:00	Opening Day	Vic Sepanski	Franklin-Douglas (ASCAP)
:45	Opening Night	Doug Wood	Franklin-Douglas (ASCAP)

14.2 Information a broadcaster might require for reporting usage to ASCAP and BMI.

might be required to assemble a list of what music you used, how long each piece is heard, who wrote and published it, and which society that publisher belongs to (Figure 14.2). For more details, check the societies' Web sites at www.ascap.com and www.bmi.com.

---

4. Yes, musicians also buy library music—CDs of prerecorded instrumental sections, playing short musical phrases, that they then use as backup elements for their own songs. Sonic Foundry's Acid program is designed for organizing, looping, and mixing this kind of element.

5. A client or station manager may attempt to convince you that it does, and that it's perfectly legal to use anything you want without paying additional fees. This just isn't true, as has been tested in court many times. The annual ASCAP and BMI fees pay the composers for playing their songs on the air as entertainment. Any copying or editing of a particular recording into a video, or using it as a background for something else, is specifically not covered.

The rights societies have been attempting to define Web sites and other new media as public performances, coupled with record companies who want new laws that would provide a fee every time one of their songs is streamed from a site. This situation is fluid, so check an independent source like DV.com for the latest news.

Using Commercial Recordings

As a producer, what are your rights regarding music from CDs you buy at a record store? Like the cops say, "You have the right to remain silent." Only three choices are guaranteed to keep you out of trouble: compose and perform the music yourself, get permission from the people who did, or don't use the music.

Copyright is a fact of life.

- Virtually any use of a music recording in any video, for any purpose other than your own personal entertainment in your home, requires written permission. In fact, dubbing a pop recording onto your own home movies is technically a violation of copyright, though there's little chance of your being sued over it. When you buy a commercial recording, you get the rights to play it for yourself and immediate friends, and to copy it to another digital recording for your own listening convenience. Period.

- It doesn't matter whether you work for a charitable or educational institution, have no budget, don't charge admission, or even intend the piece to promote the musician. You need permission.

- It doesn't matter whether the song is classical or in the public domain—if the performance is on CD, it's almost certainly protected by performance copyright. You need permission.

- It doesn't matter if you used less than eight bars: brevity was never a reliable defense in copyright cases and was specifically eliminated by Congress a quarter century ago. You need permission.

- It doesn't matter if you claim the wedding videographer's defense that "My clients will buy a copy of the CD, and I'll use that copy in the wedding album I produce." They may be a lovely couple, but when they bought the disc, they didn't buy the right to synchronize it. You need permission.

Get the message? The doctrine of "fair use" has very limited application. Unless you're quoting a brief selection in a legitimate critical review of the performance, it probably doesn't apply. Check with a lawyer before making any assumptions about it. I've heard of videographers being put out of business because they used a pop song in a wedding album, and one of the happy couple's neighbors happened to work for a giant copyright holder.

You *can* assume any music written after the first two decades of the 20th century is under copyright, and recent changes in the copyright laws will protect newer pieces a lot longer. Classical works and pop standards may be old enough for their copyrights to have expired, but newer editions and arrangements are still protected. But even if you stick to 17th-century Baroque composers, the recording of the performance itself is probably protected. Look for the sound-recording copyright symbol, the letter *P* in a circle, somewhere on the disc or label. Publishers and record labels have large and hungry business departments, and they almost always win in court. Occasionally, they even pay their composers and performers, which is the whole point of the exercise.

Written permission to use a piece of music may be absolutely necessary if you're aiming a film at TV networks or the festival circuit. Most of them won't touch a piece until the producer guarantees that copyrights have been cleared, and indemnifies them against suits for infringement.

It's entirely possible you'll sneak under the publishers' radar. Despite urban legends about lawyers coming after Boy Scouts for singing protected songs at a campfire, many casual uses are never spotted by the copyright owners. But that doesn't make it legal, it doesn't reduce their right to come after you in the future, and the fact that someone else might not have been caught isn't a defense if you're hauled to court.

The perils of pop

Even if you're not afraid of lawyers or bad karma, it's probably not a good idea to use a piece of current pop music under a video. Music is a powerful associative tool, and psychologists have found that people will pay more attention to the tune already known from the radio—and think about what happened the last time they heard it—than to the new information in your video. The reason national advertisers can get away with using rock classics in their spots is that they run their ads so many times that their message starts to overpower the memories. (And of course, they've gotten permission.)

But if you honestly believe a commercial recording might be appropriate for your project, don't be afraid to ask if you can use it. Record company promotion departments can be surprisingly generous at times—particularly if good causes are involved—and I've worked on projects that got permission to use a Beatles song for PBS, and a Leonard Bernstein recording for a music school, absolutely free. Even if the cause is less than noble, you may be able to secure limited-audience rights for a reasonable amount. It doesn't hurt to ask.

If it turns out that rights to a commercial recording aren't available or are too expensive, most large music libraries have a good selection of "soundalikes" you can use at their regular rates. These won't sound *exactly* like the original recording—that could also be a violation of copyright—but are close enough to get the message across.

Sources for source music

Some of the music libraries have excellent collections of contemporary and new recordings of generic "era" music—such as big-band, swing, or classic rock—designed to be coming from on-screen radios and TVs. If you want an authentic older style, perhaps because your characters are watching an old movie or documentary, check the archive sections of the larger needle-drop houses. Some of those companies were around in the 1940s and 1950s and will license you the same music on CD that they sold on 78s back then. They may also have appropriate music for elevators and supermarkets; between the 1950s and 1970s, a lot of background music came from the same sources.

A few of the buyout libraries have vocal cuts with the same musical and production values as current pop styles. They possibly *were* failed pop songs that the composer is trying to recoup some investment from, but we don't care.

Needle-drop libraries are frequently very good with solo piano, jazz combo, and big-band sounds for a restaurant or club. But on-screen small rock groups for a club or dance can be problematic; most library music is too well performed, or has too much of a studio sound, to be convincing. Ask the library if they have any demo or scratch tracks they'd be willing to license—or find a local band, and ask if they have any tapes of live performances of their original music you can use.

It almost always helps to start in the middle of a source cue, rather than at the front. Unless your characters are psychic, they won't be able to turn on their radios at the start of a song or walk into a club at the precise beginning of a set.

Source music always needs equalization and reverb—often with drastic settings—to make it match the ambience of a scene (see Chapter 16).

Mix and Match

You can use Hollywood's trick of mixing original and library music in your own limited-budget video, hiring a composer for specialty pieces but blending them with stock elements where it will save money. For a 10-minute humorous film about advertising, I needed (and couldn't afford) an almost continuous score. Parts of it had to be precisely timed to on-screen actions and specific words of the script, but could have the sound of a small group or sampled chamber orchestra. Other cues required a full orchestra or styles of playing that are difficult to synthesize. Still others were just to set a background or location, and could be easily found in a library.

We created a spotting list (part of it is shown in Figure 14.1) detailing 25 different musical elements ranging from a few seconds' length to slightly less than a minute. Each was designed for a particular part of the video. Then we selected 18 of the cues from a good needle-drop library and made sure they could be edited to fit picture. Finally, I gave those cues and the spotting notes to a local composer, along with reference video. She wrote and recorded the other pieces, fitting precise word or visual cues. She didn't have to charge us for 10 minutes of original music, but—since she was using the library cuts as a guide—her pieces blended with the others into a seamless whole.

Non-CD libraries

Some libraries are sold as CD-ROM, allegedly because that medium is "computer-ready" or because they can offer 48 kHz sampling for "better-than-CD" sound. This is hype. Any desktop computer can rip audio files from standard music CDs with absolutely no quality loss. And unless a 48 kHz sampled recording is both created and played back on high-end studio equipment, there won't be any difference between it and a 44.1 kHz CD. In fact, the predigitized music and effects CD-ROMs I've seen at computer stores sound like they were recorded through generic sound cards with no studio production . . . sort of "worse-than-CD" sound. But a well-recorded CD-ROM can be useful if you need a lot of music on a single disc, recorded in mono or at lower sample rates. Some also come with search engines.

Sonic Desktop's SmartSound series of programs (including Sonicfire Pro) uses music on CD-ROM with an attached database of edit points. It lets you specify a style of music from the discs in your own library, and mark the start and end points against video. Then it automatically cuts the music to fit. The program only works with CD-ROMs from Sonic Desktop, but most of the songs are encoded versions of cues from mainstream buyout libraries. You pay a premium for the encoding, and the selection is limited compared to the world of good buyout music out there, but SmartSound can be useful if you need a lot of pre-cut music in odd lengths and don't mind using the same songs over and over. Music editing isn't difficult once you've been shown the basic principles (that's the second half of this chapter), and doing it yourself is a lot more flexible.

Many libraries are now turning to the Internet. You make your selection from a Web page, listening to low-resolution samples, and then purchase the cut online. It's downloaded to you as a compressed file. This is lossy compression (Chapter 3), so the cue will never sound as good as a CD recording. But if the compression is done well, and isn't more radical than 12:1 or so (about 850 kilobytes per stereo minute), the quality should be perfectly usable. Or if you want top quality, you can have a CD shipped by overnight courier.

You may also consider buying music as MIDI files. (See "What's this MIDI?" on page 336.) These can be cheaper and a lot more flexible to edit, but the burden is on you to turn them into usable music tracks for a video. You'll need additional software, equipment, and musical skills. But if you know what you're doing, you can create acceptable tracks—certainly as good as the basic buyout libraries.

What's this MIDI?

MIDI (Musical Instrument Digital Interface) is actually a local area network (LAN) standardized by synthesizer manufacturers in the early 1980s. It works like other LANs in that messages are constantly flowing across the network and each node pays attention only to the ones that are addressed to it. Unlike Ethernet, the networks are wired in a daisy chain—computer to synth A, synth A to synth B—rather than with a common hub. Cables use two conductors of a five-pin DIN connector and carry messages in one direction only.

The messages themselves are primarily musical instructions: *Play middle C, turn C off and play the E above it*, and so on. Obviously, enough messages equals a tune. Other MIDI messages may control volume, pitch-bend, continuous pressure on sustained notes, what sound is assigned to each address (such as *piano on channel one, trumpet on channel two*), and special messages reserved by the manufacturer. Since MIDI is so ubiquitous a network standard, various manufacturers have also adopted it to control tape decks or processors, or to pass text messages.

Addressing can get convoluted. The original MIDI specification called for only 16 unique addresses, called "channels." Today's synths make different sounds simultaneously, and each may need up to a dozen channels to sort them out. This doesn't leave many for the next instrument down the line. On the other hand, multiple synths may be assigned to the same channel, so they respond to the same commands and thicken the sound.

For this reason, many MIDI music studios use multiple networks. MIDI interfaces connect each of the controlling computer's serial or USB ports to as many as eight separate networks, called "cables." A computer with two ports can then control up to 16 simultaneous sounds on each of 16 cables. Sequencer programs control what messages are sent, and try to keep track of overall timing—but this can be a problem in fast passages with lots of instruments, when the number of simultaneous musical messages exceeds MIDI's low-speed data capability.

The programs can also edit melodies, create their own harmony or rhythmic variations, and even print sheet music. Computer MIDI files follow a standard format, so files can be imported by different programs to play approximately the same song. Since they represent just the note commands, rather than digital audio, they can be quite compact: A MIDI version of a 60-second clip theme might need only 16 kilobytes, while a CD-quality recording of that same theme, played on the same synths, would eat more than 10 meg. Of course, the CD version can also include hot session players, studio mixing effects and human vocals—all impossible to encode in a MIDI file. It also doesn't need a rack full of equipment and serious production expertise to get the best sounds.

Selecting Music From a Library

Grab your notes, the script, and—if possible—the rough video edit, narration tracks, or anything else that will have to work with the music. Then head for the library.

If your facility doesn't have its own selection of discs, check larger local recording or video houses; you can probably rent time in their libraries. Bigger music publishers often have offices in major production cities, with expert librarians on tap; they charge only a nominal amount for this service because it helps them sell licenses.

Obviously, you'll want to listen to the songs you're considering. (Maybe it isn't obvious. Some libraries expect you to select—and pay for—cuts based on their text descriptions. Avoid them.) But before you listen, look at the discs. The titles won't tell you much—*Our Wedding* could be Mendelssohn or Wagner, a medley of waltzes, or even slapstick—but the descriptions can be useful. The better libraries use wordings like *brooding strings; panic stabs at :19 and :23*. Some more marginal libraries describe everything as *Great! The perfect music for financial, high tech, extreme sports, and retail* . . . uh-huh.

Check the composer, too. Bigger libraries have stables of freelancers with different styles. Two or three pieces by the same composer, even if they're on different discs, might fit perfectly as a suite. You may also find yourself enjoying the style of one particular composer and look specifically for that name.

Many publishers are putting search engines on the Web, where you can select music by categories and keywords and listen to brief excerpts. A few will send you searchable CD-ROM databases of their entire catalog, including excerpts from each cut (Figure 14.3), so you can look for music without a fast Internet connection. Either of these searching systems are a valuable time-saver. They get faster the more times you use a library because you get used to their particular keyword system.

Once you've found some cuts, start listening, and make notes on which music is best for each place in your video. Then

14.3 A CD-ROM library utility that lets you search and audition music cues from a database. This one is from Omnimusic.

turn off the sound the moment you've gotten a feel for a potentially usable cut and make some notes. *Not* listening is an important part of choosing music. Use the pause control a lot, and take frequent breaks. Human brains turn to oatmeal after extended library-music sessions—remember, most of this is music that was never designed to be in the foreground—so stop the music every 15 minutes or so, and do something else. This will make it easier to distinguish and evaluate individual pieces.

Selective listening is an important part of the process as well. The melody of a library cut often starts some 10 seconds after the intro, but there may be variations later on. If you think a piece has some merit but you don't like precisely what you're hearing, skip forward and listen for the texture to change. Include, in your notes, what parts you liked and which you'd rather avoid.

Once you've got a short list, go back and explore those pieces again. Mix the voice with music while you're listening, or play the cut while you watch video. If you don't have a mixer in the music library, put the narration on a boombox next to the CD player. Or make copies of your potential selections, and bring them back into the NLE or video suite for previewing. It's important to try the music under real circumstances.

When you think you've found the right music, keep playing the video or announcer and turn the music off. You should immediately feel, in your gut, that something's missing. If you don't, the music isn't contributing anything to the project.

Don't worry too much about synchronizing specific hits or meeting a particular length while you're auditioning. You'll be able to do all that when you edit.

No matter what you do, don't forget that music is an artistic element. No set of rules, catalog descriptions, or software can replace your best directorial judgment. Don't be afraid to go against type—I once scored a PBS documentary about jogging by using Bach fugues—and don't be afraid to make a statement. (Just be sure it's the same statement your client wants to make.)

Music Editing

No book will ever turn me into a truly good video editor. I lack the visual design skills. But, over the years, I've learned some rules of thumb (cut on motion, respect the axis . . . oh, *you* know) to make my rare video sessions a less painful experience. It's the same thing with music editing. Unless you're born with musical sensibilities and have learned how chords and beats go together to make a song, you'll never be a truly gifted music cutter.

But most of the time, what makes bad music editing not work has nothing to do with chords or melody. It's simply a broken rhythm. Every mainstream piece of music since the late Renaissance has a constant heartbeat, with accents in a regular pattern. The tempo can change, or different beats might get accented, but only according to specific rules. We learn those rules subconsciously, starting with the first lullaby our mothers sing us. If an edit breaks a rule, we know something is wrong—even if we don't know precisely what.

On the other hand, the rules about that heartbeat are simple. You can learn how to deal with it even if you can't carry a tune in a boombox. Use some simple techniques, and you'll soon be cutting like a pro—and making generic library pieces fit like a custom score.

Learn to Trust Your Ears

The first step is to forget what you've been told about looking at waveforms. Music editing requires knowing exactly where the heartbeat starts, and there's nothing in a visual waveform—no matter how tightly you zoom in—guaranteed to tell you where it is. All you'll ever find by eye is where the drums are hit loudest, and that may or may not be related to the start of a rhythmic phrase (in most rock and pop music, it isn't). Besides, if you're cutting orchestral music, there aren't any drum hits. If you're cutting world music, there

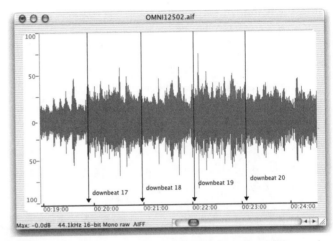

14.4 Beat it! You'd never find these downbeats by eye. I was able to mark them quickly, but only while listening to the music in real time.

are too many (Figure 14.4). Remember: all sound exists as changes of pressure over time. The only way to experience it is by taking time, not by looking at a snapshot.

Learn to Count

The most important technique is to learn to count along while you listen. Once you can count in rhythm, you'll be able to mark edits quickly and accurately on the fly . . . without bothering to redraw a screen. In fact, you can apply the same editing technique to computers that don't have particularly accurate zooms, or even nonvisual systems like MiniDisc and CMX-style edit controllers.

Most of the music you'll ever use—or hear—is made up of evenly spaced beats organized into groups. Usually there are four of them in a group, though occasionally there may be two, three, or six.[6] We'll cover those other numbers later. For now, let's stick to four.

---

6. And sometimes five, seven, or other numbers, but those are extremely rare in production music. Once you master the more common four-beat system, you'll find even this oddly counted music easier to edit.

Four beats make up a *bar* or *measure*. There is always a strong emphasis on the first beat of the bar, and a slightly weaker one on the third. This four-beat pattern keeps on ticking no matter what the melody or lyrics are doing, though most melodies are based on groups of four or eight of these bars. The pattern can change tempo, speeding up or slowing down, but it does so smoothly and without breaking the pattern.

If you don't respect the four-beat pattern, your music edits will probably sound wrong. If you *do* respect it, there's a good chance the chords and melody will fall into place.

The trick is to learn to count those four beats at the same time you're deciding where to edit. It isn't hard. All you need is enough eye-hand coordination to tap your edit system's marking buttons at the right time. It's like dancing with your fingers instead of your feet.

We'll learn how with a little Stephen Foster ditty. Everybody sing! *Camptown ladies sing this song, Doo-dah! Doo-dah! Camptown racetrack five miles long, oh the doo-dah-day!*

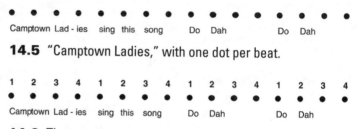

14.5 "Camptown Ladies," with one dot per beat.

14.6 The same song, counting 1–4 with the beat.

While you're singing, tap your finger along with the beat. Short syllables get one tap each. "Song" is held twice as long, so it gets two taps. The "Dahs" are held longest of all, three taps. If we print a dot for each finger tap, it looks like Figure 14.5. Notice how no matter what the words are doing, the dots are evenly spaced. The tapping should have a similarly constant rhythm.

Now sing it again, but this time count from one to four while you're tapping. (If you can't sing, tap, and count at the same time, recruit a friend to sing for you.) The loudest syllable will always be "one," like in Figure 14.6.

We're using "Camptown Ladies" because almost everybody knows it.[7] Think about the pattern of stresses in the lyric: the strongest syllables in the first line are *Camp*, *sing*, and the two *Doos* on one. The next strongest are *Lad* and *song* on three. This 1-3 stress pattern holds for almost every song in the most common time signatures. ("Camptown" was actually written in 2/4 time, but you can still count it in fours.) Practice counting along with songs on the radio, and it'll become second nature.

---

7. . . . and it's in the public domain. In fact, since we're not using anybody else's performance, no permission is necessary.

The "one" in each count is the downbeat. It's called that because if you're conducting an orchestra playing the song, this is the only time in each measure that your hand moves in a downward direction. (The movements of a conductor's hand follow a centuries-old tradition. There's a specific direction for each beat of the measure, depending on how many beats there are overall. Experienced music editors often follow the same hand patterns when marking a song, so they can feel the metric structure instead of having to count it. My clients can't really understand why I have to conduct my editing system . . .)

Listen for the accented syllables of any melody. These aren't necessarily the loudest drum hits; pop styles often accent the second and fourth beats of each measure, to make them more danceable. (If you want to sing "Camptown" in a hoe-down style, clap your hands on 2 and 4. Try it!) Don't be fooled by the drummer on these backbeats; it's just rhythmic embellishment. If you sing along with the melody, you'll always be able to find the downbeat.

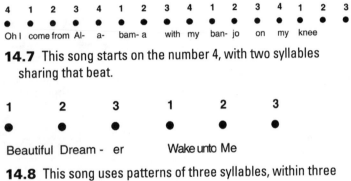

14.7 This song starts on the number 4, with two syllables sharing that beat.

14.8 This song uses patterns of three syllables, within three beats to a measure.

Some songs don't start on their loudest syllable, so you have to start counting on a different number. Others can have a few short notes sharing a beat. Figure 14.7 is another Stephen Foster song to illustrate both situations. The "Oh I" shares one beat. The syllables "come" and "bam" are much louder than any others around them, so they get the number 1.

A few songs move in threes instead of fours. The principle's the same, as you can see in Figure 14.8. The three fast syllables in "Beautiful" occupy just one count—the same way that "Dream" does. "Beau" and "Wake" are definitely the accented syllables and get the 1.

Cutting by Counting

Once you've learned to count accurately with the music, the editing part is simple. All you have to do is match the numbers. Start by loading track 24 of the book's CD into your editing system. This is one of a number of pieces written specifically for this book by Doug Wood, president of the Omnimusic Library,[8] and it's designed to be typical of the kind of straight corporate or documentary theme you'd find in most libraries. It counts in 4.

---

8. And, of course, protected by copyright. But you can license similar pieces—as well as a lot more—from Omnimusic (www.omnimusic.com).

If you're using a desktop NLE, follow the steps below. If you've got a different kind of system, the procedure will be only slightly different. Read along through these instructions, and we'll cover the differences later.

- Open the music in a clip window, start playing it, and count along. You might want to play it a few times before proceeding, to get used to the tempo.

- Start tapping the marking button very lightly on each count. When you get to each "one," tap hard enough to actually make a mark. Depending on your system, you might then have to switch to a different button to mark the next "one" without erasing the first. When you're done, you should have a bunch of marks looking something like the gray flags in Figure 14.9.

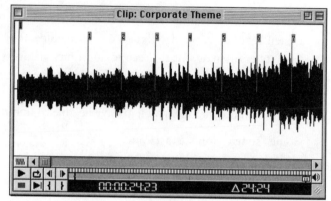

14.9 Tap hard enough to make a mark each time you count the number 1.

Move the clip to a timeline, and you're ready to edit. If you want to shorten the piece, cut out the space between two marks and butt the pieces together. In Figure 14.10, we cut from Marker 2 to Marker 4, pulling out about three seconds. (Because of the way chords

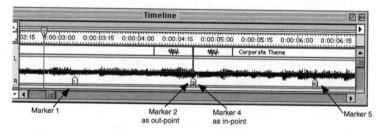
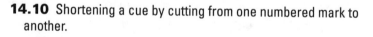

14.10 Shortening a cue by cutting from one numbered mark to another.

flow in most music, it usually sounds better to cut from an even number to another even one, or from an odd number to another odd one.) If we wanted to extend the music, we could have taken that stretch between Marker 2 and Marker 4 and laid it into the timeline twice.

This is a very short edit—there's only about three seconds between the markers—but the technique works for edits of any length. If you need to edit longer stretches of music, make the marks farther apart—say, every fourth "one."

Editing off the marks

As you listen through the sample corporate piece on the CD, notice how the horn melody begins around 12 seconds in. It actually starts on a "4," one beat ahead of the downbeat. But you'll still use those markers you made to cut the song accurately, and start that melody anywhere you want.

- Move the entire clip to one track of the timeline. Play through it, and notice the marker number *just after* you'd like the melody to start. For the sake of this example, we'll say it's Marker 3.

- Go back to the clip, and notice which marker occurs just after the melody's actual start. If your clip looks like our Figure 14.9, it'll be Marker 7. Slide the clip onto another track, lining up Marker 7 against Marker 3 (as in Figure 14.11). In most editing programs, you can temporarily call Marker 7 the in-point, and it'll align itself against the other marker automatically. Then slide the in-point forward to include the start of the melody.

In Figure 14.11, we built the edit on two tracks and added a quick fade up to make the entrance of the horn melody smoother. But you can do a similar edit on a single track, making a butt cut from one marker to the other, and then rolling the edit point forward to pick up the melody. The important thing is that, no matter where you make the edit, you still preserve that constant heartbeat—the length of time from one downbeat to the next has to stay the same.

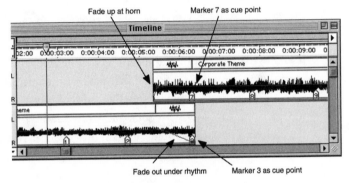

14.11 An edit can be before or after a marker, but the markers still have to line up.

When it doesn't sound good . . .

If you hear a little hiccup at the edit, chances are you didn't mark the downbeat accurately. This is usually because you were too conscious of tapping the marking button and stiffened your hand up slightly when it was time to press. Editing is like a lot of other physical activities: it helps to stay loose and relaxed. Practice counting aloud as you make the lighter and heavier taps.

If you want to verify that you've made the marks accurately, put copies of the clip on two adjacent tracks, with the first marker on one track lined up to a later marker on the other. Play them both simultaneously: if the marks were correct, you won't hear any stuttering in the drums.

Practice counting along with the beat while you're reviewing an edit as well. If the edit is accurate, your "one" should line up perfectly before and after the cut. If you have to adjust slightly while you're counting, one or both of the edit points were off the beat.

An edit can also sound odd because the chords or melody doesn't match. (This is more likely to occur when the song is strung out along two simultaneous tracks, like Figure 14.11.) Try moving one of the points an odd number of measures earlier or later. For example, if you cut Marker 3 to Marker 6 and don't like the result, you may have much better luck coming in on Marker 5, 7, or 9.

As you cut more music, you'll develop a better feel for how chords change and melodies develop, and you'll have fewer awkward edits. But don't expect to ever outgrow the idea of counting along with the rhythm. It's one of the most powerful techniques you can use.

Adapting to other systems

If your system edits sound by cutting or pasting sections, the process is very similar. Plant markers on the downbeats, then stop the playback and select an area from one marker to another. Use the cut command if you want to shorten the cue. If you want to lengthen it, use the copy command. Then place the insertion point on another marker, and paste.

If you're using a traditional multimachine online editor with in- and out-points, you just have to mark more carefully. Copy the first part of the cue, at least past the edit point, onto the master tape. Play it back, tapping the Record-in button on downbeats, until you mark the desired record-in point. Now play back the source tape, marking the source-in the same way. Preview the edit, and the beat should be constant. Then, if you want, multitrim to pick up the melody.

More practice

Not every cue is going to be as straightforward as our corporate theme. Here are two more selections for you to practice on, also both written by Doug Wood.[9]

Track 25 is a jazzier piece that counts in 4, with a syncopated melody and drum tracks that seldom line up with the downbeat. But when you mark those downbeats, the marks should have perfectly even spacing; while the melody is all over the place, the tempo

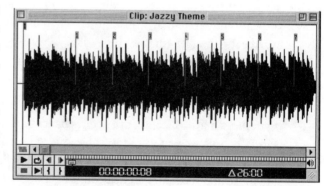

14.12 A more syncopated piece. The downbeats are regular, even though the drums and melody aren't.

never changes (Figure 14.12). The edit technique that worked for the straighter corporate

---

9. Once again, remember these pieces are protected by copyright. You have permission to copy them to your computer to practice editing techniques, but you must contact Omnimusic if you want to use them in a production. Besides, Omnimusic has a lot more selections to choose from, and almost all of them are longer than the short ones written for this book. You might find something you like better.

piece—lining up downbeats, and then sliding the edit to catch a piece of melody—is just as applicable here.

Track 26 is a waltz, played by a string orchestra. You have to count it in threes, rather than fours, but the principle is the same, and the downbeats just as regular (Figure 14.13). Since the melody starts ahead of the beat, the best way to edit this is on multiple tracks (Figure 14.14); I left track B extended up to Marker 5 so you could see how the markers still line up.

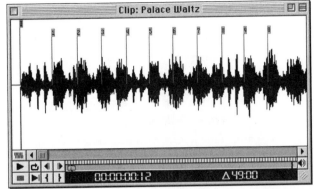

14.13 Shall we waltz? You can see how the melody is ahead of most downbeats. If you look between Markers 4 and 5, and between 8 and 9, you can see the definite one-two-three structure.

Strings, particularly when played in echoey halls, can take a moment to build up their sound. Since the notes change slowly compared to other instruments, butt cuts—even when on the right beat—can sound abrupt. The best solution is often to overlap the start of one note with the end of another (as in the first edit of Figure 14.14) or do a quick cross-fade (as in the second edit of that figure). Note the time ruler: neither overlap is longer than a quarter second.

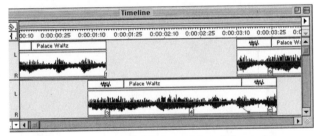

14.14 Strings usually do best with quick overlaps.

Matching Picture

Once you get comfortable editing this way, each individual cut will take very little time to execute. Then you'll be ready to create custom scores, adding or subtracting measures so that musical climaxes and changes match changes in the video. A few things will help you achieve that perfect marriage of music and picture:

- If a downbeat is almost lined up with an important visual cue, try shifting the entire music track a few frames. The earlier edits may still appear to be in sync after they've been moved slightly, and it'll be easier to catch that golden moment.

- Don't be afraid to speed up or slow down the entire piece slightly, even it means changing the pitch. Acoustic instruments can be shifted about 3% faster or slower before their timbre sounds wrong, but synthesizers can be shifted as much as 10% and still sound reasonable.

- If your software can change the tempo without affecting the pitch, you can do more radical manipulation—as much as 30% either way in a good audio program. You can also change the tempo for just part of a cue, or squeeze or stretch only a couple of bars to fit a video sequence, if the pitch doesn't change.

- If a piece has prominent drums, don't worry about matching the video perfectly. When there's an important visual hit, add a matching drum sound effect on a different track. It'll sound like the drummer was deliberately playing ahead of or behind the beat to match picture. This works with orchestral percussion as well as with jazz and rock.

A final tip

Reverberation can cause problems with sound pickup when you're shooting, but it's great stuff to have when you're editing music. A little reverb, faded up right before a cut and out right after, can make up for sounds that got lost because they extended over the barline. And if you have to fade the end of a piece quickly to match a visual fade, a little reverb can help make it sound like the musicians stopped playing on cue.

Sound Effects

We Don't Need No Stinkin' Reality

Just like music, sound effects have been a part of movies since the earliest silent blockbusters. Theater organs often included a "toy counter"—bells, bird whistles, ratchets, gun shots, and anything else that could be rigged to an organ key, designed to add convincing realism to a film. Of course, realism has more to do with convention than reality. While it's tempting to laugh at early audiences being thrilled by bird whistles accompanying grainy black-and-white panoramas, today's practices aren't much more realistic.

For example, when Gene Roddenberry first tested the opening of *Star Trek*[1] in the late 1960s, the Enterprise didn't make a sound as it flew past the camera. Space is a vacuum as well as a final frontier, so there couldn't be any noise out there. But by the time the series got to television, the ship's engines had a satisfying *woosh*. Roddenberry rewrote the laws of physics to make a scale-model spaceship more exciting. Today, Hollywood rockets scream by in digital surround . . . but the sound isn't any more realistic than those original organ-key birds.

In Hollywood, reality means, "If you can see it, you must hear something." Feature films have teams of sound editors, often spending a week on effects for each 10-minute reel. Everything is foleyed (Chapter 10) or has effects cut to it, and sound effects supervisors will walk into a mix with synchronized tracks for every rustling leaf and buzzing fly in a scene, not to mention the

---

1. The original TV series, also known as *Star Trek: Who Knew It Would Become a Dynasty?*

fantasy light swords and laser bombs. It's overkill—many of these sounds never make it to the final track—but still follows the "see it, hear it" rule.

Your video's budget may be more modest, but properly chosen and applied sound effects can add realism to stock footage or scenes shot on a limited set. They can heighten drama, provide comic relief, and command attention. A good stereo ambience, played through properly placed speakers, can even capture the space around a video screen or kiosk and isolate the user. The trick is planning how to use effects most efficiently. Unless you've got the resources to edit a specific effect for every leaf rustle and fly buzz, it makes sense to concentrate on the ones that'll make a difference.

In fact, the first step in creating a good effects track is to ignore it. Concentrate on the dialog and the music first. A lot of times, scenes that were crying out for effects will be completely covered by the score.

Pioneer sound designer Tony Schwartz once said sound effects are a waste of time. According to him, those random footsteps and rattles can never sound like real life. They get in the way more than they help. He prefers *effective sounds*—noises that might be unrelated to the story line, but trigger the audience's own memories. I work in a somewhat more commercial atmosphere than Dr. Schwartz, with more conventional clients, but I've found his rule to be more valid than Hollywood's "see it, "hear it":

The only important characteristic of a sound effect is how it makes the viewer feel. It doesn't matter where you get it,[2] what the label said, or what frames it's applied to. If an effect feels right, it *is right*. If not, change or lose it.

Choosing sound effects can be a much more casual process than choosing music. Music selection usually involves a separate auditioning session, so you can concentrate on individual cues and select them without the distractions of trying to edit them together. It's almost always more efficient to grab sound effects as you need them. That's because sound effects aren't presented as an abstraction. Until you've placed one against picture, you can't tell if it's going to work. And if you're going to that trouble, you might as well edit it accurately and move on to the next effect.

It may not be possible to do your sound effects spotting, auditioning, and editing at the same time. If you don't already have a sound effects library, you'll have to record sounds specially or get them from an outside source. You'll need to plan the effects, make a list, audition them at a library or over the Web, assemble the source material, and then cut it into the show—exactly the same process you'd follow for music. But believe me, it's a lot better if you start building your own effects library from the very first project. Get a couple of general-purpose CDs for the most common effects. Any time you have to record or buy a specific sound, make a digital dub for the

---

2. Assuming a healthy respect for copyright, of course.

15.1 Keep a database, because your library will grow quickly.

library. Keep a database (Figure 15.1), and you'll be amazed how quickly that library grows. The extra effort will pay off with every new project that needs effects.

Sources for Sound Effects

While audio professionals spend thousands of dollars for immense sound collections on audio CDs or networked hard drives, it's easy to start more modestly. In fact, you already have: the example sound effects on this book's CD can be used in your productions, courtesy of The Hollywood Edge.

You can add about a hundred more effects to your library for free, if you're a potential sound-effects buyer, by requesting Hollywood Edge's sound effects demo. This hybrid CD-ROM/audio disc includes nearly a hundred indexed, well-recorded effects and the right to use them in your productions. (It's smart marketing on their part, because the disc also includes demos of the various libraries they sell—and it's enticed me to buy a few.)

Contact them at www.hollywoodedge.com.[3] If you're not a potential customer entitled to a free disc, or you don't want to wait for them to mail you one, you can download high-quality compressed versions of most of the effects from their Web site.

Where Not to Get Effects

You may find sound effects CDs at a record store, at normal retail prices. These frequently aren't a bargain, both for copyright and technical reasons.

In 1978, U.S. law was changed to allow copyrights on sound effects. Prior to that, you could get a pre-recorded effect almost anywhere and use it with impunity. Today, almost all recordings are protected. Professional libraries come with a license for the buyer to use their sounds in any productions.

But most record store discs are legal for personal listening only. A few don't carry any copyright notice or have wording like "Your imagination is your only limit." These may be safe, but they can still make you sorry. I've heard some retail CDs that were merely copies of pre-1978 vinyl libraries, complete with record scratches and surface noise!

Professional CD Libraries

Most of the prerecorded sound effects used by professionals come from a few specialized publishers like Hollywood Edge. Their sounds are recorded digitally, without echo whenever possible, with a minimum of processing so that you've got the most flexibility to tweak them in your mix. They're then organized onto CDs and grouped into libraries. A specialized foley library might have four or five discs of nothing but footsteps. A category library might have sounds that relate just to the old West (stagecoaches, blacksmith sounds, old guns). A generalized library might include 10–40 discs with enough different sounds to cover most production needs.

Depending on how specialized a library is, how easy the sounds were to record, and how many discs are in a set, professional sound effects CDs will cost between $30–75 each. They include the right to use the sound in any way (except reselling it as a sound effect) and usually include catalog files that can be integrated into a database. Most of the publishers are accessible individually on the Web; a few resellers like Gefen Systems (www.gefen.com) represent all the major publishers and serve as a clearing house for sound effects information. Contact information for other large suppliers appears in the tutorial section of my Web site, www.dplay.com.

CD-ROM Libraries

If you don't need full broadcast rights and the highest quality, you can get compressed or low-sample-rate versions of some professional libraries on CD-ROM. These discs include cross-platform browser and decompression software, along with the right to include the sounds in corpo-

---

3. They assured me there'd be plenty of discs available when I wrote this book. But the usual fine print must apply: the offer can be withdrawn at any time, and neither Hollywood Edge, CMP, or your humble author are responsible if you can't get a copy.

rate presentations and Web sites. The discs sell for about the same prices as standard sound effects CDs, but because they're recorded as compressed files instead of stereo audio tracks, they can include many times more sounds. The more expensive ones may have as many as 2,000 separate tracks, either as 22 kHz 16-bit mono or as data-compressed full-resolution stereo.

Just like with audio sound effects CDs, you have to be careful about the source. Low-cost computer store CD-ROMs may include 8-bit sounds, badly digitized vinyl effects, collections stripped from hobby sites on the Web, or otherwise unusable tracks. The better ones are sold by professional sound effects sources, their labels indicate which large effects library the sounds came from, and they come with a proper license.

SFX on the Internet

If you really want bad sound effects, don't bother with cheap CD-ROMs. You can find almost any sound you can think of, free, somewhere on the Web. Many audio enthusiasts have put up pages of effects they've digitized from VHS movies and TV shows. Sound quality is poor to awful, and using the sounds will almost certainly violate someone's copyright. Still, some of them are fun to listen to—and listening is perfectly legal. These sites pop in and out of existence unpredictably, but your favorite search engine will probably find you a few dozen.

On the other hand, you can also buy professional-quality sound effects over the Internet. Services like Sound Dogs (www.sounddogs.com), a large Hollywood effects company, have put big chunks of their catalog on the Web (Figure 15.2). You can search and audition the sounds in low resolution. When you find one you like, enter a credit card number—cost varies with file size, but most hard effects are under a couple of dollars—and, within a few minutes, the system will e-mail back a password for an ftp site where the sounds are waiting. The scheme is too complicated and time-consuming to replace having your own CDs on hand, but is great when you need a couple of specialized effects during a late-night editing session.

Rolling Your Own

If an effect has to match an on-screen action, the best way to get it may be to record your characters or a production assistant doing the action right after you finish shooting. You'll have the microphone, recorder, and all the necessary props right there. You can also record usable effects in a studio, in your editing suite, and out in the real world. Chapter 10 has specific tips for this kind of recording.

Choosing Effects

So you've got a hundred or a thousand effects in front of you, in a collection of discs or on the screen. Here's how to choose the right ones.

15.2 You can buy high-quality sound effects over the Internet from www.sounddogs.com

- Try to hear them in your head before you look. This is a reality check to make sure the sound can actually exist. (A major ad agency once asked me for the sound of a flashing neon sign, as heard from across a busy street. I resisted the temptation to ask what color.)

- It can also help if you break the sound into easily found components. A *"Cellblock Door"* can be just a jingling key ring and a sliding metal gate, slowed and mixed with a heavy echo.

- Hard sounds (Chapter 5) are caused by physical actions. So if you can't find something in the catalog that's a perfect match, look for something else that moves in the same way. A golf club, arrow, and leather whip make a very similar *wsssh* in the air. An electric car window motor may work perfectly as a robot arm, laser printer, or spaceship door. You can occasionally make outlandish substitutions if the sound you're using isn't immediately identifiable and there's enough of a visual cue to suggest what it should be. When a cable network needed promos for the movie *Mouse Hunt*, I used a rubbed balloon's squeaks against images of the star rodent.

- Don't rely too much on the name; you actually have to listen before deciding. "Police Car" could be an old-fashioned siren or a modern electronic whooper, near or far, with or without an engine; or it could be a high-speed chase, or even a two-way radio. The better libraries use long, detailed descriptions, but details are no substitute for listening.

- Pay attention to the environment around the effect while you listen. A car door has a lot of different slams depending on whether it's outdoors or inside a parking garage, how much of a hurry the slammer is in, and how far away we are from the car. Exterior sounds can often be used for interiors if they're clean and you add echo . . . but it's almost impossible to make an interior sound match an outdoor shot. You can add distance to an exterior sound by using an equalizer to roll off the high midrange (Chapter 16).

- You can loop or repeat relatively short backgrounds to cover longer scenes. Twenty or thirty seconds' worth of original sound is usually sufficient, but see the note about looping backgrounds later in this chapter.

- Foreign cities often provide the best American walla. Look for street scenes or crowds recorded in other languages. Mixed properly, they'll fill out a scene without interfering with principal dialog. And it's a lot harder to tell when they've been looped.

Sound Effects Palettes

Hard effects generally fall into one of three categories: those made by mechanical actions (usually wood or metal, but also such things as rock scrapes); those from organic sources (crowd noises, animals, fantasy monsters); and those from electronic circuits.

It may seem strange, but I've found that montages and mixed effects seem to work best if you stay within the same source category, making exceptions only for accents. It's a lot like an artist staying in a single palette of earth tones or cool pastels.

Placing Sound Effects

The easiest way to simplify sound effects placement is to ignore a lot of it. In Hollywood, almost every action is matched by an effect, down to the tiniest foley. But on the small screen, you can often limit your efforts to just those sounds that advance the plot.

- Place the music before you worry about effects. TV mixes aren't very subtle, and if the music's going to be loud, you might not be able to hear anything else.

- Place ambiences before you worry about hard effects. Often a random movement in a background sound will work perfectly for an on-screen action if you merely move it a few frames.

- Don't worry about the little sounds—clothing rustles or pencil scratches—until you're sure they're necessary. Video sound isn't a subtle medium, and these effects may be needed only during intimate scenes that don't have any other sound.

- Always do effects spotting with the narration and/or dialog tracks up. Television is driven by dialog, and words have to take priority over other sounds. (Of course, it helps to mute other tracks while you're actually placing and trimming the effect.)

- Sometimes it's important to hear an effect, for plot or sound-design reasons, but there's simultaneous dialog. In these cases, be prepared to lower the dialog. If the words are also important, the best solution is often to re-edit the picture so they don't compete.

Planning Effects

It's important to look over the entire sequence while you're getting an idea for effects, so you can respect the dramatic arc of the scene. The effects that are part of the plot—explosions, screams, or even off-screen gasps—are most important and can help viewers forget that other sounds may be missing.

Don't make sound effects compete with each other. There's been a trend in Hollywood action pictures to mix a continuous wall of sound, with everything at maximum volume. This is wearying even in a theater. Video has a more limited range that can't handle two sounds of the same volume and timbre at the same time. A simultaneous gunshot and car crash may sound great on large studio monitors, when you know what you're listening to, but viewers will have a hard time sorting them out. Even some softer combinations, such as a cricket background mixed with a campfire, can turn to mush on many sets because the sounds are so similar.

Unfamiliar sounds work best when we know what they're supposed to be, either because we can see what's making the noise or because a character refers to it. It's best to approach this kind of issue when you're first planning the video. Chapter 5 has some tips.

Give some thought to track layout also, when you're planning effects. Leave some dead space between effects on the same track; if they're butted up against each other, they'll be difficult to keep track of on a timeline and almost impossible to control during the mix. If you keep similar sounds on the same track, you won't have to be constantly changing global echo or equalization settings.

After you've done this a few times, you'll evolve a few standard track layouts. I usually put dialog on the top tracks, hard-effect tracks below them, then background effects, and finally music tracks on the bottom. It makes mixing faster because the same kinds of sound always appear in the same place on my screen and on the same channels of my mixing console. It also makes life simpler when the producer asks for dialog, effect, and music *stems*—separate, synchronized mixes with just one category of sound—for foreign-language release.

Backgrounds

It's a good idea to edit background or ambience tracks first. A lot of times, they'll eliminate the need for more elaborate effects work. Since the mind associates what it hears with what it sees, random sounds in a stock background recording can appear to match specific on-screen actions. I usually find a few clunks and rattles in a background that serve as perfect foley or hard-effect replacements just by sliding them a few frames.

Backgrounds are also easiest to put in, since you can spot their start and end points just by looking at the timeline. Many sound editors extend their backgrounds slightly past the video out-point, so they can be faded during the mix to cover abrupt picture transitions.

Looping

If a background sound isn't long enough to cover a scene, put it in more than once. You might hear a slight break in the sound where two copies are spliced together, but there are ways to disguise where the "loop"[4] joins:

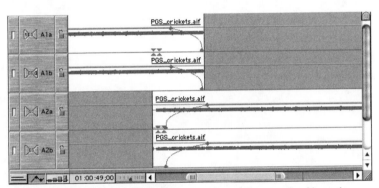

15.3 The same sound repeated on alternating tracks. Note the cross-fade where they overlap.

- Place the splice under a hard effect or loud dialog line.

- Slide the splice to where the camera angle changes.

- Put the repeats on alternate tracks, and let them overlap for a few seconds, with a cross-fade between them (Figure 15.3). This will usually make the splice imperceptible. Track 27 of this book's CD has a cricket background you can try this with.

- Some backgrounds, such as traffic, change pitch or timbre as they develop. Others, such as seawash, have a definite rhythm. In either case, a repeating loop would be obvious because the sound is different at each end of the loop, and cross-fading would mean we hear the different parts simultaneously. Hollywood's trick for that is the *flip loop* or *C-loop*, shown in Figure 15.4. At the top is an original helicopter background. Note how its volume decreases slightly over time. Looping it (Figure 15.4B) makes an obvious jump, because

---

4. The term came from the practice of cutting film background sounds into long loops—often dozens of feet long—that would continuously pass through the player. In this way, the term is related to *looping* for dialog replacement.

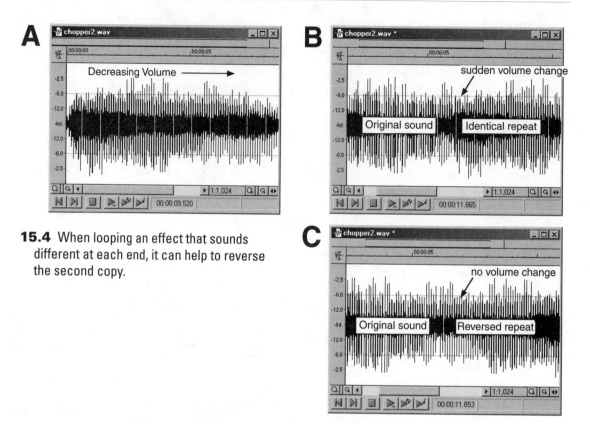

15.4 When looping an effect that sounds different at each end, it can help to reverse the second copy.

we've joined the loud start to the softer ending. To fix this, take the original sound and reverse it[5]—instead of going from loud to soft as the original did, the copy will go from soft to loud. Then copy that after the original (Figure 15.4C). Since there's no change in volume, we're not aware of where the pieces are joined. The new combined version starts and ends at the same level, so it can be looped as a whole. You'd be amazed how many background sounds can be played backwards and still sound right. Try it with the ocean waves on Track 28.

Making backgrounds seem fuller

If a background is going to be mixed with dialog, any midrange sounds in it will compete with the voices. Since most background recordings—and real-world environments—have a lot of midrange in them, you'll have to turn the track down during the mix, or equalize it so it almost disappears.

A good solution is to find two different backgrounds—one predominantly high-pitched, the other low—and use both under a scene. For example, instead of using a single busy street back-

---

5. In some programs, you do this by applying a speed of –100%; in others, apply a "Reverse" effect.

ground, combine rumbling start-and-stop traffic with pedestrian footsteps. The result can sound bigger without interfering with dialog. If you want to add some midrange honking horns, do it during pauses or unimportant words.

Stereo effects can seem much wider if you spread their tracks apart, and get rid of the middle. Delay one side of the stereo signal several seconds, but fade both sides in and out together. This is easily done in an audio workstation; in an NLE, you may have to use two separate stereo pairs, one greatly offset from the other. Use the Take Left command on one pair, so it turns into a mono signal from just the left track; and Take Right on the other. Pan one about 40% to the left, the other 40% to the right, and put matching fades on both. Or try phase-inverting software, included in some audio programs as a "solo eliminator" for eliminating the vocalist in commercial recordings. It removes sounds from the center of a stereo field.

If you've done any stereo trickery, check the result in mono when you're done. Make sure you haven't introduced a hollow sound.

Adding Hard Effects

After the backgrounds are in place, play back the sequence and see what effects still seem to be missing. This might not be too long a list. Television can ignore most foley, which gets lost through a small speaker anyway. Theatrical scenes with music and a background track can often ignore foley as well. You'll probably also find that some hard effects were picked up with dialog and just need to be boosted in the mix. While you're working at this stage, make sure you preview at the full frame rate and with any audio processing you've assigned to the clips turned on.

Usually you can insert a hard effect right on the same frame where you see an action. Jog to the single frame where the action starts, and plant a marker. Then drag the start of the effect to that marker. Some effects can be placed intuitively (it doesn't take much imagination to find the exact frame where a punch lands or a car crashes). You may be surprised how easy it is to place other effects, once you scan at the single-frame level. Guns, for example, almost always have a one-frame barrel flash exactly when they're fired, as in Figure 15.5. Mark the frame, then snap the front of the sound to it.

15.5 Only one frame has a barrel flash. That's where the *bang!* belongs.

Don't worry about compensating for the speed of sound: as soon as something happens, viewers expect to hear it. Who cares if the collapsing building is a few hundred feet away, and the crash would take half a second to reach us? If a sound is big enough, convention dictates that it will travel instantly. That's why when a laser death-cannon destroys a rebel home planet, we hear the explosion immediately . . . even though the planet is a few thousand kilometers away, through the soundless vacuum of space.

Sometimes, the editing rhythm is so fast, you can't find an appropriate frame. Consider the movie promo in Figure 15.6. We see an explosion at 9:03—but it's already started when we cut to it. There's no frame where the sound should start! This also happens frequently in fight scenes, with a cut from one shot with a fist flying, to a reverse angle where the punch has already landed. If this is the case, place the sound a frame or two ahead of its visual (starting the explosion sound around 9:01). The sound can even help smooth the visual discontinuity.

15.6 This fast-cut sequence didn't leave room for the explosion sound, so put it a frame or two ahead of the cut.

If the video is moving very quickly, there may not be enough time for big effects to die out, either. In this sequence, it would be perfectly reasonable for the picture to cut to a hospital a second or so later. That's too short for the sound of an explosion to register. Keep the explosion over the cut while you add a hospital background; then fade it under the first dialog so the background shows through.

As you're placing effects, consider that many should be cued to their middle instead of their front. Figure 15.7 shows a typical explosion. There's a rumble at the

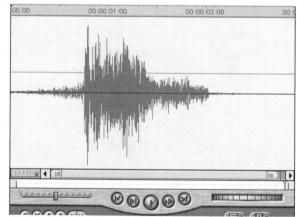

15.7 Things don't start exploding until almost a second in.

start of the sound, before we hear the big crunch. But you'd want the crunch to sync with the first frame of fireball. Plant a marker on the big sound, in this case about 24 frames in. Line the marker up with the visual frame, and let the front of the effect fall where it will. If the scene doesn't have enough time to fit the entire intro before the part you've marked, trim the sound's in-point.

Many sounds are based on multiple actions, and an effect may need some internal editing to fit picture. For example, "closing a door" can consist of a hinge squeal, a latch strike and release, and a rattle against the frame. While you might be able to place the strike and release as one edit, you'll probably have to use the razor tool to separate the squeal onto into a separate clip. Then slide it on a different track to match the door's movement.

A few technical tricks can help as you're working with effects.

- Effects should be digitized at full volume, even if they're from actions that don't make much noise. You can lower their level with a rubber band or other playback-volume control, but don't do anything that lowers the level of the sound file itself. This prevents noise buildup, and prevents problems if you want to add echo or other processes at the mix.

- Don't be afraid to vary the speed. A small increase can add excitement to a sound. A large decrease can make a sound bigger. If you're slowing a sound down in an audio program with a Preserve Pitch option, try it both ways and see which you like better. If you're lowering pitch by more than an octave, try it in multiple programs: a badly-designed algorithm can add aliasing distortion which in this case, helps keep the sound bright.[6]

- Try the slowing-down trick on an impact like a car crash or explosion, and then mix it with the original to make the sound much bigger. Add a fade to the end of the slower copy, so they both end at the same time. There's a crash on Track 29 of this book's CD for you to try this with, followed by the same effect with this process added.

- You can add a *feeling* of speed to steady sounds like auto engines by applying a flanging effect (Chapter 16). If you don't have a flange processor in your software, put the sound on two tracks, delay one track a few frames, speed the delayed one up so it ends in sync with the other, and mix both tracks together.

- Use pitch shift on just one channel of a stereo effect to make it bigger. You'll usually want less than a 3% change, but the right amount depends on the sound. Try different settings and check the result on mono speakers as well as in stereo.

- Make hard effects, such as explosions or door slams, wider in stereo by changing the pitch or speed of just one channel a few percent. If you're mixing for broadcast or home video, compatibility is important, so check the result in mono before committing. Try this on the splash effect, Track 30 of the CD.

---

6. I often use the ancient SoundEdit 16—its last full update was in the early 1990s—for slowdowns, just to get this aliasing.

Processing

Few audio tools are as useful or abused as effects processors. A professional studio will have thousands of dollars invested in these units. They use them to change the tonal balance of a sound, change its dynamics, manipulate its apparent environment, or even change the sound into something totally different. In every case, the real goal is improving communication by making the track easier to understand or a dramatic premise easier to accept.

But for these processors to do any good at all, you have to know what's going on inside them. You can't just grab a knob and twist until it sounds good . . . that's as likely to harm one aspect of the track as improve another. Learning how to use processors properly isn't difficult. All it takes is a little knowledge of how sound works, some imagination, and the next few pages.

The previous chapter was about sound effects—recordings you add to a track to heighten its realism. This one is about effects processors like equalizers and compressors. In a busy studio both the recordings and the processors are referred to simply as *effects*. Which kind you mean should be obvious from the context.[1]

---

1. Many NLEs refer to all of their audio effects as *filters*. In the audio world, a filter is a specific kind of equalizer.

How Any Effect Can Wreck a Sound

A couple of warnings before we begin. These apply to every kind of processor, from hardware-based analog units to NLE plugins, but are particularly important in the desktop environment.

Watch Out for Overloads

Somewhere, inside virtually any effects processor, the signal level has to get boosted. If you boost things too high, the system will distort—adding fuzziness to an analog signal, or crackling to a digital one. The amount of boost is often controlled by something other than a volume knob, and the distortion might not show up until the loudest part of a track, so it can be easy to cause serious damage without noticing. Pay attention to OVERLOAD or CLIP indicators on the front panel or control screen, and listen for distortion or crackling on loud signals while you're previewing an effect. If you see or hear a problem, turn down the input volume control until the distortion goes away. Then adjust the output volume control until the output meter reads correctly.

If you're working in audio software with a plugin that lets you hear only a limited-length preview, select the loudest part of the track while you're making these adjustments. Save the settings, select the entire section you want to process, go back to the plugin and process with the settings you've saved. Then review the section to listen for problems while you can still Undo.

In most NLEs, you can't easily select just the loud part of a clip. Fortunately, most NLEs apply effects *non-destructively* on the timeline: the original file isn't changed, but a new one is rendered with the effect. If you're working in a system like this, don't worry about reviewing for distortion until you're ready to mix the final track. Effects that don't sound good can be removed or changed any time before you render the final output.

Watch Out for Sounds that are Too Soft

If you're working in an NLE, your system probably has only 16-bit resolution. This isn't a problem when you're editing, but can affect sound quality as you add effects and cross-fades. These processes use a lot of math, multiplying and dividing parts of the signal by various factors. Each calculation requires additional bits to reflect the softest or loudest sounds accurately.

If a system doesn't have enough bits for the loudest sounds, you get the distortion described above and can turn down the volume. But if it doesn't have enough bits for the softest ones, it will add subtle noises that aren't apparent until you play the final mix on a good speaker. Each additional processing step makes things worse.

Professionals use 24- or 32-bit effects to guard against this. The best you can do in a 16-bit NLE is make sure you've digitized or recorded at a good level (Chapter 12), and avoid doing anything that'll permanently reduce a sound's volume until the final mix stage.

Use Good Monitors

You can't adjust a processor unless you can hear what it's doing accurately. You need good monitors (see Chapter 11 for some tips on choosing them). If you don't have good speakers at your editing setup, save processing decisions until you're ready to mix. If you don't have good speakers at all, get some.

The small monitors bundled with many NLEs may be adequate for adjusting compression and reverb, if you listen carefully and there aren't other computer noises interfering, but they can lead you to make major mistakes when using an equalizer. A set of very good headphones can be useful for adjusting an equalizer or noise-reduction software, but won't give you an accurate picture of how viewers will hear compression or reverb.

Take Advantage of Presets

Most third-party NLE plugins, and many of the effects built into audio-only programs, come with a library of prebuilt settings. These often have names like "vocal enhance" or "small room reverb." They're written by people who know the software and what each of its controls can do. Load them, listen to what they do to your tracks, and see what happens to the sound as you change each knob.

Once you learn how to use an effect, think of the factory presets as a starting place. Load them, tweak the controls until they work best with your elements, and then save the result as your own new preset. Also, save the settings you come up with for one-time situations like correcting a particularly noisy location. If you ever have to go back to the original tape, you'll have no trouble matching the sound quality.

> There are a lot more musicians buying effects than videographers, so most of the presets are designed for that kind of production.[2] They're not much use in video production, but you can learn from how they've been put together.

The effects built into most NLEs don't have presets, or even any way to store your settings. Until you get very familiar with processing, keep a notebook and write down how you've adjusted the effects for each clip. Or, if your software allows this, use the Copy Filters function to save settings to a dummy clip—any short soundfile—with a name that'll help you remember the effect. Keep these clips in a separate bin labeled *effects presets*, and copy their filters to new clips as you need them. Either method will help you keep a consistent sound throughout your projects, and make it easier to match the processing if you have to re-edit.

---

2. Frequency ranges are much wider in music, but they don't care about the midrange as much as we do. Reverbs are often too big to simulate normal interior spaces.

Be Wary of Commitment

Standalone software and most of the effects in audio programs can be *destructive*; they change the file, and the original unprocessed sound is lost. Before you apply a destructive effect, make sure there's a clean copy elsewhere on your hard drive or a backup disc. It will be invaluable if you have to re-edit, if you have to use the elements in some other project, or when you discover that you had one of the many effects settings in the wrong position.

Most of the effects in NLEs are non-destructive. The original clip isn't affected, and processing is applied in realtime when you preview. You can change settings or try different combinations of effects as you develop the project.

Processing Can Take Time

The downside of non-destructive processing in NLEs is that a lot of simultaneous effects can load down the CPU. This can cause problems with playback during previews, either as stuttering sound or warning beeps. Most NLEs let you render a temporary audio preview file with all the effects in place; some won't let you preview without making one automatically. Rendered files are handy if you're going to be previewing a sequence many times, or need to be sure of how multiple effects will work together. But the files get discarded as soon as you make an edit in the section, and have to be re-rendered before the next preview. If you're going to be doing a lot of cutting and don't have a very fast computer, look for an Ignore Audio Filters checkbox in the project's Render or Preview settings. Or don't apply any effects until the sequence is edited.

Final Cut Pro lets you preset different rendering qualities for quick previews or high-quality client review. Apple assumes you've got a fast Mac, and its factory default includes audio filters with every rendering quality. But if you're stacking lots of filters on multiple audio tracks, this can slow down your picture editing. Edit the lowest-quality rendering mode to turn the Include Filters checkbox off. (This affects video filters as well as audio ones.)

Each Effect Affects the Next

If you're applying multiple effects to a track, the order in which you use them can make a major difference. We'll discuss how to take advantage of this at the end of this chapter.

Equalizers

These ubiquitous audio processors were invented to boost the highs that got lost over long telephone lines, and their name comes from the fact that they made a line equally efficient at all frequencies. Some brilliant sound engineer brought them into an early film mixing suite to equalize the sound from multiple microphones. They're now considered an essential part of any audio production facility.

What an equalizer does is the same whether it's a multiknob wonder in a recording studio, a couple of on-screen sliders in your NLE, or the tone controls on your car radio: it emphasizes or suppresses parts of the audio spectrum, picking out the elements of the signal that will be most useful, and changing the harmonic structure of a sound. The only difference between individual equalizers—other than the noise or distortion a specific model introduces—is how precisely they let you specify the frequency and how it will be boosted or lowered. Precision is important because sounds you want to keep can be close to ones you want to lose. But precision requires complexity, and a good equalizer is a lot more than a simple bass and treble control.

You can use the equalizer to do the following:

- Increase intelligibility of a voice track.

- Make music more exciting under a montage.

- Tailor both the voice and the music so you can make both of them seem louder in the mix.

- Change the character of background sounds and some hard effects.

- Fix some types of distortion, and correct for boominess or some on-set noises.

- Improve intelligibility on badly-miked sequences. This doesn't make the audio actually sound better, but may make it easier to understand.

- Simulate telephones, intercoms, and awful multimedia speakers.

But equalizers have their limits:

- They can't pick out one voice from a crowd.

- They can't eliminate complex noises like air conditioner motors, or harmonically-rich ones like power-line buzzing.[3]

- They can't generate parts of the band that were never recorded. If you turn up the treble on a track that has no highs because of a low sample rate, all you'll do is boost noise.

- They can't turn lightweight voices into deep-voiced giants.

- They can't compensate for bad monitors in your NLE setup, or bad speakers in a viewer's set.

---

3. But a comb filter, which is actually a delay technique rather than an equalizer, can be very effective for this. Details later in the chapter.

Equalizer Types

There are dozens of different equalizer types in equipment catalogs and software specs, but they're really just combinations of three basic functions.

Peaking equalizer

Peaking equalizers affect the volume of the sound around a particular frequency. They'll always have a level control, most of them have frequency controls, and a few also let you adjust the bandwidth (or Q). The Q determines how sharply the equalizer chooses its frequencies. A very high Q can emphasize a single note while not affecting notes next to it, and you can definitely hear the equalization effect. A low Q lets you control an octave or more at once, and the effect can be subtle enough to sound like a characteristic of the original sound. Figures 16.1 and 16.2 show the response curve of a typical peaking equalizer. (All the equalizer curves in this chapter were lifted from screenshots of Waves' Renaissance plug-ins. You can see what the program's full screen looks like in Figure 16.8.)

As the Q gets higher and the equalizer gets more selective, it will add a small amount of distortion to frequencies just outside its range. This is a fact of equalizer life and has nothing to do with the particular brand or design. A very high-Q boost can be so sharp it resonates, ringing like a bell when its exact frequency is sounded. A similarly high Q, set to cut instead of boost, can pick out some kinds of noises and eliminate them completely from a dialog track. This is most effective if the noise doesn't have many harmonics or starts at a very high frequency. A peaking equalizer, set for a low Q and moderate cut, can help dialog recordings that have too much boominess because of room reverb. A moderate Q and boost around the 5 kHz range can increase the perceived brightness of a track without increasing the noise.

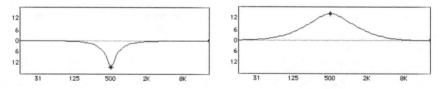

16.1 Equalizers set for 12 dB loss *(left)* and boost *(right)* at 500 Hz, with a low Q

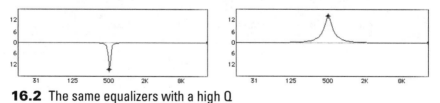

16.2 The same equalizers with a high Q

How to tune an equalizer to correct problems   If you want to use a high Q and large cut to eliminate a pitched noise, or a lower Q and moderate cut to remove boominess, it's important to find the precise frequency. Not even a trained engineer can listen to a track and immediately dial up the right one. But there's a trick professionals use:

1. Set the equalizer for maximum Q and maximum *boost*, even though you're intending to eventually cut.

2. Start the track playing, and sweep the frequency control slowly around the area where you think the problem might exist. For room boominess, try 100–300 Hz. For whistles, try 1–3 kHz.

3. At one point while you're sweeping, you'll hear the noise or room resonance jump out at you. It may even burst into crackling distortion. Move the control up and down very slowly around there to find the exact frequency.

4. Now, adjust for the amount of cut you'll want. If you're removing a single whistle or other tone, leave the Q high. If you're trying to compensate for room acoustics, lower the Q until things sound good.

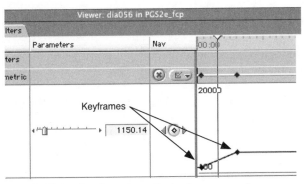

16.3 Using keyframes to find a frequency for equalization. These settings will sweep from around 500 Hz to 2 kHz over about ten seconds.

Some NLEs don't let you listen to an equalizer while you're adjusting its frequency. But you can use a workaround. Set keyframes on the frequency adjustment, so it will sweep the range you're interested in while the clip plays (Figure 16.3). Preview the effect. When you hear the sound jump out, stop and note the exact frequency; this may require jogging back or forth a few frames to find where the sound is the loudest. Remove the keyframes, and set the equalizer to that frequency.

Graphic equalizer

A graphic equalizer is really just a bunch of peaking equalizers with fixed frequencies and overlapping bandwidths (Figure 16.4 shows one from Bias' Deck, a multitrack music program). Graphics are the easiest kind of equalizer to use, since the knobs draw a graph of the volume at different frequencies. But they're also the least useful because factory-set frequencies on a graphic are seldom the best ones for a specific use, and the Q is determined by the number of bands and can't be adjusted.

Graphic equalizers are often set to a "smiley" curve by beginners (and boombox owners), boosting the extreme highs and lows as much as 12 dB while not affecting the mids. It does make some kinds of music listening more exciting, but is almost never a good idea in video production. Dialog lives in the midrange, and equalizing a mixed track with a smiley will make it hard to understand. Applying the smiley just to music tracks isn't much better: the extreme boosts can add noise and distortion, and the extra level can cause TV station processors to make the entire track softer when the project is broadcast.

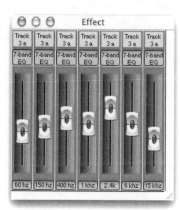

16.4 A graphic equalizer is just a bunch of peaking equalizers with fixed frequencies and Qs.

Shelving equalizer

Shelving equalizers (Figure 16.5) apply a controllable amount of boost or cut to sounds above or below the specified frequency. They always have a level

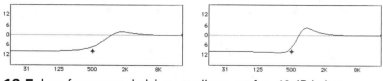

16.5 Low-frequency shelving equalizers set for −10 dB below 500 Hz, with low Q *(left)* and high Q *(right)*

control and may have frequency and Q controls. The bass and treble controls on your stereo are fixed-frequency shelving equalizers. Shelving equalizers are most useful when you want to apply a broad, gentle correction; but too much of a shelf can run the risk of boosting noises at the extremes of the spectrum.

Filters

Cutoff filters, also known as high- or low-pass filters (Figure 16.6) are extreme shelving equalizers, throwing away any sound above (when they're low-pass) or below (highpass) the cutoff frequency. Their design lets them have much sharper slopes than shelving equalizers, with-

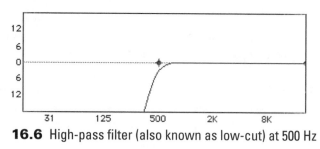

16.6 High-pass filter (also known as low-cut) at 500 Hz

out the disadvantages of a high Q. In fact, cutoff filters don't have level or Q controls;[4] they can be used only to reject sounds beyond a desired frequency. They're useful for noise control or removing parts of a sound that can interfere in the mix. Low-pass filters above 8 kHz or so can be helpful for removing distortion from acoustic instrument recordings.

The cutoff filters in most NLEs are fairly gentle, reducing 6 dB per octave (as opposed to the 18 dB/octave filters I used to make Track 2 of the CD). If you're using one to reject a sound, this gentle slope can affect desired sounds as well. You can increase the slope by using multiple passes through the filter; each additional pass adds 6 dB/octave. If you're using an audio program, apply the process multiple times (but keep a backup of the original audio in case you go too far). If you're using an NLE, assign multiple filters at the same frequency to the clip. Figure 16.7 shows how this can look with three high-pass followed by a low-pass. The frequencies shown will simulate a telephone conversation. Be aware that multiple filters can stress a program's real-time capacity. You might not be able to hear the effect until you render a preview.

Parametric equalizer

A parametric equalizer gives you complete control, usually with three or more peaking sections, and individual controls for frequency, level, and Q. A software-based parametric like Waves' Renaissance (shown in its entirety in Figure 16.8) lets you change the function of each section, so you can have cutoffs, shelving, and peaking at the same time.

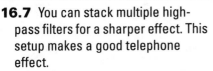

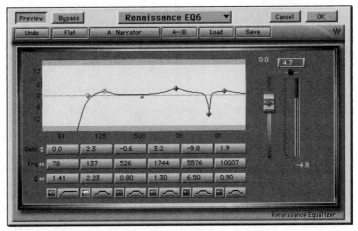

16.8 A parametric equalizer set for one cut and five shelving sections

16.7 You can stack multiple high-pass filters for a sharper effect. This setup makes a good telephone effect.

---

4. Final Cut Pro's cutoff filters have a Q control. Leave it at 1 or below for filtering; anything higher can cause boxy or peaky resonances.

Learning the Bands

The best tool for learning how to equalize is the equalizer itself. Grab a short voice clip, such as Track 30 on the book's CD, and set it to play continuously. Start with all of the level controls in their neutral position (usually marked 0 dB) and the Q around 7. Pick a section, raise its level about 6 dB, and listen to the audio while you sweep the frequency control very slowly. The changes will be subtle as you move from one frequency to the next, but try to give a name to what you hear: *boomy, powerful, harsh, bright*—whatever comes to mind. Then turn the section's level as far down as it'll go, and sweep through its frequencies again. Lowering a few frequencies can make some signals sound better. Then try the whole thing again with some music (Tracks 24–26 on the CD). You'll hear different effects depending on the type of material.

Ears get used to equalization very quickly, so keep going back to the unequalized sound as a reference, and don't spend more than 10 or 15 minutes at a time on this exercise. Do this a few times, and you'll start to learn exactly where to set those equalizer knobs for the sound you want.

Overequalization

Once you learn how to hear subtle differences, you can avoid the most common equalizer mistake: setting the knobs too high. Equalizers are volume controls, and too much volume causes problems—particularly in digital systems. Check volumes along the entire equalized track. A 12 dB boost at 5 kHz may help the strings at the start of a piece of music, but it'll cause an awful clatter when the cymbal comes in. (Far better to use a 6 dB boost around 10 kHz.)

As a general rule, don't raise any control higher than 6 dB—one bit, in digital terms—and remember that overlapping bands have their levels added together. Save the more radical settings for special effects, or to rescue badly recorded tracks.

You usually shouldn't turn all the knobs in the same direction. If everything's boosted, the signal won't sound better—just more distorted.

The logical extension of these two rules is to remember that equalizers can be turned down as well as up. If a voice is getting lost under the music track, don't look for a way to boost it. Instead, dip the music around 1.5–2 kHz. The overall mix will be cleaner and more natural sounding.

Unless you're fixing specific noises at the extremes of the band, most equalization will take place in the 200 Hz–10 kHz range. If you set the frequency much higher than that, you're likely to be adding noise.

Equalizer Tips

If you're in a hurry, these ideas can help you get started, but don't treat the settings as gospel. Every track is slightly different, and every equalizer contributes its own sound.

- Strengthen an announcer. Cut off everything below 90 Hz—those frequencies are just wasting power. Then try a gentle peak (3 dB, Q = 7) around 240 Hz for warmth, and a similar boost around 1.8 kHz for intelligibility. A sharp dip (–18 dB, Q = 100) around 5 kHz can help sibilance.

- Help muddy dialog with a cutoff below 150 Hz, and a 3–6 dB boost (Q = 7) around 2 kHz.

- If there's no voice, you can make the music sound more exciting: boost the bass notes (6 dB, Q = 3) around 100 Hz, and add a 6 dB high-frequency shelf around 3 kHz.

- Simulate a telephone conversation with the setup in Figure 16.7.

- Tune out hum or whistles with multiple sections of a parametric. Turn on just the lowest frequency section, and tune it using the technique explained in "Peaking equalizer" on page 366. Then turn on the next higher section and tune it the same way, starting around twice the frequency you found for the first. Continue, doubling frequencies, until the sound is fixed or you run out of sections.

- Reduce distortion. If a natural sound doesn't have many harmonics (Chapter 2), you can often clean up bad recordings by applying a sharp high-frequency cutoff filter. This not only eliminates hiss; it also reduces the artificial harmonics that a bad analog recording can generate. Start with the equalizer as low at 5 kHz, and then slowly raise its cutoff frequency until the recording doesn't seem muddy.

Compressors

In the real world, the difference between loud and soft adds excitement to what we hear. But in the electronic world of a video track, loud causes distortion and soft gets lost in electronic noise. Used properly, a compressor can control those pesky level changes—and make a track sound louder—without affecting its dynamic feel. But used the wrong way, a compressor can turn tracks into bland, unlistenable mush.

It's easy to misuse these things. That's because the best compressors have a daunting array of knobs with relatively nonintuitive names. You need this much control to properly shape your sound: every element in a track has its own dynamic footprint and should be handled differently. But once you understand exactly how a compressor does its magic, you'll reach for the right knob every time.

What Happens Inside a Compressor

You can understand how a compressor works by using a little visual math; but don't worry, there's no calculating involved. The graphs starting with Figure 16.9 are a map of how volumes can be affected by a circuit. Incoming sound (the vertical axis) travels to the black diagonal line (the RATIO knob on a compressor) and is reflected down to the output. So in Figure 16.9, a loud sound at the input (dotted line a) crosses the ratio line and becomes a loud sound at the output. A soft sound (dotted line c) stays soft when it comes out. This trivial graph isn't a compressor at all. The slope of the diagonal line is one unit up for each unit sideways, or a ratio of 1:1.

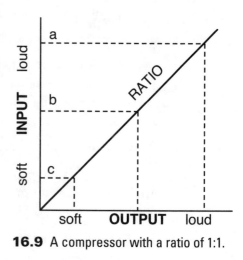

16.9 A compressor with a ratio of 1:1.

But in Figure 16.10, we've turned the RATIO knob to 3:1, tilting the diagonal three units up for each unit sideways. A loud incoming sound crosses the diagonal sooner and is reflected down to be only medium-loud at the output. The softer input of the bottom dotted line is reflected later and becomes louder at the output. What was a large volume range going in becomes a small one coming out. Ratios can get as high as 100:1 when a compressor is being used to control peak levels.

The compressor in Figure 16.10 also boosts things that *should* stay soft, like room noise or camera hiss, so we fix the problem by putting a little kink in the ratio line. Figure 16.11 shows how it works. Below

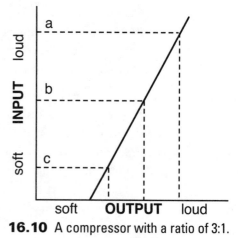

16.10 A compressor with a ratio of 3:1.

the bend, the ratio is still 1:1 . . . and soft sounds aren't affected. The location of this bend is usually set by a THRESHOLD control, and its abruptness may be adjusted by a KNEE control. Some compressors have a fixed threshold and let you adjust the overall INPUT level around it. The effect is the same.

You'll notice that the outputs of Figures 16.10 and 16.11 don't get very loud. They've been lowered by the action of the ratio slope, so we compensate with an OUTPUT or MAKEUP GAIN control (Figure 16.12), which preserves compression while making the entire signal louder.

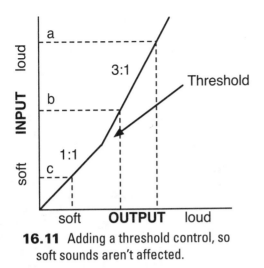

16.11 Adding a threshold control, so soft sounds aren't affected.

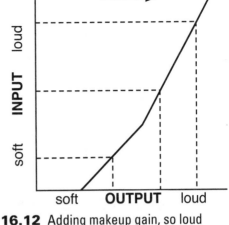

16.12 Adding makeup gain, so loud sounds stay loud.

You might also have a GATE adjustment to control noise. Signals softer than its setting are totally cut off. You can see this in Figure 16.13, where a very soft signal doesn't make it to the output at all. A *noise gate* is a processor with this function only, and no gain reduction circuit. It works like a fast on-off switch, totally silencing a signal when it falls below the THRESHOLD but leaving it unaffected when it gets louder. This total silence can sound unnatural, so noise gates often have BYPASS or THROUGH controls to let a little signal through when they're in the off condition.

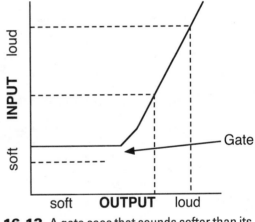

16.13 A gate sees that sounds softer than its threshold never reach the output at all.

Some compressors have a "gated compression" feature, which isn't the same as a noise gate. In a real compressor circuit, the slope of our drawings is replaced by an amplifier with continuously-variable gain. Gated compression freezes the gain of that amplifier whenever the input drops below a preset level, so soft sounds can pass through it without being boosted unnaturally.

Using the Compressor

- The best way to adjust a compressor is by ear, with a sample of the actual program material. If you can, keep looping the same 5- or 10-second section so you can be sure you're hearing differences in the compression rather than changes in the source. Adjust only one knob at a time, until you're sure of its effect.

- Good compressors also have a GAIN REDUCTION meter to tell you how much the signal is being lowered. Keep an eye on it. The meter should be bouncing in time with the input. If the meter stays at a fixed value, the threshold or time constants (see below) are set wrong, or you're overloading the input. In either case, the compressor isn't doing much to the signal other than providing distortion.

- If you set a high THRESHOLD (or low INPUT), high RATIO, and sharp or hard KNEE, the compressor will just regulate extreme peaks to avoid overloads. This setting preserves most of the dynamic range, and is often used during original recording. There's an example on Track 32 of this book's CD. Listen carefully because the effect is subtle.

- On the other hand, a lower THRESHOLD and RATIO squeezes the volumes together, making a narration stronger or music easier to mix. Since this affects the overall feel of a track, it's best left for postproduction. Hear it on Track 33.

- High ratios tend to emphasize any distortion in the sound. Even the distortion of an extra analog-to-digital conversion can become audible in a heavily compressed track.

- Don't obsess about MAKEUP GAIN while you're adjusting other knobs. After you've got things set the way you want, fine-tune the makeup to get a good level on the compressor's output.

Compression in the Fourth Dimension

Those graphs can't illustrate one important aspect of compression: time. Remember *envelopes* from Chapter 2? A compressor has to be set so it responds to the volume of a sound (black wavy line in Figure 16.14), but not be so fast that it reacts to individual waves. This requires two additional controls: ATTACK determines how long it takes to pull the volume down when the input crosses the threshold; DECAY sets how long it takes to recover normal volumes after the input goes down. If there's a gate, it might have its own time controls.

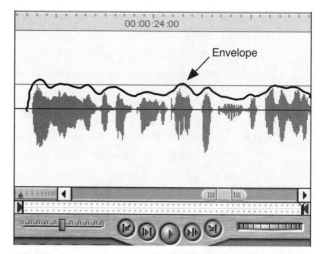

16.14 A compressor's time controls let it pay attention to the envelope but not individual waves.

- A fast ATTACK will protect you from momentary distortion or digital overloads, particularly with percussive sounds or sharp consonants. But too fast an attack can destroy the impact of these sounds.

- A fast DECAY can extend echoes and other sustained sounds by making them louder as they're fading out. (A guitarist's sustain pedal is really a compressor with a fast decay.) You can often increase the effect of reverberation in a recording by compressing it and changing the decay time.

- If both settings are too fast, low-pitched sounds will distort as the compressor tries to smooth out waves instead of the envelope. The fundamental wavelength of a male narrator's voice—around 10 milliseconds—is within the range of most compressors.

- A slow ATTACK lets the initial hit of a musical instrument show through in a mix, while keeping the overall track under control. Too slow an attack on a voice track can result in a spitty sound because vowel sounds will be lowered more than initial consonants.

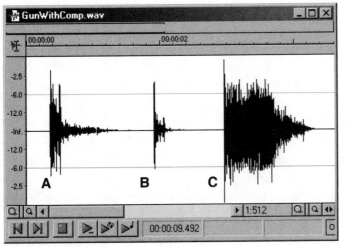

16.15 Changing the attack and decay controls can completely change a sound.

Figure 16.15 shows how these time settings can change a sound effect. The first envelope (A) is a 0.357 Magnum shot at medium range, with no compression. B is the same shot with a slow attack and decay; only the initial sound gets through, so the result is more of a pile-driver clank than a bang. C has a very fast attack and decay; the hit is suppressed and the reverb emphasized, making it sound more like a big explosion. Track 34 of the CD lets you hear all three versions.

Sidechains

Compressors adjust their timing by applying filters to a control voltage, which is basically just a DC version of the input signal. By connecting other circuits to this voltage—called a sidechain—they can add some useful functions:

- The left and right sidechains of a stereo compressor can be linked together, so both channels are controlled identically and the stereo image is preserved. Or they can be unlinked to make the whole image swing away from any loud off-center sounds.

- The sidechain can be filtered to make the compressor react more to specific frequencies. Tuning it for sibilance turns a compressor into a de-esser.

- The sidechain can be patched to a different signal entirely. Put a compressor on a music track but give it the narration for a sidechain, and the music will automatically fade down whenever the narrator talks.

- You can even make a compressor predict the future, by putting a delay in the main signal path but none in the sidechain. A gunshot, for example, will cause the overall track to fade down before the gun is fired . . . so the impact is preserved, without any overload.

Sidechain inputs are often found in hardware compressors, but are almost impossible to implement in an NLE because they require extra signal paths. Some high-end software compressors include separate equalizers in the sidechain; a few multitrack audio programs allow assignable sidechains.

Multiband Compression

A compressor reacts to volume changes across the entire bandwidth of the signal; a loud sound at any frequency, low or high, will make it turn down the volume. This works fine for many applications. But imagine a mixed track with a narrator speaking over music that has a strong bass drum beat. Each time the drum is hit, a compressor would turn the entire track down and the narrator would get momentarily softer. The solution is to break the audio signal into multiple bands by using cutoff and bandpass filters. Each band is processed through its own compressor, usually with different timings to be most effective while avoiding distortion, and then the multiple outputs are mixed together. In our imaginary mix, the bass drum would only trigger the low-frequency compressor, and the announcer's voice—primarily midrange—wouldn't be affected.

Radio stations pioneered the use of extreme equalization and multiband compression to make their music appear louder than the competition's. The extreme highs and lows are boosted and then compressed separately so they blast through on good receivers, while the midrange has its own compression to stay as loud as possible on smaller radios. Five separate bands are typically used.

Following the same principle, hardware-based combination equalizers and multiband compressors are sold as final "loudness" generators in music production. A few audio companies make them available in software as well. You may find these units effective in video mixes,[5] if you watch out for two things:

- Every other part of your signal chain has to be absolutely clean. The extreme processing emphasizes noise and distortion that would be normally hidden by midrange signals.

---

5. I use one on just about everything: a hardware-based TC Electronics FinalizerPlus.

- You must build your own presets. The factory-set frequency bands and compression characteristics are designed for rock music, not for soundtracks where the midrange is most important.

Multiband compression can destroy many of the masking cues used by data reduction algorithms like MP3 and AAC (Chapter 3). If you're going to be combining these techniques, plan to spend a lot of time fine-tuning how they interact.

Reverberation

Real rooms have walls that bounce sound back to us. Recording studios don't, because the walls have been treated to reduce reflections. Lavaliere mics—even in real rooms—tend to ignore reflections from the walls because they're so much closer to the speakers' mouths. In both cases, the reverb-free sound can seem artificial.

This may be a good thing, if a spokesperson is talking directly to camera or a narrator lives in the nonspace of a voice-over. But reverb is essential if you want dramatic dialog to seem like it's taking place in a real room. It can be the real reverb of the room, picked up by a boom mic along with the voices. Or it can be artificially generated, to make lavs and studio ADR sessions feel like they're taking place in the same room we see on the screen.

Today's digital reverberators use memory to delay part of the sound and send it back a fraction of a second later. There may be dozens of delays, each representing a different reflecting surface in an imaginary room. Since real surfaces reflect highs and lows differently—a thin windowpane may reflect highs and absorb lows, while a bookshelf does the opposite—equalizers are included for the delays. To adjust the sound of a reverb, you have to control these delays and equalizers.

Real Reflections

The speed of sound might be impressive for an airplane, but in terms of human perception—or even of video frames—it's pretty slow stuff. Sound travels about 1,100 feet per second, depending on air temperature.[6] That means it takes about 1/30th of a video frame to move one foot. It can take a couple of frames for a drumbeat to reach the back of a large concert hall by the most direct path. When you sit in that hall you also hear the drum over other paths, each taking a different length of time—that's reverb.

Figure 16.16 shows how it works. Imagine a concert hall roughly 45 feet wide by 70 feet deep. You're about 20 feet from the drum. There's no way you can hear that drum sooner than 20 milliseconds after it's played—two-thirds of a frame—because it takes that long for the first sound to reach you. I drew that direct 20-foot path as a heavy black line between the drum and you.

---

6. There was an exhaustive discussion of this in Chapter 2.

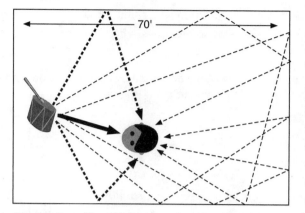

16.16 Reverb paths in a concert hall. It's the longer (dotted) paths that give the room its rich sound.

But sound also bounces off the side walls and then to your ears. I've drawn two of those possible paths as heavy dashed lines. The lower one is about 40 feet long, and the upper one is almost 60 feet. You hear a second drumbeat at 40 ms, and a third at 60 ms. If these were the only paths, you'd hear a drum and two distinct echoes—it could sound like a giant stadium. A well-designed concert hall has plenty of other relatively direct paths, so these early echoes are mixed with others and you hear a richer sound instead.

Sound fills the room. Reflections bounce off the back wall, off the side to the back and to the ceiling, from one side to another, and so on. All of these paths—the dashed thinner lines—eventually reach your ears, but you hear so many of them that they merge into a barrage of late reflections. The longer the path, the softer the sound gets; in a well-designed hall, it can take many seconds to die out.

Of course, there are other factors. A concert hall, a gymnasium, and a hotel lobby can all have the same size and shape but sound completely different. That's because multiple surfaces determine how far apart the reflections are when they reach you. Also, their shape and the material of each surface affects the tone of the reverb: Hard surfaces reflect more highs. Complex shapes disperse the highs and reflect more lows.

A good reverb device lets you simulate all these factors. You can adjust

- The timing and number of early reflections (up to about 1/10th of a second)

- The density of late reflections and how quickly they build

- The relative bass and treble of late reflections

- How long it takes late reflections to die out

- The relative levels of initial sound and early and late reflections

By controlling those factors, you can simulate just about any acoustic space. Figure 16.17 shows some of the controls in one good software reverb, Waves' TrueVerb plug-in. You can see individual early reflections over the first 50 ms, and then a fairly fast decay of late reflections in this relatively small but rich-sounding room. (A separate panel lets you equalize the late reflections and control the overall mix.)

16.17 Waves' TrueVerb includes a graph of the reflections it generates.

Evaluating Reverbs

Accurately simulating every one of the thousands of different surfaces in a real room requires too much processing to be practical. Fortunately, it isn't necessary; we could never distinguish all those echoes in any case. Instead, reverb designers rely on how we hear and give us just enough reflections to think that a space is real. This is as much art as science and is limited by how much processing power is available, which is why different reverb hardware or effects plugins will have totally different sounds. A basic echo—the kind you might find thrown in with a low-end video program—will sound very different than a well-written plugin on the same computer. And modern studio reverbs use dedicated DSP chips for the best simulations.

You can judge the quality of a reverb by playing a sharp, nonpitched sound with an abrupt ending—like the burst of white noise on Track 35 of the CD—through the reverb. You shouldn't be able to hear individual early reflections, and there shouldn't be any flutter or vibration in the initial sound. There shouldn't be any particular pitch to the late reflections. The tail of the echo should die out smoothly, rather than suddenly stopping. Even if a reverb device has excellent characteristics, it might not be right for video production. Most are designed for music, with long echoes that simulate a concert hall rather than the very short echoes of a smaller room where dialog takes place.

Practical Reverb

The first place to control reverb is at the original recording, using the tips in Chapter 7. Unless you have a skilled boom operator on your crew, it makes sense to avoid original reverb all together. Most shooting areas are more echoey than the space implied by the lens. If you record a tight track with a lav, you can add visually appropriate reverb at the mix. This also makes it easier to match the reverb on foley elements.

To adjust a reverb for normal dialog situations, turn its MIX control to about 75% reverb. If you have a choice of algorithms, choose SMALL ROOM. Then start PREVIEWING. Adjust the REVERB TIME for something fairly short that doesn't interfere with intelligibility. Set DIFFUSION fairly high for most rooms, but a large totally empty room—say, a new house with no furniture—will have lower diffusion. Set the EQUALIZER or BRIGHTNESS toward the middle, with more highs in a room with plaster walls and fewer in a room with lots of curtains or wooden walls. Then lower the MIX until it seems right for the room and matches a boom sound; usually this will be around 20% reverb.

I believe reverb doesn't belong in voice-overs. Reverb implies a room around the voice, and a voice-over exists in limbo where it can talk intimately to us or reflect a character's inner thoughts. Unless you've visually established a place for the voice-over to be coming from, keep it as clean as possible.

Be careful using reverb in a clip-based editing program, which includes all NLEs. If the reverb is applied as a "filter," it can last only as long as the edited clip. Add some silence at the end of the clip so late reflections have time to die out. This may require exporting a new audio element that includes the silence, and then replacing the clip with the new version. Also, consider that reverbs exist in three-dimensional space. If your project is stereo, make sure the reverb—even on mono dialog clips—has a stereo path to the final mix. This may mean putting the same clip on two tracks at once.

REVERB and ECHO are different things. REVERB (at least in a good program) is a complex simulation of all the reflections in a real space, with various timings. ECHO is a single or multiple repeat of a sound, with a fixed timing. The only time an ECHO effect can sound natural is in a large exterior setting with only one reflective surface—a canyon wall or a large building—or in hard-walled, perfectly cube-shaped rooms with no furniture or other features.

Reverbs in an audio program often have separate controls for the early reflections. Set them longer and farther apart to simulate very large spaces. NLE reverbs frequently lack this feature, but you can simulate it by putting the same clip on two separate tracks. Apply an echo effect to one track for the early reflections. Slide the second track later—about 6 frames for every hundred feet[7] from us to the farthest wall—and apply a long reverb.

Beyond Reverb

Reverb isn't just for simulating rooms. Add it to sound effects and synthesized elements to make them richer. If you have to cut the end of an effect or piece of music to eliminate other sounds,

---

7. Three frames for the sound to get there; three to come back.

add some echo to let it end gracefully. Reverb can also help smooth over awkward edits within a piece of music.

One classic studio production trick is "preverb": echoes that come before an element instead of after it. Add some silence before a clip, and then reverse the whole thing so it plays backwards. Apply a nice, rich reverb. Then reverse the reverberated clip. The echoes will build up magically into the desired sound, which lends an eerie sound to voices and can be interesting on percussive effects (Track 36).

Always think about why the reverb is there. Early Hollywood films added reverb to exteriors to make them more "outdoorsy." But if a sound doesn't have something hard to bounce off of, there can't be an echo. In this case, Hollywood used speakers and microphones in a sealed room to generate the reverb—the exact opposite of what you'd find outdoors. The tracks felt artificial, and they quickly abandoned the practice.

Similarly, don't expect a reverb to necessarily make something sound bigger. In the real world, we associate reverb with *distance*, not size. Sure, we usually stand farther away from very big objects . . . so a large machine in the background ambience of a room would probably have reverb. But adding reverb does not make a voice-over sound bigger. It just makes it sound farther away, destroying intimacy.

Other Delay-based Effects

The same digital delays that are at the heart of reverb units can also be used for special effects. Multiple short delays, with constantly changing delay times, can be combined to make one instrument or voice sound like many; this is called a *chorus* effect. Chorus can be used to thicken a crowd or background sound, but keep the effect subtle.

A single longer delay, with a slower change in its delay time, can be combined with the original signal. As it does, different frequencies will be canceled or reinforced based on the delay time. This *flanging* effect imparts a moving wooshing character to a sound, and is often heard in pop music production. It can add a sense of motion to steady sound effects, increase the speed of automobile passbys, and is a mainstay of science fiction sound design. Chorus and flange don't need as much processing as a true reverb, so even low-cost units and simple software plug-ins can be useful.

Pitch shifters use the same memory function as a delay, but read the audio data out at a different rate than it was written. This raises or lowers the pitch by changing the timing of each sound wave, just like changing the speed on a tape playback. Unlike varispeed tape, however, the long-term timing isn't affected. Instead, many times a second, the software repeats or eliminates waves to compensate for the speed variation. Depending on how well the software is written, it may do a very good job of figuring out which waves can be manipulated without our noticing.

Comb filtering

Dimmer noise and other power-line junk can be very hard to eliminate from a track because it has so many harmonics. But one delay technique, *comb filtering*, is surprisingly effective. You need to know the precise frequency of the noise's fundamental. Divide it by one to get the period of the wave (if the noise is based on 60 Hz, then the period is 0.01666... seconds, or 16.666... ms). Then combine the signal with a delayed version of itself, exactly half that period later (for 60 Hz, that would be 8.333... ms). The delay will form nulls in the signal, very deep notches that eliminate many of the harmonics. The nulls are so deep and regularly-spaced, that if you drew a frequency response graph, they'd look like teeth of a comb.

I used ellipses in the previous paragraph to indicate repeating decimals because the delay has to be set to exactly one-half the period of the sound you're eliminating. Very few audio programs outside the lab, and no NLE software, lets you set a delay this precisely. But you can simulate the delay in an audio program that supports multiple tracks, by putting a copy of the original clip on a second track and sliding it the right amount. For the most accurate setting, locate the actual noise waveform during a pause in dialog, measure its length, and slide the copy to the halfway point. Oftentimes, there'll be an inverted noise spike halfway across the wave. This visual adjustment can be better than trying to calculate the delay, since small sample-rate differences between camera and NLE can change the noise frequency from exactly 60 Hz.

The delay necessary for comb filtering can make a track sound slightly metallic. Reduce this effect by lowering the level of the delay around 3 dB.

Vocal Elimination

In pop music production, the vocalist and most instruments are usually recorded with a individual mics, rather than in stereo, and then distributed from left to right electronically. The main vocal is put in the center of the stereo image, meaning its sound is identical on both the left and right channels.

If you invert the polarity of just one channel of the stereo pair, the vocal energy of this centered solo will produce a negative voltage on one side while producing a positive one on the other. If you then combine the channels equally into mono, positive and negative will cancel each other—eliminating the vocalist. Radio stations often use this technique when creating song parodies. It can also be used to lower the melody line in pre-produced music so dialog can show through.

This technique has limitations. It's useless on acoustic recordings, such as live performances, or if studio tricks like double-tracking have been used. It doesn't eliminate a soloist's reverb, which is usually in stereo, so the result can be a ghostlike echo of a voice that isn't there. And it also eliminates anything else that was centered in a studio recording, which often includes critical parts of the drum kit and the bass line. Still, it's an amazingly effective trick when used with the right material.

Some audio software has a solo elimination process built-in (SoundForge hides it as a preset in the CHANNEL CONVERTER). If yours doesn't support this directly, select just one channel of a stereo pair and use an Invert process. Then use a MIX process to combine the channels to mono. I don't know of any way to do this within an NLE, unless you get SFX Machine (www.sfxmachine.com), a dirt-cheap multifunction audio processor packaged as a Premiere-format plugin for Macs. One of its presets is labeled VOCAL ELIMINATION. It also has a ton of other presets that are useful in sound design.

Noise Reduction

While comb filtering can reduce power-line noises, it's not effective against most other forms of noise found at a shooting location. Fortunately, there are other techniques.

Noise Gates and Expanders

You can use a noise gate (described in the "Compressors" section) to clean up a recording, but unless the noise is very soft to begin with, you'll hear the noise clicking in under dialog and turning off again during pauses. This is a distracting effect, often heard when older movies are broadcast on TV. It can also be heard, in some shooting situations, when you use the MIC NR setting on a few cameras. One solution is to give the noise gate a slow decay setting, similar to the one on a compressor. When dialog stops, the background noise slowly fades down. Coupled with a BYPASS control—to let some of the noise through at all times—this can be effective.

It's not really noise reduction. The only true noise reducer is an equalizer or filter, set to lower the level of a constantly-pitched noise. What we normally think of as noise reduction is actually noise distraction. It uses another signal, usually dialog, to partially mask the noise. But though we're paying more attention to the dialog, the noise is still there, just as loud as before. The software uses various techniques to lower the entire level when there's no masking signal.

It's more smoke-and-mirrors than a true reduction.

A better solution is the *downward expander*, which works like an anti-compressor. Signals above a certain threshold volume aren't affected at all. Those below the threshold are attenuated, by an amount inversely proportional to their volume. A moderately loud signal below the threshold will be lowered a small amount. A soft one will be lowered a lot. The threshold is usually set just below dialog level. Prop noises and footsteps are loud enough that they don't get affected very much. Background noise, during the pauses, gets lowered.

Multiband Noise Reducers

Expanders only work well when the main signal has about the same timbre as the noise. If dialog has a high-frequency hiss mixed in, the expander will have to open for the dialog but a male voice probably wouldn't be enough to distract us from the hiss. This can be solved by splitting the signal into bands, and expanding each one separately.

16.18 Sonic Foundry Noise Reduction

Hardware-based noise reducers usually settle for a limited number of bands. One Dolby unit, popular in Hollywood during analog days (and still used) had only four bands. But non-realtime software can have hundreds of bands. Each band consists of a sharp bandpass filter and a downward expander. To use one of these programs, select a chunk of audio that has just noise and no dialog. The software measures the noise volume for each band (this takes only a few seconds), and sets the threshold just above it. Then select and process the entire clip. Two effective noise reducers of this type are Arboretum's cross-platform Ionizer, and Sonic Foundry's Noise Reduction (Figure 16.18), a Direct-X plugin.

Don't expect either of these programs to be intuitive. These are professional programs with lots of controls—the figure shows just one of two panels—and individual adjustments for each of what can be hundreds of bands. Read the software's tutorial and experiment with the included files. Expect to spend at least a couple of hours before you truly understand how to use the program. But once you do, you'll be able to perform minor miracles.

Noise-reduction Strategies

Noise reduction works best when it doesn't have too much to do. The closer noise levels get to dialog, the more the algorithms are likely to introduce metallic wooshes and other artifacts. These can be controlled by fine-tuning the software (that's why it takes so long to learn) but it's better to start with as little noise as possible.

- Don't assume that any on-set noise can be reduced in postproduction. Use the techniques in Chapter 7 to lower it as much as possible before shooting.

- Reverberation, to these programs, acts like noise. If the mic distance is too great, the extra reverb will contribute to those metallic artifacts. Use good boom technique or a lav (Chapter 8).

- Remove as much pitched noise as possible before processing, with a parametric equalizer, cutoff filter, or comb filter.

- Settle for some noise. A low-artifact, slightly noisy track is better than an artifact-filled quiet one.

Combining Effects

It takes a lot of processing to make a really good soundtrack. Voices are usually equalized and then compressed, even in dramatic scenes, so they're easier to understand. Hard effects are almost always equalized to give them more impact, and then compressed to control their overall level; a gate may be added so they begin or end cleanly. Backgrounds are usually equalized so they don't interfere with the voice, and compressed to a constant level so they'll be easier to mix. A whole dramatic scene may have reverb added, or individual elements might get their own reverb so they match better.

Music should be equalized so it doesn't interfere with voice, but while compression on a music track can make it easier to mix, it can also destroy the dynamic rhythm of the score. Sometimes a little additional reverb, following the equalization, is all a music track needs to be mixable.

Source music, on the other hand, usually needs a lot of processing before it belongs to a scene. If a song is supposed to be heard through a radio or other speaker, use a high-pass at 200 Hz and a low-pass somewhere around 7 kHz, followed by some heavy compression and then reverb with very fast early reflections and a quick decay. This may be more radical than many real-world radio speakers, but the point is to sound *more* like a speaker than the scene's dialog—which, of course, the viewers are already hearing through their own speakers.

If a broadcast mix includes dialog and music, I usually add a little low-midrange peak to bring out the voices, followed by a multiband compressor with fast attacks and decays to bring up the lower-level sounds.

In general, it's most efficient to apply equalization before compression. The equalizer affects how loud the signal will be at various frequencies, which compression can then control. If you compress before equalizing, the compressor might be reacting to extreme high- or low-frequency sounds that'll never make it to the final mix. It's usually best to apply gating—if any—before the compressor so the gate has a wider range of levels to work with.

Reverberation can be added before or after the other processes. Equalizing before a reverb will affect the source sound without changing the acoustics of the simulated room; equalizing afterwards will make the room's walls harder or softer. Low-frequency sounds can travel greater distances, so shelving out some of the highs can make a long reverb seem slightly bigger. If you compress after a reverb, it'll change how long it takes late reflections to decay and make the reverb last longer.

Learning More

Practice—particularly with good speakers—is the best way to improve your processing skills. It takes years to get the skills of a good broadcast or soundtrack mixer.

You can speed up the process somewhat by using David Moulton's *Golden Ears* training CDs (www.moultonlabs.com/gold.htm). Moulton is a noted audio educator, Grammy-nominated engineer, and speaker designer. He put these discs together based on his experience training a generation of highly-respected music mixers. While the course is oriented toward music production, the ear training can be very valuable to a videographer.

You can also speed up the process with my other book, *Audio Postproduction for Digital Video* (CMP Books, 2002). It includes six separate chapters just on processing, with lots of CD examples and cookbook recipes for common video and film situations. There's more about it in the Introduction to this book and details on my Web site (www.dplay.com/book).

Chapter 17

The Mix

There's a producer who likes to come to my studio to finish her projects. Well, actually she likes to stand outside the studio and watch me through a half-open doorway. She figures if a mix sounds good under those circumstances, it'll work well on the air. Considering how most people hear TV, she may be right.

No two television sets have the same sound quality. Even identical models will sound different, depending on their placement in the room. Different furnishings and room treatments also affect the sound—a comfortable couch really does make television better—and a program's audio has to be heard over everything from air conditioners and vacuum cleaners to crying babies. If my friend were producing theatrical films, the situation would be slightly better, but she'd still have to think about home video and network release. It's no wonder she runs out of the room in search of a good mix.

But she's the producer. My job as sound engineer is to be as intimate with the mix as possible. That means monitoring on high-quality speakers to hear even the tiniest variation in the sound, keeping the speakers in the nearfield so room acoustics aren't an influence, and making sure the monitoring levels are controlled so my ears don't get fooled.[1] Mixing is a physical activity as well, with fingers constantly tweaking the faders, and eyes constantly darting between video monitor, calibrated level meter, and spectrum analyzer.

---

1. These techniques are detailed in Chapter 11.

Yes, it can be a little stressful. But it's worth it because the mix is our last chance to get things right.

Setting Up for the Mix

Since mixing can be an intense experience, it makes sense to organize things to let you work as efficiently as possible. This requires the right tools and preparation. Most of the necessary hardware or software—monitor speakers, level meters, and effects processors—has been covered in Chapters 11 and 16.

Do You Need a Mixing Console?

Most postproduction mixes are done either on digital consoles hooked up to multiple outputs of an audio workstation, or on a consolelike controller for the workstation itself. Both systems look similar: there's a panel with sliding faders for each track, some knobs to control effects, and a computer screen. They're both operated about the same way, too: the beginning of each track is previewed while equalizers and other processors are adjusted, faders are preset to a good starting mix, and then everything is recued and rolled. The levels are then adjusted as the scene plays through. If there's a mistake or you want to change something, you back up and fix it.

Mixing for video or film has to be dynamic. The relationship between sounds depends on a lot of things—what the sounds are doing at the moment, what we want to convey, how the characters are feeling. But the one thing it doesn't depend on is how a fader has been set, or where a volume-control line is on a clip. A sound's envelope is constantly changing, even if its track fader isn't moving. So you have to constantly tweak those faders to keep the most important sounds on top of the mix, without pushing other sounds so low that they get lost.

It's typical for a mix engineer to keep one finger on each of the principal dialog faders, twitching them up and down a few decibels for individual words as necessary. The other fingers fly around to adjust hard effects, backgrounds, and music. If a system has mix automation, you can refine these fader movements and then have the computer play them all back to mix the scene for you. If not, common practice is to record the mixed audio in sync with the individual tracks; pickups and remixes are then overlaid on the mix in realtime.

The one thing that's almost never done is to put the faders in a fixed position, start the mix, and not change them until the final fadeout.

Mixing without a mixer

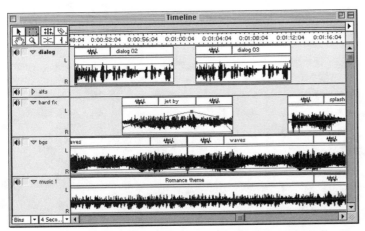

17.1 It can take a long time to fine-tune all those rubber bands.

If your setup limits you to using "rubber bands" or volume handles superimposed on tracks in a timeline, it's going to be difficult—or at least very time consuming—to do a good mix. Figure 17.1 shows 20 seconds of a work in progress. While there's a lot of movement in those volume lines, it isn't anywhere near finished. We need to trim the background so it doesn't interfere with other effects, swell the music at the climax, and then fine-tune the whole thing so we're not aware of the mix when we concentrate on the drama. What takes the most time is the mouse-to-ear connection; each adjustment requires you to find or create a keyframe, click near it, drag, and then play over the section to decide if you like the result.

If you must mix with rubber bands and a mouse, you'll save time if you do a screen full of settings at once. Play back, change every track that needed adjustment, check your changes, and move on.

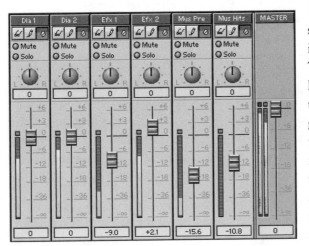

17.2 The on-screen mixing console in Premiere.

Virtual mixers On-screen mixing consoles like the one in Figure 17.2 are an improvement over using rubber bands. The fader knobs are a bigger target than a keyframe or volume line, so you can grab the right one faster. But from the program's point of view, this is just a different user interface for the same actions: as you move the virtual faders with automation turned on, the software plants keyframes and manipulates rubber bands on the timeline. If you go back to the timeline, you'll see each of your movements on the track and can edit them rubber-band style.

17.3 A more elaborate virtual mixer from an audio program.

Virtual mixers are a visual improvement over timeline rubber bands, and make it easier to understand how volumes and stereo panning are being manipulated in a mix. All have controls for the program's mix automation, usually on a track-by-track basis so you can play the fades on most tracks while writing new moves on selected ones. Many have realtime meters for each track, *mute* buttons to turn a track off without losing its automation data, or *solo* buttons to mute every other track so you can concentrate on one at a time. Audio programs will add effects for each track, and routing and record buttons. Figure 17.3 shows the mixer from Bias' Deck multitrack audio program.

There's another important difference between the mixers in an NLE and an audio program. The clips on an NLE track may be mono or stereo. When they're mono, the round knob above the fader lets you pan the signal from left to right. When they're stereo, the knob turns into a balance control. But most audio programs can accept only one channel of sound per track. A stereo clip has to be put on two tracks, with each panned to a different side. Note how the tracks on the right half of Figure 17.3 are set this way.

While virtual mixers have been a boon to music producers, where tracks tend to stay at the same volume setting for a long time, they're less useful in video production. Tracks are constantly shifting their relationship, depending on what's most important at any moment. Consider: feature films are typically mixed on giant consoles, with three people—and as many as 30 fingers on fader knobs—working simultaneously.

Mouse-based mixing lets you move only one fader at a time. But in the best film mixes, crossfades between two tracks respect the envelopes of each, as well as their combined sound. Each track affects how the other should be faded. The only way to do this is to move both faders simultaneously. Even single-fader adjustments are harder with a mouse. We've all gotten used to the concept of mousing, but consider what it involves: you have to move a physical object in response to a moving mark on a screen, reach a specific point, press a button, and then perform the desired action. This eye-hand coordination, with no tactile feedback, is more distracting than grabbing and moving physical faders and takes your attention away from the video.

Hardware controllers   If you have to mix more than one or two simple projects in a computer, it's worth investing in an accessory hardware controller. These devices connect to a computer via USB, and have between four and a dozen sliders to control individual tracks. On some, the sliders are motorized so you can see the effect of automation playback. There are usually transport controls and a jog/shuttle wheel, and there may also be knobs to control effects.

As of this writing, none of these controllers work with popular NLE programs. But almost all of them come bundled with multi-track audio software that supports video playback, and it's easy to move tracks from your NLE to the audio program when it's time to mix. Figure 17.4 shows a typical unit, Tascam's US428. For less than $600, it also provides high-quality stereo analog and digital connections for your computer, XLR mic preamps, and MIDI.

17.4 A hardware controller like this can help you do better mixes.

Not mixing

Many producers choose a middle ground, using their mouse-based NLEs for the simplest mixes and taking the complex ones to a separate audio facility. This can give you the advantages of better monitoring, higher-quality effects, and an experienced engineer.[2] There are some tips for getting the most from out-of-house mixes later in this chapter.

---

2. And pays my salary when I'm not writing books.

Track Layout

It makes sense to adopt a consistent format for track layouts, with dialog always on certain tracks and music on others. But you might have to make compromises from time to time. One scene might require three tracks for voices, while the next has many tracks of overlapping effects. Unless you have unlimited tracks, some tracks may end up being used for more than one kind of element.

If you must put different kinds of sounds on the same track, try to choose sounds whose stereo panning, equalization, and other effects will be the same. This way you can apply the effects once, then concentrate on level changes during the mix, instead of having to stop and reset things. Leave some room between adjacent elements on a track, particularly if they'll need different fader settings.

File Interchange

Moving edited tracks from an NLE to an audio program is usually transparent if you follow a few rules. There shouldn't be any problems with sync, and no loss of audio quality. Two different methods are popular: transferring individual tracks as audio files, and transferring the entire project via OMF.

Track transfers   Syncing multiple tracks requires a consistent reference, so the first thing you should do is add a *2-pop* to your project. This is usually a 1-frame, 1 kHz beep inserted on every track at the same timecode, before the first audio or video. It got its name because the pop is usually lined up with the number 2 on the countdown leader, exactly two seconds before the project starts. But you can use any short, loud sound with an abrupt start: the rectangular leading edge of the envelope makes it easier to find its exact beginning. You can also use any distinctive visual for the cueing frame, even a single all-white frame in the black before a program.

Once you've got a 2-pop, export video and the first audio track to a QuickTime or AVI. Mute the other tracks. The video can be smaller than fullframe, but must run at full-frame rate. Make sure the export settings for audio match the project's: 48 kHz or 44.1 kHz sampling, 16 bits, stereo. This movie will be what you watch while mixing, as well as providing the first track for mixing in the audio program. Then export the other tracks as stereo .wav or AIFF files, using similar settings.

Import the movie to your multitrack audio program and assign its sound to the first one or two tracks, depending on whether the NLE's track was mono or stereo. Then import the remaining audio files to additional tracks. Finally, slide the audio-only imports so they match the pop and cue frame on the movie.

Audio programs are organized with just one channel per track, unlike NLEs, which can accommodate mono or stereo clips on a single track. You can take advantage of this to save time and file space during the transfer process. If an NLE track has only mono clips on it—such as a dialog or hard-effect track—export it as mono and assign it to only one track in the audio program. Or if your NLE is capable of this, route one mono track to the left side of a stereo pair before exporting, and another mono track to the right.

Include the 2-pop while you're mixing. Save the finished mix as an audio file, open a copy of the project in your NLE, import the mix and sync its pop, and then delete all the original tracks.

OMF   Avid's Open Media Framework (OMF) was developed to share projects between their high-end NLEs and their Digidesign audio software. It greatly simplifies the process, creating a single file with all of the audio clips already in sync on their proper tracks. While the system is proprietary, it's been adopted by some other NLE manufacturers (including Apple), and many multitrack audio programs can import its files. Depending on what software you use, you may have to render a separate video file if you want to watch picture while you're mixing.

If your system supports OMF export, check its options. You may be able to automatically strip off any audio filters or fades, a good idea since you'll be able to do them better in the audio program. You may also be able to add *handles*, audio extensions of a few seconds or so on either side of an edit, for smooth fades between scenes.

While OMF files can get very big, they're usually smaller than the total size of multiple audio-only exports. That's because they don't waste data on the silence between clips in a track.

Some other high-end NLE manufacturers have been developing a competing interchange system based on Broadcast WAVE (BWF), a variation on the Windows audio format that's standardized by the European Broadcast Union. BWF files can be stamped with timecode, so a transfer system based on them would have the flexibility of individual files while exporting only the relevant parts of a track. When the BWFs are imported to the multitrack program, a database assigns them to tracks, and their individual timestamps locate them on the timeline. However, this system has not yet made it to the world of desktop production.

Before You Mix, Don't

Wine tasters rinse their mouths out with water between critical sips, so they can detect every subtle aspect of the vintage they're examining. You should cleanse your ears for the same reason. Don't listen to anything at all for a while before starting a mix.

Chances are, you've just spent hours editing individual elements against the picture. It's only natural that you'll be extra aware of each one of those gems of editorial art, and want them to sparkle in the finished product—even if they get in the way of your message. Plan for some breathing room between when you build the track and when you mix it. If you can't wait overnight or take a meal break, at least go for a short walk. Don't begrudge the extra few minutes this takes; it can save you from having to come back for a remix. Even though I charge by the hour, I'll willingly stop the clock and lose a few bucks to take this kind of a break. It always results in a better mix.

The Mix

A soundtrack can be thought of as a physical space, with mixing simply being the process of putting everything in its place. Things can be close to you or far away, and they can spread (to a limited extent, depending on the final delivery medium) across the left-to-right axis. If you're mixing for theatrical or DVD release, sounds can even be behind you. But if two sounds try to occupy the exact same space, both will suffer.

Mix engineers use three specific ways to place sounds in acoustic space.

1. Volume

Obviously, louder sounds are closer. Just remember that only one sound can predominate at a time. Don't try to make *everything* close.

Don't try to make things very far, either, unless your project will be shown only in theaters. Video mixing is not a subtle medium. If a sound effect or music cue seems to work best when the track is barely open, try turning it off entirely. You might discover it's not needed. If you miss it, try to find some way—using effects or timing changes—to bring it forward slightly. Otherwise there's a chance most viewers won't get to hear it on their sets.

2. Equalization

Music engineers frequently call the midrange equalizer a "presence" control. It makes a big difference in how close a sound appears.

Boosting the midrange, particularly between around 1.2–2.5 kHz, tends to bring voices forward. If you turn a music track down in these frequencies, it'll leave more room for the dialog. Mid-low frequencies, between 100–250 Hz, can add warmth and intimacy to a voice. Be careful about adding too many extreme low frequencies; they just add muddiness in most video tracks.

While you usually can't use an equalizer to move individual instruments forward or back in a piece of mixed music, you can control groups of harmonics. Dipping the frequencies noted in the previous paragraph can make a piece of music work with dialog better, letting you bring the entire music track forward. This works for background sounds as well.

High frequencies get absorbed as sound travels through the air. It's not enough to be noticeable in interior spaces, but turning down the highs can add distance to exterior sounds.

3. Reverberation

This might seem counterintuitive, but reverberation makes things smaller by sending them farther away. Reverb is primarily an interior effect. When you go outside, the reflecting surfaces tend to be much farther away than the sound source, and unless you're in a situation where echoes could realistically be expected—in a courtyard, next to buildings, or shouting into a canyon—exterior reverb can sound artificial.

Adding reverb to a voice-over, particularly to one that's selling us something, is a dated cliché. If someone really wants to sell us something, they'll come closer rather than stand far away and yell.

There is more about equalization and reverb in Chapter 16.

Direction

Music and film mixers can also *pan*—adjust the relative left/right position in a stereo field, or surround position in more complex tracks—to help define physical space. You don't have as much freedom for this when mixing for broadcast or VHS. Even if a viewer has a stereo receiver, chances are they're not sitting exactly centered between the speakers. Most people keep their TV sets off to one side of the room, where they might as well be mono. Low-cost small color TVs usually are mono, even if they have two speakers on the front panel. Things can get flipped or one channel lost at a TV station. VHS decks—even stereo ones—are usually connected through their mono antenna connection. And while many cable networks broadcast in stereo, you never know which local cable systems will carry the signal that way.

Television shows that advertise stereo in their opening credits are usually glorified mono. All the dialog, and any important sound effects, are strictly center stage. Only the music, background sounds, and audience reactions are mixed in stereo. This keeps the sound consistent and avoids the disconcerting situation of having characters cross the picture from left to the right while their voices go in the other direction. Surround, in most cases, merely means that some ambiences and reverb from the music track are directed to the back of home theater systems.

If you're mixing video for an environment where the playback system can be controlled, such as a theatrical release or corporate meeting video, you can do more with stereo. But it's still not a good idea to pan dialog, since people on the left side of the auditorium will lose dialog that's directed solely to the right. On the other hand, you can put hard effects anywhere you want. Kiosk mixes can be full stereo—you know the viewer will be standing in front of the monitor, with a speaker on either side. Using stereo in a kiosk can help capture the space, defining an area that's separate from the museum or office lobby where the kiosk exists. Just be careful of creating an image that's much wider than the screen itself.

There are two philosophies for surround mixing. One is to keep all the action in front of us, and let the surround channels reflect just the environmental background and reverb. This reflects the traditional position of an audience at a dramatic performance. The other is to put the action all around you. It can be more exciting, but also disorienting since what we're watching is only in one direction. A reasonable compromise is to keep the action up-front, but let the musicians and large effects surround us.

Principal dialog in theatrical tracks, whether they're stereo or surround, is always directed to the center. (In fact, most theaters have a speaker behind the center of the screen, just for dialog.) This may not be realistic when a character is on the far side of the screen, but the convention is less distracting than sudden shifts would be, particularly for ticket holders in the first few rows of the theater.

If you're mixing surround on a project that might also be used for broadcast, be wary of putting important sounds behind you. For mono listeners, those sounds might completely disappear.

The Time Dimension

A mix's acoustic space also uses the fourth dimension, and every element should have its own place in time. Music isn't the only audio element with rhythm, and you should keep aware of stress patterns in the dialog and effects as well. If two stresses happen at the same time, they'll interfere with each other.

Watch out for voice rhythms that match the music exactly; this can happen during long stretches of narration. It makes the track sound dull, and detracts from both voice and music. The same thing can happen in a song, so pop singers often bring some words in slightly ahead of the beat and others slightly behind. You can do the same with a narration track, sliding paragraphs when they land too squarely on the beat.

Traditional movie mixing used 35mm magnetic film, which had four sets of perforations per frame, for the individual tracks. This meant that a piece of mag film could be taken out of its sprocket and moved a quarter-frame at a time to change the synchronization slightly. Music tracks were sometimes slipped this way to make them work better with dialog. If you're mixing in an audio program, try the same thing. If you're working in a video program that constrains edits to the frameline, try a full frame in either direction.

If sliding the music disturbs a carefully panned hit against picture, copy the music onto two tracks and slide only one of them. Crossfade between the two during a sustained note, and you get the best of both placements.

Six Quick Rules for Better Mixes

These apply whether you're the producer, director, or hands-on mix engineer. Ignore them at your peril.

1. Saving time on the mix wastes time.

If you can't afford enough hours to do it right, take shortcuts while you're building individual tracks; a good mix will hide them. But don't take shortcuts while you're mixing, or else you'll have to remix it tomorrow.

2. Shh!

Working with the speakers very loud may be exciting, but it has nothing to do with what your audience will hear unless they're in a movie theater. Pump *down* the volume.

3. All distortion hurts.

Listening at reasonable levels also helps you track down any fuzziness in the sound because the ear expects (and forgives) distortion in loud sounds. Turn down the volume, find the distortion, and fix it. Otherwise, subsequent broadcasting or duplicating will only make things worse.

4. It's never too soon to fix a problem.

As soon as you hear something you don't like, back up and remix it while you're still conscious of the overall flow. If you finish the mix and then go back, the new section may not blend in so well. You'll also run the risk of forgetting some of the places you wanted to touch up.

5. Don't be seduced by stereo.

It may sound impressive on the nearfield speakers in a well-designed mixing setup with good acoustics, but most of your listeners will never hear things that wide.

6. Watch TV with your eyes closed.

Listen to the finished mix at least once without picture. You may hear a lot of rough spots that were easy to ignore while the images were distracting you.

Hearing Two Things at Once

Humans have an amazing ability to follow multiple sound streams based on how close they are to the listener. While this function probably evolved so we could keep track of predators in the jungle, you can use it to separate individual sounds in a track. Since we're using basic presence cues, this trick works equally well in mono or stereo. A simple demonstration will help you understand the effect:

1. Start with two different, well-recorded narrations. Use two different narrators, but both should have similar deliveries. There shouldn't be any echo in the original recording.

2. Mix both at the same level, and listen to the babble that results. You'll find it takes a lot of concentration to make sense out of either narration.

3. Now process the "B" narration to make it seem farther away. Using a cutoff filter, turn down the frequencies below 300 Hz and above 9 kHz. Add a tiny amount of room reverberation to increase the apparent distance. You may also want to lower the overall level about 3 dB.

4. Mix the processed "B" with the original "A" narration and listen again. Chances are, you'll now find it easier to follow *both*. Not only is the up-front "A" voice easier to understand, but you can also make more sense out of the distant "B"!

Track 37 of this book's CD has some voice tracks you can use to try this experiment, along with a before-and-after demonstration.

You can use this presence phenomenon in documentaries to separate an overlapping narration from the interview without having to lose either. Or use it to push crowd walla further into the background, so it doesn't interfere with dialog. One handy trick is to patch a single track to two different faders in a mixer, or copy it to two tracks in software. Apply the equalization and reverb to only one of them, and then crossfade between faders to move the sound closer or farther.

Mix Distortion

When two tracks are mixed together, the result is usually slightly louder than either one of them.[3] As you add more tracks to the mix, things get even louder. If you let them get out of hand, they'll be louder than the system can handle. If your studio hasn't been set up with proper gain-staging (Chapter 11), there's very little margin for error.

When things get much too loud because you've combined a lot of loud tracks, you hear gross distortion and know to stop mixing. But the distortion can be subtle, occurring only on momentary peaks. Your eyes—and a calibrated digital level meter—are the best way to spot this. Don't rely on your ears alone because you can fool yourself into thinking that distortion has gone away by raising the monitor level. If you're mixing in a clip-based NLE, you might not even know there's distortion until you play back the final rendered mix and look for clipped waveforms.

---

3. How much louder depends on the individual waveforms and their relationship to each other.

The best way to avoid distortion during the mix is to remember that faders go down as well as up. Build your final track by lowering some sounds as you boost others. While the two mixers in

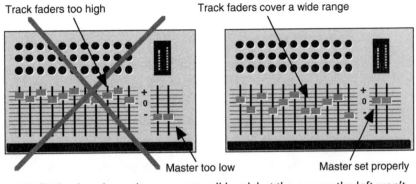

17.5 Both mixes have the same overall level, but the one on the left won't sound as good. This applies to software-based mixers also.

Figure 17.5 have the same output level on their meters, the one on the left is probably seriously overloaded; the fact that its master faders are set very low should be an immediate giveaway. Besides, lowering some of the levels gives you a wider physical range in which you can set the faders, for a more subtle mix.

This works for rubber-band mixing in an NLE as well. Check the settings in Figure 17.1. You'll see that most tracks there have been lowered; only the dialog is consistently raised.

Preparing for Someone Else to Mix

If you don't have good monitoring and mixing equipment, or the mix is particularly tricky and will require special skills, it makes sense to take your tracks elsewhere. This can be an outside studio that specializes in postproduction audio, a local general-purpose music studio, or your company's sound specialist down the hall. Most of the preparation will be the same.

Ask the Expert

Many audio facilities try to standardize pre-production by assigning it to account executives or an operations manager, but this only works for standard situations. If your project is anything out of the ordinary (of course it is—who wants to do ordinary video?), you should talk to the engineer who'll actually do the work. Five minutes with the right person, a few days before the session, will save an hour of scrambling for equipment or experimenting with special setups.[4]

Start with the basics. How long does the video run? Is it dramatic, talking heads, vérité, or voice-over? Discuss how it will be shown, since mixing for a desktop VCR is very different from mix-

---

4. Besides, we engineering types love to solve problems. Get us thinking about your project ahead of time, and we'll be more committed to doing it creatively.

ing for a theater or hotel ballroom. And don't forget subsequent uses, such as cutting the show into modules or a foreign-language version. These considerations affect what kind of equipment and procedures will work best.

Then talk about specific elements. If dialog or voice-over is simple, you've probably already cut them in your NLE. But fine-tuning sounds may be faster, more precise, and possibly cheaper on an audio workstation. Even damaged or noisy production audio may be fixable; a good sound editor will check alternate takes, or lift specific syllables from elsewhere in dialog, and insert them on-camera without disturbing sync. Many audio setups also include noise-reduction tools.

Obviously, let the engineers know if you're planning to record a new voice-over or ADR. Warn them if you want to record narration while watching pictures, in case they need to set up monitors or a playback deck. You might have to arrive a few minutes earlier than the talent, so video can be transferred to a hard-disk playback system.

File and tape interchange

The one factor you absolutely can't forget to discuss is formats. Betacam SP is almost universally accepted for analog video and has very few interchange problems. But some facilities may require analog on 3/4-inch tape, VHS, or S-VHS—all of which have variability in how timecode and audio tracks are handled. (Some editorial houses in Hollywood have ditched BetaSP, and support only 3/4-inch analog and Digital Betacam.) Digital video comes in a variety of noninterchangeable formats, but MiniDV is not one of the professional ones. On the other hand, many studios have audio and video patchbays: you may be able to show up with your camera and dub to their tape deck or hard disc video recorder. Or a studio might prefer reference video as a file on removable hard drive or CD-ROM.

Audio interchange has its own considerations. DAT—particularly timecode DAT—is a universal standard but can be inefficient if you have a lot of tracks to bring to the mix. Eight-track timecode DTRS (also known as DA-88) is standard in sophisticated postproduction studios, though music-based studios may prefer ADAT format instead. But any audio tape format will suffer if you can't get signals in and out of your editing system cleanly, and you need a digital connection between NLE and recorder to do this right.

OMF files, discussed earlier, aren't natively supported in the high-end audio workstations you'll find in many professional audio post suites. But the format is so common that third-party translators are often used. Or a studio may have Digidesign's ProTools on hand, just so they can transfer files.

While you're verifying file formats, check that the studio will be able to handle the medium you bring them on. See if you should be using a removable hard drive cartridge or CD-ROM, or bringing your own hard drive, and if there is a preferred operating system. Also verify that the studio will transfer your audio directly as digital data; some facilities rely on analog wiring to move audio from computer to workstation. If this is the case, sound quality will be proportional to the level of maintenance the studio does.

Be aware of track assignment in your NLE's audio setup pages, before you start transferring tracks to tape or rendering them to files. If you've routed two overlapping tracks to the same channel, their sounds will be mixed at full volume, and there'll be no way to separate them.

Synchronization

If you're bringing timecode tapes to an outside studio, sync shouldn't be an issue. Make sure you've done all your transfers digitally, or with recorder and NLE sharing a common video sync source. It's a good idea to tell the studio what timecode format you're using, in case they want to preformat a tape.

Timecode is a standard in the professional world. If your system supports it, you'll find it's also handy for communicating with the mixing engineer: "There's a noise coming up at 9:07," or "I took 15 frames out in the middle of the cutaway at 13:54." (Usually, spoken timecode identifies the minutes and seconds; hours are assumed, and frames aren't necessary.)

But sync is never a sure thing, even with timecode. It's always a good idea to provide a sync reference. Most common is the 2-pop discussed earlier. If you've got any reason to doubt that sync will be absolutely stable over the length of the program, it's wise to provide similar audio and video "post pops" at the tail.

What to Bring to a Mix

Obviously you should bring your edited tracks and video when you're mixing at an outside studio, in the file formats you've all agreed on. It may even make sense to ship these before the mix session if the studio can preload them into their workstation.

But there are a few other things you should also pack. If there's any chance you'll need to rebuild dialog or grab effects, take the original shoot tapes and logs. If you're bringing master videotape for the sound studio to lay their final mix onto, make sure they'll be dubbing it to another medium before the session or bring a

Digital Playroom

Producer: Custom Productions
Client: KMCG Radio
Project: :30 tv "Raindrops"

Time	Mono 1	Mono 2	Stereo 1	Stereo 2
00.01			Raindrops (fx)	Raindrops (clean)
00.19	VO line 1		II	II
03.09	II	latch	II <spin effect>	II
05.29		chain lift		
07.10	VO line 2	chain on table		
09.26	II	"aah"	wind	harp gliss
12.02	II		teeth <mono>	bla bla <mono>
15.00	II	CD drop	II	II
17.02	II	CD drop #2	II	II
18.27			sweep foley	crash!
21.14	VO 3 (short)		hinge <mono>	
22.06		latch	Sexual Healing	Cruising
24.19	VO tag		II	II
29.29			<out>	<out>

17.6 A chart can save time by helping the mixer figure out what's on each track.

protection copy. Let them whip the copy around while they're mixing, so there's no chance of ruining the master.

You'll also need some paperwork. If your tracks are more complicated than just voice and music, go through them in your NLE, and create a layout chart so the mixer can figure out where things are (Figure 17.6 shows a typical format). Bring contracts or a purchase order if necessary to keep the studio manager happy. And don't forget the phone and beeper numbers of anyone you might need to call during the session for changes or approvals.

After the Mix

If you're mixing in an NLE, check the final rendered version carefully for sync and distortion. It may help to open the finished mix in a waveform viewer or clip window, to verify there is sufficient level and no overloads. It should look similar to the properly digitized files in Chapter 12.

Mixing in a separate system, or at an outside studio, requires a couple of extra steps. If you haven't rendered a final NLE output, the best plan is to put the finished mix back into your editing system. Have the studio make a compatible file with the same sync pops you gave them in the edited tracks, load it into your editor, and line up the pops. Once you've done that, you can move the mix's in- and out-points so the beeps don't make it to the final rendering.

If you've brought a master videotape on BetaSP or one of the professional digital formats (and verified that the studio can handle it), they'll probably be able to dub your mix right onto the Dolby tracks of the master. Be aware that the higher-quality FM audio tracks on analog BetaSP can't be dubbed without erasing the picture.

Most professional productions will also be copied to timecode DAT. Be sure the studio sets the DAT's sample rate to 48 kHz, and both timecode and sample rate are locked to the same video reference; otherwise, it might not be possible to use the tape without an analog generation. Most professional video decks will reject digital audio signals that aren't synchronized this way.

Dub Levels

If you're outputting your mix on a professional digital video format, dub it to the pro standard discussed in Chapter 12: –20 dBFS nominal level and –10 dBFS maximum for broadcast; –2 dBFS maximum for theatrical. Record a –20 dBFS tone at 1 kHz along with color bars at the front of the tape.

If you're dubbing to MiniDV, use –12 dBFS for the nominal level and tone. Don't let the maximum exceed –2 dBFS.

If you're dubbing to analog, tone and nominal level should be 0 VU. Peaks shouldn't exceed +4 VU on VHS, though BetaSP can handle very short transients as high as +6 VU.

M&E Mixes

Networks often request that a producer provide an *M&E* mix with just music and effects, or *D/M/E stems* with separate mixes for dialog, music, and effects. Common practice is to put all the on-camera audio and narration on separate mono tracks, all the sound effects on a stereo pair, and all the music on another pair. This is so they can create foreign-language versions easily. Since it's impossible to predict how much time each line of a foreign narration will take, the music and effects should stay at a constant level and not be prefaded for the announcer. M&E mixes are usually provided on DAT or DTRS/DA-88 tapes, with the same digital audio and time-code specs as the master.

Backups

If you habitually copy NLE tracks to a data-archiving medium, and you haven't done much editing in an audio workstation at the professional facility, the only other backup you might want is a spare copy of the finished mix on DAT or CD-ROM. If there's a lot of additional editing or effects in the audio workstation, back up the workstation's project as well. The time it takes will not only protect you against catastrophic hard-drive failure, but also make life easier when the client requests changes.

If you've developed special sound effects or sequences you might want to use in other projects, copy them as a separate audio DAT or separate files. It's a lot faster to find and reuse them this way than to reload a backup tape and look for them in the original tracks.

The Last Thing You Should Do

Put the tape on a shelf. Come back to it a month later, listen to it, and figure out what you'd do differently. Now start the process all over again.

Glossary

Every specialty creates its own jargon, verbal shortcuts to express precise situations quickly. Audio jargon can be confusing, particularly if you're coming from the more peaceful environment of desktop video.

Jargon is also sometimes used to create an aura of mystery that keeps outsiders from knowing what's going on. But that's not what this book is about, so here's a practical guide to what we audio engineers are talking about. If you don't find a term here, check the index.

ADAT Alesis Digital Audio Tape, an eight-track format using S/VHS cassettes and named for the company that invented it. ADATs were the first practical, low-cost digital multitracks and became a favorite of scoring composers. A similar but more robust eight-track format, Tascam's DTRS (also known as DA8 or DA88), uses Hi-8 cassettes. The DTRS format was adopted by Sony and is the standard in feature production. Both systems allow multiple decks to be linked for unlimited tracks. The two formats are not compatible.

ADR Automatic (or Automated) Dialog Replacement, also sometimes known as "looping." Production audio can be noisy and, even if recorded on a quiet sound stage, can be inconsistent from shot to shot. ADR systems let actors go into a sound studio, hear short pieces of their own dialog repeated over and over in a constant rhythm, and then recreate the performance—line by line—in sync with picture. See Chapter 10.

AES/EBU Literally, the Audio Engineering Society and European Broadcasting Union. But the combination of initials almost always refers to the standard for interconnecting digital audio devices. See Chapter 4.

AIFF Audio Interchange File Format, the standard for Macintosh audio- and video-editing systems. Different from Microsoft's .wav format. Fortunately, most programs are smart enough to open either, and there are plenty of shareware converters for both platforms.

ATTC Address Track Time Code. LTC recorded on a special track of an analog video tape or down the center of an analog audio tape.

auto-conform In the dark days of analog video editing, each generation would add noise to the soundtrack. Since a video master could be three or four generations removed from the original, the production audio was often treated just as reference. An automatic conforming system (or hapless audio engineer) would use the original field recordings and an edit list, and rebuild the sound. Modern nonlinear and online systems keep audio as 16-bit or higher digital data, so this step usually isn't necessary.

BGs Background sounds (the term is pronounced like the disco group). Usually a track or two of stock environments, such as crowds or traffic noises, edited to fit the length of a scene. Careful choice of BGs can eliminate the need for a lot of foley.

bump To adjust the timing between sound and picture in precise frame or subframe units, while both are running. While this is most often used to fine-tune lipsync and sound-effects placement, bumping a piece of music a frame or two can have amazing results.

burn-in A videotape with timecode numbers superimposed on the picture.

BWF Broadcast Wave Format, an audio interchange format standardized by the European Broadcasting Union. It's similar to Microsoft .wav and can be read by standard audio programs, but software designed for this format also lets you embed sync and other information.

CD-quality Properly speaking, a digital audio signal or device capable of 20 Hz–20 kHz bandwidth with little deviation, very low distortion, and a 96 dB dynamic range. Many manufacturers use the term improperly to imply a quality that isn't justified by a system's design. Unless

you can verify specifications using some of the measurements in Chapter 9, the term is meaningless.

click track An electronic metronome played into headphones, or a track on a tape with that signal, so that musicians can perform to precise timing.

DA8, DA88, DTRS See ADAT.

DAW Digital Audio Workstation, software or integrated software and hardware for editing, processing, and mixing sound. Most DAWs include a way to play video in sync.

dBm Decibels, referenced to 1 milliwatt across 600 Ω.

dBv Decibels, referenced to 0.775 volts.

dBV Decibels, referenced to 1 volt.

decibel A precise, and often misunderstood, measurement of the ratio between two signals. See Chapter 2.

distortion Anything that changes the output of an audio system so it no longer reflects the input signal. Noise and changes in frequency response can be forms of distortion, though the term is usually reserved for unintentional, gross changes in the waveform.

dither Specially shaped random noise added to a digital signal to improve its quality at low levels.

D/M/E Dialog, music, and effects stems, separate tracks carrying only one kind of sound, used for foreign translations. More flexible than an *M&E* mix.

double system   Recording production sound on a separate audio tape recorder while a video or film camera is running. This is often looked at as a way to improve the sound of MiniDV camcorders, but Chapter 9 suggests other things you should try first.

dropframe   A way of counting timecode so that frame numbers stay, on average, in sync with real-world time. No actual frames are dropped in the process. See Chapter 12.

dynamic range   The range between the loudest signal a system can carry without distortion, and its low-level noise that would obscure any softer signals, expressed in decibels. In a purely digital signal, each bit is worth 6 dB dynamic range. But when you start involving analog circuits, dynamic range gets harder to pin down. Low-level noise is contributed by the electronics itself, and high-level distortion sets in gradually as the volume increases.

foley   Generating sound effects by duplicating the actors' on-screen movements in a sound studio. A team of good foley artists can watch a scene once, gather armloads of props, and then create everything from footsteps to fist fights in perfect sync. *Digital foley* refers to the process of matching those little sounds in an audio workstation (usually because good foley artists are expensive). The name honors Jack Foley, a Hollywood second-unit director and sound genius of the 1940s.

hard effects   Also known as spot effects. Sounds that are impractical to foley (such as telephone bells, explosions, and 25th-century laser guns) and usually important to the story. These are often drawn from large CD effects libraries, but may be created for the project. In feature-film production, the term often refers to *any* sound effects that are in sync with picture.

high fidelity   An ambiguous term. It often refers to somewhere near a 20 Hz–20 kHz frequency range with less than 2 dB variation between sounds of different frequencies, and a dynamic range of at least 70 dB with less than 0.3% distortion—but the bar keeps getting raised as technology improves. Has nothing to do with whether a system is analog or digital.

hitting a post   audio people use this term to refer to the cues within a long sound effect or music track. It's not enough to make a sound begin and end in sync with the picture; you also have to make sure that internal elements match the on-screen actions. A good sound editor will make lots of tiny edits and use other tricks to hit as many posts as possible.

house sync   In large facilities, a single video signal (usually an all-black picture in color TV format) is distributed to just about every audio and video device. House sync is not the same as timecode. The former is a precise heartbeat, accurate to microseconds. It keeps signals compatible, but can't tell one frame from another. Timecode identifies frames for editing but is only precise to a few dozen milliseconds. It's usually a mistake to control critical audio- or videotape speeds with it.

ISDN   Integrated Services Digital Network. A way of combining standard telephone wiring with special equipment to create 128 kilobit/second dial-up connections as needed. It's more reliable (as well as faster) than high-speed analog modems, and more flexible than other systems like DSL or cable modems. In the world of audio, the term usually refers to real-time transfers and remote recording sessions using ISDN wiring along with audio data reduction equipment.

layback Copying a finished mix from an audio workstation or separate audiotape back to a videotape master.

layup Transferring production sound from edited videotape to an audio medium for further manipulation. Networked nonlinear editing systems can make both layback and layup unnecessary.

LTC Longitudinal Time Code. SMPTE timecode data is actually a biphase digital stream in the audio range, sounding something like a fax machine signal. When it's recorded on an analog audio track, it's called "longitudinal," since it runs parallel to the tape instead of slanting like a videotape track. LTC also refers to the biphase signal itself, so the wire that plugs into a timecode input is actually carrying LTC—even if the data came from a digital data track or VITC. See Chapter 12.

M&E Music and Effects, a submix of a production's soundtrack with no dialog to make foreign translations easier.

masking A phenomenon where sounds at one frequency make it difficult or impossible to hear other simultaneous (or, in the case of *temporal* masking, closely occurring) sounds at a nearby frequency. The basis behind every system of perceptual encoding. See Chapter 3.

mid-side (M-S) Stereo microphone technique with excellent control of width and mono compatibility. See Chapter 7.

MIDI Musical Instrument Digital Interface, a common language and electrical standard for describing events such as the turning on or off of a note. See Chapter 14.

mono Short for *monaural*, literally "one ear." An audio signal with no directional information,

frequently recorded with a single mic. In most systems, mono signals are automatically placed in the center of a stereo field. Dialog is almost always recorded and mixed in mono.

MOS Scenes that are videotaped or filmed without any audio, usually because the camera setup or location makes sound impractical. The expectation is that a track will be created using foley and other effects. This is often a bad idea in video production, since any track—even one from a camera-mounted microphone far from the action—is better than nothing and may be usable for sound effects or a sync reference. Rumor has it, the term MOS originated when an early German-speaking film director wanted to work "mitout sound."

MP3 MPEG II Layer 3, the most common file format and data-reduction scheme for delivering audio over the Internet.

NLE Non-Linear Editor, a computer program or integrated hardware and software for editing and finishing video.

noise, pink Electronic noise with an equal likelihood of a signal in each octave. Since any octave has twice as many frequencies as the octave below it, pink noise is created by filtering white noise so there's less energy as the frequency gets higher. It reflects how we hear better than white noise and is used for acoustic testing.

noise, white Random electronic noise with an equal likelihood of a signal at any frequencies. This is the kind of noise commonly generated by analog circuits.

octave The musical interval of 12 semitones, or a frequency ratio of 2:1.

offset The difference in timecode between any two tapes. Video editors typically start their programs at 1:00:00:00 (one hour; no minutes, seconds, or frames) to allow for color bars and slates. If an audio operator decides to start that same program at 00:01:00:00, the sound would have a –59 minute offset. Some digital audio processors introduce delays to handle the sound more intelligently, so small offsets are sometimes necessary.

pan To move a mono audio signal across the stereo field, or place it in a specific left/right position.

production audio Sounds recorded in the field while the picture is being shot, usually dialog. May be recorded directly on the videotape, or as *double system*.

R-DAT Exactly the same as a standard or timecode DAT tape. When it was first invented, some digital audio systems used stationary heads (like an analog audio tape deck), and others used rotating heads (like a helical-scan video deck). Our ubiquitous DAT was originally called "Rotating Digital Audio Tape."

SMPTE Short for SMPTE timecode, the frame-accurate time data recorded on video and audio tapes to control editing and keep elements together. It stands for the Society of Motion Picture and Television Engineers, who invented the format.

s/pdif A standard for interconnecting stereo digital audio devices, similar to AES/EBU but using a lower-cost wiring scheme and carrying information that's appropriate for consumer audio. See Chapter 3.

stereo An audio signal that includes two distinct channels of information, one intended for the left ear and one for the right, to help the listener locate sound sources across an imaginary line in front of them. This is not the same thing as two channels of identical information, which is just a mono signal with redundant data.

timbre A characteristic of a sound wave that has to do with the number and strength of a wave's harmonics (Chapter 2), often referred to as its *brightness* or *richness*. Timbre is different from volume or pitch, though an untrained ear can easily be tricked into confusing these characteristics.

VITC Vertical Interval Time Code. Time data encoded as a series of dots at the top of each video field. Unlike LTC, it can be read when the tape is paused. This makes it easier to jog a tape to find a specific action, and then match a sound to it. Unfortunately, VITC can't be read when the picture is distorted because of high-speed winding. Most professional analog video systems put identical VITC and LTC data on a tape and choose the most appropriate for the speed.

walla Voices of people in a crowd, recorded at an event or studio or taken from a sound effects CD. On-camera crowds are usually told to mime their conversations to make dialog pickup easier; walla is then added in post. Walla can also be used to simulate an off-camera crowd to make a scene larger.

wet/dry Refers to echoes. Most foley, hard effects, and ADR are recorded dry, without any natural reverberation. Appropriate echoes are then added during the mix, to make the sounds appear to belong to the on-screen environment. But some effects are recorded wet—that is, with natural (or artificial) reverb. These have to be chosen carefully so the echo's quality matches the scene, and they can be harder to edit because you can't cut into the reverberations.

wild   Recorded without synchronization. Sound effects are usually gathered this way and matched up in an editing system. But some things are wild by mistake and have to be carefully resynced. This can happen when a timecode generator or low-end audio workstation isn't locked to house sync, or when audio has been stored on an unstable medium such as audio cassette.

XLR   The standard connector for high-end analog and digital audio, originally known as Cannon's XLR product line. It was universally accepted and is now supported by most other connector manufacturers. It's rugged and has low contact resistance, but its primary advantage is that it can carry balanced wiring (Chapter 4). This makes cables more immune to noise and hum.

zero level   Means two different things depending on whether you're working in analog or digital. Analog zero is a nominal volume near the top of the scale, and loud sounds are expected to go above it. Digital zero is an absolute limit, the loudest thing that can be recorded. Depending on the facility and style of audio mixing, analog zero is equivalent to somewhere between 12–20 dB below digital zero. See Chapter 12.

Resources

Many commercial and nonprofit organizations and individuals maintain Web sites where you can learn more about electronics, digital audio, and sound for video. Because the Web is an ever-changing thing, these sites may also contain links to other resources that evolved after I wrote this book. Of course, some of them may also have disappeared by the time you read this . . .

American Radio Relay League

www.arrl.org

This amateur radio organization publishes many books about electronics, including an excellent primer, *Understanding Basic Electronics*, for $20. Their *ARRL Handbook* ($75) is a 1,200-page technical encyclopedia, updated every year.

Cinema Audio Society

www.ideabuzz.com/cas

This organization of production sound mixers and boom operators has an informative journal, which is available online, and an active discussion board.

Digital Playroom

www.dplay.com

My Web site, which has a large tutorial section as well as some spoofs of our industry in streaming audio formats.

DV magazine

www.dv.com

This authoritative magazine posts information resources, equipment reviews, and the complete text of a few years' worth of back issues, including my monthly column on audio techniques. The Communities section contains active forums about many DV production issues, many of which are moderated by noted professionals.

Equipment Emporium

www.equipmentemporium.com

A commercial site for an equipment rental house, with lots of useful articles on aspects of soundtrack production.

Tomi Engdahl's Audio and Hifi page

www.hut.fi/Misc/Electronics/audio.html

Anybody interested in audio should know about this site, with indexed links to enough technical articles to write a few textbooks.

Quantel Digital Fact Book

www.quantel.com/domisphere/infopool.nsf/html/DFB

Incredibly informative glossary—almost an encyclopedia—about every aspect of digital video and audio, from a leading manufacturer of high-end studio equipment.

Rane Corporation

www.rane.com

Rane makes equipment for commercial sound installations. But their site includes valuable information about all forms of audio, including a library of downloadable booklets about topics such as reducing hum and interconnecting equipment, and the Rane Pro Audio Reference, a complete dictionary.

Video University

www.videouniversity.com

This site has a few basic articles on audio, plus a lot of information about the technology and business of video.

Organizations

Audio Engineering Society (AES)

60 East 42nd Street
New York, NY 10165
212/661-8528
Fax 212/682-0477
www.aes.org

American Federation of Television and Radio Artists (AFTRA)

260 Madison Avenue
New York, NY 10016
212/532-0800
Fax 212/532-2242
www.aftra.org

Media Communications Association (Formerly ITVA)

9202 North Meridian Street
Indianapolis, IN 46260
317/816-6269
Fax 800/801-8926
www.itva.org

National Association of Broadcasters (NAB)

1771 N Street, NW
Washington, DC 20036
202/429-5300
Fax 202/429-4199
www.nab.org

Society of Motion Picture and Television Engineers (SMPTE)

595 West Hartsdale Avenue
White Plains, NY 10607
914/761-1100
Fax 914/761-3115
www.smpte.org

Appendix C

CD Contents

I decided to include a standard audio CD with this book, rather than a CD-ROM, for a couple of reasons. I wanted you to be able to play it on the best speakers you have, which are more likely to be part of your stereo system than connected to your computer. I also didn't want to limit the CD's usefulness to a particular platform or software generation—there's nothing colder than last year's shareware. Most of the examples on this disc will be valid as long as CDs are playable.

Of course, you should also use this CD as source material for the exercises and tutorials. I suggest you transfer it digitally—most NLEs have a way to strip audio tracks from their CD-ROM drive—to preserve sound quality and to keep the waveforms looking like the examples in this book.

Track 1. Instrumental waves with and without harmonics *2:16*

Most of what we hear as the characteristic sound of an instrument is its harmonics. Here are digitally generated waveforms for an oboe, violin, and trumpet along with a pure sine wave, all at concert A (440 Hz). When you can hear their full range, it's easy to identify the sources.

The second part of this track has the exact same waves, but played through a sharp filter at 600 Hz to eliminate all the harmonics. You may be surprised at how similar they sound.

Track 2. High-frequency response tests *2:06*

The same short piece of music is played five times. Each time, it starts playing through a very sharp filter to eliminate everything above a specific frequency. The filter is switched off twice during each passage, to let the music's full range play through. If you don't hear a difference when the filter turns on or off, it's because sounds higher than the filter frequency aren't passing through your system anyway.

Don't be alarmed if you can't hear any difference at the higher frequencies; many speakers that are rated "full range" really aren't. Consider also that the system you're listening with includes your own ears, and high-frequency hearing deteriorates with age.

The filter frequencies are 18 kHz, 15 kHz, 12 kHz, 9 kHz, and 6 kHz. If you want to continue this experiment with other frequencies and source material, remember that the filter itself will influence the results. I used a DSP-driven one with a steep, 18 dB per octave cutoff; ordinary parametric or graphic equalizers will start affecting sounds considerably below their nominal frequency.

Track 3. 7.5 kHz sine wave on one channel, for acoustic testing *0:28*

Track 4. 7.5 kHz and 400 Hz sine waves equally mixed on one channel *0:38*

Track 5. The effects of low bit-depth sampling *2:06*

Music and narration, recorded at 44.1 kHz and 16-bits depth, then truncated to 12 bits, 8 bits, 7 bits, and 4 bits. The resulting audio was then resampled at 16 bits so it would be playable on a standard CD.

The 8-bit version probably sounds a lot better than you've heard in 8-bit multimedia files. That's because only the bit depth was limited; early computer sound equipment also suffered from analog noise and distortion.

Track 6. Aliasing distortion *0:26*

This is 16-bit music and voice downsampled to 5 kHz, but with no filter to prevent sounds from exceeding the Nyquist limit; then resampled at 44.1 kHz for the CD. The distortion is takes the form of an annoying whistle accompanying the music and voice. The voice has also acquired a lisp, buy that's because the very low sample rate won't pass the high frequencies that make up sibilants.

It's doubtful that any modern equipment will have aliasing this severe, but many MiniDV cameras show a similar distortion on very high frequency, loud signals.

Track 7. Delta encoding demo *0:26*

Music and voice, processed through IMA 4:1 encoding and then decoded for the CD.

Track 8. Perceptual encoding (MP3) demo *3:23*

Music and voice, processed through MPEG Layer 3 at various degrees of compression and then decoded for the CD. The original file was 16-bit, 44.1 kHz stereo, with a file size of 4,147 kilobytes (KB).

Bitrate (kbps)	Coding ratio	File size (KB)
160	8.8:1 (11.3% of original)	471
64	22:1 (4.5%)	189
32	44:1 (2.3%)	94
16	86:1 (1.1%)	48
8	173:1 (0.6%)	24

Track 9.   Various mic patterns, on and off axis *2:15*

The same voice, recorded in a quiet but somewhat reverberant room, through omnidirectional, cardioid, and short shotgun microphones. Each mic is used head-on and then at a 90° angle to the voice.

Track 10   Boom versus lav, in well-treated studio and on location *1:09*

These are recorded as split tracks, with the boom mic (a short shotgun) on the left channel and a collar-mounted lavaliere on the right.

Track 11   Restaurant background from two mic positions *0:43*

The first recording uses stereo omnis mounted at table height; the second has the mics in the corner of a banquette. Notice how they're equally live-sounding, but there's much less clatter in the second version.

Track 12   1 kHz sine @ −20 dBfs. *0:50*

This and the following track can be used for lineup tones at the head of a tape.

Track 13.   1 kHz sine @ −12 dBfs. *0:50*

Track 14.   1 kHz sine @ 0 dBfs *1:02*

For comparison, here's digital zero: the loudest tone that can be recorded without distortion. It's the loudest thing on this disk, so it would be a good idea to turn down your speakers before playing it.

You might hear distortion when playing this track, in the form of a second softer tone an octave higher. If so, it's happening in the digital-to-analog converter or audio amplifier circuits of your sound card or CD player. The circuit designer probably never expected a CD to get this loud.

This music selection, and the two that follow, are © 1999 Franklin-Douglas, Inc., and used here by permission. They were written for the first edition of this book by Doug Wood, who is also president of the Omnimusic library. You may copy them to your editing system and use them when trying the techniques in this book, but you can't incorporate them in a finished videotape without a specific license from Omnimusic.

For more information on the Omnimusic library, see Track 40 of this disc.

This track, and the sound effects that follow, are © 1991 The Hollywood Edge, Inc., and used here by permission. You may copy them to your editing system to try the techniques in this book.

If you'd like about a hundred equally good sound effects, along with license to use them in your production—free!—see Track 41.

The three sounds in this track are from one recording of a single 0.357 Magnum shot. The only processing done to them was compression; there was no editing, echo, or equalization.

This eerie effect is easy to do in almost any editing system.

First the two separate voices, then the voices mixed without any processing, then the processing described in Chapter 14.

Wes is the acknowledged master of vocal sounds. He created all of these effects using just a microphone and his mouth. For more about Wes and his techniques, see Chapter 8.

This is a brief excerpt from his full-length CD, *The One and Only*—a compilation of live recordings of the nightclub act he performs as "Mr. Sound Effects" around the world. (The recordings were done over a number of years, so quality may be uneven.) For a copy of the CD, send $10 to Wes Harrison, Post Office Box 901, Park Ridge, IL 60068.

Don is one of the busiest narrators in the Boston area and a regular voice on the PBS network. He contributed a lot of information about voice-over sessions in this book, along with voice tracks for the CD. He also wrote and is the only voice in the two parodies here. For booking information, contact him at 413-698-3561.

Track 40. Omnimusic demo *6:05*

Omnimusic is one of the better midsized libraries (about 180 discs, as of this writing) and has supplied music for many of my recent productions along with virtually all of the music on this CD. For more information, contact them at 800/828-6664, 516/883-0121, or 52 Main St, Port Washington, NY 11050. www.omnimusic.com.

Track 41. Hollywood Edge sound effects demo *2:15*

This is one of many demos of various category sound effects from the Hollywood Edge. They'll send potential customers a free CD with more demos... and about a hundred additional clean sound effects, fully licensed for you to use in your productions. Contact them at 800/292-3755, 323/603-3252, or 7080 Hollywood Blvd, Hollywood, CA 90028. Even if you're not likely to buy one of their professional libraries, you can still download most of the effects from www.hollywoodedge.com.

They figure that once you've heard and used the free sample, you'll purchase some of their commercial sound effects libraries. It worked for me.

Track 42. Good-bye *0:03*

Credits and Caveats

The elegant voice in the editing tutorials is popular PBS announcer Don Wescott. For booking information, see the description of Track 39. The corporate-sounding female in the microphone demonstrations is my wife Carla Rose. For a funny story about her experiences voicing national commercials, see the beginning of Chapter 10; for booking information contact Carla@graphicalcat.com. The unpolished voice describing the CD's tracks is yours truly. I was cheap and handy.

The disc was edited and mastered on the Orban Audicy audio workstation in my studio, the Digital Playroom, with special effects processing using custom software on an Eventide DSP-4000. Multimedia files were manipulated in Bias' Peak software on a Macintosh. Additional recording was by Timm Keleher at Soundworks, Watertown, MA; and by Bill Wangerin at The Stable, Cambridge, MA.

Contact information, prices, and freebies were accurate when I wrote the book but subject to change.

Index

The Authority on Digital Video Technology
DV MEDIA GROUP

The **DV Media Group** provides video professionals technical insight, inspiration, and knowledge to improve their skills, productivity, and make informed buying decisions.

DV Expo West
December 9-13, 2002
Los Angeles Convention Center, CA

DV.
PRINT

DV.com
ONLINE

DV.expo
EVENTS

www.DV.com

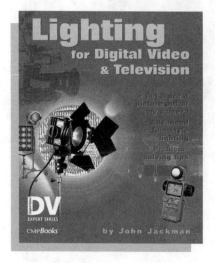

What's on the Audio CD?

The audio CD for *Producing Great Sound for Digital Video, Second edition*, features platform-independent diagnostics, demonstrations, and tutorial tracks that you can use to polish your skills. You can play the tracks on the best speakers you've got and load them into your NLE. The tutorials, of course, should be loaded into your computer.

For more information on the audio CD's contents, tracks, as well as licensing and copyright information, see the Introduction (page xii) and Appendix C beginning on page 415.